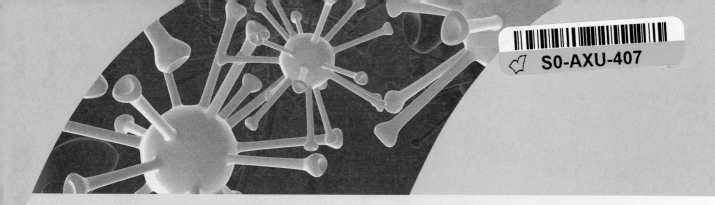

Epidemiology 101

Robert H. Friis, PhD

Professor and Chair
Department of Health Science
California State University, Long Beach
Long Beach, California

Series Editor: Richard Riegelman

JONES & BARTLETT
LEARNING

World Headquarters

Jones & Bartlett Learning
40 Tall Pine Drive
Sudbury, MA 01776
978-443-5000
info@jblearning.com
www.jblearning.com

Jones & Bartlett Learning
Canada
6339 Ormindale Way
Mississauga, Ontario L5V 1J2
Canada

Jones & Bartlett Learning
International
Barb House, Barb Mews
London W6 7PA
United Kingdom

Jones & Bartlett Learning books and products are available through most bookstores and online booksellers. To contact Jones & Bartlett Learning directly, call 800-832-0034, fax 978-443-8000, or visit our website www.jblearning.com.

Substantial discounts on bulk quantities of Jones & Bartlett Learning publications are available to corporations, professional associations, and other qualified organizations. For details and specific discount information, contact the special sales department at Jones & Bartlett Learning via the above contact information or send an email to specialsales@jblearning.com.

This publication is designed to provide accurate and authoritative information in regard to the Subject Matter covered. It is sold with the understanding that the publisher is not engaged in rendering legal, accounting, or other professional service. If legal advice or other expert assistance is required, the service of a competent professional person should be sought.

Some images in this book feature models. These models do not necessarily endorse, represent, or participate in the activities represented in the images.

Production Credits
Publisher: Michael Brown
Associate Editor: Katey Birtcher
Editorial Assistant: Catie Heverling
Senior Production Editor: Tracey Chapman
Marketing Manager: Sophie Fleck
Manufacturing and Inventory Control Supervisor: Amy Bacus
Composition: Auburn Associates, Inc.
Cover Design: Kristin E. Parker
Photo Research Manager and Photographer: Kimberly Potvin
Assistant Photo Researcher: Jessica Elias
Cover Image: © Gregor Buir/ShutterStock, Inc.; © Suravid/ShutterStock, Inc.; © Lee O'Dell/ShutterStock, Inc.;
    © Scott Bowlin/ShutterStock, Inc.
Printing and Binding: Malloy, Inc.
Cover Printing: John Pow Company

Library of Congress Cataloging-in-Publication Data
Friis, Robert H.
  Epidemiology 101 / Robert H. Friis.
      p. ; cm.
  Includes bibliographical references and index.
  ISBN-13: 978-0-7637-5443-3 (pbk.)
  ISBN-10: 0-7637-5443-9 (pbk.)
  ISBN-10: (invalid) 0-7637-5443-3 (pbk.) 1. Epidemiology. I. Title. II. Title: Epidemiology one hundred and one.
  III. Title: Epidemiology one hundred one.
  [DNLM: 1. Epidemiology. 2. Epidemiologic Methods. WA 105 F9118e 2009]
  RA651.F687 2009
  614.4—dc22
                                                                                    2008041624

6048

Printed in the United States of America
17 16 15 14 13   10 9 8

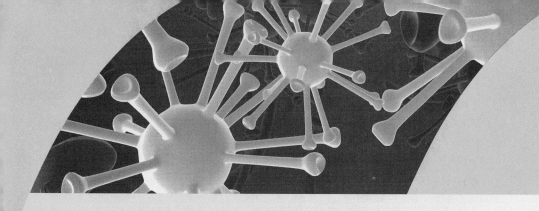

Contents

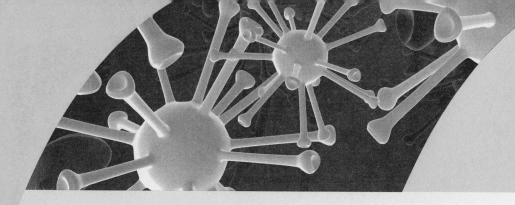

The Essential Public Health Series

ABOUT THE EDITOR:

Richard K. Riegelman, MD, MPH, PhD, is Professor of Epidemiology-Biostatistics, Medicine, and Health Policy, and Founding Dean of The George Washington University School of Public Health and Health Services in Washington, DC. He has taken a lead role in developing the Educated Citizen and Public Health initiative which has brought together arts and sciences and public health education associations to implement the Institute of Medicine of the National Academies' recommendation that "…all undergraduates should have access to education in public health." Dr. Riegelman also led the development of George Washington's undergraduate major and minor and currently teaches "Public Health 101" and "Epidemiology 101" to undergraduates.

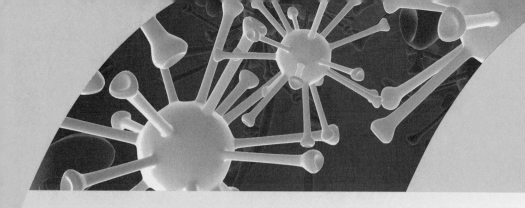

Prologue

Robert Friis's *Epidemiology 101* introduces you to the world of epidemiology—the basic science of public health—and shows you the many ways that epidemiology affects all of our lives. *Epidemiology 101* clearly conveys the key concepts with a minimum of mathematics. It presents epidemiology as a scientific way of thinking applicable to a wide range of fields from basic and clinical sciences to public policy.

Epidemiology 101 builds upon Robert Friis's many years of teaching and writing about epidemiology and environmental health, bringing alive the excitement of these fields. You will come away from *Epidemiology 101* with an enduring understanding that you can use and build upon in a wide range of careers for many years to come.

In 2006, a Consensus Conference on Undergraduate Public Health Education attended by arts and sciences, public health, and clinical health professions educators recommended that all undergraduates have access to a curriculum such as *Epidemiology 101* as part of their general education. Epidemiology was also recommended as a core component of an undergraduate public health curriculum.[1]

Epidemiology 101 follows the basic curriculum framework recommended by the Consensus Conference. In addition, an "epidemiology laboratory" was suggested for institutions that require a laboratory as part of science courses. *Epidemiology 101* fulfills that goal by providing references to exercises from the Young Epidemiology Scholars (YES) program developed by the Robert Wood Johnson Foundation.

Robert Friis's book *Essentials of Environmental Health* was the first book to be published as part of our *Essential Public Health* book series. It set a high standard for the series that is now rapidly expanding to provide introductory textbooks that cover the full spectrum of public health. In *Epidemiology 101*, Dr. Friis has done it again. Here, you will find the work of a true educator, a real pro. Take a look and see for yourself.

Richard Riegelman MD, MPH, PhD
Series Editor—Essential Public Health

1. The Educated Citizen and Public Health: Report of the Consensus Conference on Undergraduate Public Health Education, Council of Colleges of Arts and Sciences, Williamsburg VA, 2007. Available at: http://www.ccas.net/i4a/pages/index.cfm?pageid=3351.

Acknowledgments

The concept for *Epidemiology 101* originated with Dr. Richard Riegelman, professor and founding dean of the School of Public Health and Health Services, at The George Washington University. I would like to thank Dr. Riegelman for his encouragement and support. This work is part of the *Essential Public Health* series, which offers a comprehensive curriculum in public health. This is the fourth textbook that I have completed. Each project begins with enthusiasm, anxiety, and an ocean of blank pages. From the author's perspective, the input of colleagues and students was essential in completing the work. My colleagues and students were extremely helpful in providing comments. I wish to thank the following students from California State University, Long Beach: Sarah Long, Paula Griego, and Che Wankie. Students aided with literature searches, reviewed written text materials, and provided feedback. I also acknowledge the helpful comments and other contributions of Ibtisam Khoury-Sirhan, Claire Garrido-Ortega, Dr. Javier Lopez-Zetina, and Dr. Veronica Acosta-Deprez of California State University, Long Beach. These professional colleagues reviewed chapters that were relevant to their areas of expertise. Mike Brown, publisher for Jones & Bartlett, provided continuing encouragement and motivation for completion of the project; Jones & Bartlett staff offered much helpful expertise. Finally, my wife, Carol Friis, was involved extensively with this project; for example, she critiqued the manuscript, typed final versions of the document, provided detailed editorial comments, verified the accuracy of the references, and helped with many other aspects of the book. Without her support and assistance, completion of the text would not have been possible.

R. H. F.

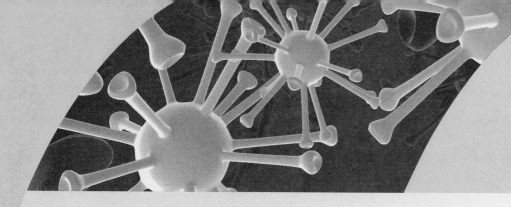

About the Author

Robert H. Friis, PhD, is Professor and Chair of the Department of Health Science at California State University, Long Beach (CSULB), and Director of the CSULB-Veterans Affairs Medical Center, Long Beach, Joint Studies Institute. He is a past president of the Southern California Public Health Association and member of the governing council. He serves or has served on the advisory boards of several health-related organizations, including the California Health Interview Survey. Previously, he was an Associate Clinical Professor in the Department of Medicine, Department of Neurology, and School of Social Ecology, University of California, Irvine, from which he has retired. He is an epidemiologist by training and profession.

As a health department epidemiologist, he led investigations into environmental health problems such as chemical spills and air pollution. He has taught courses on epidemiology, environmental health, and statistics at universities in New York City and southern California. In addition to previous employment in a local health department, he has conducted research and published and presented numerous papers related to tobacco use, mental health, chronic disease, disability, minority health, and psychosocial epidemiology. Dr. Friis has been principal investigator or coinvestigator on grants and contracts from the University of California's Tobacco-Related Disease Research Program, the National Institutes of Health, and other agencies. This funding has supported investigations into topics such as geriatric health, depression in Hispanic populations, and nursing home infections. His research interests have led him to conduct research in Mexico City and European countries. He has been a visiting professor at the Center for Nutrition and Toxicology, Karolinska Institute, Stockholm, Sweden; the Max Planck Institute, Munich, Germany; and Dresden Technical University, also in Germany. In 2008, he was a visiting professor at the Medizinische Fakultät Carl Gustav Carus of the Dresden Technical University. He reviews articles for scientific journals, including *International Migration Review*, *Social Science and Medicine*, and *Public Health*. Dr. Friis is a member of the Society for Epidemiologic Research and the American Public Health Association. Among his awards were a postdoctoral fellowship for study at the Institute for Social Research, University of Michigan, and the Achievement Award for Scholarly and Creative Activity from California State University, Long Beach. His biography is listed in *Who's Who in America*.

He is author/coauthor of the following books with Jones & Bartlett:

- *Epidemiology for Public Health Practice*, with Thomas A. Sellers (editions one through four), published by Jones and Bartlett Publishers
- *Essentials of Environmental Health*, published by Jones and Bartlett Publishers

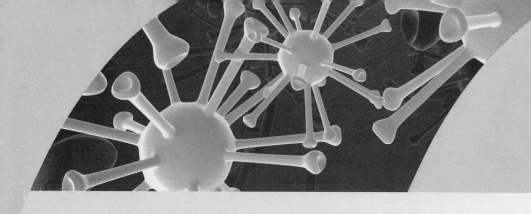

Preface

I wrote *Epidemiology 101* in response to a call to increase the epidemiologic content of undergraduate programs. A growing movement advocates for incorporating epidemiology into undergraduate curricula as a liberal arts subject. Consequently, students in undergraduate liberal arts programs, as well as those with limited public health or mathematical backgrounds, are the target audience for *Epidemiology 101*. No extant epidemiologic textbook is tailored exactly for this audience.

Epidemiology is suited ideally as a topic for liberal arts because habits of mind such as problem analysis, deductive and inductive reasoning, and creating generalizations are key features of epidemiology. The discipline provides reinforcement of basic skills acquired in the natural sciences, mathematics and statistics, and the social sciences. Thus, a course in epidemiology might be taken in order to fulfill a distribution requirement in one of the basic or applied sciences. Furthermore, knowledge of epidemiology equips citizens with informed opinions regarding crucial health issues that appear daily in the media.

In addition to covering basic epidemiologic concepts, the text will demonstrate how these concepts can be applied to problems encountered in everyday life, e.g., hazards posed by the food supply, risks associated with lifestyle choices, and dangers associated with youth violence. One of the features of *Epidemiology 101* is its emphasis on socially related determinants of health. This text is one in the series *Essential Public Health* published by Jones and Bartlett and edited by Richard Riegelman.

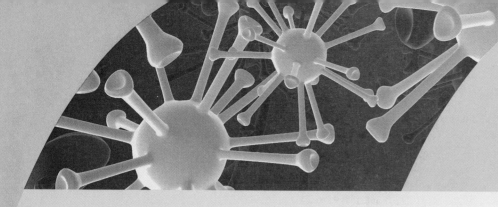

Introduction

This textbook has been created for students who would like to study epidemiology in order to fulfill a requirement for a science course. Increasingly, curriculum designers recognize that as a discipline, epidemiology embodies many useful critical thinking skills, which include gathering facts, forming hypotheses, and drawing conclusions. These processes are the hallmark of the scientific method and embody modes of thinking that benefit well-educated citizens even if they do not intend to become public health professionals.[1] In this respect, epidemiology resembles a liberal art.[2]

Epidemiology may be approached from a nontechnical point of view that students from a variety of backgrounds can appreciate. Examples of epidemiologic investigations into such problems as bird flu and studies of lifestyle and chronic disease are inherently appealing. Although epidemiology has strong quantitative roots, this text emphasizes the nonquantitative aspects of the discipline by creating a linkage with traditional liberal arts concepts, including social justice and health disparities. A background in mathematics and statistics is not required in order to use the book. The text incorporates numerous case studies, text boxes, vignettes, exhibits, photographs, figures, and illustrations to gain the interest of readers.

Epidemiology has evolved into a discipline that has applications in many fields. Once thought of as being confined to the investigation of infectious disease outbreaks, epidemiologic methods are used increasingly in such diverse health-related areas as traditional clinical medicine, healthcare administration, nursing, dentistry, and occupational medicine. In addition, the applications of epidemiologic methods are expanding to manufacturing processes, law, and control of international terrorism. *Epidemiology 101* will provide examples of these applications.

The content of this book follows the outline of the curriculum titled Epidemiology 101, recommended by the Consensus Conference on Undergraduate Public Health Education, November 7–8, 2006, Boston, Massachusetts. Web address: http://www.aptrweb.org/resources/pdfs/Curriculum_Guide_Version3.pdf.

In some instances, for didactic purposes, the arrangement of the topics departs somewhat from the order presented in the conference's *Working Group Reports*. However, the content of this textbook is similar to the content shown in the curriculum suggested for Epidemiology 101.

This text contains a total of ten chapters, which begin with coverage of basic principles and then increase in complexity. Chapters 9 and 10 illustrate current applications of epidemiology. Examples chosen are recent and command the attention of students. Selected chapters are keyed to exercises from the College Board's Young Epidemiology Scholars (YES) Program. These exercises may be found on the Web at http://www.collegeboard.com/yes/ (accessed July 8, 2008). The course content can be covered during an academic quarter or a semester.

A full set of supportive learning materials, e.g., PowerPoint slides, flashcards, and a test bank, is available online at http://www.jbpub.com/essentialpublichealth for students and instructors to access. Each chapter concludes with study questions for additional reinforcement. Students should be encouraged to use the flashcards and other supportive materials that are available on the Web site for this textbook. The interest level of students can be increased by using group exercises, lectures from public health experts, and field visits. The Robert Wood Johnson Foundation's YES exercises can be implemented as a laboratory component of an epidemiology course.

REFERENCES

1. Weed DL. Epidemiology, the humanities, and public health. *Am J Public Health.* 1995;87:914–918.
2. Fraser DW. Epidemiology as a liberal art. *N Engl J Med.* 1987;316:309–314.

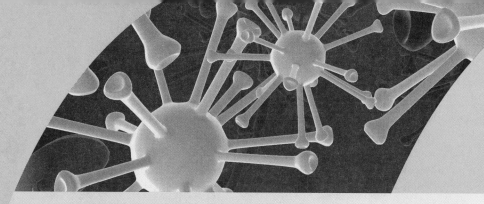

CHAPTER 1

History, Philosophy, and Uses of Epidemiology

LEARNING OBJECTIVES

By the end of this chapter you will be able to:

- Define the term *epidemiology*
- Describe two ways in which epidemiology may be considered a liberal arts discipline
- State three important landmarks in the history of epidemiology
- Describe three uses of epidemiology

CHAPTER OUTLINE

INTRODUCTION

As a member of contemporary society, you are besieged constantly with information about the latest epidemic, which now ranges from HIV/AIDS to the obesity and diabetes epidemics

---

TABLE 1-1 List of Important Terms Used in This Chapter

Analytic epidemiology	Exposure	Pandemic
Descriptive epidemiology	John Snow	Population
Determinant	Morbidity	Prevention of disease
Distribution	Mortality	Risk
Epidemic	Natural experiment	Risk assessment
Epidemiologic transition	Observational science	Risk factor
Epidemiology	Outcome	Uses of epidemiology

to outbreaks of foodborne illness such as the 2008 outbreak of salmonellosis that occurred during spring and summer.

Epidemiology is an exciting field with many applications that are helpful in solving today's health-related problems. (Refer to Figure 1-1.) For example, epidemiology can demonstrate the risks associated with smoking, as well as those related to exposure to second-hand cigarette smoke among nonsmokers. Currently, youth violence is an issue that confronts students, teachers, and administrators at both urban and suburban schools; epidemiologic research can identify factors related to such violence and suggest methods for its prevention. Other contributions of epidemiology include the identification of factors associated with obesity and substance abuse, both of which are major societal issues. Epidemiology can provide insights into these problems as well.

Now, let's consider the outbreak of foodborne salmonellosis mentioned previously. Salmonellosis is an infection caused by *Salmonella* bacteria, which can produce gastrointestinal symptoms (cramping, diarrhea, and fever) that begin 12 to 72 hours after the onset of infection. The majority of patients recover without treatment, but in some cases the condition is life-threatening.

The 2008 outbreak affected more than 1,400 persons and is believed to have contributed to two deaths. Cases appeared in 43 states, most frequently in Texas, Arizona, and Illinois. The source of contamination was mysterious. All patients were affected with an uncommon strain of *Salmonella* Saintpaul that had a distinctive genetic fingerprint. Initially, epidemiologic investigations implicated raw tomatoes. The public was advised not to eat red plum (red Roma) and round red tomatoes, which had been linked to the outbreak. This news was indeed disturbing; tomatoes generally are considered to be a healthful vegetable. They are used extensively in many popular items of the American diet, including salads, ketchup, spaghetti sauce, pizza, and salsa.

Investigators searched for contaminated tomatoes in Mexico, where many of the vegetables destined for its northern neighbor are grown, and also in the United States. Despite this diligent work, the origin of the bacteria that sickened so many persons was never definitively linked to tomatoes. Eventually, jalapeño and serrano peppers were targeted as the offending foods, but only those harvested or packed in Mexico.

The *Salmonella* outbreak illustrates a foodborne-disease episode that reached epidemic proportions. Individual *Salmonella* cases may arise sporadically; usually such occurrences are not epidemics. However, because in this instance a large number of persons were affected across the United States, the *Salmonella* outbreak could be considered an epidemic.

What is meant by the term epidemic? An **epidemic** refers to "the occurrence in a community or region of cases of an illness, specific health-related behavior, or other health-related events clearly in excess of normal expectancy."[1] Figure 1-2 demonstrates the concept of an epidemic in the case of the annual occurrence of a hypothetical disease. The "normal expectancy" is six cases per year. In three years, 2016, 2019, and 2020, the occurrence of the disease was in excess of normal expectancy.

It is possible in some instances for a single case of a disease to represent an epidemic. With respect to a new occurrence of an infectious disease not previously found in an area or the occurrence of an infectious disease that has long been absent, a single case or a few cases of that disease would be regarded as an epidemic. At present, examples of infrequently occurring diseases in the United States are measles and polio. A small outbreak of measles, polio, or other infrequently occurring infectious disease requires the immediate attention of public health officials and would be treated as an epidemic.

FIGURE 1-1 Examples of the types of questions that can be answered by epidemiologic research.

Questions for Epidemiology

Is it safe to eat the tomatoes?

Will I get lung cancer if I smoke?

How can youth violence be prevented?

What's causing the obesity epidemic?

Who's at risk for substance abuse?

Source: © adsheyn/ShutterStock, Inc.; © Zdenka Micka/ShutterStock.com; © Yuri Areurs/ShutterStock, Inc.; Courtesy of Bill Branson/National Cancer Institute; © Photos.com.

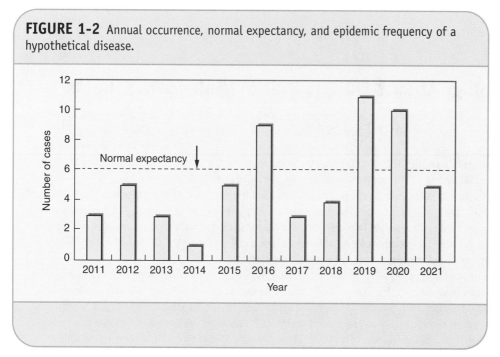

FIGURE 1-2 Annual occurrence, normal expectancy, and epidemic frequency of a hypothetical disease.

they formulate hypotheses, and they explore causal relationships between exposures and health outcomes. A special concern of the discipline is causality: do research findings represent cause-and-effect associations or are they merely associations? A simple example of a causal association would be whether a specific contaminated food such as tomatoes caused an outbreak of gastrointestinal disease; a more complex example is whether there is a causal association between smoking during the teenage years and the subsequent development of lung cancer later in life.

Although the foregoing examples of the applications of epidemiology are primarily health related, epidemiology is a body of methods that have general applicability to many fields. Exhibit 1-1 provides an example of school-related violence, a topic of public health and societal concern.

The aforementioned exhibit regarding violence in schools illustrates the potential applications of epidemiology for solving a broad range of problems that affect the health of populations. Specifically, epidemiology can be used as a research tool that seeks answers to the following types of questions with respect to violence in schools:

- Violent episodes are most likely to affect which types of schools and universities?
- What are the characteristics of victims and perpetrators of violent acts?
- What interventions might be proposed for the prevention of violent acts and how successful are they likely to be?

DEFINITION OF EPIDEMIOLOGY

"**Epidemiology** is concerned with the distribution and determinants of health and diseases, morbidity, injuries, disability, and mortality in populations. Epidemiologic studies are applied to the control of health problems in populations."[2] (p6) The term epidemiology originates from the Greek: *epi* (upon) + *demos* (people) + *logy* (study of). The key characteristics of epidemiology are discussed below.

The use of the word *epidemic* is not limited to communicable diseases. The term is applied to chronic diseases and other conditions as well. Illustrations are the "epidemic of obesity," the "epidemic of diabetes," or the "epidemic of heart disease." Related to epidemic is **pandemic**, defined as "an epidemic occurring worldwide, or over a very wide area, crossing international boundaries, and usually affecting a large number of people."[1] The 1918 influenza pandemic discussed later in the chapter and periodic less-severe global influenza epidemics illustrate this concept.

The previous discussion leads to the question: what is the scope of epidemiology? This chapter will begin with a definition of the term epidemiology and illustrate how the study of epidemiology imparts skills that are useful in a variety of pursuits. As part of this exploration, the author will highlight the key historical developments in epidemiology and demonstrate how these developments have influenced the philosophy and practice of epidemiology. Some of these historical developments include concerns of the ancient Greeks about diseases caused by the environment, the observations of Sir Percival Pott on scrotal cancer among chimney sweeps in England, the work of John Snow on cholera, and modern work on the etiology of chronic diseases.

Epidemiology is one of the basic sciences of public health; epidemiologic methods are applied to a variety of public health-related fields: health education, health care administration, tropical medicine, and environmental health. Epidemiologists quantify health outcomes by using statistics;

Exhibit 1-1

What Is Epidemiology About? The Example of Violence in Schools

An episode of violence on a school or university campus represents a tragic event that all too frequently rivets the attention of the national media. Since the mid-1960s, more than a dozen fatal shootings have occurred on U.S. college campuses. Among the most deadly were shootings at the University of Texas at Austin on August 1, 1966 (17 dead, including the gunman, and 31 injured), and at Virginia Tech University on April 16, 2007 (33 dead, including the gunman, and 26 injured). On February 15, 2008, a gunman killed five students and injured 16 others at Northern Illinois University in DeKalb, Illinois.

At the secondary-school level, highly publicized shootings also have grabbed the headlines. One of these was the 1999 violence at Columbine High School in Littleton, Colorado; this shooting took 15 lives and injured 23 persons. Although they command our attention, violent episodes that cause multiple homicides on school premises are actually highly unusual. Nevertheless, the National Academy of Sciences declared that youth violence "reached epidemic levels" during the 1990s. A total of 35 shooting incidents transpired at secondary schools or school-sponsored events from 1992 to 2001.

In what sense can school violence be regarded as an epidemic? Perhaps the answer is that any incident of violence (especially shootings) on school premises is significant. The U.S. Centers for Disease Control and Prevention produced epidemiologic data on school-associated student homicides that occurred during the years 1992 to 2006 (see Table 1-2 and Figure 1-3). These data suggest that the preponderance of homicide victims were male students and students in urban areas. The table also demonstrates an approach of epidemiology—comparing data according to the characteristics of homicides and the settings in which the homicides occurred.

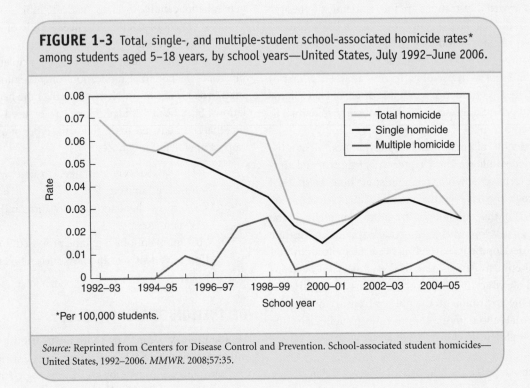

FIGURE 1-3 Total, single-, and multiple-student school-associated homicide rates* among students aged 5–18 years, by school years—United States, July 1992–June 2006.

*Per 100,000 students.

Source: Reprinted from Centers for Disease Control and Prevention. School-associated student homicides—United States, 1992–2006. *MMWR.* 2008;57:35.

TABLE 1-2 Total, Single-, and Multiple-Student School-Associated Homicide Rates* among Students Aged 5–18 Years, by Sex and Selected School Characteristics—United States, July 1999–June 2006

Characteristic	Total				Single victim				Multiple victims			
	No. of deaths	Rate	Rate ratio	(95% CI[†])	No. of deaths	Rate	Rate ratio	(95% CI)	No. of deaths	Rate	Rate ratio	(95% CI)
All students	116[§]	0.03	—	—	101	0.03	—	—	15	<0.01	—	—
Sex												
Female	23	0.01	1.00	—	17	0.01	1.00	—	6	<0.01	1.00	—
Male	93	0.05	4.39	(2.78–6.93)	84	0.04	5.37	(3.19–9.04)	9	<0.01	1.63	(0.58–4.58)
School level/ grade												
Elementary/ middle	25	<0.01	1.00	—	22	<0.01	1.00	—	3	<0.01	1.00	—
Secondary	90	0.08	18.47	(11.86–28.73)	78	0.07	18.19	(11.34–29.20)	12	0.01	20.53	(5.79–72.74)
NCES school locale[¶]												
Central city	50	0.06	3.47	(1.80–6.66)	45	0.05	3.81	(1.86–7.80)	5	0.01	1.91	(0.37–9.82)
Urban fringe/ large town	17	0.02	0.86	(0.40–1.84)	15	0.01	0.93	(0.41–2.12)	2	<0.01	0.56	(0.08–3.95)
Rural small town	11	0.02	1.00	—	9	0.01	1.00	—	2	<0.01	1.00	—
School type												
Private	5	0.01	1.00	—	5	0.01	1.00	—	0	<0.01	—	—
Public	110	0.02	1.22	(0.50–2.99)	95	0.01	1.05	(0.43–2.59)	15	<0.01	—	—

*Per 100,000 students.

[†]Confidence interval. (This term is defined in Chapter 5.)

[§]Associated with 109 events.

[¶]National Center for Education Statistics. Includes only data from 1999 to 2004 because information on the number of students enrolled in private schools in various locales during 2004–2006 is not available.

Source: Reprinted from Centers for Disease Control and Prevention. School-associated student homicides—United States, 1992–2006. *MMWR.* 2008;57:35.

Population Focus

The unique focus of epidemiology is upon the occurrence of health and disease in the population. The definition of a **population** is "all the inhabitants of a given country or area considered together. . . ."[1] The population approach contrasts with clinical medicine's concern with the individual; hence epidemiology is sometimes called population medicine. The examples of the *Salmonella* outbreak and violence in schools demonstrated epidemiologic investigations that were focused on entire populations groups (such as the United States). A third example involves epidemiologic studies of lung disease; these investigations might examine the occurrence of lung cancer mortality across counties or among regional geographic subdivisions known as census tracts. Investigators might want to ascertain whether lung cancer mortality is higher in areas with higher concentrations of "smokestack" industries in comparison with areas that have lower levels of air pollution or are relatively free from air pollution. In contrast with the population approach used in epidemiology, the alternative approach of clinical medicine would be for the clinician to concentrate on the diagnosis and treatment of specific individuals for the sequelae of foodborne illnesses, injuries caused by school violence, and lung cancer.

Distribution

The term **distribution** implies that the occurrence of diseases and other health outcomes varies in populations, with some subgroups of the populations more frequently affected than others. Epidemiologic research identifies subgroups that have increased occurrence of adverse health outcomes in comparison with other groups. In the present text, we will encounter many illustrations of differential distributions of health outcomes: for example, variations in the occurrence of cancer, heart disease, and asthma in populations.

Determinants

A **determinant** is defined as "any factor that brings about change in a health condition or other defined characteristic."[1] Examples of determinants are biologic agents (e.g., bacteria and viruses), chemical agents (e.g., toxic pesticides and chemical carcinogens), and less specific factors (e.g., stress and deleterious lifestyle practices).

Related to determinants are **exposures**, which pertain either to contact with a disease-causing factor or to the amount of the factor that impinges upon a group or individuals.[1] Epidemiology searches for associations between exposures and health outcomes. Examples of exposures are contact with infectious disease agents through consumption of contaminated foods and environmental exposures to toxic chemicals, potential carcinogens, or air pollution. In other cases, exposures may be to biological agents or to forms of energy such as radiation, noise, and extremes of temperature. For an epidemiologic research study to be valid, the level of exposure in a population must be defined carefully; the task of exposure assessment is not easily accomplished in many types of epidemiologic research. Also related to determinants are risk factors, which are discussed later in the chapter.

Outcomes

The definition of **outcomes** is "all the possible results that may stem from exposure to a causal factor. . . ."[1] The outcomes examined in epidemiologic research range from specific infectious diseases to disabling conditions, unintentional injuries, chronic diseases, and other conditions associated with personal behavior and lifestyle. These outcomes may be expressed as types and measures of **morbidity** (illnesses due to a specific disease or health condition) and **mortality** (causes of death). Accurate clinical assessments of outcomes are vitally important to the quality of epidemiologic research and the strength of inferences that can be made. Without such assessments, it would not be possible to replicate the findings of research.

Quantification

Epidemiology is a quantitative discipline; the term **quantification** refers to counting of cases of illness or other health outcomes. Quantification means the use of statistical measures to describe the occurrence of health outcomes as well as to measure their association with exposures. The field of descriptive epidemiology quantifies variation of diseases and health outcomes according to subgroups of the population (refer to Chapter 4).

Control of Health Problems

Epidemiology aids with health promotion, alleviation of adverse health outcomes (e.g., infectious and chronic diseases), and prevention of disease. Epidemiologic methods are applicable to the development of needs assessments, the design of prevention programs, and the evaluation of the success of such programs. Epidemiology contributes to health policy development by providing quantitative information that can be used by policy makers. Chapter 7 describes the role of epidemiology in the policy arena.

Here is a brief comment about public health, epidemiology, and the prevention of disease (with the linkage between prevention and the natural history of disease). The **natural history of disease** refers to the course of disease from its beginning to its final clinical endpoints. The period of prepathogenesis is the time period in the natural history of disease before a disease agent (e.g., a bacterium) has interacted with a host (the person who develops the disease). The agent simply exists in the environment. Pathogenesis occurs after the agent has interacted with a host. Three modes of prevention are directed toward the periods of prepathogenesis and pathogenesis.

From the public health point of view, the three types of prevention are primary, secondary, and tertiary. **Primary prevention** involves the prevention of disease before it occurs; primary prevention targets the stage of prepathogenesis and embodies general health promotion and specific prevention against diseases. Methods of primary prevention include the creation of a healthful environment, implementation of health education programs, and administration of immunizations against specific infectious diseases. **Secondary prevention** takes place during the early phases of pathogenesis and includes activities that limit the progression of disease. Illustrations are programs for cancer screening and early detection of other chronic diseases. Finally, **tertiary prevention** is directed toward the later stages of pathogenesis and includes programs for restoring the patient's optimal functioning; examples are physical therapy for stroke victims and fitness programs for recovering heart attack patients.

THE EVOLVING CONCEPTION OF EPIDEMIOLOGY AS A LIBERAL ART

Epidemiology is often considered to be a biomedical science that relies on a specific methodology and high-level technical skills.[3] Nevertheless, epidemiology in many respects also is a "low-tech" science that can be appreciated by those who do not specialize in this field.[4] The text box lists skills acquired through the study of epidemiology; these skills enlarge the appreciation of many academic fields: laboratory sciences, mathematics, the social sciences, history, and literature.

Skills acquired through training in epidemiology

1. Use of the interdisciplinary approach
2. Use of the scientific method
3. Enhancement of critical thinking ability
   a. Reasoning by analogy and deduction
   b. Problem solving
4. Use of quantitative and computer methods
5. Communication skills
6. Inculcation of aesthetic values

The Interdisciplinary Approach

Epidemiology is an **interdisciplinary science**, meaning that it uses information from many fields. Here are a few examples of the specializations that contribute to epidemiology and the types of contribution that they make:

- Mathematics and biostatistics (for quantitative methods)
- History (for historical accounts of disease and early epidemiologic methods)
- Sociology (social determinants of disease)
- Demography and geography (population structures and location of disease outbreaks)
- Behavioral sciences (models of disease; design of health promotion programs)
- Law (examining evidence to establish causality; legal bases for health policy)

Many of the issues of importance to contemporary society do not have clearly delineated disciplinary boundaries. For example, prevention of school violence requires an interdisciplinary approach that draws upon information from sociology, behavioral sciences, and the legal profession. In helping to develop solutions to the problem of school violence, epidemiology leverages information from mathematics (e.g., statistics on the occurrence of violence), medicine (e.g., treatment of victims of violence), behavioral and social sciences (e.g., behavioral and social aspects of violence), and law (legal basis for development of school-related antiviolence programs). Through the study of epidemiology, one acquires an appreciation of the interdisciplinary approach and a broader understanding of a range of disciplines.

Use of the Scientific Method

Epidemiology is a scientific discipline that makes use of a body of research methods similar to those used in the basic sciences and applied fields including biostatistics. The work of the epidemiologist is driven by theories, hypotheses, and empirical data. The scientific method employs a systematic approach and objectivity in evaluating the results of research. Comparison groups are used to examine the effects of exposures. Epidemiology uses rigorous study designs: cross-sectional, ecologic, case-control, and cohort. Chapter 6 will provide more information about these designs.

Enhancement of Critical Thinking Ability

Critical thinking skills include the following: reasoning by analogy, making deductions that follow from a set of evidence, and solving problems. We will learn that epidemiologists use analogical reasoning to infer disease causality. Suppose there are two similar diseases. The etiology of the first disease is known, but the etiology of the second disease is unknown. By analogy, one can reason that the etiology of the second disease must be similar to that of the first.

Also, epidemiologists gather descriptive information on the occurrence of diseases; they use this information to develop hypotheses regarding specific exposures that might have been associated with those diseases. Finally, epidemiologists are called into action to solve problems, for example, trying to control the *Salmonella* outbreak that was believed to be associated with tomatoes.

Use of Quantitative and Computer Methods

Biostatistics is one of the core disciplines of epidemiology. Because of the close linkage between the two fields, epidemiology and biostatistics sometimes are housed in the same academic department in some universities. Through your training in epidemiology, you will acquire quantitative skills such as tabulating numbers of cases, making subgroup comparisons, and mapping associations between exposures and health outcomes. In research and agency settings, epidemiologists use computers to store, retrieve, and process health-related information and to perform these types of analyses.

Communication Skills

As a core discipline of public health, epidemiology is an applied field. Information from epidemiologic analyses can be used to control diseases, improve the health of the community, evaluate intervention programs, and inform public policy. One of the skills needed by applied epidemiologists is the ability to disseminate information that could be useful for controlling health problems and improving the health status of the population.

Inculcation of Aesthetic Values

Aesthetic values are concerned with the appreciation of beauty, which would seem to have no relevance to epidemiology.

Nevertheless, you can hone your aesthetic values by reading about the history of epidemiology and descriptions of epidemics and health problems found in literature. The writings of the great thinkers such as Hippocrates and John Snow, who contributed so greatly to epidemiology, are compelling as works of literature. Many other writings relevant to epidemiology are extant. Two are *The Jungle* (by Upton Sinclair), which describes deplorable sanitary conditions in Chicago slaughterhouses in 1906, and Camus' *The Plague*, an account of the ravages of disease.

APPLICATION OF DESCRIPTIVE AND ANALYTIC METHODS TO AN OBSERVATIONAL SCIENCE

In examining the occurrence of health and disease in human populations, researchers almost always are prohibited from using experimental methods because of ethical issues such as potential harm to subjects. Studies of the population's health present a challenge to epidemiologic methods. First and foremost, epidemiology is an **observational science** that capitalizes upon naturally occurring situations in order to study the occurrence of disease. Thus, in order to study the association of cigarette smoking with lung diseases, epidemiologists might examine and compare the frequency of lung cancer and other lung diseases among smokers and nonsmokers.

The term **descriptive epidemiology** refers to epidemiologic studies that are concerned with characterizing the amount and distribution of health and disease within a population. Health outcomes are classified according to the variables: person, place, and time. Examples of person variables are demographic characteristics such as sex, age, and race/ethnicity. Place variables denote geographic locations including a specific country or countries, areas within countries, and places where localized patterns of disease may occur. Some time variables are a decade, a year, a month, a week, or a day. Descriptive studies, regarded as a fundamental approach by epidemiologists, aim to delineate the patterns and manner in which disease occurs in populations.[5] These studies, which are focused on the development of hypotheses, set the stage for subsequent research that examines the etiology of disease.

Analytic epidemiology examines causal (etiologic) hypotheses regarding the association between exposures and health conditions. The field of analytic epidemiology proposes and evaluates causal models for etiologic associations and studies them empirically. "Etiologic studies are planned examinations of causality and the natural history of disease. These studies have required increasingly sophisticated analytic methods as the importance of low-level exposures is explored and greater refinement in exposure-effect relationships is sought."[6(p945)]

One approach of analytic epidemiology is to take advantage of naturally occurring situations or events in order to test causal hypotheses. These naturally occurring events are referred to as **natural experiments**, defined as "naturally occurring circumstances in which subsets of the population have different levels of exposure to a supposed causal factor in a situation resembling an actual experiment, where human subjects would be randomly allocated to groups."[1] However, in a natural experiment persons usually are not assigned randomly to the groups. An example is the work of John Snow, discussed later in this chapter. Many past and ongoing natural experiments are relevant to environmental epidemiology. When new public health-related laws are introduced, these laws become similar to natural experiments that could be explored in epidemiologic research. For example, epidemiologists could study the effects of the 2008 California law that requires adult drivers to use hands-free cellular telephones upon the frequency of automobile crashes. Other examples of natural experiments that have evolved from laws are the addition of fluoride to the public water supply in order to prevent tooth decay and the requirement that children wear safety helmets while riding bicycles.

HISTORY OF EPIDEMIOLOGY AND DEVELOPMENT OF EPIDEMIOLOGIC PRINCIPLES

The history of epidemiology originated as early as classical antiquity (before about 500 AD), and later during the medieval period was marked by bubonic plague epidemics in Europe. The Renaissance was the time of Paracelsus (toxicologist) and John Graunt, pioneering compiler of vital statistics. During the eighteenth and nineteenth centuries, breakthroughs occurred in the development of a vaccination against smallpox and the formulation of epidemiologic methods. The period from the beginning of the twentieth century to the present has seen a rapid growth in epidemiology; two of the achievements of this period were identification of smoking as a cause of cancer and eradication of smallpox. (Refer to Figure 1-4 for a brief epidemiology history time line.)

The Period of Classical Antiquity (before 500 AD)

Hippocrates (460 BC–370 BC).

The ancient Greek authority Hippocrates contributed to epidemiology by departing from superstitious reasons for disease outbreaks. Until Hippocrates' time, supernatural explanations were used to account for the diseases that ravaged human populations. In about 400 BC, Hippocrates suggested that environmental factors such as water quality and the air were implicated in the causation of diseases. He authored the historically important book *On Airs, Waters, and Places*. Hippocrates' work and the writings of many of the ancients did not delineate specific known agents involved in the causality of health problems but referred more generically to air, water, and food.

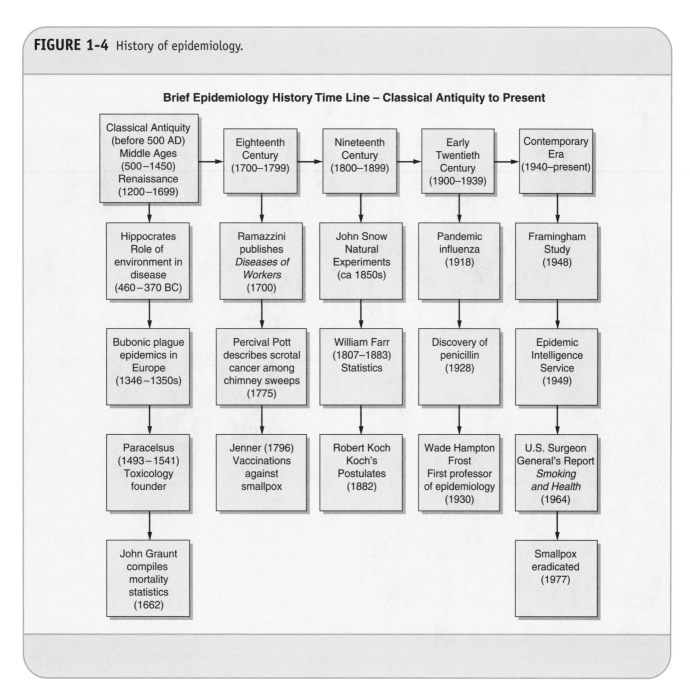

FIGURE 1-4 History of epidemiology.

In this respect, early epidemiology shares with contemporary epidemiology the frequent lack of complete knowledge of the specific agents of disease, especially those associated with chronic diseases.

Middle Ages (approximately 500–1450)

Black Death.

Of great significance for epidemiology is the Black Death, which occurred between 1346 and 1352 and claimed up to one-third of the population of Europe at the time (20 to 30 million out of 100 million people). The Black Death was thought to be an epidemic of bubonic plague, a bacterial disease caused by *Yersinia pestis*. (Refer to Figure 1-5 for a drawing of plague victims during a later period.) Bubonic plague is characterized by painful swellings of the lymph nodes (buboes) in the groin and elsewhere in the body. Other symptoms often include fever and the appearance of black splotches on the skin. (Refer to Figure 1-6.) Untreated, bubonic plague kills up to 60% of its victims. The bites of fleas harbored by rats and some other types of rodents can transmit plague.

FIGURE 1-5 Black Death.

Source: © National Library of Medicine.

FIGURE 1-6 This patient presented with symptoms of plague that included gangrene of the right foot causing necrosis of the toes.

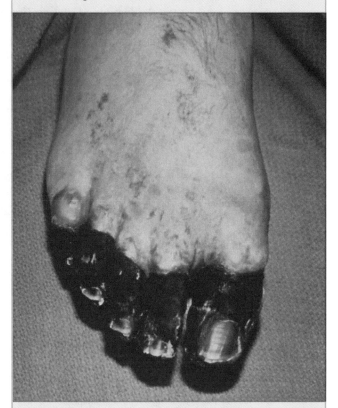

Source: Reprinted from Centers for Disease Control and Prevention. Public Health Image Library, ID# 4139. Available at: http://phil.cdc.gov/phil/home.asp. Accessed August 2, 2008.

Renaissance (approximately 1200–1699)

Paracelsus (1493–1541).

Paracelsus was one of the founders of the field of toxicology, a discipline that is used to examine the toxic effects of chemicals found in environmental venues such as the workplace. Active during the time of da Vinci and Copernicus, Paracelsus advanced toxicology during the early sixteenth century. Among his contributions were several important concepts: the dose-response relationship, which refers to the observation that the effects of a poison are related to the strength of its dose, and the notion of target organ specificity of chemicals.

John Graunt (1620–1674).

In 1662, John Graunt published *Natural and Political Observations Mentioned in a Following Index, and Made Upon the Bills of Mortality*. This work recorded descriptive characteristics of birth and death data, including seasonal variations, infant mortality, and excess male over female mortality. Graunt is said to be the first to employ quantitative methods to describe population vital statistics by organizing mortality data in a mortality table. Because of his contributions to vital statistics, Graunt has been called the Columbus of statistics.

Eighteenth Century (1700–1799)

Ramazzini (1633–1714).

Bernardino Ramazzini is regarded as the founder of the field of occupational medicine.[7] He created elaborate descriptions of the manifestations of occupational diseases among many different types of workers.[8] His descriptions covered a plethora of occupations, from miners to cleaners of privies to fabric workers. The father of occupational medicine is also considered to be a pioneer in the field of ergonomics, by pointing out the hazards associated with postures assumed in various occupations. Ramazzini authored *De Morbis Artificum Diatriba* (Diseases of Workers), published in 1700. His book highlighted the risks posed by hazardous chemicals, dusts, and metals used in the workplace.

Sir Percival Pott (1714–1788).

Sir Percival Pott, a London surgeon, is thought to be the first individual to describe an environmental cause of cancer. In 1775, Pott made the astute observation that chimney sweeps had a high incidence of scrotal cancer (in comparison with male workers in other occupations).[9] He argued that chimney sweeps were prone to this malady as a consequence of their contact with soot.

In a book entitled *Chirurgical Observations Relative to the Cataract, the Polypus of the Nose, the Cancer of the Scrotum, the Different Kinds of Ruptures, and the Mortification of the Toes and Feet*, Pott developed a chapter called "A Short Treatise of the Chimney Sweeper's Cancer." This brief work of only 725 words is noteworthy because "… it provided the first clear description of an environmental cause of cancer, suggested a way to prevent the disease, and led indirectly to the synthesis of the first known pure carcinogen and the isolation of the first carcinogenic chemical to be obtained from a natural product. No wonder therefore that Pott's observation has come to be regarded as the foundation stone on w[h]ich the knowledge of cancer prevention has been built!"[10(p521)] In Pott's own words,

> … every body … is acquainted with the disorders to which painters, plummers, glaziers, and the workers in white lead are liable; but there is a disease as peculiar to a certain set of people which has not, at least to my knowledge, been publickly noteced; I mean the chimney-sweepers' cancer. … The fate of these people seems singularly hard; in their early infancy, they are most frequently treated with great brutality, and almost starved with cold and hunger; they are thrust up narrow, and sometimes hot chimnies, where they are bruised, burned, and almost suffocated; and

> when they get to puberty, become peculiary [sic] liable to a noisome, painful and fatal disease. Of this last circumstance there is not the least doubt though perhaps it may not have been sufficiently attended to, to make it generally known. Other people have cancers of the same part; and so have others besides lead-workers, the Poictou colic, and the consequent paralysis; but it is nevertheless a disease to which they are particularly liable; and so are chimney-sweepers to the cancer of the scrotum and testicles. The disease, in these people … seems to derive its origin from a lodgment of soot in the rugae of the scrotum.[10(p521–522)]

Following his conclusions about the relationship between scrotal cancer and chimney sweeping, Pott established an occupational hygiene control measure—the recommendation that chimney sweeps bathe once a week.

Edward Jenner (1749–1823).

In 1798, Jenner's findings regarding the development of a vaccine that provided immunity to smallpox were published. Jenner had observed that dairymaids who had been infected with cowpox (transmitted by cattle) were immune to smallpox. The cowpox virus, known as the vaccinia virus, produces a milder infection in humans than does the smallpox virus. Jenner created a vaccine by using material from the arm of a dairymaid, Sarah Nelmes, who had an active case of cowpox. In 1796, the vaccine was injected into the arm of an eight-year-old boy, James Fipps, who was later exposed to smallpox and did not develop the disease. Concluding that the procedure was effective, Jenner vaccinated other children including his own son. Figure 1-7 displays an 1802 cartoon by British satirist James Gillray. The cartoon implied that people who were vaccinated would become part cow.

Nineteenth Century (1800–1899)

John Snow and cholera in London during the mid-nineteenth century.

Over the centuries, cholera has inspired great fear because of the dramatic symptoms and mortality that it causes. Cholera is a potentially highly fatal disease marked by profuse watery stools, called rice water stools. The onset of cholera is sudden and marked by painless diarrhea that can progress to dehydration and circulatory collapse; severe, untreated cholera outbreaks can kill more than one-half of affected cases. At present, the cause of cholera is known (the bacterium *Vibrio cholerae*); the level of fatality is often less than

FIGURE 1-7 The Cow Pock—or—the Wonderful Effects of the New Inoculation.

Source: Drawing by James Gillray, 1802. Reprinted from National Institutes of Health, National Library of Medicine. Smallpox: A Great and Terrible Scourge. Available at: http://www.nlm.nih.gov/exhibition/smallpox/sp_vaccination.html. Accessed August 2, 2008.

1% when the disease is treated. One of the methods for transmission of cholera is through ingestion of contaminated water (see Figure 1-8).

John Snow (1813–1858) was an English anesthesiologist who innovated several of the key epidemiologic methods that remain valid and in use today. For example, Snow believed that the disease cholera was transmitted by contaminated water and was able to demonstrate this association. In Snow's time, the mechanism for the causation of infectious diseases such as cholera was largely unknown. The Dutchman Anton van Leeuwenhoek had used the microscope to observe microorganisms (bacteria and yeast). However, the connection between microorganisms and disease had not yet been ascertained. One of the explanations for infectious diseases was the **miasmatic theory of disease**, which held that ". . . disease was transmitted by a miasm, or cloud, that clung low on the surface of the earth."[11(p11)] This theory was applied to malaria, among other diseases.

FIGURE 1-8 Typical water supply that is contaminated with *Vibrio cholerae,* the infectious disease agent for cholera.

Source: Reprinted from Centers for Disease Control and Prevention. Public Health Image Library, ID# 1940. Available at: http://phil.cdc.gov/phil/home.asp. Accessed August 3, 2008.

John Snow, M.D., the forerunner of modern epidemiologists

Snow's contributions included:

- Powers of observation and written expression
- Application of epidemiologic methods
  - Mapping (spot maps)
  - Use of data tables to describe infectious disease outbreaks
- Participation in a natural experiment
- Recommendation of a public health measure to prevent disease (removal of the pump handle; see text)

Snow noted that an outbreak of "Asiatic" cholera had occurred in India during the early 1800s. Snow wrote, "The first case of decided Asiatic cholera in London, in the autumn of 1848, was that of a seaman named John Harnold, who had newly arrived by the *Elbe* steamer from Hamburgh, where the disease was prevailing."[12(p3)] Subsequently, cholera began to appear in London.

During the mid-1800s, Snow conducted an investigation of a cholera outbreak in London. A section of London, designated the Broad Street neighborhood (now part of the Soho district), became the focus of Snow's detective work (refer to the map shown in Figure 1-9). His procedures for investigating the cholera outbreak demonstrated several important innovations (summarized in the text box titled "John Snow, M.D., the forerunner of modern epidemiologists").

Here is Snow's graphic description of the cholera outbreak that occurred in 1849. "The most terrible outbreak of cholera which ever occurred in this kingdom, is probably that which took place in Broad Street, Golden Square, and the adjoining streets, a few weeks ago. . . . The mortality in this limited area probably equals any that was ever caused in this country, even by the plague; and it was much more sudden, as the greater number of cases terminated in a few hours. . . . Many houses were closed altogether, owing to the death of the proprietors; and, in a great number of instances, the tradesmen who remained had sent away their families: so that in less than six days from the commencement of the outbreak, the most afflicted streets were deserted by more than three-quarters of their inhabitants."[12(p38)]

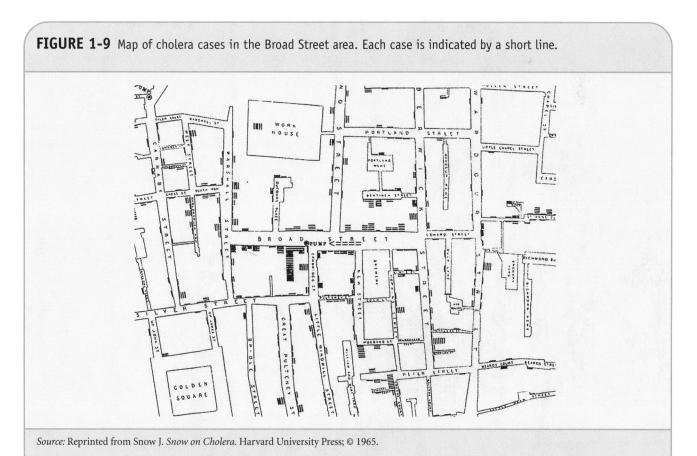

FIGURE 1-9 Map of cholera cases in the Broad Street area. Each case is indicated by a short line.

Source: Reprinted from Snow J. *Snow on Cholera.* Harvard University Press; © 1965.

Snow's pioneering approach illustrated the use of both descriptive and analytic epidemiology. One of his first activities was to plot the cholera deaths in relation to a pump that he hypothesized was the cause of the cholera outbreak. Each death was shown on the map (Figure 1-9) as a short line. An arrow in the figure points to the location of the Broad Street pump. "As soon as I became acquainted with the situation and the extent of this irruption of cholera, I suspected some contamination of the water of the much-frequented street-pump in Broad Street, near the end of Cambridge Street; . . . On proceeding to the spot, I found that nearly all the deaths had taken place within a short distance of the pump."[12(pp38–39)] The handle of the pump was later removed—a public health measure to control the outbreak. In Snow's time, many European cities took water for domestic use directly from rivers, which often were contaminated with microorganisms. (Refer to Figure 1-10, which suggests that pumps that dispensed river water were sources of deadly contamination.)

FIGURE 1-10 Death lurks at the pump.

Source: © SPL/Photo Researchers, Inc.

The natural experiment: Two water companies, the Lambeth Company and the Southwark and Vauxhall Company, provided water in such a manner that adjacent houses could receive water from two different sources. In 1852, one of the companies, the Lambeth Company, relocated its water sources to a section of the Thames River that was less contaminated. During a later cholera outbreak in 1854, Snow observed that a higher proportion of residents who used the water from the Southwark and Vauxhall Company developed cholera than did residents who used water from the Lambeth Company. The correspondence between changes in the quality of the water supply and changes in the occurrence of cholera became known as a natural experiment.

Collection and presentation of data in tabular format: Data from the outbreak of 1854 are presented in Table 1-3. The Lambeth Company provided cleaner water than the Southwark and Vauxhall Company. "The mortality in the houses supplied by the Southwark and Vauxhall Company was therefore between eight and nine times as great as in the houses supplied by the Lambeth Company. . . ."[12(p86)]

Here is a second example of Snow's contributions to epidemiology. In addition to utilizing the method of natural experiment, Snow provided expert witness testimony on behalf of industry with respect to environmental exposures to potential disease agents.[13] Snow attempted to extrapolate from the health effects of exposures to high doses of environmental substances to the effects of exposure to low doses. On January 23, 1855, a bill was introduced in the British Parliament called the Nuisances Removal and Diseases Prevention Amendments bill. This bill was a reform of Victorian public health legislation that followed the 1854 cholera epidemic.[13] The intent of the bill was to control release into the atmosphere of fumes from operations such as gas works, silk-boiling works, and bone-boiling factories. Snow contended that these odiferous fumes

TABLE 1-3 The Proportion of Deaths per 10,000 Houses—Cholera Epidemic of 1854

	Number of houses	Deaths from cholera	Deaths in each 10,000 houses
Southwark and Vauxhall Company	40,046	1,263	315
Lambeth Company	26,107	98	37
Rest of London	256,423	1,422	59

Source: Reprinted from Snow J. *Snow on Cholera.* Harvard University Press; © 1965;86.

were not a disease hazard in the community.[14] The thesis of Snow's argument was that deleterious health effects from the low levels of exposure experienced in the community were unlikely, given the knowledge about higher-level exposures among those who worked in the factories. Snow argued that the workers in the factories were not suffering any ill health effects or dying from the exposures. Therefore, it was unlikely that the much lower exposures experienced by the members of the larger community would affect their health.

William Farr (1807–1883).

A contemporary of John Snow, William Farr assumed the post of "Compiler of Abstracts" at the General Register Office (located in England) in 1839 and held this position for forty years. Among Farr's contributions to public health and epidemiology was the development of a more sophisticated system for codifying medical conditions than that which was previously in use. Also noteworthy is the fact that Farr used data such as census reports to study occupational mortality in England. In addition, he explored the possible linkage between mortality rates and population density, showing that both the average number of deaths and births per 1,000 living persons increased with population density (defined as number of persons per square mile).

Robert Koch (1843–1910).

The German physician Robert Koch (Figure 1-11) verified that a human disease was caused by a specific living organism. He isolated the bacteria that cause anthrax (*Bacillus anthracis*) and cholera (*Vibrio cholerae*). One of his most famous contributions was identifying the cause of tuberculosis (*Mycobacterium tuberculosis*); this work was described in 1882 in *Die Aetiologie der Tuberkulose*. Koch's four postulates to demonstrate the association between a microorganism and a disease were formatted as follows:

1. The organism must be observed in every case of the disease.
2. It must be isolated and grown in pure culture.
3. The pure culture must, when inoculated into a susceptible animal, reproduce the disease.
4. The organism must be observed in, and recovered from, the experimental animal.[15]

Early Twentieth Century (1900–1940)

Pandemic influenza.

Also known as the Spanish Flu, this pandemic raged from 1918 to 1919 and killed 50 to 100 million persons globally. Estimates

FIGURE 1-11 Image of Robert Koch.

Source: © National Library of Medicine.

suggest that one-third of the world's population, which then was 1.5 billion, became infected and developed clinically observable illness. Instead of primarily attacking the young and the elderly as is usually the situation with influenza, the Spanish Flu took a heavy toll on healthy young adults. One hypothesis is that the influenza virus interacted with respiratory bacteria, causing numerous deaths from bacterial pneumonias. The death rate was so high that morgues were overflowing with bodies awaiting burial; adequate supplies of coffins and the services of morticians were unavailable. To handle the influx of patients, special field hospitals were set up. (See Figure 1-12.)

Discovery of penicillin.

Scottish researcher Alexander Fleming (1881–1955) discovered the antimicrobial properties of the mold *Penicillium notatum* in 1928. This breakthrough led to development of the antibiotic penicillin, which became available toward the end of World War II.

The Contemporary Era (1940 to the present)

From the mid-twentieth century to the present (first decade of the twenty-first century), epidemiology has made numerous contributions to society. These innovations include:

FIGURE 1-12 Emergency hospital during influenza epidemic, Camp Funston, Kansas.

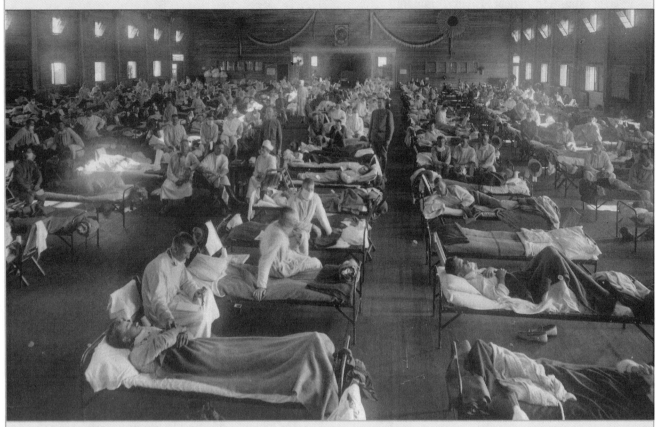

Source: © National Museum of Health and Medicine, Armed Forces, Institute of Pathology, (NCI, 1903).

- Framingham Study. Begun in 1948, this pioneering research project is named for Framingham, Massachusetts. Initially, a random sample of 6,500 persons aged 30 to 59 years participated. This project has been responsible for gathering basic information about aspects of health such as the etiology of coronary heart disease. Chapter 6 will present more information on the Framingham study.
- Epidemic Intelligence Service. Alexander Langmuir was hired by the Centers for Disease Control and Prevention as the first chief epidemiologist. One of Langmuir's contributions was the establishment in 1949 of the Epidemic Intelligence Service (EIS). In the beginning, the mission of EIS was to combat bioterrorism. Presently, EIS officers aid in the rapid response to public health needs both domestically and internationally.
- Smoking and health. By the mid-twentieth century, a growing body of evidence suggested that cigarette smoking contributed to early mortality from lung cancer as well as other forms of morbidity and mortality. In 1964, the U.S. Surgeon General released *Smoking and Health*,[16] which stated that cigarette smoking is a cause of lung cancer in men and is linked to other disabling or fatal diseases.
- Smallpox eradication. As noted previously, Jenner pioneered development of a smallpox vaccine during the 1800s. Smallpox is an incurable disease caused by a virus. One form of the virus *variola major* produces a highly fatal infection in unvaccinated populations. Because of a highly effective surveillance and vaccination program that was intensified during the late 1960s, the ancient scourge of smallpox was brought under control. The last known naturally acquired case was reported in Somalia in 1977.
- Some newer developments. More recent contributions of epidemiology include helping to discover the associ-

ation between the human papillomavirus and cervical cancer, the correspondence between a bacterium (*Helicobacter pylori*) and peptic ulcers, and the correlation between genetic factors and cancers (e.g., breast cancer).

BRIEF OVERVIEW OF CURRENT USES OF EPIDEMIOLOGY

Epidemiologists are indebted to J.N. Morris,[17] who published a list of seven uses of epidemiology; five of these uses are shown in the text box.

Among the principal uses of epidemiology are the following:

- Historical use: study the history of the health of populations
- Community health use: diagnose the health of the community
- Health services use: study the working of health services
- Risk assessment use: estimate individuals' risks of disease, accident, or defect
- Disease causality use: search for the causes of health and disease

Source: Adapted from Morris JN. *Uses of Epidemiology.* 3rd ed. Edinburgh, UK: Churchill Livingstone; 1975:262–263.

Historical Use

The historical use of epidemiology documents the patterns, types, and causes of morbidity and mortality over time. Since the early 1900s, in developed countries the causes of mortality have shifted from those related primarily to infectious and communicable diseases to chronic conditions. This use is illustrated by changes over time in the causes of mortality in the United States. For example, Figure 1-13 shows the decline in the rate of infectious disease mortality between 1900 and 1996. Mortality from infectious diseases rose sharply during the influenza pandemic of 1918 and then continued its downward trend. In the early 1980s, mortality from infectious diseases increased again because of the impact of human immunodeficiency virus (HIV) disease. Mortality from HIV disease subsequently declined and caused 12,543 deaths in 2005; during that year, the leading causes of death were heart disease, cancer, and stroke. (Refer to Chapter 2 for more information.)

The term **epidemiologic transition** describes a shift in the patterns of morbidity and mortality from causes related primarily to infectious and communicable diseases to causes

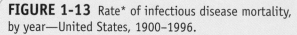

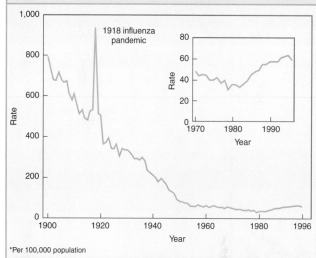

FIGURE 1-13 Rate* of infectious disease mortality, by year—United States, 1900–1996.

*Per 100,000 population

Source: Adapted from Armstrong GL, Conn LA, Pinner RW. Trends in infectious disease mortality in the United States during the 20th century. *JAMA.* 1999;281:63. Copyright © 1999 American Medical Association. All rights reserved. Insert: Reprinted from Centers for Disease Control and Prevention. CDC's 60th Anniversary: Director's Perspective—James O. Mason, M.D., Dr.P.H., 1983–1989. *MMWR.* 2006;55:1356.

associated with chronic, degenerative diseases. The epidemiologic transition coincides with the **demographic transition**, a shift from high birth rates and death rates found in agrarian societies to much lower birth and death rates in developed countries. Figure 1-14 shows the stage of epidemiologic transition across the top and the stage of demographic transition across the bottom. These two kinds of transition parallel one another over time. The figure is subdivided into four segments: pre-, early, late, and post-. Refer to the figure for the definitions of these stages. At present, the United States is in the posttransition stage, which is dominated by diseases associated with personal behavior, adverse lifestyle, and emerging infections.

Community Health Use

Morris described this use as follows: "To *diagnose the health of the community* and the condition of the people, to measure the true dimensions and distribution of ill-health in terms of incidence, prevalence, disability and mortality; to set health problems in perspective and define their relative importance; to identify groups needing special attention."[17(p262)]

Examples of characteristics that affect the health of the community are age and sex distributions, racial/ethnic makeup, socioeconomic status, employment and unemployment rates, access to healthcare services, population density, and residential

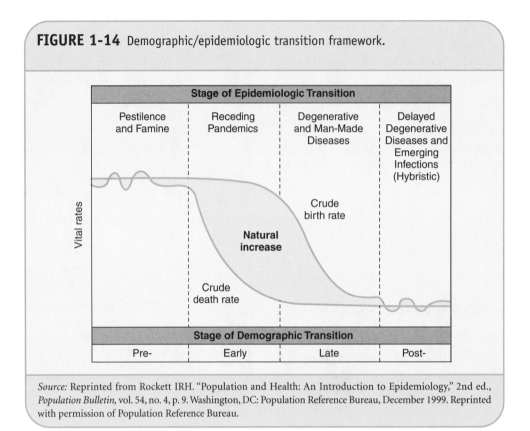

FIGURE 1-14 Demographic/epidemiologic transition framework.

Source: Reprinted from Rockett IRH. "Population and Health: An Introduction to Epidemiology," 2nd ed., *Population Bulletin*, vol. 54, no. 4, p. 9. Washington, DC: Population Reference Bureau, December 1999. Reprinted with permission of Population Reference Bureau.

mobility. These variables are reflected in a wide range of outcomes: life expectancy, social conditions, and patterns of morbidity and mortality. These characteristics will be covered in more detail in Chapter 4 (descriptive epidemiology) and Chapter 6 (analytic epidemiology—section on ecologic studies).

Health Services Use

Morris also proposed that epidemiology could be used "to study the *working of health services* with a view to their improvement. Operational research translates knowledge of (changing) community health and expectations in terms of needs for services and measure [sic] how these are met."[17(p262)]

Operations research is defined as a type of study of the placement of health services in a community and the optimum utilization of such services. Epidemiology helps to provide quantitative information regarding the availability and cost of healthcare services. Epidemiologic studies aid planners in determining what services are needed in the community and what services are duplicated unnecessarily. Provision of healthcare services is exceedingly costly for society; epidemiologic methods can be used to weigh cost issues against quality of services in order to maximize cost effectiveness.

Epidemiologic findings are relevant to the current era of managed care through **disease management**; this term refers to a method of reducing healthcare costs by providing integrated care for chronic conditions, e.g., heart disease, hypertension, and diabetes.

Risk Assessment Use

According to Morris, this application was "to estimate from the group experience what are the *individual* risks on average of disease, accident and defect, and the *chances* of avoiding them."[17(p262)]

Risk is "the probability that an event will occur, e.g., that an individual will become ill or die within a stated period of time or by a certain age."[1] A **risk factor** is an exposure that is associated with a disease, morbidity, mortality, or adverse health outcome. For example, cigarette smoking increases the risk of contracting certain forms of cancer including lung cancer. Epidemiologic studies provide quantitative measurements of risks to health through a methodology known as **risk assessment**. One of the major cornerstones of health policy development, risk assessment (and its four components) will be covered in Chapter 7.

Disease Causality Use

With respect to this use, Morris wrote, "To *search for causes* of health and disease by computing the experience of groups defined by their composition, inheritance and experience, their behaviour [sic] and environments."[17(p263)]

The search for causes of disease and other health outcomes is one of the most important uses of epidemiology. In order to assess potential causal associations, epidemiologists need to consider a set of criteria that must be satisfied; refer to Chapter 2 for more information. Possible associations can be evaluated by analytic study designs; these designs include case-control and cohort studies. Other analytic studies involve natural experiments, randomized controlled clinical trials, and community trials. Analytic study designs are discussed in Chapter 6. We will learn that study designs, whether observational or analytic, can be arranged in a hierarchy according to our confidence in the validity of the information that they provide.

ETHICS AND PHILOSOPHY OF EPIDEMIOLOGY

Description of Ethics in Research

The final topic in this chapter relates to ethics and epidemiology. The term **ethics** refers to "... **norms for conduct** that distinguish between ... acceptable and unacceptable behavior."[18] David B. Resnik, bioethicist for the National Institute of Environmental Health Sciences, has written the following statement about ethics in research:

> When most people think of ethics (or morals), they think of rules for distinguishing between right and wrong, such as the Golden Rule ("Do unto others as you would have them do unto you"), a code of professional conduct like the Hippocratic Oath ("First of all, do no harm"), a religious creed like the Ten Commandments ("Thou shalt not kill ..."), or a wise aphorisms [sic] like the sayings of Confucius. This is the most common way of defining "ethics": ethics are **norms for conduct** that distinguish between ... acceptable and unacceptable behavior ....
>
> Many different disciplines, institutions, and professions have norms for behavior that suit their particular aims and goals. These norms also help members of the discipline to coordinate their actions or activities and to establish the public's trust of the discipline. For instance, ethical norms govern conduct in medicine, law, engineering, and business. Ethical norms also serve the aims or goals of research and apply to people who conduct scientific research or other scholarly or cre-

ative activities, and there is a specialized discipline, research ethics, which studies these norms.

> There are several reasons why it is important to adhere to ethical norms in research. First, some of these norms **promote the aims of research**, such as knowledge, truth, and avoidance of error. For example, prohibitions against fabricating, falsifying, or misrepresenting research data promote the truth and avoid error. Second, since research often involves a great deal of cooperation and coordination among many different people in different disciplines and institutions, many of these ethical standards promote the **values that are essential to collaborative work**, such as trust, accountability, mutual respect, and fairness. For example, many ethical norms in research, such as guidelines for authorship, copyright and patenting policies, data sharing policies, and confidentiality rules in peer review, are designed to protect intellectual property interests while encouraging collaboration. Most researchers want to receive credit for their contributions and do not want to have their ideas stolen or disclosed prematurely. Third, many of the ethical norms help to ensure that researchers can be held **accountable to the public**. For instance, federal policies on research misconduct, on conflicts of interest, on the human subjects protections, and on animal care and use are necessary in order to make sure that researchers who are funded by public money can be held accountable to the public. Fourth, ethical norms in research also help to build **public support** for research. People [are] more likely to fund research project [sic] if they can trust the quality and integrity of research. Finally, many of the norms of research promote a variety of other important **moral and social values**, such as social responsibility, human rights, animal welfare, compliance with the law, and health and safety. Ethical lapses in research can significantly [do] harm to human and animal subjects, students, and the public. For example, a researcher who fabricates data in a clinical trial may harm or even kill patients, and a researcher who fails to abide by regulations and guidelines relating to radiation or biological safety may jeopardize his health and safety or the health and safety ... [of] staff and students.[18]

A description of syphilis

A sexually transmitted disease associated with the bacterial agent *Treponema pallidum*, syphilis can have both acute (having sudden onset) and chronic (long-term) phases. The initial infection (primary lesion) produces a painless sore (called a chancre) that appears approximately three weeks after exposure. After the primary lesion seems to resolve, a secondary infection (e.g., a rash on the palms of the hands and soles of the feet) may appear in about two months. This secondary infection resolves several weeks or months later and then becomes a latent infection. Some infections will remain latent for life and others will progress to tertiary syphilis, resulting in diseases of the central nervous system, cardiovascular system (see Figure 1-15), or other organs of the body.[20] At present, syphilis is treatable with penicillin and other antibiotics. Before the advent of modern antibiotics, compounds that contained mercury or arsenic were used to treat syphilis. These treatments were not completely effective and often were harmful.

Ethical Violation: U.S. Public Health Service Syphilis Study at Tuskegee

The U.S. Public Health Service in conjunction with the Tuskegee Institute began a syphilis investigation in 1932 that spanned forty years. (Refer to the text box for a description of syphilis.) The purpose of the study was to ". . . record the natural history of syphilis in hopes of justifying treatment programs for blacks. It was called 'The Tuskegee Study of Untreated Syphilis in the Negro Male.'"[19] A total of 600 African American Men (399 syphilis cases and 201 syphilis-free controls) participated in the study.

The participants in the Tuskegee Study never gave informed consent to participate. "Researchers told the men that they were being treated for 'bad blood,' a local term used to describe several ailments, including syphilis, anemia, and fatigue."[19] Appropriate treatment for syphilis was never offered, despite the fact that as early as 1947 penicillin was known to be efficacious. A class-action suit filed on behalf of the men in 1973 resulted in a $10 million settlement plus medical and health benefits. Figure 1-16 shows a nurse conversing with some of the participants in the study.

FIGURE 1-15 Stenosis (narrowing) of the coronary arteries due to cardiovascular syphilis.

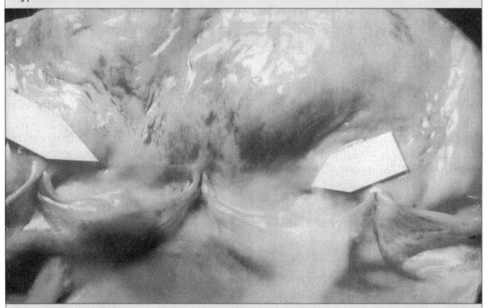

Source: Reprinted from Centers for Disease Control and Prevention, Public Health Image Library, ID# 2339. Available at: http://phil.cdc.gov/phil/home.asp. Accessed August 3, 2008.

FIGURE 1-16 Tuskegee syphilis study participants with Nurse Rivers.

Source: Photo from the U.S. Public Health Service. Reprinted from the National Archives, Southeast Region. Available at: http://www.archives.gov/southeast/exhibit/popups.php?p=6.1.5. Accessed August 3, 2008.

Nowadays, universities maintain Human Subjects Review Boards to ensure that all research protocols that involve human beings and animals are reviewed to make certain that the procedures meet the requirements for informed consent and other ethical standards. In addition, many professional organizations have adopted codes of professional ethics to prevent ethical lapses by their members. For example, epidemiologists operate according to a set of core values that guide practice in the field. The American College of Epidemiology (ACE) has developed a statement of ethics guidelines.[21] Five of the guidelines have been abstracted from the ACE ethics statement (refer to text box).

CONCLUSION

Epidemiologists study the occurrence of diseases and health outcomes in populations. Findings from epidemiologic research are reported frequently in the popular media. For example, disease outbreaks such as those caused by foodborne illnesses often command public attention. Chapter 1 defined some of the terms that are used to describe disease outbreaks, discussed the scope and applications of epidemiology, and presented information on its interdisciplinary composition. Epidemiologic methods are applicable to many types of health-related issues,

Ethics guidelines for epidemiologists

- Minimizing risks and protecting the welfare of research subjects
- Obtaining the informed consent of participants
- Submitting proposed studies for ethical review
- Maintaining public trust
- [Meeting] obligations to communities

Source: Adapted and reprinted from American College of Epidemiology, Ethics Guidelines. This article was published in *Annals of Epidemiology,* Vol 10, No 8, 2000, pp. 487–497, "Ethics guidelines." Available at: http://www.acepidemiology2.org/policystmts/EthicsGuide.asp. Accessed August 7, 2008.

from infectious diseases to violence in schools. Although many people consider epidemiology to be primarily a medical subject, it is also a liberal arts discipline in many respects; epidemiology provides training in generally applicable skills such as critical thinking ability and use of the scientific method.

Epidemiology is primarily an observational science that involves describing the occurrence of disease in populations (descriptive epidemiology) and researching the etiology of diseases (analytic epidemiology). The history of epidemiology extends over many centuries, beginning during classical antiquity at the time of the ancient Greeks. Subsequent historical events included the identification of infectious disease agents and Snow's use of methods such as case mapping and data tabulation that remain relevant today. Recent history has included eradication of smallpox and development of improved procedures to control chronic diseases. Chapter 1 concluded with a review of the uses of epidemiology and a discussion of the ethical aspects of epidemiologic research.

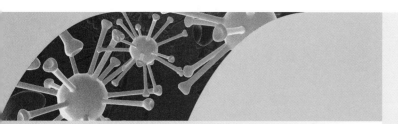

Study Questions and Exercises

1. Define the following terms:
   a. epidemic
   b. pandemic
   c. epidemiology

2. Define and discuss three of the key characteristics of epidemiology.

3. In what respects does epidemiology differ from clinical medicine?

4. What are some examples of risk factors for disease that you experience in your life? Be sure to define what is meant by a risk factor.

5. Check your local library or go online to find works of literature that describe epidemics and epidemic detective work.

6. Distinguish between the descriptive and analytic approaches to epidemiology.

7. The following list shows individuals who contributed to the history of epidemiology. Describe each of their contributions.
   a. Hippocrates
   b. John Graunt
   c. Sir Percival Pott
   d. John Snow
   e. Robert Koch

8. Discuss four uses of epidemiology. For each use, give examples that were not mentioned in the textbook.

9. Find an article in the popular media (either in the print media or online) that illustrates one or more uses of epidemiology. Be prepared to discuss the article in class.

Young Epidemiology Scholars (YES) Exercises

The Young Epidemiology Scholars Web site provides links to teaching units and exercises that support instruction in epidemiology. The YES program is administered by the College Board and supported by the Robert Wood Johnson Foundation. The Web address of YES is www.collegeboard.com/yes. The following exercises relate to topics discussed in this chapter and can be found on the YES Web site.

History of epidemiology:

1. McCrary F, Stolley P. Examining the plague: An investigation of epidemic past and present.

2. McCrary F, St. George DMM. Mortality and the transatlantic slave trade.

3. McCrary F, Baumgarten M. Casualties of war: The short- and long-term effects of the 1945 atomic bomb attacks on Japan.

Uses of epidemiology:

1. Huang FI, Bayona M. Disease outbreak investigation.

Ethical issues:

1. Kaelin MA, St. George DMM. Ethical issues in epidemiology.

2. Huang FI, St. George DMM. Should the population be screened for HIV?

3. McCrary F, St. George DMM. The Tuskegee Syphilis Study.

REFERENCES

1. Porta M, ed. *A Dictionary of Epidemiology*. 5th ed. New York: Oxford University Press; 2008.

2. Friis RH, Sellers TA. *Epidemiology for Public Health Practice*. 4th ed. Sudbury, MA: Jones and Bartlett Publishers; 2009.

3. Oppenheimer GM. Comment: Epidemiology and the liberal arts—toward a new paradigm? *Am J Public Health*. 1995;85:918–920.

4. Fraser DW. Epidemiology as a liberal art. *N Engl J Med*. 1987;316: 309–314.

5. Grufferman S. Methodological approaches to studying environmental factors in childhood cancer. *Environ Health Perspect*. 1998;106(Suppl 3): 881–886.

6. Wegman DH. The potential impact of epidemiology on the prevention of occupational disease. *Am J Public Health*. 1992;82:944–954.

7. Franco G. Ramazzini and workers' health. *Lancet*.1999;354:858–861.

8. Gochfeld M. Chronologic history of occupational medicine. *J Occup Environ Med*. 2005;47:96–114.

9. National Institutes of Health, National Institute of Environmental Health Sciences. Medicine for the layman environment and disease. Available at: http://www.mindfully.org/Health/Layman-Medicine.htm. Accessed August 10, 2008.

10. Doll R. Pott and the path to prevention. *Arch Geschwulstforsch*. 1975; 45:521–531.

11. Gordis L. *Epidemiology*. 3rd ed. Philadelphia: Elsevier Saunders; 2004.

12. Snow J. *Snow on Cholera*. New York: Hafner Publishing Company, by arrangement with Harvard University Press; 1965.

13. Lilienfeld DE. John Snow: the first hired gun? *Am J Epidemiol*. 2000; 152:4–9.

14. Sandler DP. John Snow and modern-day environmental epidemiology. *Am J Epidemiol*. 2000;152:1–3.

15. King LS. Dr. Koch's postulates. *J Hist Med*. Autumn 1952:350–361.

16. U.S. Department of Health, Education and Welfare, Public Health Service. *Smoking and Health, Report of the Advisory Committee to the Surgeon General of the Public Health Service*. Public Health Service publication 1103, Washington, DC: Government Printing Office; 1964.

17. Morris JN. *Uses of Epidemiology*. 3rd ed. Edinburgh, UK: Churchill Livingstone; 1975.

18. Resnik DB. What is ethics in research and why is it important? National Institute of Environmental Health Sciences. Available at: http://www.niehs.nih.gov/research/resources/bioethics/whatis.cfm. Accessed July 11, 2008.

19. Centers for Disease Control and Prevention. U.S. Public Health Service Syphilis Study at Tuskegee: The Tuskegee Timeline. Available at: http://www.cdc.gov/tuskegee/timeline.htm. Accessed July 10, 2008.

20. Heymann DL, ed. *Control of Communicable Diseases Manual*. 19th ed. Washington, DC: American Public Health Association; 2008.

21. American College of Epidemiology. Ethics Guidelines. Available at: http://www.acepidemiology.org/policystmts/EthicsGuide.asp. Accessed August 7, 2008.

Epidemiologic Measurements Used to Describe Disease Occurrence

INTRODUCTION

This chapter introduces the concept of measurement in epidemiology. The chapter begins by introducing four key mathematical terms that are applied to epidemiologic constructs; these terms involve the use of fractions and numerators and denominators. Then the chapter relates these terms to basic epidemiologic measures that pertain to the frequency of diseases in populations and risks associated with exposures to disease agents. Chapter 2 discusses conclusions that can be drawn by examining existing and

TABLE 2-1 List of Important Mathematical and Epidemiologic Terms Used in This Chapter

Data presentation	Mathematical terms	Epidemiologic terms: frequency	Epidemiologic terms: risk	Measures related to morbidity and mortality
Enumeration and tabulation	Percentage	Count	Incidence	Case fatality rate
Histogram	Proportion	Period prevalence	Incidence rate	Crude rate
Line graph	Rate	Point prevalence	Population at risk	Death rate
Pie chart	Ratio	Prevalence	Reference population	Specific rate and adjusted rate

new cases of disease and subsequently defines basic measures of morbidity and mortality. Refer to Table 2-1 for a list of the major terms and concepts covered in Chapter 2.

PRESENTATION OF EPIDEMIOLOGIC DATA

Counting and Tabulating Cases

Counting and tabulating cases is one of the first steps in presenting data after they have been reviewed for accuracy and completeness (a process called data cleaning). A clean data set contains a group of related data that are ready for coding and data analysis. Table 2-2 presents a data set for twenty patients with hepatitis C virus infection.

Across the top row are shown the column headings that designate the study variables (e.g., case number, interview status, age, sex, and race). Each subsequent row contains the data for a single case. What can be done with the data at this stage? One possibility is to tabulate the data. Computers simplify this task; here is what is involved. The process of tabulation creates

a frequency table for a particular study variable, for example, "Interviewed." This variable is called a categorical variable, meaning that it has a fixed number of categories—"yes" and "no." The tabulated variable is:

Yes: L̶H̶1 L̶H̶1 I   Total number of "yes" responses: 11

No: L̶H̶1 IIII   Total number of "no" responses: 9

Total number of cases = 11 + 9 = 20

Similar tabulations could be performed for the other study variables. Refer to Table 2-3 for the results.

Graphical Presentations

After tabulating the data, an epidemiologist might plot the data graphically as a bar chart, line graph, or pie chart. Such graphical displays summarize the key aspects of the data set. Although visual displays facilitate an intuitive understanding of the data, they omit some of the detail contained in the data set.

TABLE 2-2 Demographic Characteristics, Risk Factors, Surveillance Status, and Clinical Information for Twenty Patients with Hepatitis C Virus (HCV) Infection—Postal Code A, Buffalo, New York, November 2004–April 2007*

Case	Interviewed	Age (yrs)	Sex	Race	Date of diagnosis	Reason for test	IDU[†]	Shared needles	Noninjection-drug use
1	Yes	17	Male	White	11/3/04	Risk factors	Yes	Yes[††]	Yes
2	No	23	Female	White	1/25/05	Symptomatic	Yes	—	Yes
3	No	26	Male	White	3/9/05	Risk factors	Yes	—	—
4	Yes	28	Male	White	12/6/05	Symptomatic	Yes	Yes	Yes
5	Yes	17	Male	White	12/29/05	Risk factors	Yes	Yes[††]	Yes
6	No	19	Male	White	1/20/06	Symptomatic	Yes	Yes[††]	Yes
7	Yes	17	Male	White	1/24/06	Risk factors	Yes	Yes[††]	Yes
8	Yes	16	Female	White	2/17/06	Risk factors	Yes	Yes[††]	Yes
9	Yes	21	Male	White	2/23/06	Risk factors	Yes	Yes[††]	Yes
10	No	22	Male	White	3/2/06	Risk factors	Yes	—	—
11	Yes	18	Female	White	5/17/06	Risk factors	Yes	Yes	Yes
12	Yes	19	Male	White	5/24/06	Risk factors	Yes	Yes	Yes
13	No	19	Male	White	5/24/06	Risk factors	Yes	—	—
14	No	20	Male	White	5/26/06	Symptomatic	Yes	Yes[††]	Yes
15	Yes	17	Female	White	8/14/06	Risk factors	No	No	No
16	Yes	23	Male	White	10/10/06	Risk factors	Yes	Yes[††]	Yes
17	No	19	Male	White	12/19/06	Risk factors	Yes	Yes[††]	Yes
18	No	26	Female	White	1/6/07	Risk factors	Yes	Yes	Yes
19	No	17	Female	White	3/13/07	Risk factors	Yes	Yes[††]	Yes
20	Yes	19	Male	White	4/26/07	Risk factors	Yes	Yes[††]	Yes

*Data were compiled from standard surveillance forms and patient interviews.
[†]Injection-drug use.
[††]Shared needles with a person known or believed to be HCV positive.
Source: Adapted and reprinted from Centers for Disease Control and Prevention. Use of enhanced surveillance for hepatitis C virus infection to detect a cluster among young injection-drug users—New York, November 2004–April 2007. *MMWR.* 2008;57:518.

TABLE 2-3 Tabulations of Discrete (Categorical) Variables by Using Data in Table 2-2

Variable	Frequency	Variable	Frequency
Interviewed	—	IDU	—
Yes	11	Yes	19
No	9	No	1
Unknown	0	Unknown	0
Total	20	Total	20
Sex	—	Shared needle	—
Male	14	Yes	15
Female	6	No	1
Unknown	0	Unknown	4
Total	20	Total	20
Race	—	Noninjection drug use	—
White	20	Yes	16
Other	0	No	1
Unknown	0	Unknown	3
Total	20	Total	20

Source: Author created. Compiled from data in Table 2-2.

A **bar chart** is a type of graph that shows the frequency of cases for categories of a categorical (discrete) variable such as the Yes/No variable described in the foregoing example. Along the base of the bar chart are categories of the variable; the height of the bars represents the frequency of cases for each category. Histograms are similar types of charts that are used to display the frequency distributions for grouped categories of a continuous variable. The definition of a **continuous variable** is a variable that could have an infinite number of values along a continuum; examples of continuous variables are height, weight, and blood sugar level. When continuous variables are plotted as histograms, coding procedures have been applied to convert them into categories. Because of their similarity to bar charts, histograms are not discussed further in this chapter. Selected data from Table 2-3 are graphed in Figure 2-1, which shows a bar chart.

Figure 2-2 presents another example of a bar chart—the percentage of nutrient-fortified wheat flour processed in roller mills in seven World Health Organization (WHO) regions for 2004 and 2007. Fortification of wheat increases the nutritional value of this commodity. The chart demonstrates that the highest percentage of fortified wheat was produced in the Americas and that the percentage showed an increasing trend in all regions between 2004 and 2007.

A second type of graphical display is a line graph, which enables the reader to detect trends in the data; an example is a time trend. A single point represents the frequency of cases for each category of a variable. By using more than one line, the epidemiologist is able to demonstrate comparisons among subgroups. Figure 2-3 shows a line graph of childhood cancer deaths by race and ethnicity between 1990 and 2004. In almost all subgroups, the lines show a declining trend.

FIGURE 2-1 Graph of selected information from Table 2-3.

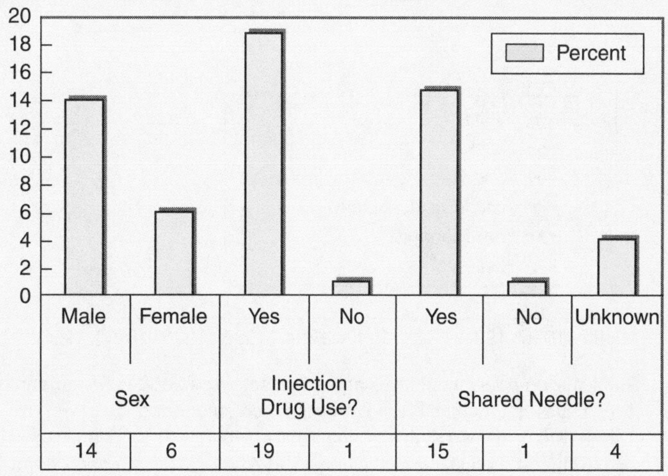

Source: Author created from data in Table 2-3.

A third method for the graphical presentation of data is to construct a pie chart, which is a circle that shows the proportion of cases according to several categories. The size of each piece of "pie" is proportional to the frequency of cases. The pie chart demonstrates the relative importance of each subcategory. For example, the pie chart in Figure 2-4 represents the percentage of childhood cancer deaths by primary site/leading diagnosis for the United States in 2004. The data reveal that leukemias and brain/nervous system cancers accounted for the most frequent percentages of childhood cancer deaths.

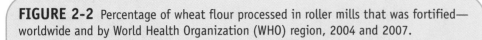

FIGURE 2-2 Percentage of wheat flour processed in roller mills that was fortified—worldwide and by World Health Organization (WHO) region, 2004 and 2007.

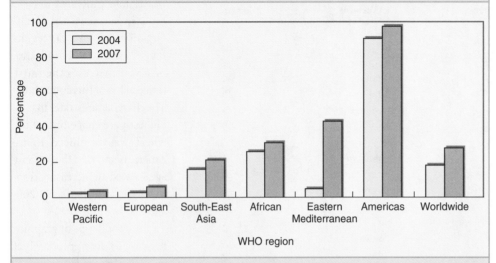

Source: Reprinted from Centers for Disease Control and Prevention. Trends in wheat-flour fortification with folic acid and iron—worldwide, 2004 and 2007. *MMWR.* 2008;57:9.

FIGURE 2-3 Rates* of childhood cancer deaths, by race and ethnicity†—United States, 1990–2004.

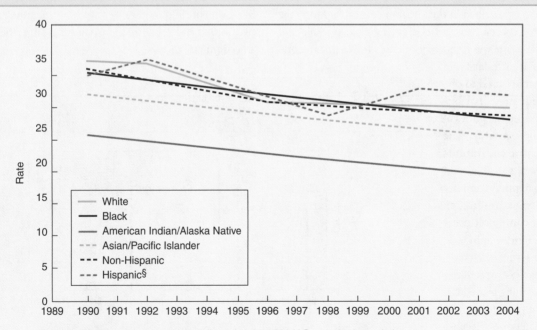

* Per 1 million population; rates age adjusted to the 2000 U.S. standard population.
† Ethnicity is not mutually exclusive from race categories.
§ Death rate remained stable during 1990–1992 (p = 0.53), declined significantly during 1992–1998.
(p = 0.01), and then stabilized during 1998–2001 (p = 0.32) and during 2001–2004 (p = 0.57).

Source: Reprinted from Centers for Disease Control and Prevention. Trends in childhood cancer mortality—United States, 1990–2004. *MMWR.* 2007;56:1260.

FIGURE 2-4 Percentage of childhood cancer deaths,* by primary cancer site/leading diagnosis†—United States, 2004.

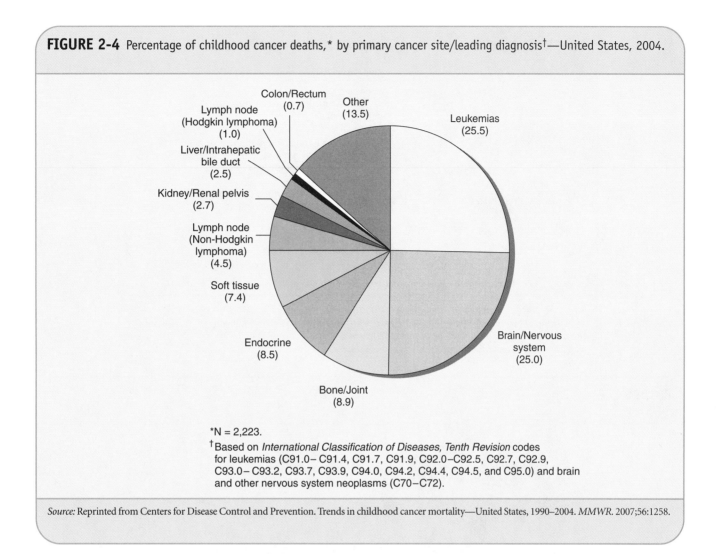

*N = 2,223.

†Based on *International Classification of Diseases, Tenth Revision* codes for leukemias (C91.0– C91.4, C91.7, C91.9, C92.0–C92.5, C92.7, C92.9, C93.0– C93.2, C93.7, C93.9, C94.0, C94.2, C94.4, C94.5, and C95.0) and brain and other nervous system neoplasms (C70–C72).

Source: Reprinted from Centers for Disease Control and Prevention. Trends in childhood cancer mortality—United States, 1990–2004. *MMWR.* 2007;56:1258.

MATHEMATICAL TERMS USED IN EPIDEMIOLOGY

Some important mathematical terms applied to epidemiologic measures are rate, proportion, and percentage; these measures are types of ratios. (Refer to Figure 2-5.) The following section defines these terms and gives calculation examples of ratios, proportions, and percentages for mortality from AIDS. The topic of rates will be covered later in the chapter. Here are some data that will be used for the calculations: for the five-year period, 2002 through 2006, the estimated cumulative number of deaths in the United States from AIDS among adults and adolescents was 450,541 for males and 89,895 for females.[1]

Ratio

A **ratio** is defined as "the value obtained by dividing one quantity by another. RATE, PROPORTION, and percentage are types of ratios."[2] Although a ratio consists of a numerator and a denominator, its most general form does not necessarily

have any specified relationship between the numerator and denominator.

A ratio is expressed as follows: ratio = X/Y.
Calculation example of a ratio:

Example l: With respect to AIDS mortality, the sex ratio of deaths (male to female deaths) = X/Y, where:

$X = 450,451$ and $Y = 89,895$. The sex ratio = 450,451/89,895 = 5 to 1 (approximately).

Example 2: Referring to the data in Table 2-3, you can observe that the ratio of users of intravenous drugs to nonusers is 19 to 1.

Example 3: In demography, the sex ratio refers to the number of males per 100 females. In the United States, the sex ratio in 2005 was 96.5, meaning that there were more women and girls than men and boys.[3] At the same time, there were considerable variations by state; Alaska and Nevada had the highest sex ratios (refer to Figure 2-6.)

FIGURE 2-5 Definitions of mathematical terms that are used in epidemiology.

– Ratio (R)	$R = \dfrac{X}{Y}$	X and Y can be any number, including ratios.
– Rate (r)*	$r = \dfrac{X}{\Delta t}$	Type of ratio where the numerator is usually a count, and the denominator is a time elapsed.
– Proportion (p)	$P = \dfrac{A}{A + B}$	Type of ratio where the numerator is part of the denominator.
– Percent (P)	$P = \left(\dfrac{A}{A + B} \right) \times 100$	A proportion is multiplied by 100.

*Note: This is the mathematical formula for a rate. Refer to text for epidemiologic measures of rates.

Source: Modified with permission from Aragón T. *Descriptive Epidemiology: Describing Findings and Generating Hypotheses.* Center for Infectious Disease Preparedness, UC Berkeley School of Public Health. Available at: http://www.idready. org/slides/feb_descriptive.pdf. Accessed August 16, 2008.

FIGURE 2-6 Sex ratios by state: 2005.

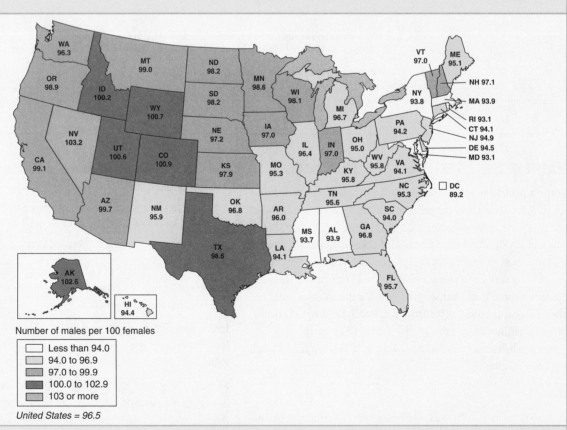

Number of males per 100 females

- Less than 94.0
- 94.0 to 96.9
- 97.0 to 99.9
- 100.0 to 102.9
- 103 or more

United States = 96.5

Source: Reprinted from U.S. Census Bureau. Age and sex distribution in 2005. Population Profile of the United States: Dynamic Version. Available at: http://www.census.gov/population/pop-profile/dynamic/AgeSex.pdf. Accessed July 12, 2008.

Proportion

A **proportion** is a type of ratio in which the numerator is part of the denominator; proportions may be expressed as percentages.

A proportion is expressed as follows: proportion = $A/A + B$

Calculation example of a proportion:

Example 1: Proportion of AIDS deaths

Suppose that A = the number of male deaths from AIDS
A = 450,451
B = the number of female deaths from AIDS
B = 89,895

The proportion of deaths that occurred among males = 450,451/(450,451 + 89,895) = 0.83

Example 2: Proportion of IDU users (data from Table 2-3)

Proportion = 19/(19+1) = 0.95

Percentage

A percentage is a proportion that has been multiplied by 100. The formula for a percentage is as follows: percentage = $(A/A + B) \times 100$

Example 1: The percentage of male deaths from AIDS was (0.83 × 100) = 83%.

Example 2: The percentage of IDU users was (0.95 × 100) = 95%.

Example 3: Refer to Figure 2-7, which is a graph of the percentage of adults who reported joint pain or stiffness in the United States, 2006. The figure demonstrates that slightly less than one-third of adults had symptoms of joint pain within the preceding 30-day period. The most frequently reported form of pain was knee pain. "During 2006, approximately 30% of adults reported experiencing some type of joint pain during the preceding 30 days. Knee pain was reported by 18% of respondents, followed by pain in the shoulder (9%), finger (7%), and hip (7%). Joint pain can be caused by osteoarthritis, injury, prolonged abnormal posture, or repetitive motion." [4(p467)]

Let's consider how a proportion (as well as a percentage) can be helpful in describing health conditions. A proportion indicates how important a health outcome is relative to the size of a group. Refer to the foregoing examples; suppose there were ten college dorm residents who had infectious mononucleosis (a virus-caused disease that produces fever, sore throat, and tiredness). How large a problem did these ten cases represent? To answer this question, one would need to know whether the dormitory housed twenty students or 500 students. If there were only 20 students, then 50% (or 0.50) were ill. Conversely, if there were 500 students in the dormitory, then only 2% (or

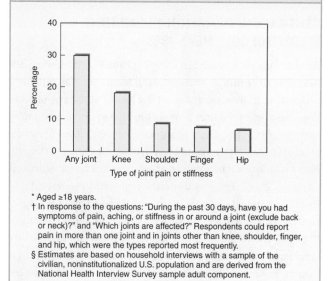

FIGURE 2-7 Percentage of adults* reporting joint pain or stiffness,[†]—National Health Interview Survey,[§] United States, 2006.

* Aged ≥18 years.
† In response to the questions: "During the past 30 days, have you had symptoms of pain, aching, or stiffness in or around a joint (exclude back or neck)?" and "Which joints are affected?" Respondents could report pain in more than one joint and in joints other than knee, shoulder, finger, and hip, which were the types reported most frequently.
§ Estimates are based on household interviews with a sample of the civilian, noninstitutionalized U.S. population and are derived from the National Health Interview Survey sample adult component.

Source: Reprinted from Centers for Disease Control and Prevention. QuickStats: Percentage of adults* reporting joint pain or stiffness,[†] —National Health Interview Survey,[§] United States, 2006. *MMWR.* 2008;57:467.

0.02) were ill. Clearly, these two scenarios paint a completely different picture of the magnitude of the problem. In this situation, expressing the count as a proportion is indeed helpful. In most situations, it will be informative to have some idea about the size of the denominator. Although the construction of a proportion is straightforward, one of the central concerns of epidemiology is to find and enumerate appropriate denominators to describe and compare groups in a meaningful and useful way.

Rate

Also a type of ratio, a **rate** differs from a proportion because the denominator involves a measure of time, indicated by Δt in Figure 2-5. The rate measure shown in the figure is the mathematical formula. As an epidemiologic measure, a rate modifies the terms shown in the numerator and denominator; nevertheless, time is an important component of epidemiologic rates. In epidemiology, rates are used to measure risks associated with exposures and provide information about the speed of development of a disease. Also, rates can be used to make comparisons among populations. More detailed information on rates is provided in the section on crude rates.

Medical publications may use the terms ratio, proportion, and rate without strict adherence to the mathematical definitions for these terms. Hence, one must be alert as to how a measure is defined and calculated.[5]

GENERAL INFORMATION REGARDING EPIDEMIOLOGIC MEASURES

As noted previously, epidemiologic measures represent an application of common mathematical terms such as ratio and proportion to the description of the health of the population. Epidemiologic measures provide the following types of information: (1) the frequency of a disease or condition; (2) associations between exposures and health outcomes; and (3) strength of the relationship between an exposure and a health outcome. Chapters 2 and 3 will focus on the first topic; the second and third topics will be covered in Chapter 5 and Chapter 6, respectively. Figure 2-8 gives an overview of the principal epidemiologic measures covered in Chapter 2; these are count, rate (incidence rate), and prevalence. See Chapter 6 for information on risk, or odds. Keep in mind that time is a component of rates.

The following considerations are important to the expression of epidemiologic measures:

- Defining the numerator.
  - Case definition (condition)—For epidemiologic measures to be valid, the case of disease or other health phenomenon being studied must be defined carefully and in a manner that can be replicated by others.
  - Frequency—How many cases are there?
  - Severity—Some epidemiologic measures employ morbidity as the numerator and others use mortality.

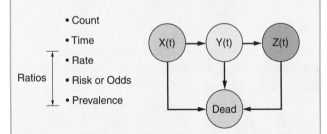

FIGURE 2-8 Epidemiologic measures—measures of occurrence.

- Count
- Time
- Rate
- Risk or Odds
- Prevalence

Ratios

Source: Reprinted with permission from Aragón T. *Descriptive Epidemiology: Describing Findings and Generating Hypotheses.* Center for Infectious Disease Preparedness, UC Berkeley School of Public Health. Available at: http://www.idready.org/slides/feb_descriptive.pdf. Accessed August 16, 2008.

- Defining the denominator—Does the measure make use of the entire population or a subset of the population? Some measures use the population at risk (defined later in the chapter).
- Existing (all cases) versus new cases.

The following sections will define the foregoing terms and concepts.

TYPES OF EPIDEMIOLOGIC MEASURES

A number of quantitative terms, useful in epidemiology, have been developed to characterize the occurrence of disease, morbidity, and mortality in populations. Particularly noteworthy are the two terms *incidence* and *prevalence*, which can be stated as frequencies or raw numbers of cases. (These terms are defined later.) In order to make comparisons among populations that differ in size, statisticians divide the number of cases by the population size.

Counts

The simplest and most frequently performed quantitative measure in epidemiology is a count. As the term implies, a **count** refers merely to the number of cases of a disease or other health phenomenon being studied. As shown in Table 2-4, an example of counts is the number of cases of infrequently reported notifiable diseases per year.

The previous discussion may leave the reader with the impression that counts, because they are simple measures, are of little value in epidemiology; this is not true, however. In fact, case reports of patients with particularly unusual presentations or combinations of symptoms often spur epidemiologic investigations. In addition, for some diseases even a single case is sufficient to be of public health importance. For example, if a case of smallpox or Ebola virus were reported, the size of the denominator would be irrelevant. That is, in these instances a single case, regardless of the size of the population at risk, would stimulate an investigation.

Incidence

The term **incidence** refers to the occurrence of new disease or mortality within a defined period of observation (e.g., a week, month, year, or other time period) in a specified population. Incidence is expressed as a number, e.g., the number of new cases of lung cancer reported during a year. Those members of the population who are capable of developing the disease or condition being studied are known as the **population at risk**.

The **incidence rate** denotes a rate formed by dividing the number of new cases that occur during a time period by the number of individuals in the population at risk. (Several variations of incidence rates exist, but a discussion of all of them

TABLE 2-4 Provisional Cases of Infrequently Reported Notifiable Diseases (<1,000 Cases Reported during the Preceding Year)—United States, Week Ending January 12, 2008 (2nd Week)*

| Disease | Total cases reported for previous years | | | | |
	2007	2006	2005	2004	2003
Cholera	7	9	8	6	2
Hansen disease[†]	62	66	87	105	95
Rabies, human	—	3	2	7	2
Tetanus	20	41	27	34	20

—: No reported cases.
*Incidence data for reporting years 2007 and 2008 are provisional, whereas data for 2003, 2004, 2005, and 2006 are finalized.
†Not notifiable in all states.
Source: Data from Centers for Disease Control and Prevention. *MMWR.* 2008;57:46.

is beyond the scope of this chapter.) Figure 2-9 presents the incidence rates for tuberculosis by state in the United States. The author notes that, statistically speaking, the incidence rate is a rate because of the specification of a time period during which the new cases occur.

$$Incidence\ rate = \frac{Number\ of\ new\ cases}{Total\ population\ at\ risk}\ over\ a\ time\ period \times multiplier\ (e.g.,\ 100,000)$$

Incidence measures are central to the study of causal mechanisms with regard to how exposures affect health outcomes.

FIGURE 2-9 Rate* of tuberculosis cases, by state/area—United States, 2007.[†]

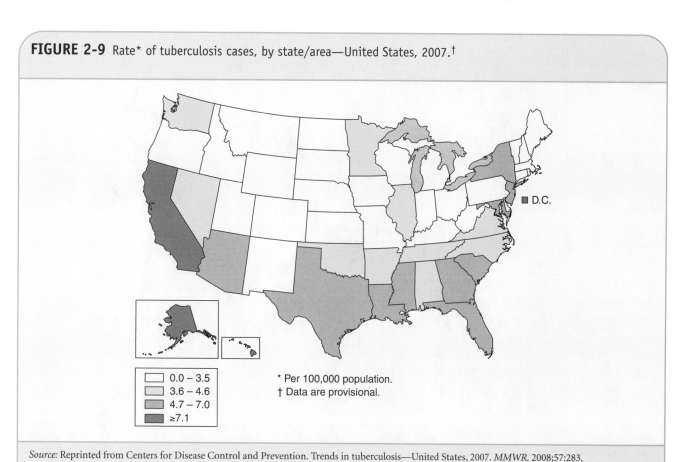

* Per 100,000 population.
† Data are provisional.

0.0 – 3.5
3.6 – 4.6
4.7 – 7.0
≥7.1

Source: Reprinted from Centers for Disease Control and Prevention. Trends in tuberculosis—United States, 2007. *MMWR.* 2008;57:283.

Incidence measures are used to describe the risks associated with certain exposures; they can be used to estimate in a population "... the probability of someone in that population developing the disease during a specified period, conditional on not dying first from another disease." [6(p23)]

Prevalence

The term **prevalence** refers to the number of existing cases of a disease or health condition, or deaths in a population at some designated time. A type of prevalence, **point prevalence**, refers to all cases of a disease, health condition, or deaths that exist at a particular point in time relative to a specific population from which the cases are derived.

Refer to Figure 2-10 for information on the prevalence of asthma among children. During the period 1980 to 2005, asthma prevalence tended to be higher among children in the Northeast region of the United States in comparison with other sections of the country. Data were from the National Health Interview Survey. Researchers stated that "current asthma prevalence estimates are based on the questions 'Has a doctor or other health professional ever told you that {child's name} had asthma?' and

'Does {child's name} still have asthma?' Estimates for Delaware, the District of Columbia, Mississippi, Nebraska, Nevada, and New Hampshire [are unreliable] . . . and should be interpreted with caution. . . . The estimates for Alaska, Idaho, Maine, Montana, North Dakota, South Dakota, Vermont, West Virginia, and Wyoming . . . are not represented in this figure." [7(p1)]

Other variations of prevalence are period prevalence and lifetime prevalence. **Period prevalence** refers to all cases of a disease within a period of time, whereas **lifetime prevalence** denotes cases diagnosed at any time during the person's lifetime. Refer to Figure 2-11 for illustrations of prevalence. The line called "asthma period prevalence" refers to the percentage of people in the United States who had asthma during the past 12 months of any particular year. The line designated as "lifetime asthma diagnosis" indicates the percentage of children who have ever been diagnosed with asthma. The remaining two lines, "current asthma prevalence" and "asthma attack prevalence," respectively, portray the percentage of children who had the diagnosis of asthma at the time of interview (similar to point prevalence) and the percentage of children who had asthma attacks during the past 12 months.

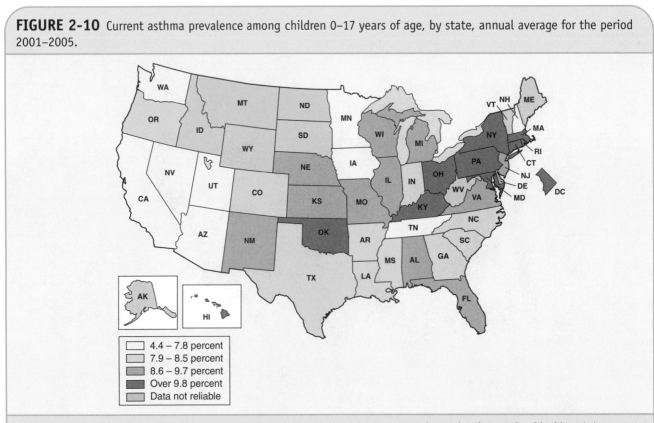

FIGURE 2-10 Current asthma prevalence among children 0–17 years of age, by state, annual average for the period 2001–2005.

Legend:
- 4.4 – 7.8 percent
- 7.9 – 8.5 percent
- 8.6 – 9.7 percent
- Over 9.8 percent
- Data not reliable

Source: Reprinted from Akinbami LJ. The state of childhood asthma, United States, 1980–2005. Advance data from vital and health statistics; no 381, Hyattsville, MD: National Center for Health Statistics. 2006:1.

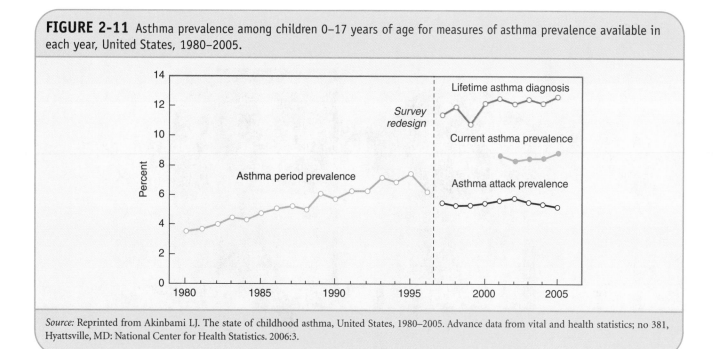

FIGURE 2-11 Asthma prevalence among children 0–17 years of age for measures of asthma prevalence available in each year, United States, 1980–2005.

Source: Reprinted from Akinbami LJ. The state of childhood asthma, United States, 1980–2005. Advance data from vital and health statistics; no 381, Hyattsville, MD: National Center for Health Statistics. 2006:3.

Prevalence measures are used to describe the scope and distribution of health outcomes in the population. By offering a snapshot of disease occurrence, prevalence data contribute to the accomplishment of two of the primary functions of descriptive epidemiology: to assess variations in the occurrence of disease and to aid in the development of hypotheses that can be followed up by analytic studies.

Comparisons among populations that differ in size cannot be accomplished directly by using frequency or prevalence data. In order to make such comparisons, prevalence (usually referring to point prevalence) may be expressed as a proportion formed by dividing the number of cases that occur in a population by the size of the population in which the cases occurred.

$$Point\ prevalence = \frac{Number\ of\ persons\ ill}{Total\ number\ in\ the\ group}\ at\ a\ point\ in\ time$$

The result is only a proportion and should not be called a rate.

Interrelationships between Incidence and Prevalence

Incidence and prevalence are interrelated concepts, as demonstrated by Figure 2-12. When the incidence of a disease increases, the prevalence also increases. Other factors that cause the prevalence of a disease to increase are its duration, inmigration of new cases, and development of treatments for the disease including methods for extending the lives of patients who may not actually be cured. An example of how the duration of a disease affects its prevalence would be two diseases (A—long duration and B—short duration) that have similar incidence rates; we would expect disease A to have a higher prevalence than disease B.

EPIDEMIOLOGIC MEASURES RELATED TO MORBIDITY AND MORTALITY

This chapter will conclude with four epidemiologic measures of morbidity (illness) and mortality (death): crude rates, death rates, case fatality rates, and cause-specific rates.

Crude Rates

The basic concept of a rate can be broken down into three general categories: crude rates, specific rates, and adjusted rates. A **crude rate** is a type of rate that has not been modified to take account of any of the factors such as the demographic makeup of the population that may affect the observed rate. Remember that rates include a time period during which an event occurred. Crude rates are summary rates based on the actual number of events in a population over a given time period. The numerator consists of the frequency of a disease over a specified period of time, and the denominator is a unit size of population (Exhibit 2-1). An example is the crude death rate, which approximates the proportion of a population that dies during a time period of interest.[2] It is critical to remember

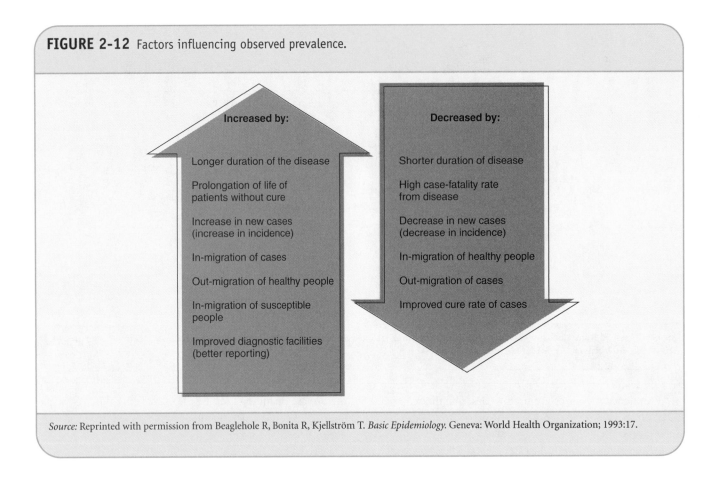

FIGURE 2-12 Factors influencing observed prevalence.

Increased by:	Decreased by:
Longer duration of the disease	Shorter duration of disease
Prolongation of life of patients without cure	High case-fatality rate from disease
Increase in new cases (increase in incidence)	Decrease in new cases (decrease in incidence)
In-migration of cases	In-migration of healthy people
Out-migration of healthy people	Out-migration of cases
In-migration of susceptible people	Improved cure rate of cases
Improved diagnostic facilities (better reporting)	

Source: Reprinted with permission from Beaglehole R, Bonita R, Kjellström T. *Basic Epidemiology.* Geneva: World Health Organization; 1993:17.

that to calculate a rate, two periods of time are involved: the beginning of the period and the end of the period.

In the formula shown in Exhibit 2-1, the denominator also is termed the **reference population**, which is defined as the population from which cases of a disease have been taken. For example, in calculating the annual death rate (crude mortality rate) in the United States, one would count all the deaths that occurred in the country during a certain year and assign this value to the numerator. The value for the denominator would be the size of the population of the country during that year. The best estimate of the population would probably be the population around the midpoint of the year, if such information could be obtained. Referring to Exhibit 2-1, one calculates the U.S. crude mortality rate as 825.9 per 100,000 persons for 2005 (the most recently available data as of this writing).

Rates improve one's ability to make comparisons, although they also have limitations. For example, rates of mortality for a specific disease (see the section on cause-specific mortality rates later in this chapter) reduce the standard of comparison to a common denominator, the unit size of pop-

ulation. To illustrate, the U.S. crude death rate for diseases of the heart in 2005 was 220.0 per 100,000. One also might calculate the heart disease death rate for geographic subdivisions of the country (also expressed as frequency per 100,000 individuals). These rates then could be compared with one another and with the rate for the United States for judging whether the rates found in each geographic area are higher or lower. For example, the crude death rates in 2005 for diseases of the heart in New York and Texas were 270.0 and 175.6 per 100,000, respectively. On the basis of the crude death rates, it would appear that the death rate was higher in New York than in Texas or the United States as a whole. This may be a specious conclusion, however, because there may be important differences in population composition (e.g., age differences between populations) that would affect mortality experience. Later in this chapter, the procedure to adjust for age differences or other factors is discussed.

Rates can be expressed in terms of any unit size of population that is convenient (e.g., per 1,000, per 100,000, or per 1,000,000). Many of the rates that are published and routinely used as indicators of public health are expressed ac-

Exhibit 2-1

Rate Calculation

Rate: A ratio that consists of a numerator and a denominator and in which time forms part of the denominator. Epidemiologic rates contain the following elements:

- disease frequency
- unit size of population
- time period during which an event occurs

Example:

$$Crude\ death\ rate = \frac{Number\ of\ deaths\ in\ a\ given\ year}{Reference\ population\ (during\ midpoint\ of\ the\ year)} \times 100,000$$

(Either rate per 1,000 or 100,000 is used as the multiplier)

Calculation problem (crude death rate in the United States):

Number of deaths in the United States during 2005 = 2,448,017

Population of the United States as of July 1, 2005 = 296,410,404

Crude death rate = 2,448,017/296,410,404 = 825.9 per 100,000

Source: Adapted and reprinted from Friis RH, Sellers TA. *Epidemiology for Public Health Practice.* 4th ed. Sudbury, MA: Jones and Bartlett Publishers; 2009:96.

cording to a particular convention. For example, cancer rates are typically expressed per 100,000 population, and infant mortality is expressed per 1,000 live births. One of the determinants of the size of the denominator is whether the numerator is large enough to permit the rate to be expressed as an integer or an integer plus a trailing decimal (e.g., 4 or 4.2). For example, it would be preferable to describe the occurrence of disease as 4 per 100,000 rather than 0.04 per 1,000, even though both are perfectly correct. Throughout this chapter, the multiplier for a given morbidity or mortality statistic is provided.

Case Fatality Rate

An additional measure covered in this section is the case fatality rate (CFR). The **case fatality rate** refers to the number of deaths due to a disease that occur among persons who are afflicted with that disease. The CFR (%), which provides a measure of the lethality of a disease, is defined as the number of deaths due to a specific disease within a specified time period divided by the number of cases of that disease during the same time period multiplied by 100. The formula is expressed as follows:

$$CFR\ (\%) = \frac{Number\ of\ deaths\ due\ to\ disease\ "X"}{Number\ of\ cases\ of\ disease\ "X"} \times 100\ during\ a\ time\ period$$

The numerator and denominator refer to the same time period. For example, suppose that 45 cases of hantavirus infection occurred in a western U.S. state during a year of interest. Of these cases, 22 were fatal. The CFR would be:

$$CFR\ (\%) = \frac{22}{45} \times 100 = 48.9\%$$

An example of an infectious disease that has a high case fatality rate is primary amebic meningoencephalitis, which is extremely rare and nearly always fatal. The causative organism is a type of amoeba (*Naegleria fowleri*) found in bodies of fresh water such as hot springs. This uncommon infection occurs when amoeba-contaminated water enters the nose and the parasites migrate to the brain via the optic nerve.[8]

Proportional Mortality Ratio

The **proportional mortality ratio** (PMR) is the number of deaths within a population due to a specific disease or cause divided by the total number of deaths in the population.

$$PMR\ (\%) = \frac{Mortality\ due\ to\ a\ specific\ cause\ during\ a\ period\ of\ time}{Mortality\ due\ to\ all\ causes\ during\ the\ same\ time\ period} \times 100$$

Sample calculation: Refer to Table 2-5 for data used in this calculation. In the United States, there were 652,091 deaths due to coronary heart disease in 2005 and 2,448,017 deaths due to all causes in that year. The PMR is (652,091/ 2,448,017) × 100 = 26.6%.

Table 2-5 presents mortality data for 2005 for the ten leading causes of death in the United States In Figure 2-13, a pie chart illustrates the percentage of total deaths for each of the ten leading causes of death listed in Table 2-5.

SPECIFIC RATES

The three examples of specific rates discussed in this chapter are cause-specific rates, age-specific rates, and sex-specific rates.

Cause-Specific Rate

The **cause-specific rate** is a measure that refers to mortality (or frequency of a given disease) divided by the population size at the midpoint of a time period times a multiplier. An example of a cause-specific rate is the cause-specific mortality rate, which, as the name implies, is the rate associated with a specific cause of death. Refer to data in Table 2-5 for a sample calcula-

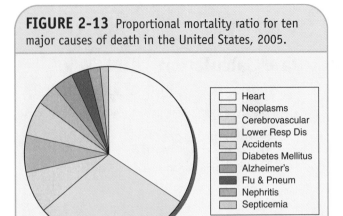

FIGURE 2-13 Proportional mortality ratio for ten major causes of death in the United States, 2005.

Heart
Neoplasms
Cerebrovascular
Lower Resp Dis
Accidents
Diabetes Mellitus
Alzheimer's
Flu & Pneum
Nephritis
Septicemia

Source: Author created. Compiled from data in Table 2-5.

tion for 2005. The number of deaths for accidents (unintentional injuries) was 117,809, whereas the population total on July 1, 2005, was estimated to be 296,410,404. The crude cause-specific mortality rate due to accidents (unintentional injuries) per 100,000 was 117,809/296,410,404, or 39.7 per 100,000.

The formula for a cause-specific rate is shown in the text box.

$$Cause\text{-}specific\ rate = \frac{Mortality\ (or\ frequency\ of\ a\ given\ disease)}{Population\ size\ at\ midpoint\ of\ time\ period} \times 100,000$$

TABLE 2-5 Number and Percentage of Deaths for the 10 Leading Causes of Death in the United States, 2005

Rank	Cause of death	Number	Percentage of total deaths	2005 crude death rate
...	All causes	2,448,017	100.0	825.9
1	Diseases of heart	652,091	26.6	220.0
2	Malignant neoplasms	559,312	22.8	188.7
3	Cerebrovascular diseases	143,579	5.9	48.4
4	Chronic lower respiratory diseases	130,933	5.3	44.2
5	Accidents (unintentional injuries)	117,809	4.8	39.7
6	Diabetes mellitus	75,119	3.1	25.3
7	Alzheimer's disease	71,599	2.9	24.2
8	Influenza and pneumonia	63,001	2.6	21.3
9	Nephritis, nephrotic syndrome, and nephrosis	43,901	1.8	14.8
10	Septicemia	34,136	1.4	11.5

Source: Data from Kung HC, Hoyert DL, Xu JQ, Murphy SL. Deaths: Final data for 2005. *National vital statistics reports*; vol 56 no 10. Hyattsville, MD: National Center for Health Statistics; 2008:5.

Age-Specific Rates

An **age-specific rate** refers to the number of cases of disease per age group of the population during a specified time period. Age-specific rates help in making comparisons regarding a cause of morbidity or mortality across age groups. A more precise definition of an age-specific rate is the frequency of a disease (or health condition) in a particular age stratum divided by the total number of persons within that age stratum during a time period. The formula for an age-specific rate is shown in the text box.

Age-Specific Rate (R)

Age-specific rate: The number of cases per age group of population (during a specified time period).

Example:

$$R = \frac{\text{Number of deaths among those aged 15–24 years}}{\text{Number of persons who are aged 15–24 years (during time period)}} \times 100,000$$

Sample calculation:
In the United States during 2005, there were 1,717 deaths due to malignant neoplasms among the age group 15 to 24 years, and there were 42,076,849 persons in the same age group. The age-specific malignant neoplasm death rate in this age group is 1,717/42,076,849 = 4.1 per 100,000.

Figure 2-14 illustrates data for age-specific rates of hospitalization for kidney disease. For people 45 years of age and older, the age-specific hospitalization rates have shown an increasing trend. The highest rates of hospitalization and the sharpest increase in rates occurred among people aged 75 years and older.

Sex-Specific Rates

A **sex-specific rate** refers to the frequency of a disease in a gender group divided by the total number of persons within that gender group during a time period times a multiplier. For example, in 2005, the following information was recorded about mortality and the population size:

- Number of deaths among males—1,207,675
- Number of deaths among females—1,240,342

- Estimated number of males in the population as of July 1, 2005—145,999,746
- Estimated number of females in the population as of July 1, 2005—150,410,658

The sex-specific crude rate for males in 2005 per 100,000 was 1,207,675/145,999,746 × 100,000 = 827.2 per 100,000.

The sex-specific crude rate for females in 2005 per 100,000 was 1,240,342/150,410,658 × 100,000 = 824.6 per 100,000.

Thus, in 2005, the sex-specific mortality rate for males was 827.2 per 100,000 population versus 824.6 per 100,000 population for females.

ADJUSTED RATES

An adjusted rate is a rate of morbidity or mortality in a population in which statistical procedures have been applied to permit fair comparisons across populations by removing the effect of differences in the composition of various populations. A factor in rate adjustment is age adjustment. Calculation of age-adjusted rates is a much more involved procedure than that required for crude rates. A weighting process is used that entails the use of detailed information about the age structure of the population for which the rates are being age adjusted. For example, "age-adjusted death rates are constructs that show what the level of mortality would be if no changes occurred in the age composition of the population from year to year."[9 (p3)] The direct method of age adjustment involves multiplying the age-specific rates for each subgroup of a population to be standardized by the number in a comparable subgroup of a standard population.

To age-adjust the crude mortality rate in the United States, we would use the standard population, which for the United States is the year 2000 population. For example, suppose you wanted to standardize the crude mortality data for the United States for 2003. You would multiply the age-specific death rate for the population under age 1 (700.0 per 100,000) in 2003 by the number in the year 2000 standard population under age 1 (3,794,301). This calculation would need to be repeated for each age stratum. The results for each stratum would then be summed to create a weighted average—the age-adjusted death rate. For additional information regarding the computations involved in age adjustment, the reader is referred to *Epidemiology for Public Health Practice*, 4th edition.[10]

According to the National Center for Health Statistics, the age-adjusted death rate in the U.S. in 2005 was 798.8 deaths per 100,000 U.S. standard population. This figure compares with a crude rate of 825.9 per 100,000 population. In most years since 1980 (with the exception of 1983, 1985, 1988, 1993, and 1999), the age-adjusted death rate in the United States has declined. There was a 23.1 percent decline in the age-adjusted death rate between 1980 and 2005. Refer to Figure 2-15 for information on trends in age-

FIGURE 2-14 Age-specific hospitalization rates* for kidney disease,† by age group—National Hospital Discharge Survey, United States, 1980–2005.

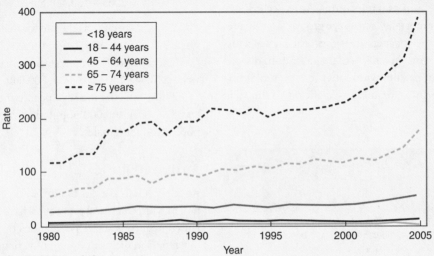

*Per 10,000 population.

†Based on *International Classification of Diseases, Ninth Revision, Clinical Modification* codes 580–589, which include acute kidney disease, acute renal failure, end-stage renal disease, chronic kidney failure, and other kidney diseases.

Source: Reprinted from Centers for Disease Control and Prevention. Hospitalization discharge diagnoses for kidney disease—United States, 1980–2005. *MMWR.* 57:311.

adjusted and crude mortality rates over time.

Returning to the example in which we compared mortality in New York and Texas, the crude mortality rate for diseases of the heart was 270.0 per 100,000 in New York; in Texas, the rate was 175.6 per 100,000. The corresponding age-adjusted rates were 239.6 per 100,000 and 219.5 per 100,000, respectively. The higher crude mortality rate observed in New York in comparison with Texas was due largely to differences in the age structures of the two states. You can see that when the rates were age adjusted, the differences in mortality for diseases of the heart diminished substantially.

FIGURE 2-15 Crude and age-adjusted death rates: United States, 1960–2005.

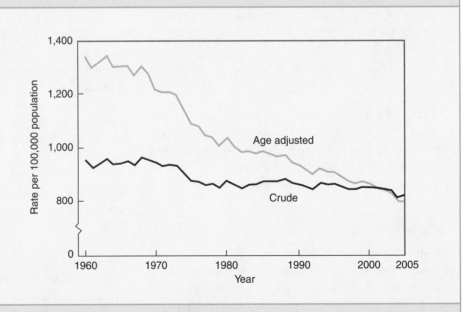

Source: Reprinted from Kung HC, Hoyert DL, Xu JQ, Murphy SL. Deaths: Final data for 2005. *National vital statistics reports;* vol 56 no 10. Hyattsville, MD: National Center for Health Statistics; 2008:4.

CONCLUSION

Chapter 2 provided information on measures that are used in epidemiology; these were derived from ratios such as rates, proportions, and percentages. Types of epidemiologic measures included counts and crude rates as well as case fatality rates, proportional mortality ratios, specific rates, and adjusted rates. These measures are helpful in making descriptive statements about the occurrence of morbidity and mortality and demonstrating risks of adverse health outcomes associated with particular exposures. Two important measures used in epidemiology are prevalence and incidence, which are interrelated terms. Rates are measures that specify a time period during which health events have occurred. A common epidemiologic rate is a crude rate, which allows comparisons of populations that differ in size but not in demographic composition. Specific rates and adjusted rates may be used to overcome some of the problems inherent in crude rates and thus can be used to make comparisons among populations.

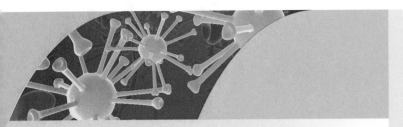

Study Questions and Exercises

1. What are the main advantages of using each of the following types of data presentation: bar chart, line graph, and pie chart?

2. Define what is meant by the term **ratio**. Compare and contrast rates, proportions, and percentages. Give an example of each one.

3. An epidemiologist presented information regarding the annual prevalence (number of cases per 1,000) of adolescent pregnancy to a local health planning board. The epidemiologist compared data for the local county with data for the United States as a whole. One of the members of the planning board objected that this comparison was not valid because the county is much smaller than the entire country. Do you agree with the objection?

4. How does a prevalence proportion (expressed as number of cases per unit size of population) differ from an incidence rate?

5. Distinguish between period prevalence and incidence. What is the definition of lifetime prevalence?

6. What are the advantages and disadvantages of crude and adjusted rates? What is one of the main purposes of adjusted rates?

7. What types of information are found by using specific rates such as cause-specific, age-specific, and sex-specific rates instead of crude rates?

Questions 8 through 10 refer to Table 2-6.

8. What is the sex ratio for total injuries?

9. What is the crude mortality rate per 100,000 population?

10. What is (a) the cause-specific mortality rate for injuries and (b) the case fatality rate (%) for injuries?

Answers:

8. 1.78 to 1, male to female

9. 291.2 per 100,000

10. (a) 85.7 per 100,000; (b) 4.4%

Young Epidemiology Scholars (YES) Exercises

The Young Epidemiology Scholars Web site provides links to teaching units and exercises that support instruction in epidemiology. The YES program is administered by the College Board and supported by the Robert Wood Johnson Foundation. The Web address of YES is www.collegeboard.com/yes. The following exercises relate to topics discussed in this chapter and can be found on the YES Web site.

1. Bayona M, Olsen C. Measures in epidemiology.

2. Huang FI, Baumgarten M. Adolescent suicide: The role of epidemiology in public health.

3. McCrary F, St. George DMM. Mortality and the transatlantic slave trade.

TABLE 2-6 Hypothetical Data for Unintentional Injuries

	Total injuries	Fatal injuries	Non-fatal injuries	Number in population	Total deaths from all causes
Men	73	3	70	2,856	9
Women	41	2	39	2,981	8

REFERENCES

1. Centers for Disease Control and Prevention. *HIV/AIDS Surveillance Report, 2006.* Vol. 18. Atlanta: U.S. Department of Health and Human Services, Centers for Disease Control and Prevention; 2008:1–55.

2. Porta M, ed. *A Dictionary of Epidemiology.* 5th ed. New York: Oxford University Press; 2008.

3. U.S. Census Bureau. Age and sex distribution in 2005. Population Profile of the United States: Dynamic Version. Available at: http://www.census.gov/population/pop-profile/dynamic/AgeSex.pdf. Accessed July 12, 2008.

4. Centers for Disease Control and Prevention. QuickStats: Percentage of adults reporting joint pain or stiffness,—National Health Interview Survey, United States, 2006. *MMWR.* 2008;57:467.

5. Hennekens CH, Buring JE. *Epidemiology in Medicine.* Boston, MA: Little, Brown; 1987.

6. Morgenstern H, Thomas D. Principles of study design in environmental epidemiology. *Environ Health Perspect.* 1993;101(Suppl 4):23–38.

7. Akinbami LJ. The state of childhood asthma, United States, 1980-2005. Advance data from vital and health statistics; no 381, Hyattsville, MD: National Center for Health Statistics. 2006.

8. Centers for Disease Control and Prevention. Primary amebic meningoencephalitis—Arizona, Florida, and Texas, 2007. *MMWR.* 2008;57:573–577.

9. Kung HC, Hoyert DL, Xu JQ, Murphy SL. Deaths: Final data for 2005. *National vital statistics reports*; vol 56 no 10. Hyattsville, MD: National Center for Health Statistics; 2008.

10. Friis RH, Sellers TA. *Epidemiology for Public Health Practice.* 4th ed. Sudbury, MA: Jones and Bartlett Publishers; 2009.

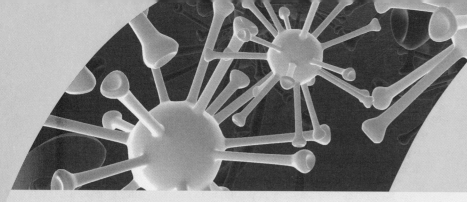

CHAPTER 3

Data and Additional Measures of Disease Occurrence

INTRODUCTION

Chapter 2 introduced data presentation and epidemiologic measures, which were derived from ratios such as rates, proportions, and percentages. The epidemiologic measures that were described included counts and crude rates as well as case fatality rates, proportional mortality ratios, specific rates, and adjusted rates. All of these measures are used to describe morbidity and mortality in populations. In addition, the terms

---

TABLE 3-1 List of Important Terms Used in This Chapter

Criteria for data quality	Data sources	Health status measures
Appropriate uses of data	Health insurance programs	Crude birth rate
Availability of data	Registries	Fetal death rate
Completeness of data	Specialized morbidity surveys	General fertility rate
Content of data	Surveillance programs: reportable disease statistics	Infant mortality rate
Representativeness of data	U.S. Census	Life expectancy
Source of data	Vital events	Maternal mortality rate

incidence and *prevalence* were defined. Chapter 3 extends this coverage by providing information about sources of data and additional measures of morbidity and mortality. Two vital concerns of epidemiology are, first, the quality of data available for describing the health of populations and, second, the appropriate applications of these data. Chapters 5 and 6 will extend this discussion further, particularly with respect to evaluation of associations between exposures and health outcomes and study designs employed in epidemiologic research. Refer to Table 3-1 for a list of important terms used in this chapter.

ONLINE SOURCES FOR RETRIEVAL OF EPIDEMIOLOGIC INFORMATION

Extensive resources are available for online retrieval of epidemiologic information, and the number of Web sites seems to be growing exponentially. Among the numerous Web sites that may be researched for data and other pertinent epidemiologic information are the following:

- Google: http://www.google.com. The Google site facilitates rapid access to epidemiologic documents and links. One may search for reports in written text as well as for images.
- Centers for Disease Control and Prevention (CDC): http:// www.cdc.gov. This site is the portal to many of the federal government's publications related to infectious and chronic diseases. One of these publications is the *Morbidity and Mortality Weekly Reports.*
- MEDLINE, National Library of Medicine (NLM), National Institutes of Health (NIH): http://www.nlm.nih.gov. MEDLINE is a site for performing bibliographic searches of the health-related literature.
- Web sites of organizations and publications related to epidemiology, for example, the American Public Health Association: http://www.apha.org. The American Public Health Association publishes the *American Journal of Public Health.* A second example is the Society for Epidemiologic Research (http://www.epiresearch.org), which sponsors the *American Journal of Epidemiology.* Professional organizations such as these sponsor health-related conferences and in some cases publish journals that can be searched for epidemiologic information.
- World Health Organization Statistical Information System (WHOSIS): http://www3.who.int/whosis/menu.cfm. The World Health Organization Web site provides data on the occurrence of morbidity and mortality from a worldwide perspective.

Navigate through the Web and access these sites. Not only are they interesting in themselves but also they will link you to many other related Web sites.

FACTORS THAT AFFECT THE QUALITY OF EPIDEMIOLOGIC DATA

The quality of epidemiologic data is a function of the sources from which they were derived as well as how completely the data cover their reference populations. Data quality affects the permissible applications of the data and the types of statistical analyses that may be performed. Four questions that should be raised with respect to the quality of epidemiologic data are the following:

- What is the nature of the data, including sources and content? Examples of data that this chapter will cover are vital statistics (data from recording births and deaths), surveillance data, reportable disease statistics, and data from case registries. Other data that are important for epidemiologic research are the results of specialized surveys, records from health care and insurance programs, and information from international organizations.
- How available are the data? Release of personally identifiable information is prohibited in the United States and many other developed countries. In the United States, epidemiologic data that might identify a specific person may not be released without the person's consent. The Health Insurance Portability and Accountability Act of 1996 (HIPAA) protects personal information contained in health records. Thus, individual medical records that disclose the patient's identity, reveal his or her diagnoses and treatments, or list the source of payment for medical care are confidential. On the other hand, data banks that collect information from surveys may release epidemiologic data as long as individuals cannot be identified.
- How complete is the population coverage? The completeness of the population coverage affects the representativeness of the data. The term **representativeness** (also known as **external validity**) refers to the generalizability of the findings to the population from which the data have been taken. Some data sources (for example, mortality statistics) cover the population extensively. Other data sources such as those from health clinics, medical centers, heath maintenance organizations (HMOs), and insurance plans may exclude major subsets of the nonserved or noncovered population.
- What are the appropriate and inappropriate uses of the data? In some instances the data may be used only for cross-sectional analyses. In others, the data may be used primarily for case-control studies. And in still others, the data may provide information about the incidence of disease and may be used to assess risk status. Chapter 4 will present information on cross-sectional studies. Chapter 6 will cover other epidemiologic study designs.

U.S. BUREAU OF THE CENSUS

Measures of morbidity and mortality require accurate information about the size and characteristics of the population. One of the applications of this information is the clarification of denominators used in epidemiologic measures. Also, descriptive and other epidemiologic studies classify health outcomes according to sociodemographic variables; consequently, accurate information about these characteristics is needed. The U.S. Bureau of the Census (http://factfinder.census.gov/home/saff/main.html?_lang=en) provides a wealth of data that can be used to define the denominator in rates with respect to official estimates of the total population size and subdivisions of the population by geographic area. The U.S. Bureau of the Census conducts a census of the population every ten years (the decennial census—e.g., 1980, 1990, 2000, 2010) and calculates estimates of the population size during the nondecennial years.

Exhibit 3-1

Data Collected during Census 2000

Census 2000 was the largest peacetime effort in the history of the United States. Information about the 115.9 million housing units and 281.4 million people across the United States will be available in a variety of formats and media, including the Internet, CD-ROMs, DVDs, and printed reports. This brochure provides a brief introduction to the information available from Census 2000, Census 2000 geography, maps, and data products. Visit our Web site at http://www.census.gov for more information.

Information Available from the 22nd Census of Population and Housing

100-percent characteristics (short form): *A limited number of questions were asked of every person and housing unit in the United States.*

Information is available on:

Household relationship	Race
Sex	Tenure (whether the home is owned or rented)
Age	Vacancy characteristics
Hispanic or Latino origin	

Sample characteristics (long form): *Additional questions were asked of a sample (generally 1-in-6) of persons and housing units. Data are provided on:*

Population

Marital status	Disability
Place of birth, citizenship, and year of entry	Grandparents as caregivers
School enrollment and educational attainment	Labor force status
Ancestry	Place of work and journey to work
Migration (residence in 1995)	Occupation, industry, and class of worker
Language spoken at home and ability to speak English	Work status in 1999
Veteran status	Income in 1999

Housing

Value of home or monthly rent paid	Telephone service
Units in structure	Vehicles available
Year structure built	Heating fuel
Number of rooms and number of bedrooms	Farm residence
Year moved into residence	Utilities, mortgage, taxes, insurance, and fuel costs
Plumbing and kitchen facilities	

Source: Reprinted from U.S. Department of Commerce, U.S. Bureau of Census. Available at: http://www.census.gov/prod/2001pubs/mso-oliedp.pdf. Accessed June 26, 2008.

"The Population Estimates Program prepares estimates of the total population; estimates of the population by age, sex, race, and Hispanic origin; and estimates of the number of housing units. The 2007 population estimates start with a base population for April 1, 2000 and calculate population estimates for July 1 for years 2000 to 2007. The population estimates use a variety of administrative records data to measure the population change including data on births, deaths, migration, and housing units."[1] Both short and long questionnaire forms were used in Census 2000. (Refer to Exhibit 3-1.) Data products may be obtained by accessing the Census Web site.

THE VITAL REGISTRATION SYSTEM AND VITAL EVENTS

Vital events are deaths, births, marriages, divorces, and fetal deaths. The vital registration system in the United States collects information routinely on these events. The legal authority for the registration of vital events within the United States is held by individual states, five U.S. territories (e.g., Puerto Rico), the Commonwealth of the Northern Mariana Islands, New York City, and Washington, D.C. These jurisdictions are charged with keeping records of vital events and providing certificates of marriage and divorce as well as birth and death certificates. In many instances, certificates that document vital events are also available from local health departments in the United States.

Deaths

Data are collected routinely on all deaths that occur in the United States. Mortality data have the advantage of being almost totally complete because deaths are unlikely to go unrecorded in the United States. In many instances, the funeral director completes the death certificate. Then the attending physician completes the section on date and cause of death. If the death occurred as the result of accident, suicide, or homicide, or if the attending physician is unavailable, then the medical examiner or coroner completes and signs the death certificate. Finally, the local registrar checks the certificate for completeness and accuracy and sends a copy to the state registrar. The state registrar also checks for completeness and accuracy and sends a copy to the National Center for Health Statistics (NCHS), which compiles and publishes national mortality rates (e.g., in Vital Statistics of the United States).

Death certificate data in the United States include the following information about the decedent:

- demographic characteristics
  - age
  - sex
  - race
- date and place of death—hospital or elsewhere

- cause of death
  - immediate cause
  - contributing factors

One of the most commonly used indices of public health, mortality data are readily available and in most cases fairly complete. Nevertheless, they are hampered by the fact that the specified cause of death may not be entirely accurate. When an older person with a chronic illness dies, the primary cause of death may be unclear. Death certificates list multiple causes of mortality as well as the underlying cause. However, assignment of the cause of death sometimes may be arbitrary. In illustration, diabetes may not be given as the immediate cause of death; rather, the certificate may list the cause of death as heart failure or pneumonia, which could be complications of diabetes. Another factor that detracts from the accuracy of death certificates is lack of standardization of diagnostic criteria employed by various physicians in different hospitals and settings. Yet another problem is the stigma associated with certain diseases. For example, if the decedent died as a result of AIDS or alcoholism and was a long-time friend of the attending physician, the physician may be reluctant to specify this information on a document that is available to the general public.

An example of a death certificate and the type of data collected are shown in Figure 3-1.

Birth Statistics

Birth statistics include live births and fetal deaths. Presumably, birth and fetal death statistics are nearly complete in their coverage of the general population. (Refer to Table 3-2 for a list of information collected by certificates of live birth and reports of fetal death.) One of the uses of birth certificate data is for calculation of birth rates; information also is collected about a range of conditions that may affect the neonate, including conditions present during pregnancy, congenital malformations, obstetric procedures, birth weight, length of gestation, and demographic background of the mother. Some of the data may be unreliable, reflecting possible inconsistencies and gaps in the mother's recall of events during pregnancy. It is also possible that certain malformations and illnesses that affect the neonate may not be detected at the time of birth. Many of the foregoing deficiencies of birth certificates also apply to the data contained in certificates of fetal death. In addition, variations from state to state in requirements for fetal death certificates further reduce their utility for epidemiologic studies. Nevertheless, birth and fetal death certificate data have been used in many types of epidemiologic research. One of these is studies of environmental influences upon congenital malformations. For example, these data have been used to search for clusters of birth defects in geographic areas where mothers may have been exposed to possible teratogens (agents that cause fetal malformation), such as pesticides or toxic pollutants.

FIGURE 3-1 U.S. Standard Certificate of Death—Rev. 11/2003.

U.S. STANDARD CERTIFICATE OF DEATH

LOCAL FILE NO. STATE FILE NO.

NAME OF DECEDENT
For use by physician or institution

To Be Completed/ Verified By: FUNERAL DIRECTOR:

1. DECEDENT'S LEGAL NAME (Include AKA's if any) (First, Middle, Last)
2. SEX
3. SOCIAL SECURITY NUMBER
4a. AGE-Last Birthday (Years)
4b. UNDER 1 YEAR Months Days
4c. UNDER 1 DAY Hours Minutes
5. DATE OF BIRTH (Mo/Day/Yr)
6. BIRTHPLACE (City and State or Foreign Country)
7a. RESIDENCE-STATE
7b. COUNTY
7c. CITY OR TOWN
7d. STREET AND NUMBER
7e. APT. NO.
7f. ZIP CODE
7g. INSIDE CITY LIMITS? □ Yes □ No
8. EVER IN US ARMED FORCES? □ Yes □ No
9. MARITAL STATUS AT TIME OF DEATH □ Married □ Married, but separated □ Widowed □ Divorced □ Never Married □ Unknown
10. SURVIVING SPOUSE'S NAME (If wife, give name prior to first marriage)
11. FATHER'S NAME (First, Middle, Last)
12. MOTHER'S NAME PRIOR TO FIRST MARRIAGE (First, Middle, Last)
13a. INFORMANT'S NAME
13b. RELATIONSHIP TO DECEDENT
13c. MAILING ADDRESS (Street and Number, City, State, Zip Code)
14. PLACE OF DEATH (Check only one: see instructions)
IF DEATH OCCURRED IN A HOSPITAL: □ Inpatient □ Emergency Room/Outpatient □ Dead on Arrival
IF DEATH OCCURRED SOMEWHERE OTHER THAN A HOSPITAL: □ Hospice facility □ Nursing home/Long term care facility □ Decedent's home □ Other (Specify):
15. FACILITY NAME (If not institution, give street & number)
16. CITY OR TOWN , STATE, AND ZIP CODE
17. COUNTY OF DEATH
18. METHOD OF DISPOSITION: □ Burial □ Cremation □ Donation □ Entombment □ Removal from State □ Other (Specify):
19. PLACE OF DISPOSITION (Name of cemetery, crematory, other place)
20. LOCATION-CITY, TOWN, AND STATE
21. NAME AND COMPLETE ADDRESS OF FUNERAL FACILITY
22. SIGNATURE OF FUNERAL SERVICE LICENSEE OR OTHER AGENT
23. LICENSE NUMBER (Of Licensee)

To Be Completed By: MEDICAL CERTIFIER

ITEMS 24-28 MUST BE COMPLETED BY PERSON WHO PRONOUNCES OR CERTIFIES DEATH
24. DATE PRONOUNCED DEAD (Mo/Day/Yr)
25. TIME PRONOUNCED DEAD
26. SIGNATURE OF PERSON PRONOUNCING DEATH (Only when applicable)
27. LICENSE NUMBER
28. DATE SIGNED (Mo/Day/Yr)
29. ACTUAL OR PRESUMED DATE OF DEATH (Mo/Day/Yr) (Spell Month)
30. ACTUAL OR PRESUMED TIME OF DEATH
31. WAS MEDICAL EXAMINER OR CORONER CONTACTED? □ Yes □ No

CAUSE OF DEATH (See instructions and examples)
32. PART I. Enter the chain of events--diseases, injuries, or complications--that directly caused the death. DO NOT enter terminal events such as cardiac arrest, respiratory arrest, or ventricular fibrillation without showing the etiology. DO NOT ABBREVIATE. Enter only one cause on a line. Add additional lines if necessary.
Approximate interval: Onset to death

IMMEDIATE CAUSE (Final disease or condition ---------> resulting in death) a. ______
Due to (or as a consequence of):
Sequentially list conditions, if any, leading to the cause listed on line a. Enter the **UNDERLYING CAUSE** (disease or injury that initiated the events resulting in death) **LAST** b. ______
Due to (or as a consequence of):
c. ______
Due to (or as a consequence of):
d. ______

PART II. Enter other significant conditions contributing to death but not resulting in the underlying cause given in PART I
33. WAS AN AUTOPSY PERFORMED? □ Yes □ No
34. WERE AUTOPSY FINDINGS AVAILABLE TO COMPLETE THE CAUSE OF DEATH? □ Yes □ No
35. DID TOBACCO USE CONTRIBUTE TO DEATH? □ Yes □ Probably □ No □ Unknown
36. IF FEMALE: □ Not pregnant within past year □ Pregnant at time of death □ Not pregnant, but pregnant within 42 days of death □ Not pregnant, but pregnant 43 days to 1 year before death □ Unknown if pregnant within the past year
37. MANNER OF DEATH □ Natural □ Homicide □ Accident □ Pending Investigation □ Suicide □ Could not be determined
38. DATE OF INJURY (Mo/Day/Yr) (Spell Month)
39. TIME OF INJURY
40. PLACE OF INJURY (e.g., Decedent's home; construction site; restaurant; wooded area)
41. INJURY AT WORK? □ Yes □ No
42. LOCATION OF INJURY: State: City or Town: Street & Number: Apartment No.: Zip Code:
43. DESCRIBE HOW INJURY OCCURRED:
44. IF TRANSPORTATION INJURY, SPECIFY: □ Driver/Operator □ Passenger □ Pedestrian □ Other (Specify)
45. CERTIFIER (Check only one):
□ Certifying physician-To the best of my knowledge, death occurred due to the cause(s) and manner stated.
□ Pronouncing & Certifying physician-To the best of my knowledge, death occurred at the time, date, and place, and due to the cause(s) and manner stated.
□ Medical Examiner/Coroner-On the basis of examination, and/or investigation, in my opinion, death occurred at the time, date, and place, and due to the cause(s) and manner stated.
Signature of certifier: ______
46. NAME, ADDRESS, AND ZIP CODE OF PERSON COMPLETING CAUSE OF DEATH (Item 32)
47. TITLE OF CERTIFIER
48. LICENSE NUMBER
49. DATE CERTIFIED (Mo/Day/Yr)
50. **FOR REGISTRAR ONLY**- DATE FILED (Mo/Day/Yr)

To Be Completed By: FUNERAL DIRECTOR

51. DECEDENT'S EDUCATION-Check the box that best describes the highest degree or level of school completed at the time of death.
□ 8th grade or less
□ 9th - 12th grade; no diploma
□ High school graduate or GED completed
□ Some college credit, but no degree
□ Associate degree (e.g., AA, AS)
□ Bachelor's degree (e.g., BA, AB, BS)
□ Master's degree (e.g., MA, MS, MEng, MEd, MSW, MBA)
□ Doctorate (e.g., PhD, EdD) or Professional degree (e.g., MD, DDS, DVM, LLB, JD)

52. DECEDENT OF HISPANIC ORIGIN? Check the box that best describes whether the decedent is Spanish/Hispanic/Latino. Check the "No" box if decedent is not Spanish/Hispanic/Latino.
□ No, not Spanish/Hispanic/Latino
□ Yes, Mexican, Mexican American, Chicano
□ Yes, Puerto Rican
□ Yes, Cuban
□ Yes, other Spanish/Hispanic/Latino (Specify) ______

53. DECEDENT'S RACE (Check one or more races to indicate what the decedent considered himself or herself to be)
□ White
□ Black or African American
□ American Indian or Alaska Native (Name of the enrolled or principal tribe) ______
□ Asian Indian
□ Chinese
□ Filipino
□ Japanese
□ Korean
□ Vietnamese
□ Other Asian (Specify) ______
□ Native Hawaiian
□ Guamanian or Chamorro
□ Samoan
□ Other Pacific Islander (Specify) ______
□ Other (Specify) ______

54. DECEDENT'S USUAL OCCUPATION (Indicate type of work done during most of working life. DO NOT USE RETIRED).
55. KIND OF BUSINESS/INDUSTRY

Source: Available at http://www.cdc.gov/nchs/data/dvs/DEATH11-03final-acc.pdf. Accessed June 26, 2008.

TABLE 3-2 Examples of Information Collected by Birth and Fetal Death Certificates

Variable	U.S. Certificate of Live Birth	U.S. Report of Fetal Death
Name	Child	Fetus (optional)
Disposition (e.g., burial)	Not applicable	Fetus
Location	Facility name	Where delivered
Mother Identifying information	Name, age, and place of residence	Name, age, and place of residence
Mother Socioeconomic status	Education, race, and marital status	Education, race, and marital status
Mother Health-related information	Height, weight, number of previous live births	Height, weight, number of previous live births
Conditions contributing to fetal death	Not applicable	Initiating cause and other causes (e.g., pregnancy complications, fetal anomalies)
Risk factors in pregnancy	e.g., diabetes, hypertension, infections	e.g., diabetes, hypertension, infections
Congenital anomalies	e.g., anencephaly, cleft palate, Down syndrome	e.g., anencephaly, cleft palate, Down syndrome
Father	Name and age	Name and age

Source: Author.

DATA FROM PUBLIC HEALTH SURVEILLANCE PROGRAMS: THREE EXAMPLES

Three examples of public health surveillance programs are those for communicable and infectious diseases, noninfectious diseases, and risk factors for chronic disease. **Public health surveillance** refers to the systematic and continuous gathering of information about the occurrence of diseases and other health phenomena. As part of the surveillance process, personnel analyze and interpret the data they have collected and distribute the data and associated findings to planners, health workers, and members of the community.

The public health community has been concerned with the possibility of using surveillance systems for detecting diseases associated with bioterrorism as well as early detection of disease outbreaks in general. Figure 3-2 shows a worker protected against biological disease agents. The term **syndromic surveillance** describes ". . . using health-related data that precede diagnosis and signal a sufficient probability of a case or an outbreak to warrant further public health response. Though historically syndromic surveillance has been utilized to target investigation of potential cases, its utility for detecting outbreaks associated with bioterrorism is increasingly being explored by public health officials."[2] Surveillance programs operate at the local, national, and international level. Here are some examples of surveillance systems:

- Communicable and infectious diseases. In the United States, health care providers and related workers send reports of diseases (known as notifiable and reportable diseases) to local health departments, which in turn forward them to state health departments and then to the CDC. The CDC reports the occurrence of internationally quarantinable diseases (e.g., plague, cholera, and yellow fever) to the World Health Organization.
- Noninfectious diseases. Surveillance programs often focus on the collection of information related to chronic diseases such as asthma.
- Risk factors for chronic diseases. The Behavioral Risk Factor Surveillance System (BRFSS) was established by

FIGURE 3-2 A CDC laboratorian while he's at work in a maximum containment, or "Hot Lab."

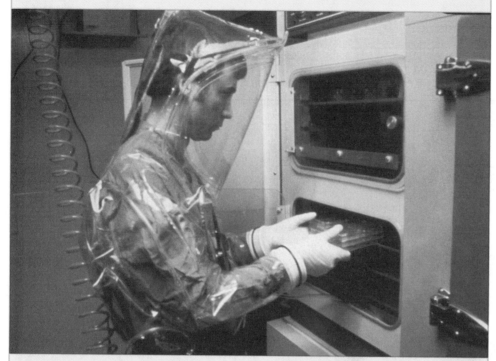

Source: Reprinted from Centers for Disease Control and Prevention. Public Health Image Library, ID# 5538. Available at: http://phil.cdc.gov/phil/home.asp. Accessed June 26, 2008.

the Centers for Disease Control and Prevention to collect information on behavior-related risk factors for chronic disease. One of the tasks of the BRFSS is the monitoring of health-related quality of life in the United States.

Figure 3-3 gives an overview of a simplified surveillance system, which shows how reports of cases of disease (e.g., infectious diseases) move up the hierarchy. Potential reporting sources are physicians and other health care providers as well as workers in clinical laboratories and other health-related facilities. Data recipients include county health departments at the primary level, state health departments at the secondary level, and federal agencies at the tertiary level. Data recipients at all of these levels are involved in feedback and dissemination of information required for appropriate public health action. Exhibit 3-2 and the section on reportable disease statistics describe these activities in more detail.

Reportable and Notifiable Disease Statistics

By legal statute, physicians and other health care providers must report cases of certain diseases, known as reportable and notifiable diseases, to health authorities. The diseases are usu-

ally infectious and communicable ones that might endanger a population; examples are the sexually transmitted diseases, rubella, tetanus, measles, plague, and foodborne disease. In addition, individual states may elect to maintain reports of communicable and noncommunicable diseases of local concern. To supplement the notifiable disease surveillance system, the CDC operates a surveillance system for several diseases of particular interest, such as salmonellosis, shigellosis, and influenza. For example, reports of influenza are tracked from October through May.

Examples of nationally notifiable infectious diseases are shown in Table 3-3. Some of the diseases and conditions are reportable in some states only; others are reportable in all states. The list changes every so often. For more information regarding United States and state requirements, refer to "Mandatory Reporting of Infectious Diseases by Clinicians, and Mandatory Reporting of Occupational Diseases by Clinicians," a publication of the Centers for Disease Control and Prevention.[3]

The major deficiency of reportable and notifiable data for epidemiologic research purposes is the possible incompleteness of population coverage. First, not every person who develops a disease that is on this list of notifiable conditions may seek medical attention; in particular, persons who are afflicted with asymptomatic and subclinical illnesses are unlikely to visit a physician. For example, an active case of typhoid fever will go unreported if the affected individual is unaware that he or she has the disease. Typhoid Mary illustrated this phenomenon (see Chapter 8). Another factor associated with lack of complete population coverage is the occasional failure of physicians and other providers to fill out the required reporting forms. This shortcoming can occur if responsible individuals do not keep current with respect to the frequently changing requirements for disease reporting in a local area. Also, as discussed earlier, a physician may be unwilling to risk compromising the confidentiality of the physician-patient

FIGURE 3-3 Simplified flow chart for a generic surveillance system.

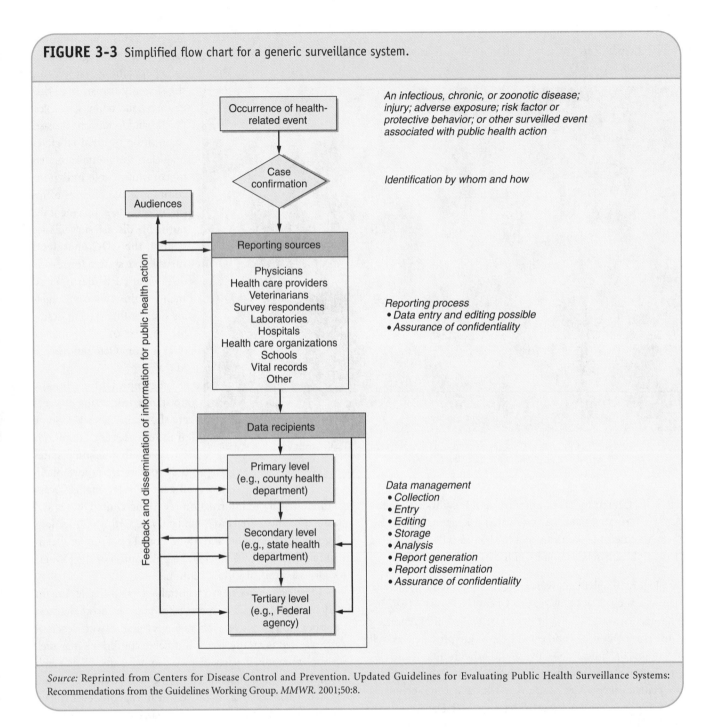

Source: Reprinted from Centers for Disease Control and Prevention. Updated Guidelines for Evaluating Public Health Surveillance Systems: Recommendations from the Guidelines Working Group. *MMWR.* 2001;50:8.

relationship, especially as a result of concern and controversy about reporting cases of diseases that carry social stigma. For example, incompleteness of AIDS reporting may stem from the potential sensitivity of the diagnosis. The author, who previously was associated with a local health department, observed that widespread and less dramatic conditions such as streptococcal pharyngitis (sore throat) sometimes are unreported.

More severe and unusual diseases, such as diphtheria, are almost always reported.

Chronic Disease Surveillance: The Example of Asthma

Asthma, a highly prevalent disease that incurs substantial medical and economic costs, is associated with inflammatory lung

Exhibit 3-2

National Notifiable Diseases Surveillance System History

In 1878, Congress authorized the U.S. Marine Hospital Service (i.e., the forerunner of the Public Health Service [PHS]) to collect morbidity reports regarding cholera, smallpox, plague, and yellow fever from U.S. consuls overseas; this information was to be used for instituting quarantine measures to prevent the introduction and spread of these diseases into the United States. In 1879, a specific Congressional appropriation was made for the collection and publication of reports of these notifiable diseases. The authority for weekly reporting and publication of these reports was expanded by Congress in 1893 to include data from states and municipal authorities. To increase the uniformity of the data, Congress enacted a law in 1902 directing the Surgeon General to provide forms for the collection and compilation of data and for the publication of reports at the national level. In 1912, state and territorial health authorities—in conjunction with PHS—recommended immediate telegraphic reporting of five infectious diseases and the monthly reporting, by letter, of 10 additional diseases. The first annual summary of The Notifiable Diseases in 1912 included reports of 10 diseases from 19 states, the District of Columbia, and Hawaii. By 1928, all states, the District of Columbia, Hawaii, and Puerto Rico were participating in national reporting of 29 specified diseases. At their annual meeting in 1950, the State and Territorial Health Officers authorized a conference of state and territorial epidemiologists whose purpose was to determine which diseases should be reported to PHS. In 1961, CDC assumed responsibility for the collection and publication of data concerning nationally notifiable diseases.

The list of nationally notifiable diseases is revised periodically. For example, a disease may be added to the list as a new pathogen emerges, or a disease may be deleted as its incidence declines. Public health officials at state health departments and CDC continue to collaborate in determining which diseases should be nationally notifiable; CSTE [The Council of State and Territorial Epidemiologists], with input from CDC, makes recommendations annually for additions and deletions to the list of nationally notifiable diseases. However, reporting of nationally notifiable diseases to CDC by the states is voluntary. Reporting is currently mandated (i.e., by state legislation or regulation) only at the state level. The list of diseases that are considered notifiable, therefore, varies slightly by state. All states generally report the internationally quarantinable diseases (i.e., cholera, plague, and yellow fever) in compliance with the World Health Organization's International Health Regulations.

Data on selected notifiable infectious diseases are published weekly in the *MMWR* and at year-end in the annual *Summary of Notifiable Diseases, United States*. [Note: Refer to Chapter 8 for examples of data and tables that report information on notifiable infectious diseases.]

Source: Reprinted from Centers for Disease Control and Prevention. National Notifiable Diseases Surveillance System. Available at: http://www.cdc.gov/ncphi/disss/nndss/nndsshis.htm. Accessed June 24, 2008.

TABLE 3-3 Examples of Nationally Notifiable Infectious Diseases—United States, 2008

- Acquired Immunodeficiency Syndrome (AIDS)
- Anthrax
- Botulism
- Gonorrhea
- Hepatitis, viral, acute
- HIV infection
- Meningococcal disease
- Mumps
- Syphilis
- Tuberculosis

Source: Data from Centers for Disease Control and Prevention. Nationally Notifiable Infectious Diseases—United States 2008. Available at: http://www.cdc.gov/ncphi/disss/nndss/phs/infdis2008.htm. Accessed June 24, 2008.

and airway conditions that can result in breathing difficulty, coughing, chest tightness, and other pulmonary symptoms. Severe asthma symptoms can be life threatening. Asthma surveillance programs provide data necessary for the development and evaluation of health care services for afflicted persons. The California Department of Health Services has established an asthma surveillance system that "uses data from a wide variety of sources to describe the burden of asthma in the state. Surveillance data include, but are not limited to: the number of people with asthma, frequency of symptoms, use of routine health care, visits to the emergency department and hospital, costs of health care utilization, and deaths due to asthma."[4 (p3)]

The Asthma Surveillance Pyramid (refer to Figure 3-4) describes the range of asthma outcomes. "The bottom of the pyramid represents asthma prevalence, or all people with asthma. This is the largest group in the pyramid and refers to

FIGURE 3-4 The asthma surveillance pyramid: A description of California's asthma data.

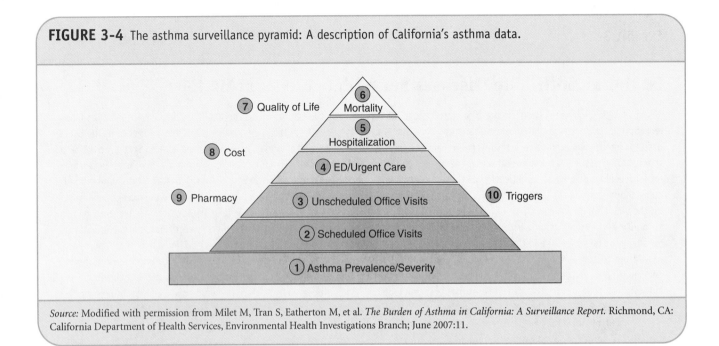

Source: Modified with permission from Milet M, Tran S, Eatherton M, et al. *The Burden of Asthma in California: A Surveillance Report.* Richmond, CA: California Department of Health Services, Environmental Health Investigations Branch; June 2007:11.

the lowest level of asthma severity. Each successively higher level in the pyramid represents an increased level of asthma severity and a smaller proportion of people affected. Outside the pyramid are quality of life, cost, pharmacy, and triggers; these are four factors that impact all of the other outcomes of the pyramid."[4(p10)]

Behavioral Risk Factor Surveillance

The Behavioral Risk Factor Surveillance System (BRFSS) is a noteworthy program used by the United States to monitor at the state level behavioral risk factors that are associated with chronic diseases. (See Exhibit 3-3 for a description of the BRFSS.) Because the BRFSS is operated at the state level, the data may not be adequate for analyses at finer levels of aggregation such as counties. Moreover, sufficient information may not be available regarding health topics not specifically addressed by the BRFSS. As a result, some states operate local versions of the BRFSS. An example is the California Health Interview Survey (CHIS), which provides information on the health and demographic characteristics of California residents who reside in geographic subdivisions of the state. From time to time, CHIS adds special topics that are of interest to Californians. CHIS is housed at the UCLA Center for Health Policy Research at the University of California, Los Angeles.

CASE REGISTRIES

A **registry** is a centralized database for collection of information about a disease. Registries, maintained for many types of conditions including cancer, are used to track patients and to select cases for case-control studies. The term **register** refers to the document that is used to collect the information.[5]

- The National Program of Cancer Registries (NPCR)—administered by CDC, United States

This program ". . . collects data on the occurrence of cancer; the type, extent, and location of the cancer; and the type of initial treatment."[6] The NPCR covers about 96% of the U.S. population through its support of cancer registries in forty-five states, the District of Columbia, and four U.S. territories. (Refer to Figure 3-5.) The purposes of the state registries are to:

- "Monitor cancer trends over time.
- Determine cancer patterns in various populations.
- Guide planning and evaluation of cancer control programs (e.g., determine whether prevention, screening, and treatment efforts are making a difference).
- Help set priorities for allocating health resources.
- Advance clinical, epidemiologic, and health services research.
- Provide information for a national database of cancer incidence."[6]

- Surveillance, Epidemiology, and End Results (SEER) Program

The SEER Program is operated by the National Cancer Institute. The program ". . . is an authoritative source of information on cancer incidence and survival in the United

Exhibit 3-3

Behavioral Risk Factor Surveillance System (BRFSS)

Established in 1984 by the Centers for Disease Control and Prevention (CDC), the Behavioral Risk Factor Surveillance System (BRFSS) is a state-based system of health surveys that collects information on health risk behaviors, preventive health practices, and health care access primarily related to chronic disease and injury. For many states, the BRFSS is the only available source of timely, accurate data on health-related behaviors.

Currently, data are collected monthly in all 50 states, the District of Columbia, Puerto Rico, the U.S. Virgin Islands, and Guam. More than 350,000 adults are interviewed each year, making the BRFSS the largest telephone health survey in the world. States use BRFSS data to identify emerging health problems, establish and track health objectives, and develop and evaluate public health policies and programs. Many states also use BRFSS data to support health-related legislative efforts.

A Brief History

By the early 1980s, scientific research clearly showed that personal health behaviors played a major role in premature morbidity and mortality. Although national estimates of health risk behaviors among U.S. adult populations had been periodically obtained through surveys conducted by the National Center for Health Statistics (NCHS), these data were not available on a state-specific basis. This deficiency was viewed as critical for state health agencies that have the primary role of targeting resources to reduce behavioral risks and their consequent illnesses. National data may not be appropriate for any given state; however, state and local agency participation was critical to achieve national health goals.

About the same time as personal health behaviors received wider recognition in relation to chronic disease morbidity and mortality, telephone surveys emerged as an acceptable method for determining the prevalence of many health risk behaviors among populations. In addition to their cost advantages, telephone surveys were especially desirable at the state and local level, where the necessary expertise and resources for conducting area probability sampling for in-person household interviews were not likely to be available.

As a result, surveys were developed and conducted to monitor state-level prevalence of the major behavioral risks among adults associated with premature morbidity and mortality. The basic philosophy was to collect data on actual behaviors, rather than on attitudes or knowledge, that would be especially useful for planning, initiating, supporting, and evaluating health promotion and disease prevention programs.

To determine feasibility of behavioral surveillance, initial point-in-time state surveys were conducted in 29 states from 1981–1983. In 1984, The Centers for Disease Control and Prevention (CDC) established the Behavioral Risk Factor Surveillance System (BRFSS), and 15 states participated in monthly data collection. Although the BRFSS was designed to collect state-level data, a number of states from the outset stratified their samples to allow them to estimate prevalence for regions within their respective states.

CDC developed [a] standard core questionnaire for states to use to provide data that could be compared across states. The BRFSS, administered and supported by the Division of Adult and Community Health, National Center for Chronic Disease Prevention and Health Promotion, CDC, is an ongoing data collection program. By 1994, all states, the District of Columbia, and three territories were participating in the BRFSS.

Source: Reprinted from Centers for Disease Control and Prevention, Behavioral Risk Factor Surveillance System. About the BRFSS. Available at: http://www.cdc.gov/brfss/about.htm. Accessed June 25, 2008.

States. . . . SEER currently collects and publishes cancer incidence and survival data from population-based cancer registries covering approximately 26 percent of the US population. The SEER Program registries routinely collect data on patient demographics, primary tumor site, tumor morphology and stage at diagnosis, first course of treatment, and follow-up for vital status. The SEER Program is the only comprehensive source of population-based information in the United States

that includes stage of cancer at the time of diagnosis and patient survival data."[7] Figure 3-5 shows federally funded cancer registries.

DATA FROM THE NATIONAL CENTER FOR HEALTH STATISTICS

The scope of information available from the National Center for Health Statistics (NCHS) is extensive. Examples of data

FIGURE 3-5 Federally funded cancer registries, 2005.

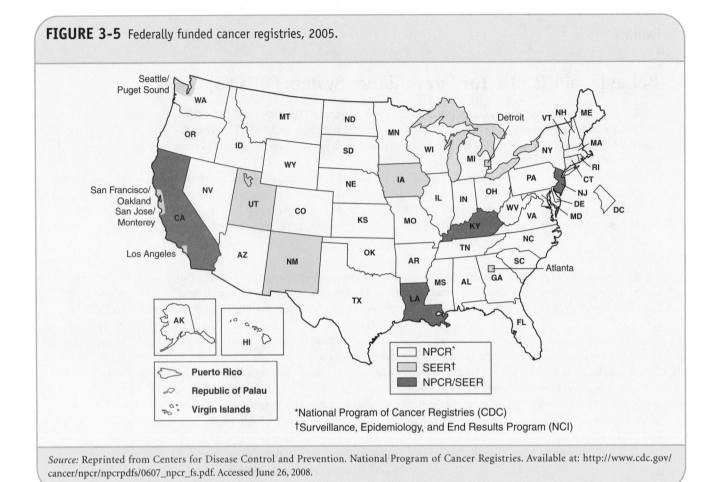

Source: Reprinted from Centers for Disease Control and Prevention. National Program of Cancer Registries. Available at: http://www.cdc.gov/cancer/npcr/npcrpdfs/0607_npcr_fs.pdf. Accessed June 26, 2008.

Exhibit 3-4

National Center for Health Statistics Surveys and Data Collection Systems

Some NCHS data systems and surveys are ongoing annual systems, whereas others are conducted periodically. NCHS has two major types of data systems: systems based on populations, containing data collected through personal interviews or examinations, and systems based on records, containing data collected from vital and medical records.

National Health Interview Survey [Table 3-4]

- **National Health Interview Survey on Disability**

National Health and Nutrition Examination Survey (NHANES) [Table 3-5]

- **NHANES I Epidemiologic Followup Study**

[Note that both the National Health Interview Survey and the National Health and Nutrition Examination Survey are examples of morbidity surveys of the population. The surveys can be designed to elicit information about issues that may not be picked up by other routinely available sources, for example, reportable disease statistics. The NHANES collects information from physical examinations. Such data may disclose undiagnosed conditions not counted by other data collection methods.]

National Health Care Survey

- **Ambulatory Health Care Data (NAMCS/NHAMCS)**
- **Hospital Discharge and Ambulatory Surgery Data**
- **National Home and Hospice Care Survey**
- **National Nursing Home Survey**
- **National Employer Health Insurance Survey**

National Vital Statistics System [Refer to Table 3-6 for information about the Vital Statistics Cooperative Program, which partially supports state costs for collecting vital statistics.]

- **Birth Data**
- **Mortality Data**
- **Fetal Death Data**
- **Linked Births/Infant Deaths**
- **National Mortality Followback Survey**
- **National Maternal and Infant Health Survey**
- **Vital Statistics Data Available Online**

National Survey of Family Growth
National Immunization Survey
The Longitudinal Studies of Aging (LSOAs)
State and Local Area Integrated Telephone Survey
Joint Canada/United States Survey of Health (JCUSH)

Source: Adapted and reprinted from Centers for Disease Control and Prevention, National Center for Health Statistics. Available at: http://www.cdc.gov/nchs/express.htm. Accessed June 14, 2008.

available from the NCHS through its survey and data collection systems are given in Exhibit 3-4.

Examples of NCHS data and survey systems are presented in Tables 3-4 to 3-6.

- Table 3-4 shows the features of the National Health Interview Survey.
- Table 3-5 describes the National Health and Nutrition Examination Survey.
- Table 3-6 describes the Vital Statistics Cooperative Program; following this table, definitions of measures listed in the table are provided.

Additional Measures of Disease Occurrence

Table 3-6 lists several terms that can be expressed as epidemiologic measures. With the exception of life expectancy, all of these are related to infant mortality, birth, and fertility. The order of the terms in this section follows their order in Table 3-6.

Life expectancy.

Life expectancy refers to the number of years that a person is expected to live, at any particular year. "Life expectancy at birth represents the average number of years that a group of infants would live if the infants were to experience throughout life the age-specific death rates present in the year of birth."[8 (p7)] In 2005, life expectancy for the population of the United States was 77.8 years overall, 80.4 years for females, and 75.2 years for males.

Causes of death.

The National Vital Statistics Reports (for example, Deaths: Final Data for 2005)[8] provides data on the mortality experience of the United States. Chapter 2 defined the terms *crude death rate* and *cause-specific mortality rate* and presented data on the ten leading causes of death. In 2005, the three leading causes of death were heart disease, cancer, and stroke. An example of causes of death is maternal mortality.

Maternal mortality.

Maternal mortality encompasses maternal deaths that result from causes associated with pregnancy. Among the factors related to maternal mortality are race, insufficient health care access, and social disadvantage. In 2005, the maternal mortality rate was 15.1 deaths per 100,000 live births (623 total deaths in 2005). The respective maternal mortality rates per 100,000

TABLE 3-4 National Health Interview Survey

Data Source/Methods
   Personal interviews
Planned Sample
   Approximately 40,000 households
   Oversample of blacks and Hispanics
Race/Ethnicity and SES
   OMB categories
   Hispanic groups
   API groups
   Family and individual income and poverty level
   Education and occupation (sample person only)
   Type of living quarters
   Acculturation questions, re: language used during interview
Selected Applications
   Annual data on:
      Health status and limitations
      Utilization of health care
      Injuries
      Family resources
      Health insurance
      Access to care
      Selected conditions
      Health behaviors
      Functioning
      HIV/AIDS testing
      Immunization

Source: Adapted from Centers for Disease Control and Prevention, National Center for Health Statistics. Summary of Surveys and Data Systems, National Center for Health Statistics, June 2004: Current NCHS Surveys and Data Systems. Available at: http://www.cdc.gov/nchs/data/NCHS_Survey_Matrix.pdf. Accessed June 26, 2008.

TABLE 3-5 National Health and Nutrition Examination Survey (NHANES)

Data Source/Methods
   Personal interview
   Physical examination
   Laboratory tests
   Nutritional assessment
   DNA repository
Planned Sample
   Approximately 5,000 persons per year, all ages
   Oversample of adolescents
   Oversample of persons 60 years of age and older
   Oversample of blacks and Mexican Americans
   Pregnant women
Race/Ethnicity and SES
   Income and poverty index
   Education
   Occupation
   Type of living quarters
   Social services
   White, black, and Mexican American
   Acculturation questions
Selected Applications
   Total prevalence of disease or conditions including those unrecognized or undetected
   Nutrition monitoring
   Heart disease
   Diabetes
   Osteoporosis
   Iron deficiency anemia and other nutritional disorders
   Environmental exposures monitoring
   Children's growth and development
   Infectious disease monitoring
   Overweight/physical fitness

Source: Adapted from Centers for Disease Control and Prevention, National Center for Health Statistics. Summary of Surveys and Data Systems, National Center for Health Statistics, June 2004: Current NCHS Surveys and Data Systems. Available at: http://www.cdc.gov/nchs/data/NCHS_Survey_Matrix.pdf. Accessed June 26, 2008.

live births for black and white women were 36.5 and 11.1; the rate for black women was about 3.3 times that for white women.[8(p12)]

$$\text{Maternal mortality rate (per 100,000 live births, including multiple births)} = \frac{\text{Number of deaths assigned to causes related to childbirth}}{\text{Number of live births}} \times 100,000 \text{ live births (during a year)}$$

Infant mortality rate.

The **infant mortality rate** is defined as the number of infant deaths among infants aged 0 to 365 days during a year divided by the number of live births during the same year (expressed as the rate per 1,000 live births).

$$\text{Infant mortality (IM)} = \frac{\text{Number of infant deaths among infants aged 0–365 days during the year}}{\text{Number of live births during the year}} \times 1,000 \text{ live births}$$

Sample calculation: In the United States during 2005, there were 28,384 deaths among infants under 1 year of age and 4,138,573 live births. The infant mortality rate was (28,384/4,138,573) × 1,000 = 6.86 per 1,000 live births. The infant mortality rate in the United States has not changed significantly since 2000. Infant mortality is related to inadequate health care and poor environmental conditions. There are substantial racial/ethnic variations. (See Figure 3-6.)

TABLE 3-6 Vital Statistics Cooperative Program (VSCP)

Data Source/Methods
   State vital registration
   Linked Birth/Infant Death Program
   Matched multiple data sets
Planned Sample
   All births (4 million records annually)
   All deaths (about 2.4 million records annually)
   Reported fetal deaths of 20+ weeks, gestation (about 30,000 annually)
   Counts of marriages and divorces
Race/Ethnicity and Socioeconomic Status (SES)
   For births, deaths, and fetal deaths:
      White, black, five Asian-Pacific Islander (API) groups, American Indian
      Five Hispanic groups
   Education
   Births and deaths: 10 API groups from 11 states
   Marital status
Selected Applications [Refer to text for definitions of the following terms.]
   Life expectancy
   Causes of death, e.g., maternal mortality
   Infant mortality (IM)
   Birth rates
   Perinatal mortality

Source: Adapted from Centers for Disease Control and Prevention, National Center for Health Statistics. Summary of Surveys and Data Systems, National Center for Health Statistics, June 2004: Current NCHS Surveys and Data Systems. Available at: http://www.cdc.gov/nchs/data/NCHS_Survey_Matrix.pdf. Accessed June 26, 2008.

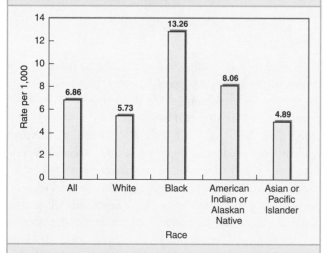

FIGURE 3-6 Infant mortality rates by race of mother, United States, 2005.

Source: Author created from data presented in Mathews TJ, MacDorman MF. Infant mortality statistics from the 2005 period linked birth/infant death data set. *National vital statistics reports;* vol 57 no 2. Hyattsville, MD: National Center for Health Statistics. 2008:14.

Fetal mortality.

Fetal mortality is defined as the death of the fetus when it is in the uterus and before it has been delivered. Two measures of fetal mortality are the fetal death rate and the late fetal death rate. The formulas for these terms are shown in the text box.

Fetal death rate (per 1,000 live births plus fetal deaths)
$$= \frac{\text{Number of fetal deaths after 20 weeks or more gestation}}{\text{Number of live births + number of fetal deaths after 20 weeks or more gestation}} \times 1,000$$

Late fetal death rate (per 1,000 live births plus late fetal deaths)
$$= \frac{\text{Number of fetal deaths after 28 weeks or more gestation}}{\text{Number of live births + number of fetal deaths after 28 weeks or more gestation}} \times 1,000$$

Birth rates.

This section defines the terms *crude birth rate* and *general fertility rate.* The **crude birth rate** refers to the number of live births during a specified period such as a year per the resident population at the midpoint of the year. The birth rate affects the total size of the population.

Crude birth rate = $\dfrac{\textit{Number of live births within a given period}}{\textit{Population size at the middle of that period}}$ × 1,000 population

Sample calculation: 4,112,052 babies were born in the United States during 2004, when the U.S. population was 293,655,404. The birth rate was 4,112,052/293,655,404 = 14.0 per 1,000.

General fertility rate (fertility rate).

Related to birth rates is the **general fertility rate**, which refers to the number of live births reported in an area during a given time interval divided by the number of women aged 15 to 44 years in the area (expressed as rate per 1,000 women aged 15 to 44). The general fertility rate is referred to more broadly as the fertility rate.

General fertility rate = $\dfrac{\textit{Number of live births within a year}}{\substack{\textit{Number of women aged 15--44 years}\\\textit{at the midpoint of the year}}}$ × 1,000 women aged 15–44

Sample calculation: During 2004, there were 62,033,402 women aged 15 to 44 in the United States. There were 4,112,052 live births. The general fertility rate was 4,112,052/62,033,402 = 66.3 per 1,000 women aged 15 to 44.

Perinatal mortality.

Perinatal mortality (known as definition I from the National Center for Health Statistics) takes into account both late fetal deaths and deaths among newborns. The **perinatal mortality rate** is defined as the number of late fetal deaths after 28 weeks or more gestation plus infant deaths within 7 days of birth divided by the number of live births plus the number of late fetal deaths during a year (expressed as rate per 1,000 live births and fetal deaths).

Perinatal mortality rate = $\dfrac{\substack{\textit{Number of late fetal deaths after}\\\textit{28 weeks or more gestation + infant}\\\textit{deaths within 7 days of birth}}}{\substack{\textit{Number of live births + number}\\\textit{of late fetal deaths}}}$ × 1,000 live births and fetal deaths

Figure 3-7 compares perinatal mortality rates by race in the United States for 2004.

DATA FROM INTERNATIONAL ORGANIZATIONS

Two examples of organizations that provide international and foreign data regarding diseases and health are the World Health Organization (WHO) (http://www.who.int)—described earlier—and the European Union. Programs and information collection supported by WHO include:

- Global infectious disease surveillance. WHO has created a "network of networks" that link existing surveillance systems such as those operated at the local and national levels in WHO member states. In addition, International Health Regulations, published by WHO, mandate legally the reporting by WHO member states of three diseases of international importance—plague, cholera, and yellow fever.[9]
- WHOSIS, an interactive database that yields data on 70 health indicators for 193 WHO member states.[10]
- Mortality data—levels and causes of mortality for children and adults.

The European Union provides statistics that cover a range of topics including public health. Access the Web site by using the following link: http://epp.eurostat.ec.europa.eu/portal/page?_pageid=1090,30070682,1090_33076576&_dad=portal&_schema=PORTAL. Some of the public health data available from this site and applicable to the member states of the European Union are related to social and health inequalities (e.g., death rates and suicide rates) and determinants of health (e.g., salmonellosis and smoking). This interactive Web site permits the user to develop customized tables, graphs, and maps.

CONCLUSION

Epidemiology is a quantitative discipline that requires data for descriptive and analytic studies. Extensive data resources are available for retrieval online. Many health-related organizations operate Web sites that can be accessed by data professionals, students, and the public. A central concern of epidemiology is data quality, which can be assessed by applying several criteria discussed in this chapter. Epidemiologists use data from a variety of sources including the vital registration system of the United States, public health surveillance systems, case registries, the National Center for Health Statistics, and international data sources. The chapter concluded with measures of health status, e.g., life expectancy, maternal mortality, and birth statistics.

FIGURE 3-7 Perinatal mortality rates, definition I, by race and Hispanic origin of mother: United States, 2004.

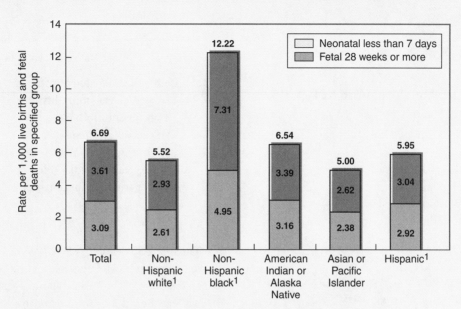

[1]Excludes data for Oklahoma, which did not report Hispanic origin for fetal deaths.

Source: Reprinted from MacDorman MF, Munson ML, Kirmeyer S. Fetal and perinatal mortality, United States, 2004. *National vital statistics reports;* vol 56 no 3. Hyattsville, MD: National Center for Health Statistics. 2007, p. 5.

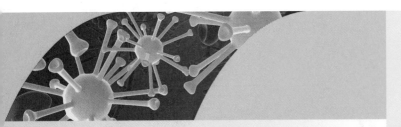

Study Questions and Exercises

1. Define the following terms:
   a. vital events
   b. public health surveillance
   c. syndromic surveillance
   d. reportable and notifiable diseases
   e. registry

2. What are some examples of Web sites where you might obtain epidemiologic data?

3. Describe the types of information that can be obtained from the vital registration system of the United States.

4. What is the purpose of surveillance systems? Describe the components of a surveillance system. Discuss the limitations of data collected from surveillance systems.

5. Describe the behavioral risk factor surveillance system. How does it differ from a surveillance system for infectious diseases?

6. What is one of the major applications of case registries?

7. Describe and discuss three data collection programs operated by the National Center for Health Statistics.

8. Define the following terms:
   a. maternal mortality rate
   b. infant mortality
   c. fetal mortality
   d. crude birth rate
   e. general fertility rate
   f. perinatal mortality rate

Young Epidemiology Scholars (YES) Exercises

The Young Epidemiology Scholars Web site provides links to teaching units and exercises that support instruction in epidemiology. The YES program is administered by the College Board and supported by the Robert Wood Johnson Foundation. The Web address of YES is www.collegeboard.com/yes. The following exercises relate to topics discussed in this chapter and can be found on the YES Web site.

1. Kaelin MA, St. George DMM. Descriptive epidemiology of births to teenage mothers.

REFERENCES

1. U.S. Census Bureau. Annual population estimates. Available at: http://factfinder.census.gov/servlet/DatasetMainPageServlet?_program=PEP&_submenuld. Accessed August 13, 2008.

2. Centers for Disease Control and Prevention. Syndromic surveillance: An applied approach to outbreak detection. Available at: http://www.cdc.gov/epo/dphsi/syndromic.htm. Accessed August 13, 2008.

3. Chorba TL, Berkelman RL, Safford SK, et al. Mandatory reporting of infectious diseases by clinicians, and mandatory reporting of occupational diseases by clinicians. *MMWR Recomm Rep.* 1990;39(RR-9):1–17.

4. Milet M, Tran S, Eatherton M, et al. *The Burden of Asthma in California: A Surveillance Report.* Richmond, CA: California Department of Health Services, Environmental Health Investigations Branch; June 2007.

5. Terracini B, Zanetti R. A short history of pathology registries, with emphasis on cancer registries. *Soz Praventivmed.* 2003;48(1):3–10.

6. Centers for Disease Control and Prevention. National program of cancer registries (NPCR). Available at: http://www.cdc.gov/cancer/npcr/about.htm. Accessed June 23, 2008.

7. National Institutes of Health, National Cancer Institute. SEER Surveillance, Epidemiology, and End Results Program. NIH Publication No. 05-4772. September 2005. Available at: http://seer.cancer.gov/about/SEER_brochure.pdf. Accessed August 13, 2008.

8. Kung HC, Hoyert DL, Xu JQ, Murphy SL. Deaths: Final data for 2005. *National vital statistics reports*; vol 56 no 10. Hyattsville, MD: National Center for Health Statistics. 2008.

9. World Health Organization. Global infectious disease surveillance. Fact sheet No 200, revised June 1998. Available at: http://www.who.int/mediacentre/factsheets/fs200/en/print.html. Accessed August 14, 2008.

10. WHO Statistical Information System (WHOSIS). Available at: http://www.who.int/whosis/en. Accessed August 14, 2008.

CHAPTER 4

Descriptive Epidemiology: Patterns of Disease— Person, Place, Time

INTRODUCTION

Human health and disease are unequally distributed throughout populations. This generalization applies to differences among population groups subdivided according to age and other demographic characteristics, among different countries, within a single country, and over time. When specific diseases, adverse health outcomes, or other health characteristics are more prevalent among one group than among another, or more prevalent in one country than in another, the logical question that follows is "Why?" To answer the question "Why," one must consider "three Ws"—Who was affected? Where did the event occur? When did the event occur?

TABLE 4-1 List of Important Terms Used in This Chapter

Descriptive epidemiology	Major descriptive epidemiologic variables		
Study design terms	**Person**	**Place**	**Time**
Cross-sectional study	Age	International	Cyclic fluctuation
Descriptive epidemiologic study	Race	Localized/spatial clustering	Point epidemic
Descriptive epidemiology	Sex	Urban-rural	Secular trends
Hypothesis	Socioeconomic status	Within country	Temporal clustering

The field of **descriptive epidemiology** classifies the occurrence of disease according to the variables of person (who is affected), place (where the condition occurs), and time (when and over what time period the condition has occurred). A **descriptive epidemiologic study** is one that is "... concerned with characterizing the amount and distribution of health and disease within a population."[1(p654)] Descriptive epidemiology provides valuable information for the prevention of disease, design of interventions, and conduct of additional research. Descriptive epidemiologic studies set the stage for more focused investigations into questions raised. Such investigations include evaluating observed trends, planning for needed services, and launching more complex research. This chapter covers the three major descriptive variables and then explores how they are used in descriptive epidemiologic studies. Table 4-1 lists the terms related to descriptive epidemiology and subcategories of variables that make up person, place, and time.

Consider the example of a descriptive epidemiologic study of children who were exclusively breastfed. The practice of breastfeeding has been recommended for reinforcing the health of babies and mothers and promoting mother-child bonding. Table 4-2 provides the characteristics (a descriptive epidemiologic statement) of babies who were breastfed. Note that the table shows person variables: sex and race/ethnicity (of child) and the mother's age, education, marital status, and socioeconomic status (as measured by income-to-poverty ratio). A place variable (location of residence of mother) is shown also.

What conclusions can you infer from this example? The table indicates that approximately 30% of infants in the United States are breastfed exclusively through three months of age and that the percentage drops to about 11% through the age of six months. Other observations include the following: non-Hispanic black mothers tend to engage in breastfeeding less often than other racial/ethnic groups and lower frequencies of breastfeeding occur among women (in comparison with the rest of the study population) who are younger, have lower levels of education and income, and are unmarried. The reader may want to speculate as to the reasons for the results that are displayed and develop hypotheses for interventions to increase breastfeeding.

USES OF DESCRIPTIVE EPIDEMIOLOGIC STUDIES

As you may have inferred from the foregoing example, descriptive epidemiologic studies aid in the realization of the following general aims, which are shown in the text box.

Aims of descriptive epidemiology

1. permit evaluation of trends in health and disease
2. provide a basis for planning, provision, and evaluation of health services
3. identify problems to be studied by analytic methods and suggest areas that may be fruitful for investigation

Source: Adapted from Friis RH, Sellers TA. *Epidemiology for Public Health Practice.* 4th ed. Sudbury, MA: Jones and Bartlett Publishers; 2009:143.

Permit Evaluation of Trends in Health and Disease

This objective includes monitoring of known diseases as well as the identification of emerging problems. Comparisons are made among population groups, geographical areas, and time periods. In the breastfeeding example, investigators reported that infants who resided in metropolitan areas were breastfed more frequently than infants who resided outside of metropolitan areas; in addition, infants from families with lower income levels (less than 100% of the income-to-poverty ratio) were breastfed less frequently than infants from families with higher income levels. These findings highlighted the relationships between the frequency of breastfeeding and both residential locations and income levels as potential emerging problems.

Provide a Basis for Planning, Provision, and Evaluation of Health Services

Data needed for efficient allocation of resources often come from descriptive epidemiologic studies. The breastfeeding example demonstrated that race (non-Hispanic African Americans), age of mother (mothers who were younger than 20 years of age), and marital status (unmarried) were associated with lower frequency of breastfeeding. An implication of this descriptive study is that an intervention program to increase the frequency of breastfeeding might target pregnant, unmarried, younger African American women.

Identify Problems to Be Studied by Analytic Methods and Suggest Areas That May Be Fruitful for Investigation

Among the phenomena identified by the breastfeeding study was a reduction in breastfeeding after infants reached three months

TABLE 4-2 Estimated Percentage of Infants Born in 2004 Who Were Exclusively Breastfed* through Ages 3 and 6 Months, by Selected Sociodemographic Characteristics—National Immunization Survey, United States

Characteristic	Exclusive breastfeeding through age 3 mos		Exclusive breastfeeding through age 6 mos	
	(%)	(95% CI§)	(%)	(95% CI)
U.S. overall (N = 17,654†)	(30.5)	(29.4–31.6)	(11.3)	(10.5–12.1)
Sex				
Male	(30.7)	(29.1–32.3)	(10.8)	(9.8–11.8)
Female¶	(30.3)	(28.7–31.9)	(11.7)	(10.5–12.9)
Race/Ethnicity (child)				
Hispanic	(30.8)	(28.3–33.3)	(11.5)	(9.7–13.3)
White, non-Hispanic¶	(33.0)	(31.6–34.4)	(11.8)	(10.9–12.7)
Black, non-Hispanic	(19.8)**	(17.0–22.6)	(7.3)**	(5.5–9.1)
Asian, non-Hispanic	(30.6)	(25.0–36.2)	(14.5)	(10.0–19.0)
Other race, non-Hispanic††	(29.3)	(24.9–33.7)	(12.2)	(9.2–15.2)
Age of mother at child's birth (yrs)				
<20	(16.8)**	(10.3–23.3)	(6.1)**	(1.5–10.7)
20–29	(26.2)**	(24.4–28.0)	(8.4)**	(7.3–9.5)
≥30¶	(34.6)	(33.2–36.0)	(13.8)	(12.7–14.9)
Education				
Less than high school	(23.9)**	(21.0–26.8)	(9.1)**	(7.1–11.1)
High school	(22.9)**	(20.9–24.9)	(8.2)**	(7.0–9.4)
Some college	(32.8)**	(30.3–35.3)	(12.3)**	(10.2–14.4)
College graduate¶	(41.5)	(39.7–43.3)	(15.4)	(14.1–16.7)
Marital status				
Married¶	(35.4)	(34.0–36.8)	(13.4)	(12.4–14.4)
Unmarried	(18.8)**	(16.9–20.7)	(6.1)**	(5.0–7.2)
Residence				
MSA,§§ central city¶	(30.7)	(29.0–32.4)	(11.7)	(10.5–12.9)
MSA, non-central city	(32.8)	(30.9–34.7)	(12.1)	(10.8–13.4)
Non-MSA	(23.9)**	(21.8–26.0)	(8.2)**	(6.9–9.5)
Income-to-poverty ratio (%)¶¶				
<100	(23.9)**	(21.6–26.2)	(8.3)**	(6.9–9.7)
100–184	(26.6)**	(23.8–29.4)	(8.9)**	(7.2–10.6)
185–349	(33.2)**	(30.9–35.5)	(11.8)**	(10.3–13.3)
≥350¶	(37.7)	(35.7–39.7)	(14.0)	(12.6–15.4)

*Defined as an infant receiving only breast milk and no other liquids or solids except for drops or syrups consisting of vitamins, minerals, or medicines.
†Weighted sample.
§Confidence interval. [This term is defined in Chapter 5.]
¶Referent group.
**p < 0.05 by chi-square test, compared with the referent group.
††Includes American Indian/Alaska Native, Native Hawaiian, other Pacific Islander, and multiple race.
§§Metropolitan statistical area, defined by the U.S. Census Bureau.
¶¶Ratio of self-reported family income to the federal threshold value, defined by the U.S. Census Bureau.
Source: Reprinted from Centers for Disease Control and Prevention. Breastfeeding trends and updated national health objectives for exclusive breastfeeding—United States, birth years 2000–2004. *MMWR.* 2007;56:762.

of age. This observation raises the question: "What caused the drop-off in breastfeeding?" You might hypothesize that when mothers return to work or other activities, breastfeeding becomes inconvenient. You might be able to think of many other hypotheses as well. The next step would be to design a more complex study—an analytic study to explore the hypotheses that have been raised. Examples of these studies are case-control, cohort, and experimental designs (covered in Chapter 6).

TYPES OF DESCRIPTIVE EPIDEMIOLOGIC STUDIES

Three of the types of descriptive epidemiologic studies are individual case reports, case series, and cross-sectional studies (e.g., a survey of a population). Case reports and case series are among the most basic types of descriptive studies.

Case Reports

Case reports are accounts of a single occurrence of a noteworthy health-related incident or small collection of such events. Here is an example of case reports that pertain to cosmetic surgery and related procedures that are typically (but not invariably) performed on healthy individuals. The use of cosmetic procedures to enhance beauty is becoming increasingly popular in many parts of the United States among all classes of people, no longer just affluent VIPs. Sometimes these procedures, which are often invasive, incur the risk of serious complications or even death.

The Centers for Disease Control and Prevention (CDC) published three case reports of women who developed adverse reactions (acute kidney failure) to injections of cosmetic soft-tissue fillers, which are substances used to improve the appearance of bodily areas such as lips and buttocks. The injections were administered by an unlicensed and unsupervised practitioner at the same clinic (facility A) in North Carolina:[2]

> "**Case 1.** On December 8, 2007, a District of Columbia woman aged 42 years, who was previously healthy except for a history of anemia, received cosmetic soft-tissue filler injections in her buttocks at facility A. . . . The woman experienced headache and vomiting within 30 minutes of these injections and noted that her urine looked like purple blood."[2(p453)] The woman was diagnosed with acute renal failure and required a 10-day stay in the hospital.

> "**Case 2.** On December 8, 2007, a previously healthy Illinois woman aged 26 years received cosmetic soft-tissue filler injections in her buttocks at facility A."[2(p453)] The patient also was diagnosed with acute renal failure and required 13 days of hospitalization and 5 weeks of hemodialysis.

> "**Case 3.** A previously healthy Maryland woman aged 26 years received soft-tissue filler injections in her buttocks at facility A on December 8, 2007, and again on December 22."[2(p454)] Afterwards, the patient became ill and required a two-week hospital stay and hemodialysis.

Follow-up interviews, investigations, and inspections of facility A were conducted. Subsequently, the Guilford County (North Carolina) Health Director mandated that facility A cease administration of all injections and initiated legal action against the unlicensed practitioner.

Case Series

In comparison with a case report, a case series is a larger collection of cases of disease, often grouped consecutively and listing common features such as the characteristics of affected patients. For example, Chapter 2 presented information on primary amebic meningoencephalitis (PAM), a disease that is caused by infection with *Naegleria fowleri* and that has a high case fatality rate. The *Naegleria* workgroup (formed by the CDC and the Council of State and Territorial Epidemiologists) reviewed all cases of PAM that were reported in the United States between 1937 and 2007. Preliminary findings were that a total of 121 cases occurred during the approximately 70-year time period. The largest number of cases reported in any one year (2007) was six. About 93% of the persons afflicted were male (median age = 12 years). The primary exposure source was described as freshwater (untreated and warm) in lakes and rivers.[3] Figure 4-1 demonstrates the number of PAM cases distributed according to the year in which they were reported.

Cross-Sectional Studies

More complex than case reports and case series are **cross-sectional studies**. This type of investigation is defined as one ". . . that examines the relationship between diseases (or other health-related characteristics) and other variables of interest as they exist in a defined population at one particular time. The presence or absence of disease and the presence or absence of the other variables . . . are determined in each member of the study population or in a representative sample at one particular time."[4] Thus, a cross-sectional study is a type of prevalence study in which exposures and distributions of disease are determined at the same time, although it is not imperative for the study to include both exposure and disease. A cross-sectional study may focus only on the latter.[1] Cross-sectional designs make a one-time assessment (similar to a snapshot) of the prevalence of disease in a study group that in most situations has been sampled randomly from the parent population of interest. As is true of descriptive studies in general, cross-sectional studies may be used to formulate hypotheses that can be followed up in analytic studies.

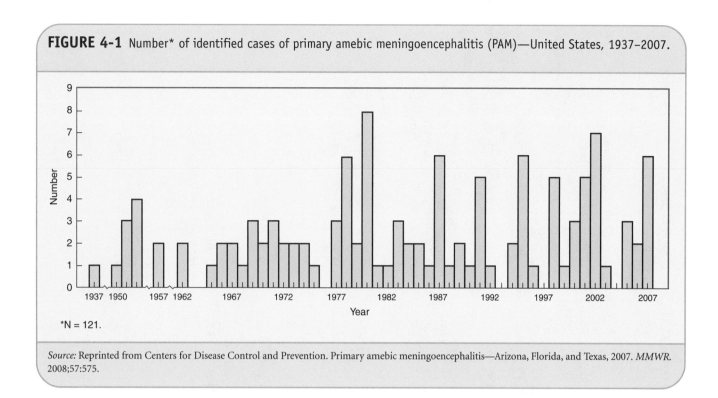

FIGURE 4-1 Number* of identified cases of primary amebic meningoencephalitis (PAM)—United States, 1937–2007.

*N = 121.

Source: Reprinted from Centers for Disease Control and Prevention. Primary amebic meningoencephalitis—Arizona, Florida, and Texas, 2007. *MMWR.* 2008;57:575.

Here is an example of a cross-sectional study: The Behavioral Risk Factor Surveillance System (BRFSS) conducts an ongoing survey of civilian, noninstitutionalized U.S. residents aged 18 years and older. (Refer also to Chapter 3.) The 2006 survey examined the problem of chronic sleep loss in four states (Delaware, Hawaii, New York, and Rhode Island). The survey question was: "During the past 30 days, for about how many days have you felt you did not get enough rest or sleep?" Responses were coded according to the following schema (0 days, 1–6 days, 7–13 days, 14–20 days, 21–29 days, and 30 days). Table 4-3 presents the results distributed according to the variables of race/ethnicity, age group, sex, education level, and employment status.

Overall, Table 4-3 shows that approximately 10% of the sample reported 30 or more days of insufficient rest or sleep. Those who were more likely to report insufficient rest or sleep were younger and unable to work. About one-third of the sample reported having no days of insufficient rest or sleep; related factors were older age, retired status, and higher levels of education.

Epidemiologic Inferences from Descriptive Data

Descriptive epidemiology and descriptive studies provide a basis for generating hypotheses; thus studies of this type connect intimately with the process of epidemiologic inference.

The process of inference in descriptive epidemiology refers to drawing conclusions about the nature of exposures and health outcomes and formulating hypotheses to be tested in analytic research. Figure 4-2 illustrates the process of epidemiologic inference.

Refer to the figure's center panel, which suggests that epidemiologic inference is initiated with observations. The observation(s) made in descriptive epidemiology (left-hand panel) culminate in hypotheses. As discussed previously, descriptive epidemiology aims to characterize health phenomena according to person, place, and time (who, where, and when). This process involves quantifying the findings (how many cases) and providing insights into what happened. After conducting a descriptive study, the epidemiologist must evaluate the findings carefully in order to rule out chance factors, biases, and confounding. (These terms are discussed in Chapter 6.) The right-hand panel is titled "analytic epidemiology," which is concerned with testing hypotheses in order to answer the questions "why?" and "how?"

PERSON VARIABLES

Examples of person variables covered in this chapter are age, sex, race, and socioeconomic status. Other person variables include marital status, nativity (place of origin), migration, and religion.

TABLE 4-3 Percentage of Adults Who Reported Insufficient Rest or Sleep during the Preceding 30 Days,* by Number of Days and Selected Sociodemographic Characteristics—Behavior[al] Risk Factor Surveillance System, Delaware, Hawaii, New York, and Rhode Island, 2006

Characteristic	0 days		1-6 days		7-13 days		14-20 days		21-29 days		30 days	
	%	(95% CI†)	%	(95% CI)	%	(95% CI)	%	(95% CI)	%	(95% CI)	%	(95% CI)
State (unweighted sample size)												
Delaware (n = 3,876)	27.7	(25.9–29.7)	32.9	(30.8–35.1)	12.6	(11.2–14.3)	11.2	(9.8–12.8)	1.5	(1.1–2.1)	14.0	(12.2–16.0)
Hawaii (n = 6,077)	38.4	(36.7–40.1)	29.8	(28.2–31.4)	11.1	(10.0–12.2)	10.3	(9.2–11.4)	1.7	(1.3–2.2)	8.8	(7.9–9.8)
New York (n = 5,293)	29.2	(27.6–30.9)	32.9	(31.2–34.6)	13.0	(11.8–14.3)	12.3	(11.1–13.6)	2.7	(2.2–3.3)	9.9	(8.9–11.1)
Rhode Island (n = 4,343)	27.7	(26.1–29.4)	31.6	(29.7–33.5)	13.3	(11.9–14.9)	12.9	(11.5–14.4)	2.6	(2.0–3.4)	11.9	(10.7–13.3)
Age group (yrs)												
18-34 (n = 3,147)	21.9	(18.9–25.3)	27.8	(24.6–31.2)	16.5	(14.0–19.3)	17.1	(14.5–20.1)	3.4	(2.3–4.9)	13.3	(11.1–15.9)
35-44 (n = 3,505)	20.9	(18.1–23.9)	38.2	(34.9–41.6)	13.5	(11.6–15.7)	14.0	(12.0–16.3)	3.4	(2.5–4.7)	10.0	(8.2–12.0)
45-54 (n = 4,195)	26.2	(23.6–29.1)	36.0	(33.2–38.9)	14.4	(12.5–16.5)	11.3	(9.7–13.2)	2.1	(1.4–3.2)	10.0	(8.3–11.9)
≥55 (n = 8,742)	44.7	(42.7–46.7)	31.7	(29.9–33.7)	8.1	(7.1–9.2)	6.6	(5.7–7.7)	1.5	(1.1–2.1)	7.3	(6.3–8.4)
Race/Ethnicity												
White, non-Hispanic (n = 13,258)	28.2	(26.8–29.7)	33.0	(31.5–34.5)	13.7	(12.6–14.9)	12.7	(11.6–13.9)	2.7	(2.2–3.3)	9.7	(8.7–10.8)
Black, non-Hispanic (n = 1,006)	27.1	(22.7–32.1)	32.5	(27.5–38.0)	13.4	(10.1–17.6)	13.9	(9.9–19.0)	—§		11.4	(8.3–15.4)
Hispanic (n = 1,258)	33.7	(28.6–39.2)	32.3	(27.2–37.8)	9.8	(7.3–13.0)	9.7	(6.7–13.8)	—		11.6	(8.6–15.4)
Other, non-Hispanic¶ (n = 4,067)	33.8	(29.4–38.5)	31.2	(26.8–36.0)	12.1	(9.0–16.0)	11.1	(8.5–14.5)	2.2	(1.3–3.8)	9.5	(7.2–12.6)
Sex												
Men (n = 7,598)	31.1	(28.8–33.4)	34.6	(32.2–37.0)	11.5	(10.1–13.1)	11.2	(9.8–12.9)	2.7	(2.0–3.7)	8.9	(7.6–10.5)
Women (n = 11,991)	28.3	(26.7–30.0)	30.8	(29.1–32.5)	14.2	(12.9–15.6)	13.1	(11.6–14.6)	2.5	(2.0–3.1)	11.2	(10.0–12.6)
Employment status												
Employed (n = 11,610)	24.0	(22.3–25.7)	37.2	(35.3–39.2)	13.7	(12.5–15.0)	12.4	(11.2–13.8)	2.8	(2.2–3.5)	9.9	(8.8–11.2)
Unemployed (n = 706)	32.9	(26.0–40.6)	27.5	(21.6–34.3)	9.5	(6.1–14.4)	14.7	(9.4–22.3)	—		12.8	(8.7–18.5)
Retired (n = 4,781)	53.5	(50.8–56.1)	28.9	(26.6–31.4)	5.9	(4.8–7.3)	4.9	(3.9–6.1)	1.2	(0.8–1.9)	5.5	(4.4–6.9)
Unable to work (n = 968)	24.6	(19.4–30.7)	15.1	(11.3–20.0)	13.6	(9.3–19.4)	17.7	(13.4–23.1)	—		24.8	(19.6–30.8)
Other** (n = 1,524)	28.1	(23.8–33.0)	23.1	(19.1–27.8)	18.8	(14.7–23.6)	16.6	(12.8–21.3)	2.8	(1.7–4.5)	10.6	(7.7–14.3)

Education level

<High school diploma or GED†† (n = 1,461)	39.7	(34.0–45.7)	27.8	(22.4–34.0)	9.8	(7.2–13.2)	10.1	(7.1–14.3)	—	—	10.4	(7.9–13.7)
High school diploma or GED (n = 5,565)	33.4	(30.8–36.1)	29.6	(26.9–32.5)	10.7	(9.0–12.7)	10.9	(9.1–13.0)	3.5	(2.4–5.2)	11.9	(10.0–14.0)
Some college or college graduate (n = 12,563)	26.3	(24.6–28.0)	34.7	(33.0–36.5)	14.4	(13.1–15.8)	13.1	(11.8–14.5)	2.2	(1.8–2.7)	9.3	(8.2–10.6)
Total (N = 19,589)	**29.6**	**(28.2–31.0)**	**32.6**	**(31.2–34.1)**	**12.9**	**(11.9–14.0)**	**12.2**	**(11.2–13.3)**	**2.6**	**(2.1–3.1)**	**10.1**	**(9.2–11.1)**

*Determined by response to the question, "During the past 30 days, for about how many days have you felt you did not get enough rest or sleep?"
†Confidence interval.
§No estimate calculated (n < 50).
¶Asian, Hawaiian or other Pacific Islander, American Indian/Alaska Native, or multiracial.
**Homemaker or student.
††General Educational Development certificate.
Source: Reprinted from Centers for Disease Control and Prevention. Perceived insufficient rest or sleep—four states, 2006. *MMWR.* 2008;57:202.

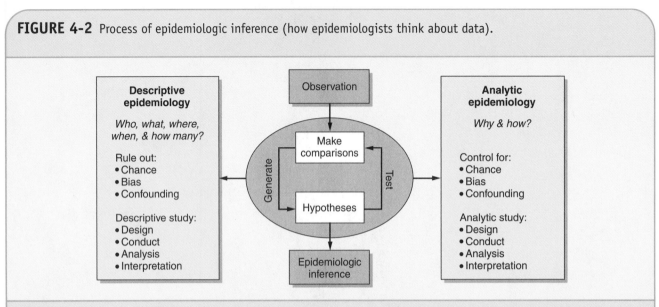

FIGURE 4-2 Process of epidemiologic inference (how epidemiologists think about data).

Source: Reprinted with permission from Aragón T. *Descriptive epidemiology: Describing findings and generating hypotheses.* Center for Infectious Disease Preparedness, UC Berkeley School of Public Health. Available at: http://www.idready.org/slides/feb_descriptive.pdf. Accessed August 16, 2008.

Age

Age is perhaps the most important factor to consider when one is describing the occurrence of virtually any disease or illness because age-specific disease rates usually show greater variation than rates defined by almost any other personal attribute. (For this reason, public health professionals often use age-specific rates when comparing the disease burden among populations.) As age increases, overall mortality increases as do the incidence of and mortality from many chronic diseases. For example, in the United States in 2005, age-specific death rates for malignant neoplasms (cancers) demonstrated substantial age-related increases, from 2.5 per 100,000 population at ages 5 to 14 years to 1,637.7 cases per 100,000 at age 85 years and older.

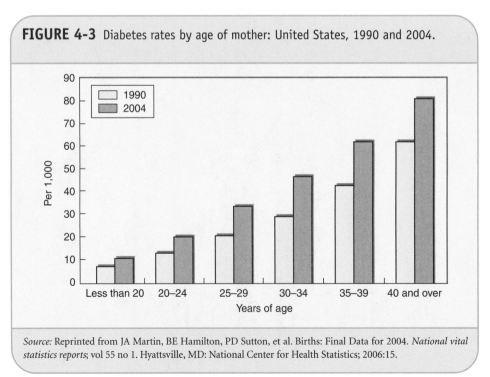

FIGURE 4-3 Diabetes rates by age of mother: United States, 1990 and 2004.

Source: Reprinted from JA Martin, BE Hamilton, PD Sutton, et al. Births: Final Data for 2004. *National vital statistics reports;* vol 55 no 1. Hyattsville, MD: National Center for Health Statistics; 2006:15.

The causes of morbidity and mortality differ according to stage of life. During childhood among unvaccinated persons, infectious diseases such as mumps and chickenpox occur most commonly. Teenagers are affected by unintentional injuries, violence, and substance abuse. Among younger adults, unintentional injury is the leading cause of death. And finally, among older adults, morbidity and mortality from chronic diseases such as heart disease and cancer take hold.

Another example of age association is the relationship between age of mother and rates of diabetes, which increases the risk of complications of pregnancy. Mothers who give birth when they are older have higher rates of diabetes than mothers who give birth at younger ages. (Refer to Figure 4-3.) In 1990, the rate of diabetes among mothers younger than 20 was less than 10 per 1,000 births. In comparison, the rate was more than six times as high among mothers who were aged 40 years and older. By 2004, the corresponding rates had increased to about 10 per 1,000 and 80 per 1,000, respectively.

A final illustration concerns age differences in birth rates for teenage mothers. In 2004, the overall teenage birth rate was 41.1 per 1,000 women aged 15 to 19 years. The birth rate (22.1 per 1,000) was lower for teenagers aged 15 to 17 years than the rate (70.0 per 1,000 women) for older teenagers aged 18 to 19 years. (See Figure 4-4.) Between 1990 and 2004, the teenage birth rate tended to decline.

Sex

Numerous epidemiologic studies have shown sex differences in a wide scope of health phenomena, including mortality and morbidity. The following discussion presents data on sex differences in mortality. With the exception of some calendar years, the population age-adjusted death rate has declined in the United States since 1980.[5] Males generally have higher all-cause age-specific mortality rates than females from birth to age 85 and older; the ratio of male to female age-adjusted death rates in 2005 was 1.4 to 1.

Figure 4-5 shows male-female age-adjusted invasive cancer incidence rates for the 10 primary sites with the highest rates within race- and ethnic-specific categories. The cancer diagnoses with the highest incidence rates per 100,000 are prostate cancer for males (150.0 per 100,000) and breast cancer for females (119.0 per 100,000). The second leading cancer incidence rate is for cancer of the lung and bronchus; the rate is somewhat higher for males than for females (86.8 versus 54.3 per 100,000). For both males and females, cancer of the lung and bronchus are the leading cause of cancer mortality.

Race/Ethnicity

Increasingly, with respect to race and ethnicity, the United States is becoming more diverse than at any time in history. Race and

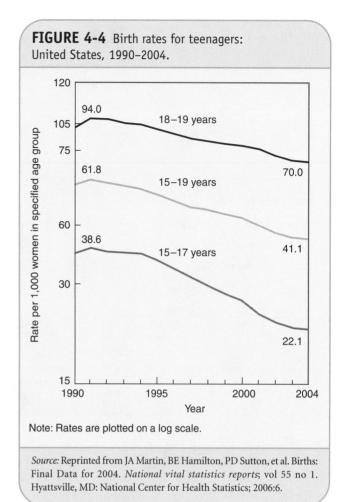

FIGURE 4-4 Birth rates for teenagers: United States, 1990–2004.

Note: Rates are plotted on a log scale.

Source: Reprinted from JA Martin, BE Hamilton, PD Sutton, et al. Births: Final Data for 2004. *National vital statistics reports*; vol 55 no 1. Hyattsville, MD: National Center for Health Statistics; 2006:6.

ethnicity are, to some extent, ambiguous characteristics that tend to overlap with nativity and religion. **Nativity** refers to the place of origin of the individual or his or her relatives. A common subdivision used in epidemiology is foreign-born or native-born. Scientists have proposed that race is a social and cultural construct, rather than a biological construct.[6] In Census 2000, the U.S. Bureau of the Census classified race into five major categories: white; black or African American; American Indian and Alaska Native; Asian; and Native Hawaiian and other Pacific Islander. To a degree, race tends to be synonymous with ethnicity because people who come from a particular racial stock also may have a common ethnic and cultural identification. Also, assignment of some individuals to a particular racial classification on the basis of observed characteristics may be difficult. Often, one must ask the respondent to elect the racial group with which he or she identifies. The responses one elicits from such a question may not be consistent: Individuals may change ethnic or racial self-identity or respond differently on different occasions, depending on their perception of the intent of the race question. Classification of persons of mixed racial

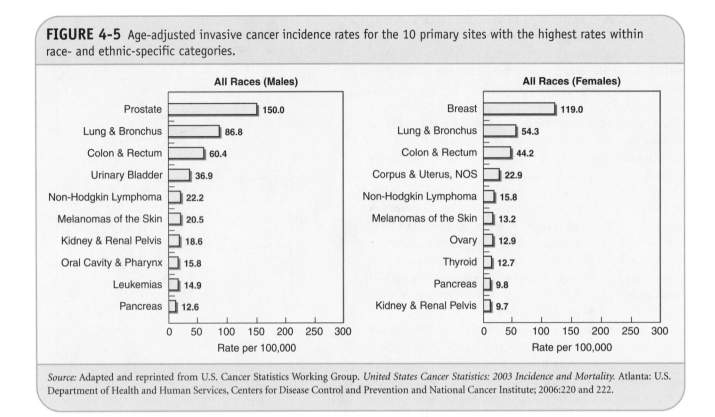

FIGURE 4-5 Age-adjusted invasive cancer incidence rates for the 10 primary sites with the highest rates within race- and ethnic-specific categories.

Source: Adapted and reprinted from U.S. Cancer Statistics Working Group. *United States Cancer Statistics: 2003 Incidence and Mortality.* Atlanta: U.S. Department of Health and Human Services, Centers for Disease Control and Prevention and National Cancer Institute; 2006:220 and 222.

parentage also may be problematic.[7] The 2000 census allowed respondents to check a multiracial category, which was used for the first time. Changes in the definitions of racial categories affect the denominators (i.e., the numbers in a particular racial subgroup) of rates used to track various health outcomes and the consequent assessments of unmet needs and social inequalities in health.[8]

Figure 4-6 demonstrates the racial/ethnic composition of the U.S. population during 2006. At that time, the total population was estimated to be 299,398,485. The largest percentage of the population was white (73.9%). Hispanics and Latinos made up 14.8% of the population (44,252,278). People who self-identify with this ethnic group can be of any race; therefore, Hispanics and Latinos are not shown in the figure.

There are many examples of racial/ethnic differences in health characteristics. The following section lists three conditions that show such variations:

- Asthma: Individuals who classified themselves as Hispanic had a lower frequency of self-reported asthma than either non-Hispanic whites or non-Hispanic blacks (Figure 4-7).
- No usual source of medical care: For persons diagnosed with diabetes, serious heart conditions, and hyperten-

sion, non-Hispanic whites and non-Hispanic blacks reported less frequently that they had no usual source of care than Hispanics (Figure 4-8).
- Gonorrhea incidence: Black, non-Hispanic individuals had the highest incidence of gonorrhea during 1991 through 2006. However, the incidence of gonorrhea among African Americans declined during this period, although in 2006 it remained above the incidence for other racial and ethnic groups. Non-Hispanic blacks in 2006 had a gonorrhea incidence that was about eighteen times greater than that reported for non-Hispanic whites (Figure 4-9).

Socioeconomic Status

Socioeconomic status (SES) is defined as a "descriptive term for a person's position in society, . . ."[4] SES is often formulated as a composite measure of three interrelated dimensions: a person's income level, education level, and type of occupation. In some instances, income level alone is used as an indicator of SES; in other cases, two or more of the foregoing dimensions are combined into composite variables. A three-factor measure would classify persons with high SES as those at the upper levels of income, education, and employment status (e.g., the learned professions). The social class gradient (variability in

FIGURE 4-6 Racial/ethnic distribution of the population of the United States, 2006 estimates. Data for individuals who declare only one race.

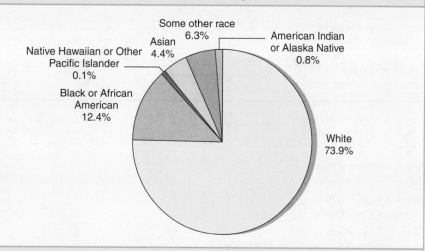

Source: Author. Data from U.S. Census Bureau. Fact Sheet: 2006 American Community Survey Data Profile Highlights. Available at: http://factfinder. census.gov/servlet/ACSSAFFFacts. Accessed August 15, 2008.

FIGURE 4-7 Estimated percentage of adults aged ≥18 years with asthma,* by sex and race/ethnicity—National Health Interview Survey, United States, 2006.[†]

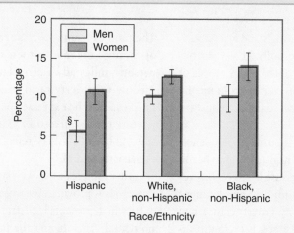

* Based on response to the following question: "Have you ever been told by a doctor or other health professional that you had asthma?"
† Estimates were age adjusted using the 2000 U.S. population as the standard population and four age groups: 18–44 years, 45–64 years, 65–74 years, and ≥75 years. Estimates were based on household interviews of a sample of the noninstitutionalized, U.S. civilian population. Persons of unknown asthma status were not included.
§ 95% confidence interval.

Source: Reprinted from Centers for Disease Control and Prevention, National Center for Health Statistics. QuickStats: Estimated percentage of adults aged ≥18 years with asthma,* by sex and race/ethnicity—National Health Interview Survey, United States, 2006[†]. *MMWR.* 2007;56:1193.

FIGURE 4-8 No usual source of care among adults 45–64 years of age, by selected diagnosed chronic conditions and race and Hispanic origin: United States, 2004–2005.

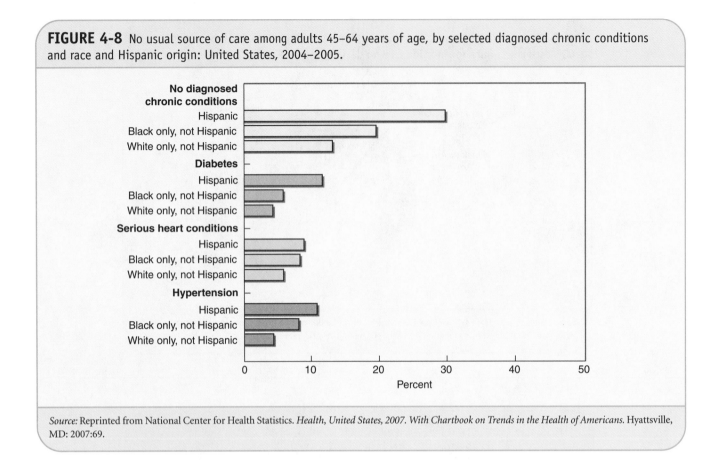

Source: Reprinted from National Center for Health Statistics. *Health, United States, 2007. With Chartbook on Trends in the Health of Americans.* Hyattsville, MD: 2007:69.

SES from high to low and vice versa) is strongly and inversely associated with levels of morbidity and mortality. Those who occupy the lowest SES positions are confronted with excesses of morbidity and mortality from numerous causes (from mental disorders to chronic and infectious diseases to the consequences of adverse lifestyle).

One of the dimensions of SES—income—may be expressed in several ways in order to assess its impact upon health outcomes. For example, poverty is a measure based on before-tax income from sources such as earnings, unemployment compensation, interest, and Social Security. Poverty exists when a single person or family has an income that is below a threshold set by the U.S. Bureau of the Census. For a single person younger than 65 years of age, the poverty level in 2006 was annual income below the threshold of $10,488. Poverty status also can be computed for families; the poverty level is a function of the total income of a family in relationship to the poverty threshold. The threshold for poverty in a family is determined by summing the poverty thresholds provided by the U.S. Bureau of the Census for each adult and child living in a family. The poverty threshold for a five-person family that comprises three adults and two children was $24,662 in 2006.

The ratio of income to poverty is the ratio of an individual's or family's income to their poverty threshold. If the five-person family had an annual income of $25,000 in 2006, their income-to-poverty ratio was $25,000/$24,662 or 1.01; this ratio can also be expressed as 101% of poverty. Similarly, all poverty ratios can also be expressed as percentages; to illustrate, 200% of poverty refers to an income that is twice the poverty threshold.[9]

An example of the association between poverty and health outcomes is provided by access to dental care. Refer to Figure 4-10, which presents U.S. data for 2005 for persons who made no dental visits during the past year. The respondents were classified according to four poverty levels. At all age levels, as the percent of poverty level increased, there was a stepwise increase in the number of persons who made no dental visits. Among all age groups shown, the largest percentage of persons who made no dental visits was for those below 100% of the poverty level.

Related to the topic of race (as well as other demographic variables including age, gender, and socioeconomic status) is the term **health disparities**, which refers to differences in the occurrence of diseases and adverse health conditions in the population.

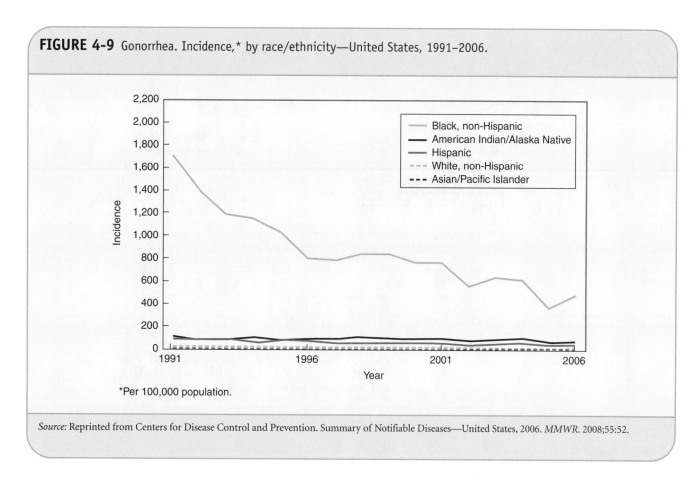

FIGURE 4-9 Gonorrhea. Incidence,* by race/ethnicity—United States, 1991–2006.

*Per 100,000 population.

Source: Reprinted from Centers for Disease Control and Prevention. Summary of Notifiable Diseases—United States, 2006. *MMWR.* 2008;55:52.

An example is cancer health disparities, defined as "…adverse differences in cancer incidence (new cases), cancer prevalence (all existing cases), cancer death (mortality), cancer survivorship, and burden of cancer or related health conditions that exist among specific population groups in the United States."[10] Currently, African Americans have the highest age-adjusted overall cancer incidence and death rates in comparison with four other racial/ethnic groups (Asian/Pacific Islander, Hispanic/Latino, American Indian/Alaska Native, and white).

PLACE VARIABLES

Morbidity and mortality vary greatly with respect to place (geographic regions that are being compared). Examples of comparisons according to place are international, national (within-country variations such as regional and urban-rural comparisons), and localized occurrences of disease.

International

The World Health Organization (WHO), which sponsors and conducts ongoing surveillance research, is a major source of information about international variations in rates of disease. WHO statistical studies portray international variations in in-

fectious and communicable diseases, malnutrition, infant mortality, suicide, and other conditions. As might be expected, both infectious and chronic diseases show great variation from one country to another. Some of these differences may be attributed to climate, cultural factors, national dietary habits, and access to health care.

Such variations are reflected in great international differences in life expectancy. The United States Central Intelligence Agency reported the ranked life expectancy at birth for 223 countries and indicated that the world life expectancy was 66.1 years (2008 estimate).[11] The three countries with the highest life expectancy in 2008 were Andorra (83.5 years), Macau—technically not a country—(83.3 years), and Japan (82.1 years); the United States ranked number 47 (78.1 years). The countries ranked as having the three lowest life expectancies were Zambia (38.6 years), Angola (37.9 years), and Swaziland (32.0 years). Life expectancy in many European countries including France, Italy, and Germany exceeded that of the United States. The United States' neighboring country, Canada, ranked seventh in life expectancy worldwide (81.2 years).

An example of an infectious disease that shows international variations and decreasing incidence is polio, which at

FIGURE 4-10 No dental visit in the past year among persons with natural teeth, by age and percent of poverty level: United States, 2005.

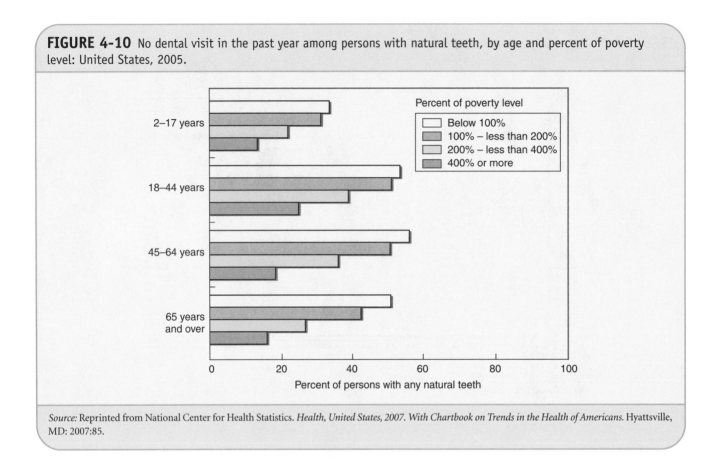

Source: Reprinted from National Center for Health Statistics. *Health, United States, 2007. With Chartbook on Trends in the Health of Americans.* Hyattsville, MD: 2007:85.

one time occurred worldwide. Polio is a viral infection that either is asymptomatic or produces a nonspecific fever in the majority of cases; about 1% of cases produce a type of paralysis known as flaccid paralysis. Immunization programs have helped to eradicate indigenous wild polio cases in the Western Hemisphere, Europe, and many other parts of the world. Figure 4-11 illustrates the spread of polio during 2002–2005. In 2002, polio was endemic in parts of Africa, Afghanistan, Pakistan, and on the Indian subcontinent. From these endemic areas, polio spread to several African and Middle Eastern countries where the wild polio virus was reestablished.

National (Within Country)

Many countries, especially large ones, demonstrate within-country variations in disease frequency. Regional differences in factors such as climate, latitude, and environmental pollution affect the prevalence and incidence of diseases. In the United States, comparisons of disease occurrence are made by geographic region (north, east, south, and west), state, or county. An example of state-level variation is the percentage of adults who reported a history of stroke in 2005. The states with the highest percentages included those in the southern United

States (e.g., Louisiana and Alabama) and Nevada. (Refer to Figure 4-12.)

Urban-Rural Differences

Urban and rural sections of the United States show variations in morbidity and mortality related to environmental and lifestyle issues. Urban diseases and causes of mortality are more likely to be those spread by person-to-person contact, crowding, and inner-city poverty or associated with urban pollution. Children's lead poisoning is an example of a health issue that occurs among urban residents who may be exposed to lead-based paint from decaying older buildings.

Agriculture is a major category of employment for the residents of rural areas. Farm workers often are exposed to hazards such as toxic pesticides and unintentional injuries caused by farm equipment. Figure 4-13 shows the distribution of nonfatal occupational farming injuries by state during 1993–1995 (the most recent data available). The highest rate of injuries occurred in Mississippi (14.5 per 100 full-time workers).

One group of employees who are at risk of health hazards associated with farming is migrant workers. Often they reside

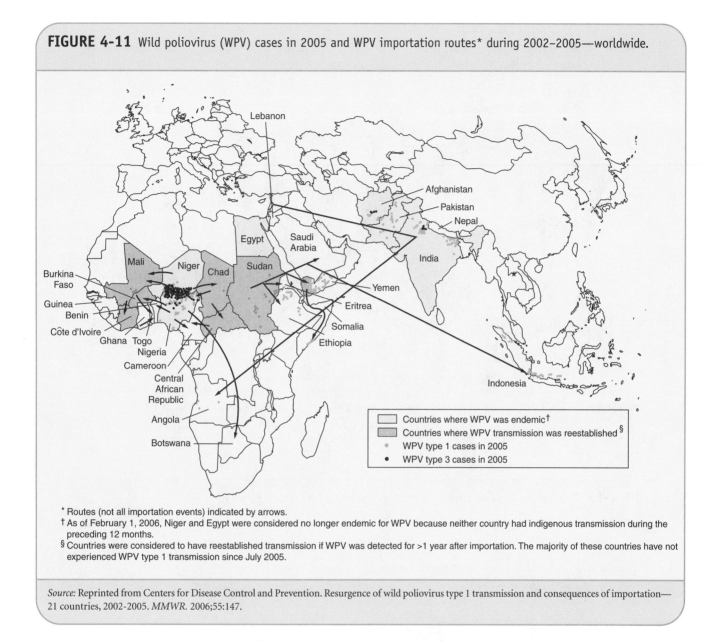

FIGURE 4-11 Wild poliovirus (WPV) cases in 2005 and WPV importation routes* during 2002–2005—worldwide.

* Routes (not all importation events) indicated by arrows.
† As of February 1, 2006, Niger and Egypt were considered no longer endemic for WPV because neither country had indigenous transmission during the preceding 12 months.
§ Countries were considered to have reestablished transmission if WPV was detected for >1 year after importation. The majority of these countries have not experienced WPV type 1 transmission since July 2005.

Source: Reprinted from Centers for Disease Control and Prevention. Resurgence of wild poliovirus type 1 transmission and consequences of importation—21 countries, 2002-2005. *MMWR.* 2006;55:147.

in crowded, substandard housing that exposes them to infectious agents found in unsanitary milieus. Many of these workers labor under extremely arduous conditions and lack adequate rest breaks, drinking water, and toilet facilities.

Localized Patterns of Disease

Localized patterns of disease are those associated with specific environmental conditions that may exist in a particular geographic area. Illustrations include lung cancer associated with radon gas found in some geographic areas and arsenic poisoning linked to high levels of naturally occurring arsenic in the water. Local environmental conditions also may support disease vectors that may not survive in other areas. (Vectors are intermediaries—insects or animals—involved in the transmission of disease agents; see Chapter 8 for a further discussion of vectors.)

An example of a localized pattern of disease is provided by dengue fever, a viral disease transmitted by a species of mosquito (a vector) that is present along the border that separates Texas from Mexico near the Gulf of Mexico. Localized populations of the mosquitoes are thought to have contributed to an outbreak of dengue fever in 2005. The affected areas are shown in Figure 4-14. Chapter 8 provides additional information about this outbreak.

FIGURE 4-12 Percentage of respondents aged ≥18 years who reported a history of stroke, by state/area—Behavioral Risk Factor Surveillance System, United States, 2005.*

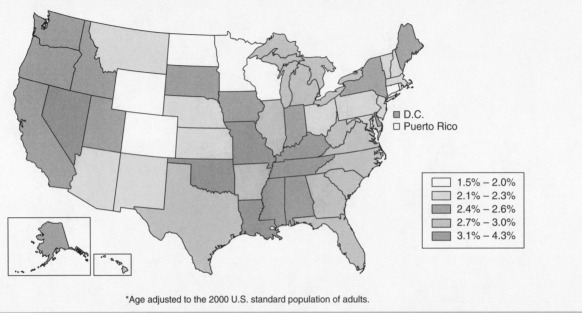

*Age adjusted to the 2000 U.S. standard population of adults.

Source: Reprinted from Centers for Disease Control and Prevention. Prevalence of stroke—United States, 2005. *MMWR.* 2007;56:473.

FIGURE 4-13 Rates of nonfatal occupational farming injuries by state, 1993–1995.

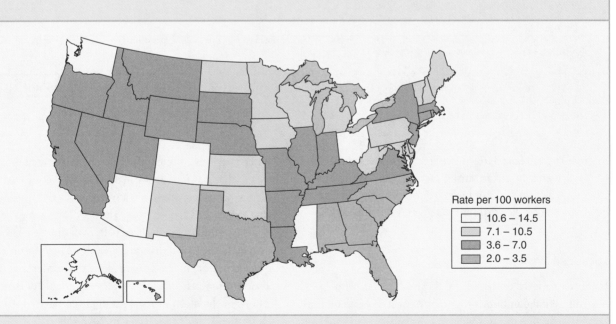

Source: Reprinted from Centers for Disease Control and Prevention, National Institute for Occupational Safety and Health. Worker Health Chartbook, 2004. DHHS (NIOSH) Publication No. 2004-146. Cincinnati, OH: National Institute for Occupational Safety and Health; 2004: 203.

FIGURE 4-14 Jurisdictions affected by dengue fever outbreak—Texas-Mexico border, 2005.

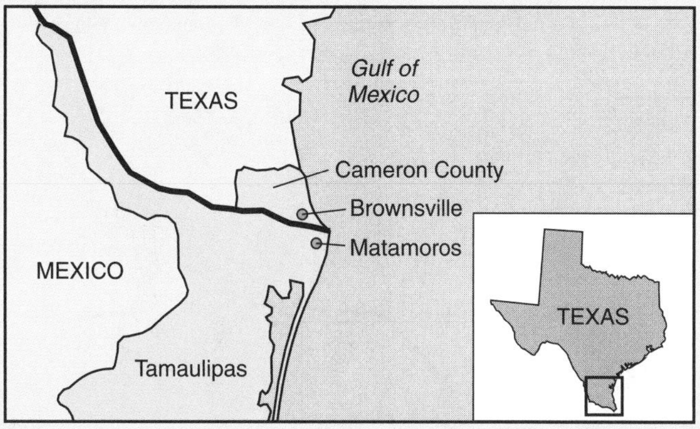

Source: Reprinted from Centers for Disease Control and Prevention. Dengue hemorrhagic fever—U.S.-Mexico border, 2005. *MMWR.* 2007;56:785.

TIME VARIABLES

Examples of disease occurrence according to time are secular trends, cyclic fluctuation (seasonality), point epidemics, and clustering.

Secular Trends

Secular trends refer to gradual changes in the frequency of diseases over long time periods. Figure 4-15 reports trends in yearly suicide rates of females. In both age groups, the frequency of suicides by firearms has declined over time, whereas suicides by hanging have increased.

Here is an example of the absence of a secular trend. Hypertension (high blood pressure) is a risk factor for stroke, cardiovascular disease, kidney disease, and other adverse health outcomes. Effective regimens and medications are available for the treatment and control of the condition; despite this fact, nearly one-third of the U.S. population has hypertension. Among all adults, this level did not change very much over the seven years shown in Figure 4-16, which tracks the age-adjusted prevalence of hypertension. The data reveal only slight variations in the age-adjusted prevalence between 1999 and 2006. Comparisons by gender, age, or race/ethnicity demonstrate that there has been no secular change.

Cyclic (Seasonal) Trends

Many phenomena (e.g., weather and health related) show cyclic trends. What is meant by a cyclic trend? **Cyclic trends** are increases and decreases in the frequency of a disease or other phenomenon over a period of several years or within a year.

Severe weather events in the Atlantic basin of the United States show cyclic trends, demonstrating a high level of seasonal activity since 1995. (Refer to Figure 4-17.) The 2005 season when Hurricane Katrina struck was the most active hurricane season on record.

With respect to health-related events, many infectious diseases and chronic adverse conditions manifest cyclical patterns of occurrence, with annual increases and decreases. Mortality from pneumonia and influenza peaks during February, decreases during March and April, and reaches its lowest level during the early summer. Enteroviruses are common viruses that affect human beings globally and are linked to a spectrum of illnesses that range from minor to severe; detections of enterovirus infections have increased in frequency during the summer months within the past two decades. (See Figure 4-18.)

Point Epidemics

A **point epidemic** may indicate the response of a group of people circumscribed in place to a common source of infection, contamination, or other etiologic factor to which they were exposed almost simultaneously.[12] An example was demonstrated by an outbreak of *Vibrio* infections that followed Hurricane Katrina in 2005.

A *Vibrio* is a bacterium that can affect the intestines (producing enteric diseases) and can cause wound infections. One of the illnesses caused by *Vibrio* is cholera (agent: *Vibrio*

FIGURE 4-15 Yearly suicide rates* for females aged 10–14 years, by method—National Vital Statistics System, United States, 1990–2004 (A); and Yearly suicide rates* for females aged 15–19 years, by method—National Vital Statistics System, United States, 1990–2004 (B).

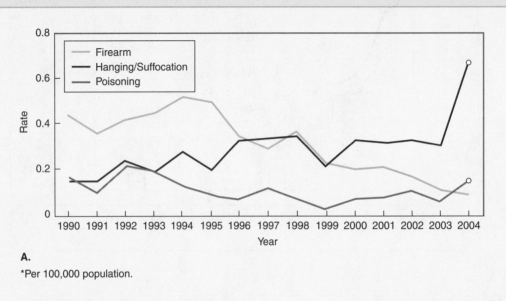

A.

*Per 100,000 population.

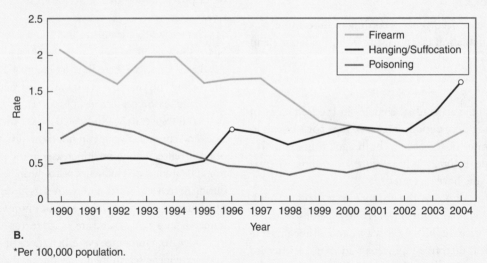

B.

*Per 100,000 population.

Source: Modified from Centers for Disease Control and Prevention. Suicide trends among youths and young adults aged 10–24 years—United States, 1990–2004. *MMWR.* 2007;56:907.

cholerae), discussed in Chapter 1. Some other types of *Vibrio* are *Vibrio parahaemolyticus* (can cause intestinal disorders) and *Vibrio vulnificus* (can cause wound infections). These bacteria can be transmitted through contaminated food and water and by many other mechanisms. During floods, public health officials need to monitor the presence of infectious disease agents such as *Vibrio* in the drinking-water supply.

Figure 4-19 shows clustering of cases of *Vibrio*-associated illnesses after Hurricane Katrina in 2005. The figure demonstrates that five persons died and 22 persons were hospitalized for *Vibrio* illness; these cases occurred among residents of Louisiana and Mississippi. The first hospital admission occurred on August 29 and the last on September 5. The frequency of cases peaked on September 3. Most of these cases

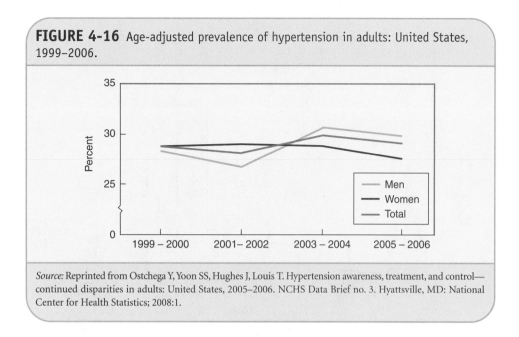

FIGURE 4-16 Age-adjusted prevalence of hypertension in adults: United States, 1999–2006.

Source: Reprinted from Ostchega Y, Yoon SS, Hughes J, Louis T. Hypertension awareness, treatment, and control—continued disparities in adults: United States, 2005–2006. NCHS Data Brief no. 3. Hyattsville, MD: National Center for Health Statistics; 2008:1.

were wound associated and believed to have been the result of an infection acquired by contact with floodwaters.

Clustering

An example of a pattern derived from descriptive studies is disease **clustering**, which refers to "a closely grouped series of events or cases of a disease or other health-related phenomena with well-defined distribution patterns in relation to time or place or both. The term is normally used to describe aggregation of relatively uncommon events or diseases (e.g., leukemia, multiple sclerosis)."[4] Clustering may suggest common exposure of the population to an environmental hazard; it also may

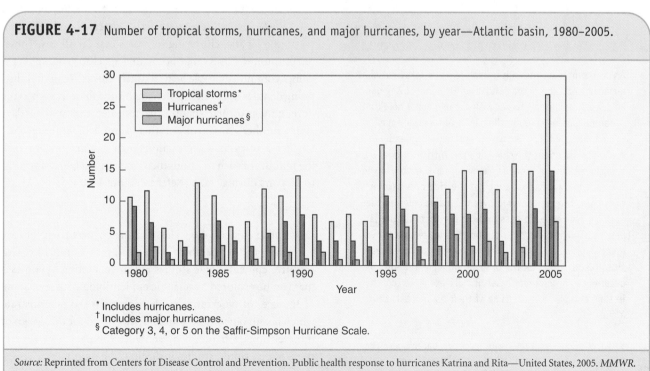

FIGURE 4-17 Number of tropical storms, hurricanes, and major hurricanes, by year—Atlantic basin, 1980–2005.

* Includes hurricanes.
† Includes major hurricanes.
§ Category 3, 4, or 5 on the Saffir-Simpson Hurricane Scale.

Source: Reprinted from Centers for Disease Control and Prevention. Public health response to hurricanes Katrina and Rita—United States, 2005. *MMWR.* 2006;55:231.

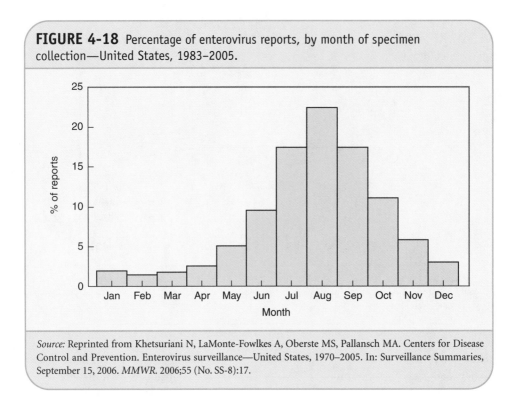

FIGURE 4-18 Percentage of enterovirus reports, by month of specimen collection—United States, 1983–2005.

Source: Reprinted from Khetsuriani N, LaMonte-Fowlkes A, Oberste MS, Pallansch MA. Centers for Disease Control and Prevention. Enterovirus surveillance—United States, 1970–2005. In: Surveillance Summaries, September 15, 2006. *MMWR.* 2006;55 (No. SS-8):17.

Texas sharpshooter effect

A traveler passing through a small town in Texas noted a remarkable display of sharpshooting. On almost every barn he passed there was a target with a single bullet hole that uncannily passed through the center of the bull's-eye. He was so intrigued by this that he stopped at a nearby gas station to ask about the sharpshooter. With a chuckle, the attendant told him that the shooting was the work of Old Joe. Old Joe would first shoot at the side of a barn and then paint targets centered over his bullet holes so that each shot appeared to pass through the center of the target. . . . In a random distribution of cases of cancer over a geographic area, some cases will appear to occur very close together just on the basis of random variation. The occurrence of a group of cases of a disease close together in time and place at the time of their diagnosis is called a cluster.

Source: Reprinted from Grufferman S. Methodologic approaches to studying environmental factors in childhood cancer. *Environ Health Perspect.* 1998;106 (Suppl. 3):882.

be purely spurious—due to the operation of chance. One cause of spurious clustering is called the Texas Sharpshooter Effect.

Clustering can refer to spatial clustering and temporal clustering. Spatial clustering indicates cases of disease (often uncommon diseases) that occur in a specific geographic region, a common example being a cancer cluster. Temporal clustering denotes health events that are related in time, such as the development of maternal postpartum depression a few days after a mother gives birth. Another example of temporal clustering is postvaccination reactions such as syncope (fainting); the number of such reactions increased among females aged 11 to 18 years during 2007. (Refer to Figure 4-20.)

CONCLUSION

Descriptive epidemiology classifies the occurrence of disease according to the variables of person, place, and time. Descriptive epidemiologic studies aid in generating hypotheses that can be explored by analytic epidemiologic studies. Some of the uses of descriptive epidemiology are to demonstrate which health outcomes should be prioritized for the design of interventions. Chapter 4 presented information on several types of descriptive studies including case reports, case series, and cross-sectional studies. The Behavioral Risk Factor Surveillance System (BRFSS) is an example of an ongoing

FIGURE 4-19 Cases of post-Hurricane Katrina *Vibrio* illness among residents of Louisiana and Mississippi,* by date of hospital admission—United States, August 29–September 11, 2005.

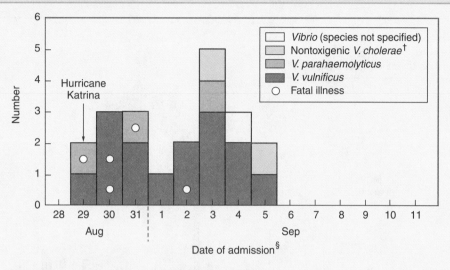

* N = 22; Alabama, a third state under surveillance, reported no cases.
† Nontoxigenic *V. cholerae* illnesses represent infections entirely distinct from the disease cholera, which is caused by toxigenic *V. cholerae* serogroup O1 or O139.
§ Date of admission was not available for one Louisiana resident. In cases that did not require hospitalization, the date represents the first contact with a healthcare provider for the illness.

Source: Reprinted from Centers for Disease Control and Prevention. *Vibrio* illnesses after Hurricane Katrina—multiple states, August–September 2005. *MMWR.* 2005;54:928.

cross-sectional study of health characteristics of the population of the United States. Person variables discussed in the chapter were age, sex, race/ethnicity, and socioeconomic status. Place variables included the following types of comparisons: international, national (within country), urban-rural, and local-ized patterns. Time variables encompassed secular time trends, cyclic trends, point epidemics, and clustering. Descriptive epidemiology is an important component of the process of epidemiologic inference.

FIGURE 4-20 Number of postvaccination syncope* episodes reported to the Vaccine Adverse Event Reporting System, by month and year of report—United States, January 1, 2004–July 31, 2007.

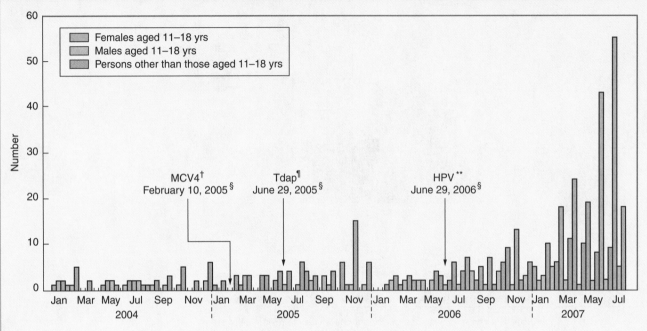

* Includes persons aged ≥5 years who had syncope onset after vaccination on the same date.
† Meningococcal conjugate vaccine.
§ Date on which the Advisory Committee on Immunization Practices decided to add this newly licensed adolescent vaccine to the Vaccines for Children Program.
¶ Tetanus toxoid, reduced diphtheria toxoid, and acellular pertussis vaccine.
** Quadrivalent human papillomavirus recombinant vaccine. HPV is licensed only for females.

Source: Reprinted from Centers for Disease Control and Prevention. Syncope after vaccination—United States, January 2005–July 2007. *MMWR.* 2008;57:458.

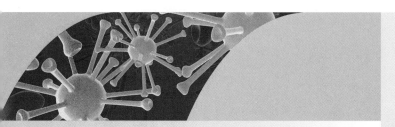

Study Questions and Exercises

1. Refer back to Table 4-2, which presents characteristics of infants who were exclusively breastfed. Describe the results shown in the table. Suppose you wanted to conduct a survey of breastfeeding in your own community:
   a. How would you choose the participants?
   b. What questionnaire items would you include in the survey?
   c. What type of study design is a survey?

2. State three uses for descriptive epidemiologic studies. How could descriptive epidemiologic studies examine the following health issues?
   a. The obesity epidemic in the United States
   b. Increases in the prevalence of type 2 diabetes among adolescents
   c. Abuse of prescription narcotic drugs

3. Define the terms case reports and case series. Indicate how they are similar and how they differ. Search the Internet for examples of case reports of disease as well as case series.

4. Refer back to Table 4-3, which gives the percentage of adults who reported insufficient rest or sleep. Provide a detailed account of the findings presented in the table. What additional information would you like to have in order to determine the reasons why people have insufficient rest or sleep?

5. Refer back to the section on sex differences. How did the top five types of invasive cancer differ in incidence between males and females? Can you hypothesize reasons for these differences?

6. What are some examples of racial/ethnic classifications used to describe health characteristics? Name two conditions that vary according to race/ethnicity.

7. What is meant by the term health disparities? What do you think could be done about them from the societal and public health points of view?

8. How does life expectancy at birth in the United States compare with that in other countries? Do you have any suggestions for improving life expectancy in the United States? What could be done to raise the life expectancies of residents in the countries that have the three lowest levels?

9. Name three characteristics of time that are used in descriptive epidemiologic studies and give an example of each one.

10. The prevalence of hypertension has remained essentially unchanged for nearly a decade. Propose a descriptive epidemiologic study to explore the reasons for this phenomenon.

Young Epidemiology Scholars (YES) Exercises

The Young Epidemiology Scholars Web site provides links to teaching units and exercises that support instruction in epidemiology. The YES program is administered by the College Board and supported by the Robert Wood Johnson Foundation. The Web address of YES is www.collegeboard.com/yes. The following exercises relate to topics discussed in this chapter and can be found on the YES Web site.

1. Kaelin MA, St. George DMM. Descriptive epidemiology of births to teenage mothers.

2. Olsen C, St. George DMM. Cross-sectional study design and data analysis.

REFERENCES

1. Friis RH, Sellers TA. *Epidemiology for Public Health Practice*. 4th ed. Sudbury, MA: Jones and Bartlett Publishers; 2009.

2. Centers for Disease Control and Prevention. Acute renal failure associated with cosmetic soft-tissue filler injections—North Carolina, 2007. *MMWR*. 2008;57:453–456.

3. Centers for Disease Control and Prevention. Primary amebic meningoencephalitis—Arizona, Florida, and Texas, 2007. *MMWR*. 2008;57:573–577.

4. Porta M, ed. *A Dictionary of Epidemiology*. 5th ed. New York: Oxford University Press; 2008.

5. Kung HC, Hoyert DL, Xu JQ, Murphy SL. Deaths: Final data for 2005. *National vital statistics reports*; 2008;56(10). Hyattsville, MD: National Center for Health Statistics.

6. Fine MJ, Ibrahim SA, Thomas SB. The role of race and genetics in health disparities research (editorial). *Am J Public Health*. 2005;95:2125–2128.

7. McKenney NR, Bennett CE. Issues regarding data on race and ethnicity: the Census Bureau experience. *Pub Health Rep*. 1994;109:16–25.

8. Krieger N. Editorial: counting accountably: implications of the new approaches to classifying race/ethnicity in the 2000 census. *Am J Public Health*. 2000;90:1687–1689.

9. U.S. Census Bureau. Poverty: How the Census Bureau measures poverty (official measure). Available at: http://www.census.gov/hhes/www/poverty/povdef.html. Accessed June 18, 2008.

10. National Cancer Institute. Factsheet: Cancer Health Disparities: Questions and Answers. Available at: http://www.cancer.gov/cancertopics/factsheet/cancer-health-disparities. Accessed August 15, 2008.

11. Central Intelligence Agency. *The World Factbook*. Rank order-life expectancy at birth. Available at: https://www.cia.gov/library/publications/the-world-factbook/rankorder/2102rank.html. Accessed August 16, 2008.

12. MacMahon B, Pugh TF. *Epidemiology Principles and Methods*. Boston, MA: Little, Brown; 1970.

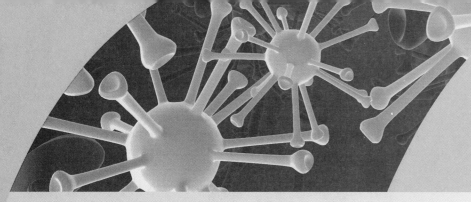

Association and Causality

CHAPTER OUTLINE

INTRODUCTION

Previously, the author distinguished between descriptive epidemiology (using epidemiologic methods to describe the occurrence of diseases in the population) and analytic epidemiology (using epidemiology to study the etiology of diseases, as in determining whether there is a causal relationship between exposures and health outcomes). Chapter 4 provided information on descriptive epidemiology, which involves three major categories: person, place, and time. Building on this foundation, Chapter 5 will launch the discussion of analytic epidemiology, beginning specifically with the concepts of noncausal associations and causal associations.

Refer to Table 5-1 for an overview of terms covered in this chapter. You will learn methods for presenting associations graphically and in contingency tables. Another issue will be

TABLE 5-1 List of Important Terms Used in This Chapter

Terms related to association	Criteria of causality	Assessing the operation of chance
Causal association	Biological gradient	Clinical significance
Contingency table	Consistency	Confidence intervals
Noncausal association	Specificity	Point estimates
Scatter plot	Strength	Power
Statistical independence	Temporality	Statistical significance

the criteria that are used to assess a causal association. Finally, when an association has been observed between an exposure and an outcome, you will need to take into account factors that can affect the validity of the observed association.

TYPES OF ASSOCIATIONS FOUND AMONG VARIABLES

Previously, the author stated that one of the concerns of analytic epidemiology is to examine associations among exposure variables and health outcome variables. A **variable** is "any quantity that varies. Any attribute, phenomenon, or event that can have different values."[1] As noted, exposure denotes contact with factors that usually may be linked to adverse outcomes such as specific forms of morbidity and mortality. The term **association** refers to a linkage between or among variables; variables that are associated with one another can be positively or negatively related. In a **positive** association, as the value of one variable increases so does the value of the other variable. In a **negative** (inverse) association, when the value of one variable increases, the value of the other variable decreases.

A measure of the strength of association (that you may have already encountered in a statistics course) is the Pearson correlation coefficient (r), used with continuous variables. A **continuous variable** is a type of variable that can have an infinite number of values within a specified range; examples are height and weight. Pearson correlation coefficients range from -1 to 0 to $+1$. When the value of r is negative, the relationship between two variables is inverse; a positive r denotes a positive association. The closer r is to either $+1$ or -1, the stronger is the association between two variables. As r approaches 0, the association becomes weaker; the value 0 means that there is no association.

Let's refer generically to variable X (exposure factor) and variable Y (outcome). Here are some possible relationships between X and Y:

- No association (X is unrelated to Y)
- Associated (X is related to Y)
  - Noncausally (X does not cause Y)
  - Causally (X causes Y)

Take the hypothetical example of non-insulin-dependent (type 2) diabetes, which appears to be occurring at earlier and earlier ages in the United States. Suppose that in a hypothetical situation an epidemiologist wanted to study whether dietary consumption of sugar (exposure variable) is related to diabetes (health outcome). There are several possible types of associations between these two variables (i.e., high levels of sugar consumption and diabetes).

- No association between dietary sugar and diabetes. The term "no association" means that the occurrence of diabetes is independent of the amount of sugar consumed in the diet.
- Dietary sugar intake and diabetes are associated. A positive association would indicate (in the example of a direct association) that the occurrence of diabetes increases with increases in the amount of dietary sugar consumed. A negative association would show that with increasing amounts of sugar in the diet, the occurrence of diabetes decreases.
  - Noncausal association between dietary sugar intake and occurrence of diabetes. In a noncausal (secondary) association, it is possible for a third factor such as genetic predisposition to be operative. For example, this third variable might have a primary association with both sugar consumption and diabetes. People who have this genetic predisposition might favor greater amounts of sugar in the diet and also may have more frequent occurrence of diabetes. Thus the association between consumption of a diet that is high in sugar is secondary to one's genetic predisposition and is a noncausal association.
  - Causal association between dietary intake of sugar and diabetes. A causal association would indicate that consumption of large amounts of sugar is a cause of diabetes. Before a causal association can be assumed, several criteria for causal relationships need to be evaluated (discussed later in this chapter) and the associations need to be examined for possible errors.

SCATTER PLOTS

Let us explore the concept of association more generally by examining a scatter plot, a method for graphically displaying relationships between variables.

A scatter diagram plots two variables, one on an X axis (horizontal axis) and the other on a Y axis (vertical axis). The measurements for each case (or individual subject) are plotted as a single data point (dot) in the scatter diagram: let's create scatter diagrams from simple data sets. The examples will indicate a perfect direct linear relationship (r = $+1$) and a perfect inverse linear relationship (r = -1); later we will examine other types of relationships. First examine the data for Study One shown in Table 5-2 and then see how the graphs turn out. The first data point (case 001) is (1,1), and the second point (case 002) is (2,2), with the final data point (case 015) ending as (15,15). Figure 5-1 demonstrates that all of the points fall on a straight line; r = 1.0. The plot of the data in Study Two is shown in Figure 5-2; the graph is also a straight line and the relationship is inverse (r = -1.0).

TABLE 5-2 Measurements Used to Create a Scatter Plot

Study One			Study Two		
Case number	X-variable	Y-variable	Case number	X-variable	Y-variable
001	1	1	001	1	15
002	2	2	002	2	14
003	3	3	003	3	13
004	4	4	004	4	12
005	5	5	005	5	11
006	6	6	006	6	10
007	7	7	007	7	9
008	8	8	008	8	8
009	9	9	009	9	7
010	10	10	010	10	6
011	11	11	011	11	5
012	12	12	012	12	4
013	13	13	013	13	3
014	14	14	014	14	2
015	15	15	015	15	1

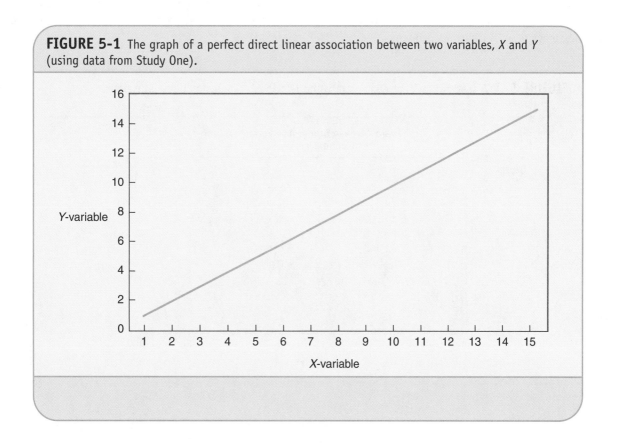

FIGURE 5-1 The graph of a perfect direct linear association between two variables, X and Y (using data from Study One).

FIGURE 5-2 The graph of a perfect inverse linear association between two variables, *X* and *Y* (using data from Study Two).

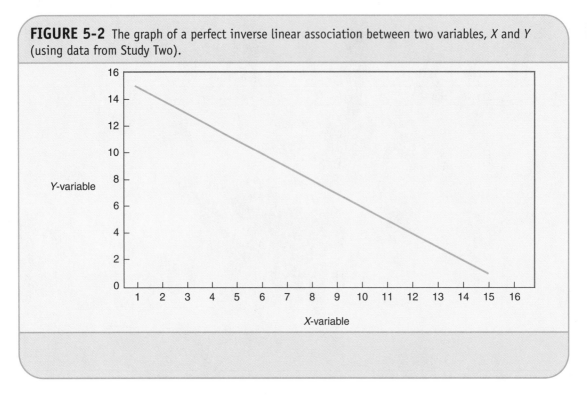

Next, we will plot the relationship between age and weight using data from a heart disease study (see Figure 5-3). The circular shape of this cloud reveals that there is no association between these two variables in the particular data set examined; the value of *r* is close to 0. When there is no association between two variables, they are statistically independent.

Figure 5-4 plots the relationship between systolic and diastolic blood pressure, which are positively related to one another ($r = 0.7$). Because this relationship is fairly strong, the points are close together and almost form a straight line. If we were to draw an oval around the points, the oval would be cigar shaped.

FIGURE 5-3 A scatter plot that demonstrates no relationship between age and weight.

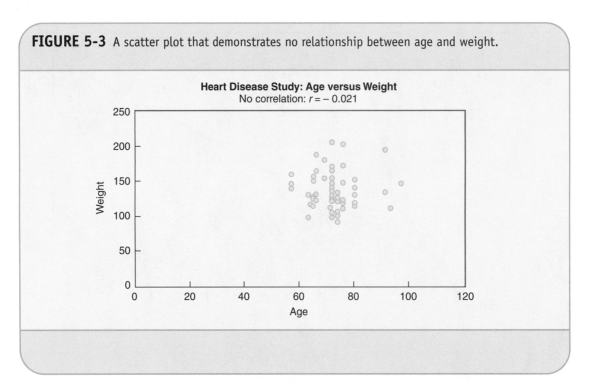

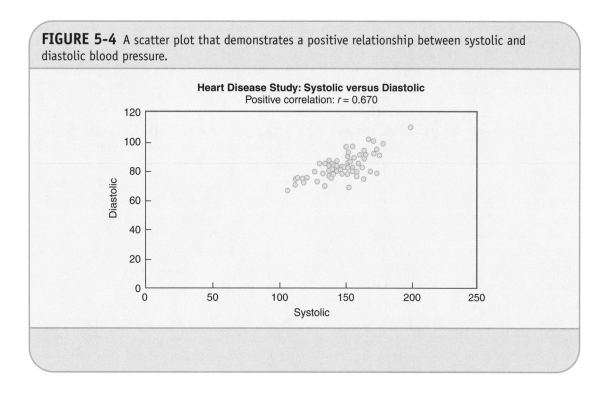

FIGURE 5-4 A scatter plot that demonstrates a positive relationship between systolic and diastolic blood pressure.

Some additional notes about scatter plots: the closer the points lie with respect to the straight line of best fit through them (called the regression line), the stronger the association between variable X and variable Y. As noted, a perfect linear association between two variables is indicated by a straight line.

It is also possible for scatter plots to conform to nonlinear shapes, such as a curved line, which suggests a nonlinear or curvilinear relationship. Figure 5-5 shows an inverted U-shaped relationship. The linear correlation between X and Y is essentially 0 (-0.09), indicating that there is no linear association. However, nonlinear curves do not imply that there

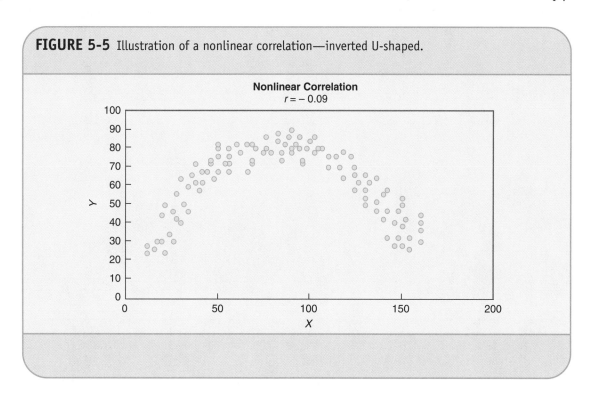

FIGURE 5-5 Illustration of a nonlinear correlation—inverted U-shaped.

is no relationship between two variables, only that their relationship is nonlinear.

DOSE-RESPONSE, MULTIMODAL, AND EPIDEMIC CURVES

Let us further explore the concepts of association by examining a dose-response curve, a multimodal curve, and an epidemic curve.

Dose-Response Curve

A **dose-response curve** is the plot of a dose-response relationship, which is a type of correlative association between an exposure (e.g., dose of a toxic chemical) and effect (e.g., a biologic outcome). Figure 5-6 illustrates a dose-response curve. The dose is indicated along the *X*-axis, with the response shown along the *Y*-axis. At the beginning of the curve, the flat portion suggests that at low levels of the dose, no or a minimal effect occurs. This is also known as the subthreshold phase. After the threshold is reached, the curve rises steeply and then progresses to a linear state in which an increase in response is proportional to an increase in dose. The **threshold** refers to the lowest dose at which a particular response occurs. When the maximal response is reached, the curve flattens out.

A dose-response relationship is one of the indicators used to assess a causal effect of a suspected exposure associated with an adverse health outcome. For example, there is a dose-response relationship between the number of cigarettes smoked daily and mortality from lung cancer.[2] As the number of cigarettes smoked per day increases, so do the rates of lung cancer mortality. This dose-response relationship was one of

the considerations that led to the conclusion that smoking is a cause of lung cancer mortality.

Multimodal Curves

A **multimodal curve** is one that has several peaks in the frequency of a condition. A **mode** is defined as the category in a frequency distribution that has the highest frequency of cases; there can be more than one mode in a frequency distribution. When plotted as a line graph, a multimodal curve takes the form shown in Figure 5-7, a multimodal distribution with three modes: A, B, and C. The figure plots age on the horizontal axis and frequency of the condition on the vertical axis.

Among the reasons for multimodal distributions are changes in the immune status or lifestyle of the host (the person who develops a disease); another explanation might be the occurrence of conditions such as chronic diseases that have long latency periods. (The term **latency** refers to the time period between initial exposure and a measurable response.) Referring back to Figure 5-7: As a purely hypothetical example, the increase at point A (for children) might be due to their relatively low immune status; the spike at point B (for young adults) might be the effect of behavioral changes that bring potential hosts into contact with other persons, resulting in person-to-person spread of disease; and the increase at point C (for the oldest persons) might reflect the operation of latency effects of exposures to carcinogens.

Epidemic Curve

An **epidemic curve** is "a graphic plotting of the distribution of cases by time of onset."[1] The concept of an epidemic curve is re-

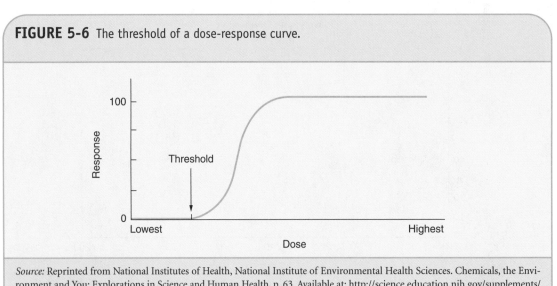

FIGURE 5-6 The threshold of a dose-response curve.

Source: Reprinted from National Institutes of Health, National Institute of Environmental Health Sciences. Chemicals, the Environment and You: Explorations in Science and Human Health, p. 63. Available at: http://science.education.nih.gov/supplements/nih2/chemicals/guide/pdfs/lesson3.pdf. Accessed July 28, 2008.

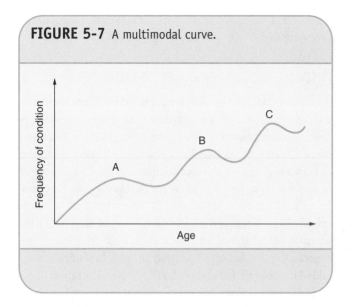

FIGURE 5-7 A multimodal curve.

CONTINGENCY TABLES

Another method for demonstrating associations is to use a **contingency table**, which is a type of table that tabulates data according to two dimensions (refer to Table 5-3).

The type of contingency table illustrated by Table 5-3 is also called a 2 by 2 table or a fourfold table because it contains four cells, labeled A through D. The column and row totals are known as marginal totals. As noted previously, analytic epidemiology is concerned with the associations between exposures and health outcomes (disease status). Two of the study designs that we will examine (refer to Chapter 6) employ variations of a contingency table to present the results. One of these designs is a case-control study and the other is a cohort study. The definitions of the cells in Table 5-3 are as follows:

A = Exposure is present and disease is present.
B = Exposure is present and disease is absent.
C = Exposure is absent and disease is present.
D = Exposure is absent and disease is absent.

Here is an example of how a contingency table can be used to study associations. Consider the relationship between advertisements for alcoholic beverages and binge drinking. We can pose the question of whether teenagers who view television commercials that promote alcoholic beverages are more prone to engage in binge drinking than teenagers who do not view such advertisements. The contingency table would be labeled

lated to point epidemics, discussed previously in Chapter 4. An epidemic curve is a type of unimodal (having one mode) curve that aids in identifying the cause of a disease outbreak. The epidemic curve for the *Salmonella* outbreak reported in Chapter 1 is shown in Figure 5-8. The figure suggests that there was a common exposure to a single etiologic agent. Disease detectives implicated *Salmonella* Saintpaul, a type of bacterium that can be transmitted by contaminated foods.

FIGURE 5-8 Infections with the outbreak strain of *Salmonella* Saintpaul, by date of illness onset* (N = 1,361 for whom information was reported) (as of Aug 7, [2008], 9 pm EDT).

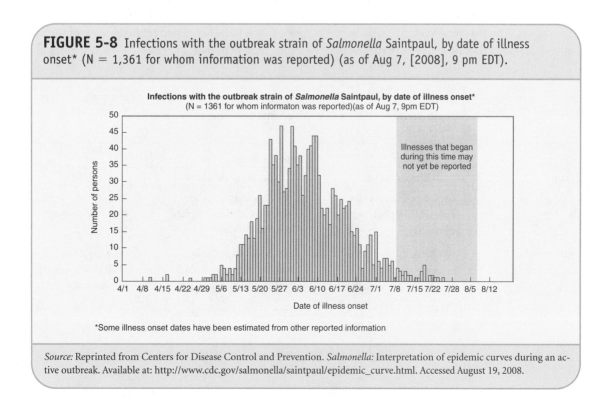

Source: Reprinted from Centers for Disease Control and Prevention. *Salmonella*: Interpretation of epidemic curves during an active outbreak. Available at: http://www.cdc.gov/salmonella/saintpaul/epidemic_curve.html. Accessed August 19, 2008.

TABLE 5-3 Generic Contingency Table

Exposure Status	Disease status		
	Yes	No	Total
Yes	A	B	A + B
No	C	D	C + D
Total	A + C	B + D	A + B + C + D

as shown in Table 5-4. In the example, the exposure status variable is viewing and not viewing alcoholic beverage commercials; the outcome variable is whether study subjects engage in binge drinking. The column totals refer to the column and row totals, respectively.

What information can we obtain from the contingency table? Here is a preview of information that we will cover later in the text: if there is an association between binge drinking and viewing alcoholic beverage commercials, the proportions of binge drinkers in each cell would be different from one another. In fact, we would expect a higher proportion of teenage binge drinkers among those who view alcoholic beverage commercials in comparison with those who do not view such commercials. However, this statement is somewhat of an oversimplification. Chapter 6 will present an in-depth discussion of measures for quantifying associations between exposure and outcome variables. The two measures that will be described in Chapter 6 are the odds ratio and relative risk. Suffice

it to say that the choice of measures of association must be appropriate to the type of study design chosen.

EPIDEMIOLOGIC RESEARCH STRATEGIES

As noted previously in Chapter 1, one of the most important uses of epidemiology is to search for the etiology of diseases. The overriding question that epidemiologists ask is whether a particular exposure is causally associated with a given outcome. "In epidemiology, as in other sciences, progress in this search results from a series of cycles in which investigators (1) examine existing facts and hypotheses, (2) formulate a new or more specific hypothesis, and (3) obtain additional facts to test the acceptability of the new hypothesis. A fresh cycle then commences, the new facts, and possibly the new hypothesis, being added to the available knowledge."[3(p29)] An illustration of the cycle of epidemiologic research is shown in Figure 5-9.

Here is an explanation of the terms used in the figure. Epidemiologic research is guided by theories and explanatory models. In epidemiology, theories are general accounts of causal relationships between exposures and outcomes. There is a close connection between theories and explanatory models; an example of an explanatory model is the web of causation discussed later in the chapter. As new information is gathered in epidemiologic studies, theories and models need to be modified to take account of these new data.

Epidemiologic research studies are initiated with research questions, which are linked to the development of hypotheses. A **hypothesis** is defined as "any conjecture cast in a form that will allow it to be tested and refuted."[1] One of the most commonly used hypotheses in research is called a negative decla-

TABLE 5-4 The Association between Viewing Alcohol Advertisements and Binge Drinking

Exposure Status	Binge drinking		
	Binge drinkers	Non-binge drinkers	Total
View alcoholic beverage commercials	(A) Binge drinkers who view alcoholic beverage commercials	(B) Non-binge drinkers who view alcoholic beverage commercials	(A + B) All viewers of alcoholic beverage commercials
Do not view alcoholic beverage commercials	(C) Binge drinkers who do not view alcoholic beverage commercials	(D) Non-binge drinkers who do not view alcoholic beverage commercials	(C + D) All nonviewers of alcoholic beverage commercials
Total	(A + C) All binge drinkers	(B + D) All non-binge drinkers	(A + B + C + D) All study subjects

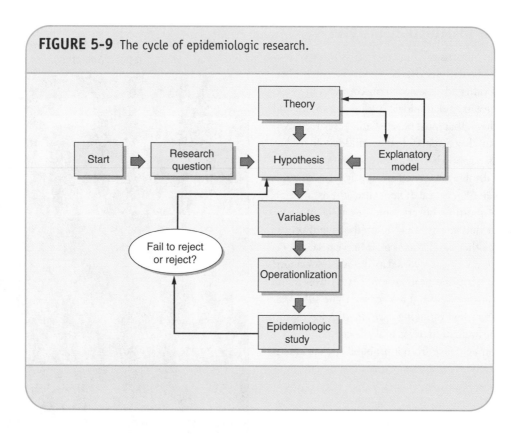

FIGURE 5-9 The cycle of epidemiologic research.

ration, or null hypothesis. For example, suppose an investigator wanted to study the association between smoking and lung cancer. The investigator could hypothesize that there is no difference in occurrence of lung cancer between smokers and nonsmokers. If an epidemiologic study found that there was a difference, then the null hypothesis would be rejected. Otherwise, the null hypothesis would fail to be rejected.

You might raise the question, "Where do hypotheses come from?" John Stuart Mill, in his writings on inductive reasoning, defined several methods for deriving hypotheses. These include the *method of difference* and the *method of concomitant variation*. The **method of difference** refers to a situation in which all of the factors in two or more domains are the same except for a single factor. The frequency of a disease that varies across the two settings is hypothesized to result from variation in a single causative factor. The method of difference is similar to a classic experimental design.

What is the linkage between the method of difference and hypotheses? An astute epidemiologist might observe that rates of coronary heart disease vary between sedentary and nonsedentary workers in a factory; he or she might hypothesize that the differences in coronary heart disease rates are due to differences in physical activity levels.

The **method of concomitant variation** refers to a type of association in which the frequency of an outcome increases with the frequency of exposure to a factor. One might hypothesize that this factor is associated with that outcome. An example from epidemiologic research is the dose-response relationship between the number of cigarettes smoked and mortality from lung cancer: the greater the number of cigarettes smoked, the higher the mortality levels from lung cancer.

Two additional terms shown in Figure 5-9 are *variables* (defined previously) and *operationalization*. Following the identification of hypotheses, the researcher needs to specify the variables that will be appropriate for the research project. After these have been specified, the measures to be used need to be identified. **Operationalization** refers to the process of defining measurement procedures for the variables used in a study. For example, in a study of the association between tobacco use and lung disease, the variables might be designated as number of cigarettes smoked and occurrence of asthma. The operationalization of these two variables might require a questionnaire to measure the amount of smoking and a review of the medical records to search for diagnoses of asthma. Using measures of association (discussed in Chapter 6), the researcher could determine how strongly smoking is related to asthma. On the basis of the findings of the study, the researcher could obtain information that would help to update hypotheses, theories, and explanatory models.

CAUSALITY IN EPIDEMIOLOGIC STUDIES

One of the central concerns of epidemiology is to be able to assert that a causal association exists between an exposure factor and disease (or other adverse health outcome) in the host. The issue of causality in epidemiologic studies is complex and includes several criteria that must be satisfied; these are known as the criteria of causality. Suppose that an epidemiologist has demonstrated an association between watching television commercials and binge drinking. As noted previously, an association can be either noncausal or causal. If noncausal, the association could be merely a one-time observation, due to chance and random factors, or due to errors in the methods and procedures used. On the other hand, there could be a causal association. What considerations are involved in a causal association?

The issue of causality has been explored extensively in the relationship between smoking and lung cancer. The 1964 U.S. Surgeon General's report *Smoking and Health* (see Figure 5-10) stated that the evaluation of a causal association does not depend solely upon evidence from a probabilistic statement derived from statistics but is a matter of judgment that depends upon several criteria.[4] Subsequently, A.B. Hill and other researchers developed an expanded list of causal criteria that augmented those presented in *Smoking and Health*. These criteria may be applied to the evaluation of the possible causal association between many types of exposures and health outcomes.

Criteria of Causality

The determination of causal relationships between exposures and outcomes remains a difficult issue for epidemiology, which relies primarily on observational studies. One reason for the difficulty is that assessment of exposures is imprecise in many epidemiologic studies, as is the delineation of the mechanisms that connect exposures with outcomes. We will return to this matter later in the text.

One of the fields that have explored the relationship between exposures and disease is environmental health, as well as the closely related field of occupational health. The noted researcher A.B. Hill pointed out that in the realm of occupational health, extreme conditions in the physical environment or exposure to known toxic chemicals is expected to be invariably injurious.[5] More commonly the situation obtains in which weaker associations have been observed between certain aspects of the environment and the occurrence of health events. An example would be the development of lung diseases among persons exposed to dusts (e.g., miners who work in dusty, unventilated mines). Hill raised the question of how one moves from such an observed association to the verdict of causation, e.g., exposure to coal dust *causes* a lung disease such as coal miners' pneumoconiosis. A second example is the perplexing

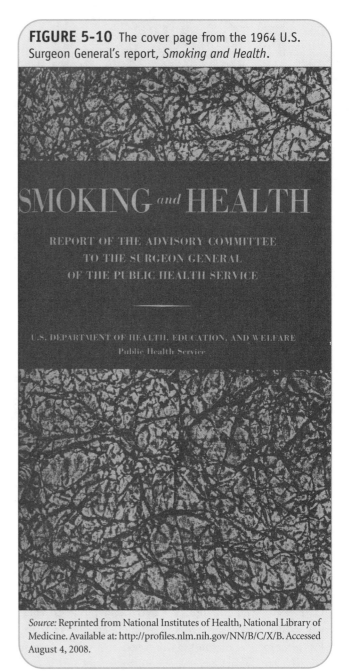

FIGURE 5-10 The cover page from the 1964 U.S. Surgeon General's report, *Smoking and Health*.

Source: Reprinted from National Institutes of Health, National Library of Medicine. Available at: http://profiles.nlm.nih.gov/NN/B/C/X/B. Accessed August 4, 2008.

question of the extent to which studies reveal a causal association between a specific environmental exposure and a particular form of cancer.[6]

Hill proposed a situation in which there is a clear association between two variables and in which statistical tests have suggested that this association is not due to chance. Under what circumstances would the association be causal? For example, data have revealed that smoking is associated with lung cancer in humans and that chance can be ruled out as being responsible for this observed association. Similarly, Hill listed several causal criteria that need to be taken into account in the assessment of a causal association between factor A and disease B. For the purposes of this text, we will consider eight of the criteria, which are included in Table 5-5.

Strength.

Strong associations give support to a causal relationship between factor and disease. Hill gives the example of the very large increase in scrotal cancer (by a factor of 200 times) among chimney sweeps in comparison to workers who were not exposed occupationally to tars and mineral oils. Another example arises from the steeply elevated lung cancer mortality rates among heavy cigarette smokers in comparison to nonsmokers (20 to 30 times higher). Hill also cautioned that we should not be too ready to dismiss the possibility of causal associations when the association is small, for there are many situations in which a causal association exists. One example would be exposure to an infectious agent (meningococcus) that produces relatively few clinical cases of meningococcal meningitis, a bacterial disease with symptoms that include headache, stiff neck, nausea, and vomiting.

Consistency.

According to Hill, a consistent association is one that has been observed repeatedly "... by different persons, in different places, circumstances and times ..."[5(p296)] An example of consistency comes from research on the relationship between smoking and lung cancer, a relationship that was found repeatedly in many retrospective and prospective studies.

Specificity.

A specific association is one that is constrained to a particular disease-exposure relationship. In a specific association, a given disease results from a given exposure and not from other types of exposures. Hill gave the example of an association that "... is limited to specific workers and to particular sites and types of disease and there is no association between the work and other modes of dying ..."[5(p297)] Returning to the smoking-lung can-

cer example, one may argue that the association is not specific, because "... the death rate among smokers is higher than the death rate of non-smokers from many causes of death ..."[5(p297)] Nevertheless, Hill argued that one-to-one causation is unusual, because many diseases have more than one causal factor.

Temporality.

This criterion specifies that we must observe the cause before the effect; Hill states that we cannot put the cart before the horse. For example, if we assert that air pollution causes lung cancer, we first must exclude persons who have lung cancer from our study; then we must follow those who are exposed to air pollution to determine whether lung cancer develops.

Biological gradient.

A biological gradient is known also as a dose-response curve, which shows a linear trend in the association between exposure and disease. An example is the dose-response association between the number of cigarettes smoked and the lung cancer death rate.

Plausibility.

This criterion requires that an association must be biologically plausible from the standpoint of contemporary biological knowledge. The association between exposure to tars and oils and the development of scrotal cancer among chimney sweeps is plausible in view of current knowledge about carcinogenesis. However, this knowledge was not available when Pott made his observations during the eighteenth century.

Coherence.

This criterion suggests that "... the cause-and-effect interpretation of our data should not seriously conflict with the generally known facts of the natural history and biology of the disease ..."[5(p298)] Examples related to cigarette smoking and lung cancer come from the rise in the number of lung cancer deaths associated with an increase in smoking, as well as lung cancer mortality differences between men (who smoke more and have higher lung cancer mortality rates) and women (who smoke less and have lower rates).

Analogy.

The final criterion relates to the correspondence between known associations and one that is being evaluated for causality. The examples Hill cites are thalidomide and rubella. Thalidomide, administered in the early 1960s as an antinausea drug for use during pregnancy, was associated subsequently with severe birth defects. Rubella (German measles), if contracted during pregnancy, has been linked to birth defects, stillbirths, and miscarriages. Given that such associations already have been demonstrated, "... we would surely be ready to

TABLE 5-5 Hill's Criteria of Causality

- Strength
- Consistency
- Specificity
- Temporality
- Biological gradient
- Plausibility
- Coherence
- Experiment
- Analogy

Source: Data from Hill AB. The environment and disease: Association or causation? *Proc R Soc Med.* 1965; 58:295–300.

accept slighter but similar evidence with another drug or another viral disease in pregnancy."[5(p299)]

So where does epidemiology stand with respect to the evaluation of causal and noncausal associations? Any one of the criteria taken alone is not sufficient to demonstrate a causal relationship. The entire set of criteria must be evaluated. Generally speaking, the more criteria that are satisfied, the more convincing is the evidence in support of a causal association. The 1964 report *Smoking and Health* stated that cigarette smoking caused lung cancer in men because the relationship satisfied many of the criteria for causality.

You can think of the assertion of causality as being similar to a trial in court. The jury must ponder each of the bits of evidence, weigh them against the causal criteria, and declare a verdict. (Refer to Figure 5-11, which shows a scale of justice.) "Innocent" means that there is no causal association; "guilty" means that there is a causal association. Sometimes, not all the evidence will support a conclusion of guilt. However, a preponderance of the evidence must support a guilty verdict. In the case of the American diet, high fat foods such as hamburgers are extremely popular and are consumed frequently. Heart disease is the leading cause of death in the United States; levels of obesity are increasing dramatically in the population. Evidence suggests that many high fat foods contain large amounts of saturated fats, which have been implicated in heart disease and other adverse health outcomes. Consequently, the weight of the evidence indicates that the scale has tipped toward a "guilty" verdict. Therefore, many authorities on nutrition and health recommend that consumption of large quantities of saturated fats should be minimized. Refer to the end of the chapter for an applicable exercise: "Young Epidemiology Scholars, Alpine fizz and male infertility: A mock trial."

Types of Causality

Many of the types of causal relationships that are involved with etiology of diseases involve more than one causal factor. This type of causality is called **multifactorial** or **multiple causality**. For example, the etiology of chronic diseases usually involves multiple types of exposures and other risk factors. These factors might include specific exposures (such as smoking), family history, lifestyle characteristics, and environmental influences. There are several models that portray multiple causality; this textbook will present two of them—the epidemiologic triangle for infectious diseases (see Chapter 8) and the web of causation, shown in Figure 5-12. The figure demonstrates that the etiology of coronary heart disease involves a complex interplay of exposures and risk factors. Note that the figure does not exhaust the list of possible factors related to coronary heart disease.

DEFINING THE ROLE OF CHANCE IN ASSOCIATIONS

Epidemiologists employ statistical procedures to assess the degree to which chance may have accounted for observed associations. For an observed association to be valid, it cannot be due to chance. As noted, an association can be merely a fortuitous event:

FIGURE 5-11 The declaration of a causal association involves a process that is similar to a jury weighing the evidence in a trial. Are foods (e.g., hamburgers) that are high in saturated fat "guilty" or "innocent" as causes of disease?

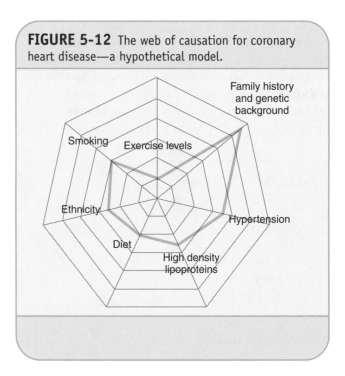

FIGURE 5-12 The web of causation for coronary heart disease—a hypothetical model.

suppose that it is Friday the thirteenth and that, on the way to class, you walked under a ladder and then a black cat crossed your path. Next, you went to class and received the results of the final you took last week; you received an "F" on the exam. Later in the day you found out that you had been laid off from your job. There was an unfortunate and chance connection between the unlucky events on Friday the thirteenth after you walked under the ladder and saw the black cat run in front of you.

The field of inferential statistics explores the degree to which chance affects the validity of conclusions that can be inferred from data. **Inference** is "the process of passing from observations and axioms to generalizations."[1] One of the goals of inference is to draw conclusions about a parent population from sample-based data. A sample is a subset of the data that have been collected from a population. An example of inference would be to estimate the average age of students in a university by randomly selecting a sample of students and calculating the average age of the sample.

Suppose we want to estimate the prevalence of multiple sclerosis in a population. We collect a random sample from the population and determine how many individuals have multiple sclerosis. The value for the population is referred to as a parameter and the corresponding value for the sample is a statistic. Suppose we know that the prevalence (parameter) of multiple sclerosis is 2.0%. The estimate (statistic) is calculated as 2.2%; this value is called a **point estimate**, which is a single value chosen to represent the population parameter. As a general rule, estimates gathered from samples do not exactly equal the population parameter because of sampling error.

As an alternative to a point estimate, an epidemiologist might use a **confidence interval estimate**, which is a range of values that with a certain degree of probability contain the population parameter. Confidence intervals are shown in Figure 5-13. To illustrate, the epidemiologist might want to be 95% certain that the confidence interval contains the population parameter. The final result for the confidence interval estimate of prevalence of multiple sclerosis might be stated in this hypothetical example as 1.5% to 2.5%. We could assert that we are 95% certain that the prevalence of multiple sclerosis in the population is from 1.5% to 2.5%.

One of the factors that affect statistical significance is the size of the sample involved in the statistical test. Larger samples are more likely to produce significant results than smaller samples. In statistics, **power** is ". . . the ability of a study to demonstrate an association if one exists."[1] Among the factors related to power are sample size and how large an effect is observed. The size of the effect is related to the strength of the association that has been observed. When the effect is small and the sample size is large, the association may be statistically significant. Conversely, if the effect is large and the sample size is

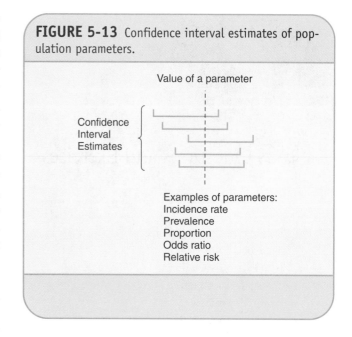

FIGURE 5-13 Confidence interval estimates of population parameters.

small, the association may not be significant merely because of the small sample size that was employed.

A final comment about statistical significance: if an observed association is statistically significant, it is not necessarily clinically significant. Suppose an epidemiologist finds that a new drug produces a significant reduction in blood pressure level, but the reduction is only slight. This slight reduction in blood pressure may not be clinically significant for an individual patient. The drug may not reduce the patient's morbidity or extend his or her life expectancy by any meaningful amount. In addition, some patients may experience side effects caused by the drug. As a result, use of the new drug may not be warranted.

CONCLUSION

Chapter 5 explored the topics of epidemiologic associations, criteria of causality, and the effect of chance upon observed relationships among variables. An association refers to a connection or linkage between or among two or more variables. A scatter plot is one of the methods for describing an association; another procedure is to construct a contingency table. The chapter defined several types of relationships between two variables including linear direct, linear inverse, and nonlinear, e.g., curvilinear. An example of a nonlinear association is an inverted U-shaped curve. An association among variables can be either noncausal or causal. The issue of causality is complex and involves the application of several causal criteria. The more of these criteria satisfied by an observed association, the greater the likelihood that a causal relationship exists. In addition to examining the criteria of causality, an epidemiologist must also rule out chance, which may account for observed associations. Statistical procedures enable one to estimate the role of chance.

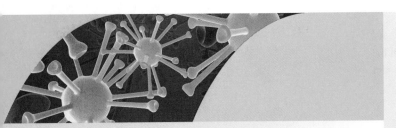

Study Questions and Exercises

1. Define the following terms:
   a. association
   b. positive association
   c. negative association
   d. nonlinear association
   e. dose-response relationship

2. Describe three types of associations (chance, non-causal, and causal) that are possible among exposures and health outcomes. Using your own experiences, give an example of each one.

3. How are a scatter plot and a contingency table helpful in demonstrating an association? Set up a contingency table that would show the association between teenage drinking and automobile crashes.

4. Define what is meant by a causal association. Table 5-5 shows Hill's criteria of causality. From your own experiences, give an example of how three criteria (strength, consistency, and temporality) might be satisfied with respect to the relationship between consumption of trans fats and heart disease. Note that trans fats are a type of liquid fat made solid through hydrogenation. Your answer might include a discussion of the health effects of eating French fries. For help with answering this question, read about the ban on trans fats in restaurants (Chapter 7).

5. Statistics are an important aspect of evaluating associations.
   a. What is the difference between a parameter and a statistic?
   b. Distinguish between a point estimate and a confidence interval estimate.
   c. How does power apply to statistical testing?
   d. How is clinical significance different from statistical significance?

6. Describe a multimodal curve. What is the significance for epidemiology of a multimodal curve? Sketch a multimodal curve.

7. Cases of gastrointestinal illness that occurred during the *Salmonella* Saintpaul epidemic were distributed as a unimodal curve. What is another name for this type of curve? Why is this type of curve important for epidemiology?

Young Epidemiology Scholars (YES) Exercises

The Young Epidemiology Scholars Web site provides links to teaching units and exercises that support instruction in epidemiology. The YES program is administered by the College Board and supported by the Robert Wood Johnson Foundation. The Web address of YES is www.collegeboard.com/yes. The following exercises relate to topics discussed in this chapter and can be found on the YES Web site.

Studying about causality:

1. Huang FI, Baumgarten M. Alpine fizz and male infertility: A mock trial.

Studying associations:

1. Kaelin M, Baumgarten M. An association: TV and aggressive acts.

2. Bayona M, Olsen C. Measures in epidemiology.

REFERENCES

1. Porta M. *A Dictionary of Epidemiology*. 5th ed. New York: Oxford University Press; 2008.

2. Doll R, Peto R. Mortality in relation to smoking: 20 years' observation on male British doctors. *BMJ*. 1976;2(6051):1525–1536.

3. MacMahon B, Pugh TF. *Epidemiology Principles and Methods*. Boston, MA: Little, Brown and Company; 1970.

4. U.S. Public Health Service. *Smoking and Health. Report of the Advisory Committee to the Surgeon General of the Public Health Service*. U.S. Department of Health, Education, and Welfare, Public Health Service, Center for Disease Control, PHS Publication No. 1103. Washington, DC: U.S. Government Printing Office; 1964.

5. Hill AB. The environment and disease: Association or causation? *Proc R Soc Med*. 1965;58:295–300.

6. DeBaun MR, Gurney JG. Environmental exposure and cancer in children. A conceptual framework for the pediatrician. *Pediatr Clin North Am*. 2001;48:1215–1221.

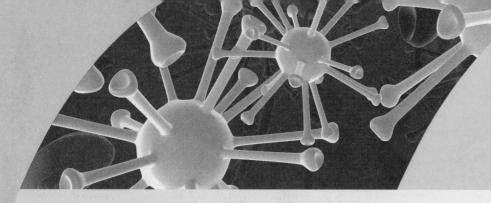

Analytic Epidemiology: Types of Study Designs

INTRODUCTION

By presenting methods for examining associations, the previous chapter provided an introduction to analytic epidemiology, which is concerned with etiology (causes) of diseases and other health outcomes. Chapter 6 further elaborates on the concept of association by applying it to the major categories of analytic designs: case-control, cohort, and ecologic study designs, and intervention studies.

    Why is analytic epidemiology important to society? One reason is that analytic studies lead to the prevention of disease. The Framingham Study (a community cohort study mentioned previously) was historically important because it contributed to our understanding of risk factors associated with coronary heart disease; modification of these risk factors has brought about reductions in morbidity and mortality from coronary heart disease. Another contribution of analytic epidemiology is the creation of quantitative evaluations of intervention programs (quasi-experimental designs) such as those directed at reduction of the

TABLE 6-1 List of Important Terms Used in This Chapter

Observational study designs			Experimental study designs (Intervention studies)	
Ecologic study	**Case-control study**	**Cohort study**	**Clinical trial**	**Community trial**
Ecologic comparison study	Matched case-control study	Cohort study	Crossover design	Hawthorne effect
Ecologic correlation	Odds ratio	Difference in risk	Prophylactic trial	Program evaluation
Ecologic fallacy	Retrospective approach	Relative risk	Therapeutic trial	Quasi-experimental study

Source: Author.

incidence of sexually transmitted diseases. Without such evaluations, it would not be possible to determine whether intervention programs are efficacious or justified socially or economically. Finally, analytic epidemiology (implemented as clinical trials) aids in determining whether new drugs, immunizations, and medical procedures are safe and work as intended.

Figure 6-1 gives an organizational chart for study designs, subdividing them into the two major branches (descriptive and analytic). To review descriptive epidemiology, refer back to Chapter 4. Here is some information about analytic epidemiology: within the panel labeled analytic studies, the two subcategories are observational and intervention (experimental) studies. Observational studies include ecologic studies, case-control studies, and cohort studies. Three types of cohort studies are prospective, retrospective, and historical prospective. The two types of intervention studies (experimental studies) are clinical trials and community interventions. These terms will be defined later in the chapter.

Analytic studies, either observational or experimental, explore the associations between exposures and outcomes. Observational studies, which typify much epidemiologic research, are those in which the investigator does not have control over the exposure factor. Additionally, usually the investigator is unable to assign subjects randomly to the conditions of an observational study. Random assignment of subjects to study groups provides a degree of control over confounding. When the results of a study have been distorted by extraneous factors, confounding is said to have taken place. (More information on confounding is presented later in this chapter.)

In comparison with observational studies, experimental designs enable the investigator to control who is exposed to a factor of interest as well as to assign the participants randomly to the groups used in the study. Random assignment of subjects is used in pure experimental designs. A quasi-experimental study is one in which the investigator is able to control the exposure of individuals or units to the factor but is unable to assign participants randomly to the conditions of the study.

Seven factors that characterize study designs

1. Who manipulates the exposure factor?
   - Observational study—exposure is not manipulated by the epidemiologist.
   - Experimental—exposure is manipulated by the epidemiologist.
2. How many observations are made?
3. What is the directionality of exposure?
4. What are the methods of data collection?
5. What is the timing of data collection?
6. What is the unit of observation?
7. How available are the study subjects?

Source: Adapted from Friis RH, Sellers TA. *Epidemiology for Public Health Practice.* 4th ed. Sudbury, MA: Jones and Bartlett Publishers; 2009: 242–243.

FIGURE 6-1 Two categories of epidemiologic studies.

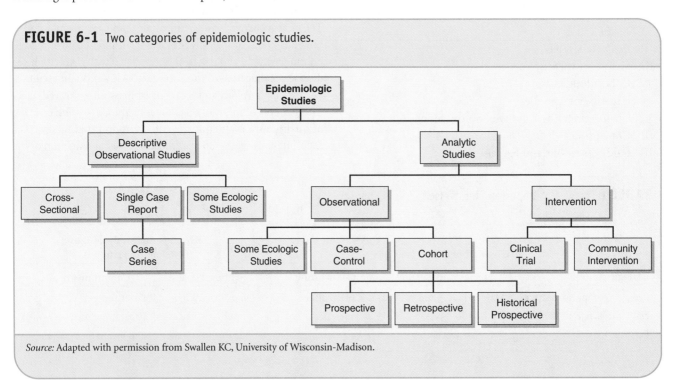

Source: Adapted with permission from Swallen KC, University of Wisconsin-Madison.

A number of factors distinguish the study designs shown in Figure 6-1 from one another. (Refer to the text box.) These factors include who manipulates the exposure factor (discussed in the foregoing paragraph), the number of observations made, directionality of exposure, data collection methods, timing of data collection, unit of observation, and availability of subjects. An explanation of these terms is as follows:

- Number of observations made
  - In some cases, observations of subjects may be made only once. This is the approach of cross-sectional studies, many ecologic studies, and most case-control studies.
  - In other cases, two or more examinations may be made. This is the approach of cohort studies and experimental studies.
- Directionality of exposure: the directionality of exposure measurement relative to disease varies according to the type of study design used.
  - Retrospective approach: the term **retrospective** means obtaining information about exposures that occurred in the past. This method is used in case-control studies. The investigator starts with subjects who already have a disease and queries them about previous exposures that may have led to the outcome under study.
  - A single point in time: the study is referenced about a single point in time, as in a survey. This approach is similar to taking a snapshot of a population. A single point in time is the time reference of a cross-sectional study (discussed previously in Chapter 4).
  - Prospective approach: information about the study outcome is collected in the future. Two study designs that use a prospective approach are experimental studies and cohort studies. In prospective cohort studies, the investigator starts with disease-free groups for which exposures are determined first. The groups are then followed prospectively for development of disease.
- Data collection methods: some methods require almost exclusive use of existing, previously collected data, whereas others require collection of new data.
  - Ecologic studies often use existing data.
- Timing of data collection: in some studies, information is obtained about exposures that occurred in the past. If long periods of time have elapsed between measurement of exposure and occurrence of disease, questions might be raised about the quality and applicability of the data. This information may be unreliable for various reasons including subjects' failure to remember past exposures. In other studies, subjects may be followed prospectively (i.e., into the future) over a period of time. Information

about the outcome variable may be lost should subjects drop out during the course of the study.
- Unit of observation: the unit of observation can be the individual or an entire group. Most epidemiologic study designs employ the individual as the unit of observation; one type, known as an ecologic study design, uses the group as the unit of observation.
- Availability of subjects: certain classes of subjects may not be available for epidemiologic research for several reasons, including ethical issues.

ECOLOGIC STUDIES

You are probably most familiar with studies in which the subjects are single individuals; this approach typifies most epidemiologic research. For example, information is collected from individual respondents by giving them a questionnaire, taking other measurements, and analyzing the data. In this situation, the individual is called the unit of analysis.

Ecologic studies are different from most research designs with which you are familiar and from other types of epidemiologic research. In ecologic studies, the group is the unit of analysis. More specifically, an **ecologic study** (also called ecological study) is ". . . a study in which the units of analysis are populations or groups of people rather than individuals."[1] For example, groups that are selected for an ecologic study might be the residents of particular geographic areas—nations, states, census tracts, or counties. An **ecologic comparison study** involves an assessment of the association between exposure rates and disease rates during the same time period.

In an ecologic study, information about both exposures (explanatory variables) and outcomes is collected at the group level. To illustrate, one could explore ". . . the relationship between the distribution of income and mortality rates in states or provinces."[1] In the hypothetical example of cancer mortality, researchers might hypothesize that persons who live in lower-income areas have greater exposure to environmental carcinogens than those who live in higher-income areas, producing differences in cancer mortality.

Figure 6-2 illustrates an **ecologic correlation**, an association between two variables measured at the group level. In the figure, infant mortality rates and average number of children per women are calculated for some African countries, which are the units of analysis. The graph portrays the strong positive linear relationship between fertility and infant mortality in sub-Saharan Africa. Countries that have high infant mortality rates (e.g., Sierra Leone) tend to have high birth rates.

One of the reasons for conducting an ecologic study is that individual measurements might not be available, but group-level data can be obtained. Often the data used have already been collected and are stored in data archives. These group measurements are called aggregate measures, which provide an overall measurement for the level, e.g., group or population, being studied. Often, ecologic studies are helpful in revealing the context of health—how demographic characteristics and the social environment contribute to morbidity and mortality.

Table 6-2 demonstrates some of the outcome variables, units of analysis, and explanatory variables (similar to exposure variables) used in ecologic studies. One of the common outcome variables of ecologic studies is mortality, either all-cause or cause-specific mortality (such as mortality from breast cancer or heart disease). In addition, outcome variables could include various types of morbidity; an example is occupational injuries. Other possible outcomes (not shown in the table)

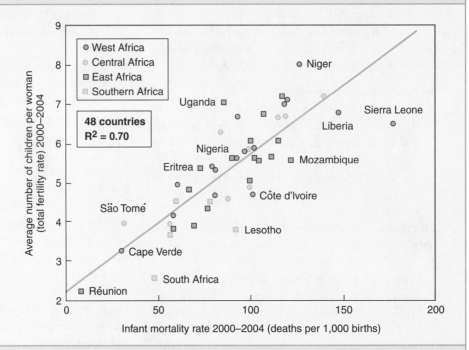

FIGURE 6-2 Relationship between fertility and infant mortality in 48 countries of sub-Saharan Africa in 2000–2004.

Source: Modified with permission from Tabutin D, Schoumaker B. The demography of Sub-Saharan Africa from the 1950s to the 2000s. *Population-E.* 2004; 59(3-4). Available at: http://www.ined.fr/ fichier/t_telechargement/13001/telechargement_fichier_en_afrique.no.6.a.1.pdf. Accessed August 19, 2008.

TABLE 6-2 Examples of Ecologic Studies

Author	Outcome variable	Unit of analysis	Representative explanatory variables
Pollán et al., 2007[2]	Breast cancer mortality	Municipalities in Spain, e.g., Madrid	Women; age group (≥ 50 and <50); socioeconomic level; % population ≥ 65
Findings: Higher levels of socioeconomic status were associated with higher levels of mortality among women aged 50 years and older.			
Shi et al., 2005[3]	All-cause mortality; heart disease mortality; cancer mortality	U.S. counties	Income inequality; primary care physicians per 10,000 population; % black; % unemployed
Findings: Mortality was from 2% to 3% lower in counties that had more available primary resources than counties with fewer resources.			
Breslin et al., 2007[4]	Occupational injuries	Regions in Ontario, Canada	Population density; residential stability; unemployment
Findings: Regional attributes such as low residential turnover were related to low injury rates.			

are rates of infectious diseases, congenital malformations, and chronic conditions.

Three examples of units of analysis are shown in Table 6-2: Spanish municipalities, U.S. counties, and regions in a Canadian province. Many other units of analysis at the group level are theoretically possible. Explanatory variables are those studied as correlates of outcome variables. The examples of explanatory variables shown are sex, socioeconomic level, age, income inequality, race, prevalence of physicians, unemployment, population density, and residential stability.

Here are the major findings of the studies shown in the table: Pollán et al.[2] reported an association between mortality and socioeconomic level among older women in Spain; Shi et al.[3] showed that availability of primary care physicians was related to a reduction in mortality; Breslin et al.[4] found that Ontario regions with stable populations had reduced levels of occupational injuries.

In addition to the examples shown in Table 6-2, what are some other examples of ecologic studies? Ecologic analyses have been applied to the study of air pollution by examining the correlation of air pollution with adverse health effects such as mortality. Instead of correlating individual exposures to air pollution with mortality, researchers measure the association between average levels of air pollution within a census tract (or other geographic subdivision) with the average mortality in that census tract. This type of study investigates whether mortality is higher in more polluted census tracts than in less polluted census tracts. (Refer to text box.)

Some statistical entities used by the U.S. Census Bureau

- Census tract: "A small, relatively permanent statistical subdivision of a county or statistically equivalent entity. . . . Census tracts generally contain between 1,000 and 8,000 people. . . . Census tract boundaries are delineated with the intention of being stable over many decades, so they generally follow relatively permanent visible features."[5(p6)]
- Census block: "An area bounded on all sides by visible and/or nonvisible features shown on a map prepared by the Census Bureau. A block is the smallest geographic entity for which the Census Bureau tabulates decennial census data."[5(p6)]
- Metropolitan area (MA): "A large population nucleus, together with adjacent communities that have a high degree of economic and social integration with that nucleus."[5(p6)]

A major problem of the ecologic technique for the study of air pollution (and for virtually all ecologic studies), however, stems from uncontrolled factors. Examples relevant to air pollution include individual levels of smoking and smoking habits, occupational exposure to respiratory hazards and air pollution, differences in social class and other demographic factors, genetic background, and length of residence in the area.[6] Nonetheless, ecologic studies may open the next generation of investigations; the interesting observations gathered in ecologic studies may provide the impetus for more carefully designed studies. The next wave of studies that build on ecologic studies then may attempt to take advantage of more rigorous analytic study designs.

Ecologic studies have examined the association between water quality and both stroke and coronary diseases. A group of studies have demonstrated that hardness of the domestic water supply is associated inversely with risk of cerebrovascular mortality and cardiovascular diseases. However, a Japanese investigation did not support a relationship between water hardness and cerebrovascular diseases. In the latter ecologic study, the unit of analysis was municipalities (population subdivisions in Japan that consisted of from 6,000 to 3,000,000 inhabitants). In analyzing the 1995 death rates from strokes in relationship to the values of water hardness, the researchers did not find statistically significant associations across municipalities.[7]

Other ecologic studies have examined the possible association between use of agricultural pesticides and childhood cancer incidence. For example, a total of 7,143 incident cases of invasive cancer diagnosed among children younger than age 15 were reported to the California Cancer Registry during the years 1988–1994. In this ecologic study, the unit of analysis was census blocks, with average annual pesticide exposure estimated per square mile. The study showed no overall association between pesticide exposure determined by this method and childhood cancer incidence rates. However, a significant increase of childhood leukemia rates was linked to census block groups that had the highest use of one form of pesticide, called propargite.[8]

Ecologic (Ecological) Fallacy

Information obtained from group-level data may not accurately reflect the relationship between exposure and outcomes at the individual level. The term **ecologic fallacy** is defined as "an erroneous inference that may occur because an association observed between variables on an aggregate level does not necessarily represent or reflect the association that exists at an individual level; . . ."[1] Here is an example: Professor Raj Bhopal writes,

> Imagine a study of the rate of coronary heart disease in the capital cities of the world relating the

rate to average income. It may be that within the cities studied, coronary heart disease is higher in the richer cities than in the poorer ones. This finding would fit the general view that coronary heart disease is a disease of affluence. We might predict from such a finding that rich people in the individual cities too have more risk of CHD than poor people. In fact, in contemporary times, in the industrialized world the opposite is the case: within cities such as London, Washington DC, and Stockholm, poor people have higher CHD rates than rich ones. The forces that cause high rates of disease at a population level are different from those at an individual level.[9(p241)]

In summary, the advantages and disadvantages of ecologic studies are the following:

- Advantages
  - May provide information about the context of health
  - Can be performed when individual-level measurements are not available
  - Can be conducted rapidly and with minimal resources
- Disadvantages
  - The ecologic fallacy
  - Imprecise measurement of exposure

CASE-CONTROL STUDIES

A case-control study is one in which subjects are defined on the basis of the presence or absence of an outcome of interest. (Refer to Figure 6-3.) The cases are those individuals who have the outcome or disease of interest, whereas the controls do not. Because having a specific outcome such as a disease is the criterion for being included in the case group, a case-control study can examine only a single outcome or a limited set of outcomes. A **matched case-control study** is one in which the cases and controls have been matched according to one or more criteria such as sex, age, race, or other variables. The reasons for matching are discussed in the section on confounding.

Case-control studies use a retrospective approach to collect information about exposure to a factor; exposure has already occurred in the past. One method to determine past exposure is for the investigator to interview cases and controls regarding their exposure history. An advantage of case-control studies is that they can examine many potential exposures, such as exposure to toxic chemicals, use of medications, or adverse lifestyle characteristics. In some variations of the case-control approach, it may be possible to conduct direct measurements of the environment for various types of exposures.

Researchers have a variety of sources available for the selection of cases and controls. For example, investigators may

FIGURE 6-3 Diagram of a case-control study.

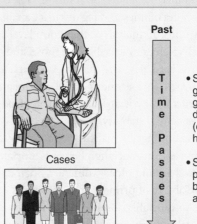

Cases

Controls

Past

Time Passes

- Start with two similar groups of people. One group (cases) has a disease and the other (controls) does not have the disease.

- Study question: Did a past exposure differ between the cases and controls?

Present

Source: Modified from Cahn MA, Auston I, Selden CR, Pomerantz KL. *Introduction to HSR, May 23, 1998.* National Information Center on Health Services Research and Health Care Technology (NICHSR), National Library of Medicine. 1998. Available at: http://www.nlm.nih.gov/nichsr/pres/mla98/cahn/sld034.htm. Accessed July 30, 2008.

use patients from hospitals, specialized clinics, or medical practices; also, they may select cases from disease registries such as cancer registries. Sometimes, advertisements in the media solicit cases. For use as controls, investigators may identify patients from hospitals or clinics—patients who have different health problems than the cases. In other instances, controls may be friends or relatives of the cases or be from the community.

Odds Ratio: Measure of Association Used in Case-Control Studies

The **odds ratio (OR)** is a measure of the association between frequency of exposure and frequency of outcome used in case-control studies. The OR is called an indirect measure of risk because incidence rates have not been used; instead, the risk of an outcome associated with an exposure is estimated by calculating the odds of exposure among the cases and controls. Table 6-3 illustrates the method for labeling cells in a case-control study. The columns are labeled as cases and controls. Cells that contain the cases are A and C; the cells that contain the controls are B and D. The total number of cases and controls are A + C and B + D, respectively. Exposure status (reading across the rows) is identified as Yes and No. A particular form of OR, the exposure-odds ratio, refers to the ratio of odds in favor of exposure among the disease group (the cases) [A/C] to the odds in favor of exposure among the no-disease group (the controls) [B/D].[1]

TABLE 6-3 Fourfold Table That Demonstrates a Case-Control Study

Exposure status	Disease status	
	Yes (Cases)	No (Controls)
Yes	A	B
No	C	D
Total	A + C	B + D

The OR is defined as (A/C) ÷ (B/D), which can be expressed as (AD)/(BC). (Multiply the diagonal cells and divide them.)

Calculation example: suppose we have the following data from a case-control study: A = 9, B = 4, C = 95, and D = 88. The OR is calculated as follows:

$$OR = \frac{AD}{BC} = \frac{(9)(88)}{(4)(95)} = 2.08$$

Interpretation: an odds ratio of more than 1.0 suggests a positive association between the exposure and disease or other outcome (provided that the results are statistically significant—a concept that will not be discussed here). In this sample calculation, the OR is 2.1, suggesting that the odds of the disease are about two times higher among the exposed persons than among the nonexposed persons. In some instances, an OR less than 1.0 indicates that the exposure might be a protective factor. When the OR is equivalent to 1.0, there is no association between exposure and outcome.

Case-control studies are used very commonly in environmental epidemiologic research. For example, environmental health researchers have been concerned about the possible health effects of exposure to electromagnetic fields. A case-control study among female residents of Long Island, New York, examined the possible association between exposure to electromagnetic fields (EMFs) and breast cancer.[10] Eligible subjects were those who were younger than 75 years of age and had lived in the study area for 15 years or longer. Cases (n = 576) consisted of women diagnosed with *in situ* or invasive breast cancer. Controls (n = 585) were selected from the same community by random digit dialing procedures. (Random digit dialing is a computerized procedure for selecting telephone numbers at random within defined geographic areas; selected respondents are called and asked to participate in telephone interviews.) Several types of measurement of EMFs were taken in the subjects' homes and by mapping overhead power lines. The investigators reported that the odds ratio between EMF exposure and breast cancer

was not statistically significantly different from 1.0; thus, the results suggested that there was no association between breast cancer and residential EMF exposure.

The advantages and disadvantages of case-control studies are as follows:

- Advantages
  - Can be used to study low-prevalence conditions
  - Relatively quick and easy to complete
  - Usually inexpensive
  - Involve smaller numbers of subjects
- Disadvantages
  - Measurement of exposure may be inaccurate
  - Representativeness of cases and controls may be unknown
  - Provide indirect estimates of risk
  - The temporal relationship between exposure factor and outcome cannot always be ascertained.

In comparison with cross-sectional study designs, case-control studies may provide more complete exposure data, especially when the exposure information is collected from the friends and relatives of cases who died of a particular cause. Nevertheless, some unmeasured exposure variables as well as methodological biases (a term discussed later in this chapter) may remain in case-control studies. For example, in studies of health and air pollution, exposure levels are difficult to quantify precisely. Also, it may be difficult to measure unknown and unobserved factors, including smoking habits and occupational exposures to air pollution, which affect the lungs.[6]

Case-control studies are often inexpensive, yield results rapidly, and involve small sample sizes. They are useful for studying low-prevalence conditions—a specific disease or outcome is the basis for selection of the cases. Disadvantages of the case-control approach include the fact that risk is estimated indirectly by using the odds ratio; in addition, relationships between exposures and health outcomes may not have been measured accurately.

COHORT STUDIES

A **cohort** is defined as a population group, or subset thereof (distinguished by a common characteristic), that is followed over a period of time. Three examples of cohorts are:

- Birth or age cohort (e.g., the baby boom generation; generations X or Y)
- Work cohort (people in a particular type of employment studied for occupational exposures)
- School/educational cohort (persons who graduated during a particular year)

In a **prospective cohort study** design, subjects are classified according to their exposure to a factor of interest and then are observed over time to document the occurrence of new cases (incidence) of disease or other health events. (Refer to Figure 6-4.) At the inception or baseline of a prospective cohort study, participants must be certified as being free from the outcome of interest. For this reason cohort studies are not helpful for researching diseases that are uncommon in the population; during the course of the cohort study, only a few cases of the disease may occur. Cohort studies are a type of prospective or longitudinal design, meaning that subjects are followed over an extended period of time. Using cohort studies, epidemiologists are able to evaluate many different outcomes (causes of death) but few exposures.[6] Exposure is the criterion used to select subjects into a cohort study; for this reason, researchers are unable to examine more than one or two exposures in a single study.

A variation of a cohort study design uses a retrospective assessment of exposure. A **retrospective cohort study** is one that makes use of historical data to determine exposure level at some baseline in the past; follow-up for subsequent occurrences of disease between baseline and the present is performed. A variation of a retrospective cohort study is a **historical prospective cohort study**, which combines retrospective and prospective approaches.

An example of a retrospective cohort study would be one that examined mortality among an occupational cohort such as shipyard workers who were employed at a specific naval yard during a defined time interval (e.g., World War II). A retrospective cohort study is different from a case-control study because an entire cohort of exposed individuals is examined. In contrast, a case-control study makes use of a limited number of cases and controls who usually do not represent an entire cohort of exposed individuals.

Measure of Association Used in Cohort Studies

The measure of association used in cohort studies is called **relative risk (RR)**, the ratio of the incidence rate of a disease or health outcome in an exposed group to the incidence rate of the disease or condition in a nonexposed group. As noted previously, an incidence rate may be interpreted as the risk of occurrence of an outcome that is associated with a particular exposure. The RR provides a ratio of two risks—the risk associated with an exposure in comparison with the risk associated with nonexposure.

> Relative risk = Incidence rate in the exposed ÷ Incidence rate in the nonexposed

The method for formatting the data from a cohort study and calculating a relative risk is shown in Table 6-4. Across the rows is the exposure status of the participants: either yes or no. The disease status of the participants is indicated in the columns and also is classified as either yes or no. The total number of subjects in the exposure group is A + B; the corresponding total for the nonexposed group is C + D.

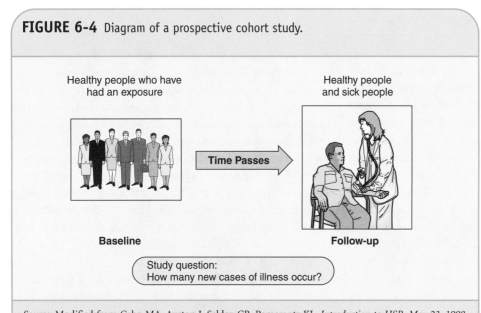

FIGURE 6-4 Diagram of a prospective cohort study.

Healthy people who have had an exposure

Healthy people and sick people

Time Passes

Baseline

Follow-up

Study question:
How many new cases of illness occur?

Source: Modified from Cahn MA, Auston I, Selden CR, Pomerantz KL. *Introduction to HSR, May 23, 1998.* National Information Center on Health Services Research and Health Care Technology (NICHSR), National Library of Medicine. 1998. Available at: http://www.nlm.nih.gov/nichsr/pres/mla98/cahn/sld034.htm. Accessed July 30, 2008.

TABLE 6-4 Fourfold Table Used to Calculate a Relative Risk

Exposure status	Disease status		
	Yes	No	Total
Yes	A	B	A + B
No	C	D	C + D

Source: Author

Mathematically, relative risk (RR) is defined as A/A + B [the rate (incidence) of the disease or condition in the exposed group] divided by C/C + D [the rate (incidence) of the disease or condition in the nonexposed group]. The formula for relative risk is:

$$RR = \frac{\dfrac{A}{A + B}}{\dfrac{C}{C + D}}$$

Calculation example: suppose that we are researching whether exposure to solvents is associated with risk of liver cancer. From a cohort study of industrial workers, we find that 3 persons who worked with solvents developed liver cancer (cell A of text box) and 104 did not (cell B). Two cases of liver cancer occurred among nonexposed workers (cell C) in the same type of industry. The remaining 601 nonexposed workers (cell D) did not develop liver cancer. The data are shown in Table 6-5.

Incidence rate in the exposed group = 3/107 = 0.02804

Incidence rate in the nonexposed group = 2/603 = 0.003317

The RR is:

$$RR = \frac{\dfrac{3}{3 + 104}}{\dfrac{2}{2 + 601}} = \frac{0.02804}{0.003317} = 8.43$$

TABLE 6-5 Data Table for Liver Cancer Example

Exposure to solvents	Liver cancer		
	Yes	No	Total
Yes	3	104	107
No	2	601	603

Source: *Author.*

We may interpret relative risk in a manner that is similar to that of the odds ratio. A relative risk of 1.0 implies that the risk (rate) of disease among the exposed is not different from the risk of disease among the nonexposed. A relative risk greater than 2.0 implies that the risk is more than twice as high among the exposed as among the nonexposed. In other words, there is a positive association between exposure and the outcome under study. In the calculation example, the risk of developing liver cancer is eight times greater among workers who were exposed to solvents than among those who were not exposed to solvents.

Sometimes a relative risk calculation yields a value that is less than 1.0. If the relative risk is less than 1.0 (and statistically significant), the risk is lower among the exposed group; for example, a relative risk of 0.5 indicates that the exposure of interest is associated with half the risk of disease. This level of risk, i.e., less than 1.0, sometimes is called a protective effect.

Accurate disease determination is necessary to optimize measures of relative risk; disease misclassification affects estimates of relative risk. The type of disease and method of diagnosis affect the accuracy of diagnosis.[6] In illustration, death certificates are used frequently as a source of information about the diagnosis of a disease. Information from death certificates regarding cancer as the underlying cause of death is believed to be more accurate than the information for other diagnoses such as those for nonmalignant conditions. Nevertheless, the accuracy of diagnoses of cancer as a cause of death varies according to the particular form of cancer.

Difference in Rates (Risks)

The two measures of risk difference discussed in this section are attributable risk and population risk difference. Remember that the relative risk is the ratio of the incidence rate of an outcome in the exposed group to the incidence rate for that outcome in the nonexposed group; for a two-group cohort study, this comparison is made by dividing the two incidence rates. An alternative to relative risk is attributable risk, which is a type of difference measure of association.

Attributable risk, in a cohort study, refers to the *difference* between the incidence rate of a disease in the exposed group and the incidence rate in the nonexposed group. Returning to the calculation example shown in Table 6-5, the incidence rate (expressed as rate per 1,000) in the exposed group was 28.03 and the incidence rate (expressed as rate per 1,000) in the non-exposed group was 3.32. The attributable risk is the difference between these two incidence rates (28.03 per 1,000 − 3.32 per 1,000) and equals 24.71 per 1,000. This is the incidence rate associated with exposure to the solvent.

A second measure that assesses differences in rates is the **population risk difference**, which provides an indication of the benefit to the population derived by modifying a risk factor. This measure is the difference between the rate of disease in the nonexposed segment of the population and the overall rate in the population.

Population risk difference = incidence in the total population − incidence in the nonexposed segment

Calculation example: What is the incidence of disease in the population attributed to smoking? Assume that the annual lung cancer incidence for men in the total population is 79.4 per 100,000 men; the incidence of lung cancer among nonsmoking men is 28.0 per 100,000 men. The population risk difference is (79.4 − 28.0), or 51.4 per 100,000 men. Among men, the incidence of lung cancer due to smoking is 51.4 cases per 100,000.

Uses of Cohort Studies

Cohort studies are applied widely in epidemiology. For example, they have been used to examine the effects of environmental and work-related exposures to potentially toxic agents. One concern of cohort studies has been exposure of female workers to occupationally related reproductive hazards and adverse pregnancy outcomes.[11]

A second example is an Australian study that examined the health impacts of occupational exposure to pesticides.[12] The investigators selected an exposure cohort of 1,999 male outdoor workers who were employed by the New South Wales Board of Tick Control between 1935 and 1995; these individuals were involved with an insecticide application program and had worked with a variety of insecticides. A control cohort consisted of 1,984 men who worked as outdoor field officers at any time since 1935 and were not known to have been exposed on the job to insecticides. The investigators carefully evaluated exposures and health outcomes such as mortality from various chronic diseases and cancer. They reported an association between exposure to pesticides and adverse health

effects, particularly for asthma, diabetes, and some forms of cancer including pancreatic cancer.

In summary, the advantages and disadvantages of cohort studies are the following:

- Advantages
  - Permit direct observation of risk
  - Exposure factor is well defined
  - Can study exposures that are uncommon in the population
  - The temporal relationship between factor and outcome is known
- Disadvantages
  - Expensive and time consuming
  - Complicated and difficult to carry out
  - Subjects may be lost to follow-up during the course of the study
  - Exposures can be misclassified

Regarding advantages, cohort studies provide information about incidence rates of disease and other health outcomes and thus provide direct assessment of risk. Exposure factors are defined at the inception of the study and are used as the basis for selection into the study. Cohort studies can examine exposures that are uncommon in the population, such as those that might be experienced by occupational groups that work with toxic chemicals and other hazardous substances. Finally, temporality between exposure variables and outcome is known; for example, in prospective cohort studies, assessment of exposures occurs before assessment of outcomes.

The disadvantages of cohort studies include the fact that they are expensive and may require several years before useful results can be obtained. Methodologically, they are difficult to carry out: frequently, the epidemiologist must account for large numbers of subjects, maintain extensive records, and follow subjects closely. Because cohort studies take place over a long period of time, subjects may be lost to follow-up because of dropping out, moving, or dying. Lastly, it is important to ascertain whether exposures have been correctly identified in cohort studies; one scenario in which misclassification of exposures can occur is in retrospective cohort studies because accurate exposure records may no longer be available.

EXPERIMENTAL STUDIES

In epidemiology, experimental studies are implemented as intervention studies. An **intervention study** is "an investigation involving intentional change in some aspect of the status of the subjects, e.g., introduction of a preventive or therapeutic regimen or an intervention designed to test a hypothesized relationship; . . ."[1] Two types of experimental study designs are randomized controlled trials and quasi-experiments.

Randomized Controlled Trial

A **randomized controlled trial** (RCT) is defined as "an epidemiological experiment in which subjects in a population are randomly allocated into groups, usually called *study* and *control* groups, to receive or not to receive an experimental preventive or therapeutic procedure, maneuver, or intervention. The results are assessed by rigorous comparison of rates of disease, death, recovery, or other appropriate outcome in the study and control groups."[1] A diagram of a randomized controlled trial (RCT) is shown in Figure 6-5. In comparison with observational studies, a randomized controlled trial is considered to use the most scientifically rigorous procedures and to have the highest level of validity for making etiologic inferences; an RCT can control for many of the factors that affect study designs, including assignment of exposures and biases in assessment of study outcomes. RCTs are limited to a narrow range

of applications; they are not as helpful for studying the etiology of diseases as are observational designs. For obvious ethical reasons, it is not possible for an investigator to run experiments that determine whether an exposure causes disease in human subjects.

An example of the difficulty in using RCTs arises in the study of environmental health hazards. For several reasons, the use of experimental methods in environmental epidemiology is difficult to achieve; consequently, observational methods are usually more feasible to implement. Rothman points out that:

> Randomized assignment of individuals into groups with different environmental exposures generally is impractical, if not unethical; community intervention trials for environmental exposures have been conducted, although seldom (if ever) with random assignment. Furthermore, the benefits of randomization are heavily diluted when the number of randomly assigned units is small, as when communities rather than individuals are

FIGURE 6-5 Diagram of a randomized controlled trial.

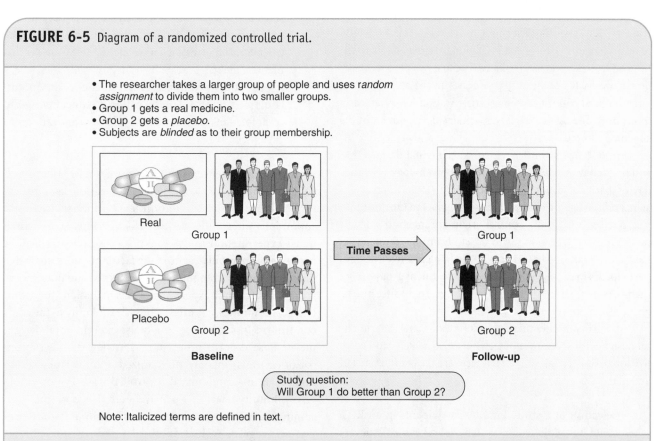

- The researcher takes a larger group of people and uses r*andom assignment* to divide them into two smaller groups.
- Group 1 gets a real medicine.
- Group 2 gets a *placebo*.
- Subjects are *blinded* as to their group membership.

Real
Group 1

Placebo
Group 2

Baseline

Time Passes

Group 1

Group 2

Follow-up

Study question:
Will Group 1 do better than Group 2?

Note: Italicized terms are defined in text.

Source: Modified from Cahn MA, Auston I, Selden CR, Pomerantz KL. *Introduction to HSR, May 23, 1998.* National Information Center on Health Services Research and Health Care Technology (NICHSR), National Library of Medicine. 1998. Available at: http://www.nlm.nih.gov/nichsr/pres/mla98/cahn/sld038.htm and http://www.nlm.nih.gov/nichsr/pres/mla98/cahn/sld039.htm. Accessed July 30, 2008

randomized. Thus, environmental epidemiology consists nearly exclusively of nonexperimental epidemiology. Ideally, such studies use individuals as the unit of measurement; but often environmental data are available only for groups of individuals, and investigators turn to so-called ecologic studies to learn what they can.[13(p20)]

Consequently, in order to study the effects of environmental exposures when dealing with human populations, researchers must use observational methods, and, in fact, the majority of research on health outcomes associated with the environment uses observational methods.[14]

Some uses of randomized controlled trials are to test the efficacy of new medications and vaccines and evaluate medical treatment regimens and health education programs. A **prophylactic trial** is designed to test preventive measures; **therapeutic trials** evaluate new treatment methods. A **clinical trial** refers to "a research activity that involves the administration of a test regimen to humans to evaluate its efficacy and safety. The term is subject to wide variation in usage, from the first use in humans without any control treatment to a rigorously designed and executed experiment involving RANDOM ALLOCATION of test and control treatments."[1] Clinical trials are conducted in three, and sometimes more, phases. The first two phases usually do not involve RCTs; the third phase does involve an RCT, called a randomized controlled clinical trial. An example of an early forerunner of a clinical trial was Jenner's development of his smallpox vaccine.

An RCT bears similarities to experimental designs that you might have studied in experimental psychology, other behavioral science courses, or biology. In an experimental design, an investigator manipulates a study factor. One or more treatment groups and a control group are involved. Participants are assigned randomly to the study groups. Some RCTs have more than one treatment group. In a **crossover design**, participants may be switched between treatment groups (e.g., members of treatment group A are transferred to treatment group B, or vice versa).

An RCT combines the features of a traditional experimental design with several unique characteristics. Refer to Figure 6-5 for an illustration of an RCT. Here are the components of an RCT:

- Selection of a study sample. Participants in an RCT could be volunteers or patients who have a particular disease. Rigorous inclusion and exclusion criteria are used in the selection of participants.
- Assignment of participants to study conditions: random assignment is used.

- The treatment group receives the new treatment, procedure, or drug.
- The control group receives an alternative, commonly used treatment or procedure or a placebo, which is a medically inactive medication or pill (e.g., sugar pill). In a study of medical procedures, the control group might receive the usual standard of care. In a study of behavioral change, the control group might be given a self-instructional booklet. (The treatment group might receive group counseling.)
- Blinding or masking to prevent biases: when the participants or the investigators know the conditions of the study (i.e., treatment and control groups) to which participants have been assigned, multiple biases can be introduced.
  - A single-blind study—the subjects are unaware of whether they are participating in the treatment or control conditions.
  - A double-blind study—neither the participants nor the investigators are aware of who has been assigned to the treatment or control conditions.
- Measurement of outcomes. Outcomes must be measured in a comparable manner in the treatment and control conditions. Outcomes of RCTs can include behavioral changes such as reduction of behaviors that increase the risk of sexually transmitted diseases, smoking cessation, and increases in exercise levels. An outcome of a clinical trial is called a clinical endpoint (examples are rates of disease, recovery, or death).

Quasi-Experimental Designs

A **community intervention** (community trial) is an intervention designed for the purpose of educational and behavioral changes at the population level. In most situations, community interventions use quasi-experimental designs. A **quasi-experimental study** is a type of research in which the investigator manipulates the study factor but does not assign individual subjects randomly to the exposed and nonexposed groups. Some quasi-experimental designs assign study units (e.g., communities, counties, schools) randomly to the study conditions. In addition, some quasi-experimental designs may not use a control group or may use fewer study subjects (or other units) that are randomized into the study conditions than in a randomized controlled trial. The operation of community trials is expensive, complex, and time consuming. An important component of community interventions is **program evaluation**, the determination of whether the program meets stated goals and is justified economically.

A specific example of a community trial was a test of the efficacy of fluoridation of drinking water in preventing tooth decay.[15] During the 1940s and 1950s, two comparable cities in

New York state—Newburgh and Kingston—were contrasted for the occurrence of tooth decay and related dental problems among children. Newburgh had received fluoride for about one decade and Kingston had received none. In Newburgh, the frequency of such problems decreased by about one-half in comparison to the period before fluoridation. Over the same period, those dental problems increased slightly in Kingston.[15] This study was an example of a quasi-experiment because the "subjects" (cities) were assigned arbitrarily and not randomly.

There are many other examples of community trials. One is the Stanford Five-City Project, which sought to reduce the risk of cardiovascular diseases. This trial was a media-based campaign directed at Monterey and Salinas, California. Control cities were Modesto and San Luis Obispo, with Santa Maria selected as an additional comparison city.[16] Another example is the Community Intervention Trial for Smoking Cessation (COMMIT), which began in 1989. This intervention trial involved 11 matched pairs of communities throughout the United States. The trial aimed to promote long-term smoking cessation.[17]

CHALLENGES TO THE VALIDITY OF STUDY DESIGNS

In addition to the type of study design chosen, several other factors affect the confidence that one may have in the results of a study. These factors are as follows:

- External validity: **external validity** refers to one's ability to generalize from the results of the study to an external population. Some studies may select subjects by taking a sample of convenience (a grab bag sample) or by using random samples of a population. Random samples are generally more representative of the parent population from which they are selected and thus are more likely to demonstrate external validity than are samples of convenience. Nevertheless, random samples may depart from (be unrepresentative of) their parent populations. **Sampling error** is a type of error that arises when values (statistics) obtained for a sample differ from the values (parameters) of the parent population.
- Internal validity: care must be taken in the manner in which a study is carried out. **Internal validity** refers to the degree to which the study has used methodologically sound procedures. For example, in an experimental design, subjects need to be assigned randomly to the conditions of the study. Appropriate and reliable measurements need to be taken. Departures from acceptable procedures such as those related to sampling and measurement as well as other errors in the methods used in the research may detract from the quality of inferences that can be made.

- Biases in outcome measurement: several types of bias can affect the results of a study. These are discussed in the section that follows.

Bias in Epidemiologic Studies

Epidemiologic studies may be impacted by **bias**, which is defined as "systematic deviation of results or inferences from truth. Processes leading to such deviation. An error in the conception and design of a study—or in the collection, analysis, interpretation, reporting, publication, or review of data—leading to results or conclusions that are systematically (as opposed to randomly) different from truth."[1] There are many types of bias; particularly meaningful for epidemiology are those that impact study procedures. Examples of such bias are related to how the study was designed, the method of data collection, interpretation and review of findings, and procedures used in data analysis. For example, in measurements of exposures and outcomes, faulty measurement devices may introduce biases into study designs.

A complete discussion of all the kinds of bias is beyond the scope of this text. One of these biases is the **Hawthorne effect**, which refers to participants' behavioral changes as a result of their knowledge of being in a study. Three other types of bias are recall bias, selection bias, and confounding. The first is particularly relevant to case-control studies. **Recall bias** refers to the fact that cases (subjects who participate in the study) may remember an exposure more clearly than controls.[14] The consequence of recall bias is a reduction in the reliability of exposure information gathered from control groups.

Selection bias is defined as "distortions that result from procedures used to select subjects and from factors that influence participation in the study. A distortion in the estimate of the effect due to the manner in which subjects are selected for the study."[1] An example of selection bias is the healthy worker effect, which may reduce the validity of exposure data. Monson states that the **healthy worker effect** refers to the "observation that employed populations tend to have a lower mortality experience than the general population."[18(p114)] The healthy worker effect may have an impact on occupational mortality studies in several ways. People whose life expectancy is shortened by disease are less likely to be employed than healthy persons. One consequence of this phenomenon would be a reduced (or attenuated) measure of effect (e.g., odds ratio or relative risk) for an exposure that increases morbidity or mortality. That is, because the general population includes both employed and unemployed individuals, the mortality rate of that population may be somewhat elevated in comparison with a population in which everyone is healthy enough to work. As a result, any excess mortality associated with a given occupational exposure is more difficult to detect when the healthy worker effect is operative. The healthy worker effect is likely to be stronger for nonmalignant causes of mortality, which usually produce worker attrition during an earlier career phase, than for malignant causes of mortality, which typically have longer latency periods and occur later in life. In addition, healthier workers may have greater total exposure to occupational hazards than those who leave the work force at an earlier age because of illness.

Confounding is another example of a type of study bias. **Confounding** denotes ". . . the distortion of a measure of the effect of an exposure on an outcome due to the association of the exposure with other factors that influence the occurrence of the outcome."[1] Confounding means that the effect of an exposure has been distorted because an extraneous factor has entered into the exposure-disease association. Confounding factors are those that are associated with disease risk (exposure factors) and produce a different distribution of outcomes in the exposure groups than in the comparison groups. A simple example of a potential confounder is age. Here is a simplified example: an epidemiologist might have studied the relationship between exposure and disease in an exposed group and a nonexposed group; the exposed group might have higher rates of morbidity and mortality than the nonexposed group. If the study participants in the exposed group are older than those in the nonexposed group, the age difference could have caused the rates of disease to be higher in the exposed group. (Keep in mind that age is associated with morbidity.) The existence of confounding factors such as age might lead to invalid conclusions.

In addition to age as a confounder, a second example is the confounding effect of smoking. Exposure of workers to occupational dusts is associated with the development of lung diseases such as lung cancer. One of the types of dust encountered in the workplace is silica, e.g., from sand used in sandblasting. Suppose we find that workers exposed to silica have a higher mortality rate for lung cancer than is found in the general population. A possible conclusion is that the workers do, indeed, have a higher risk of lung cancer. However, the issue of confounding also should be considered: it is conceivable that employees exposed to silica dusts have higher smoking rates than the general population, which might be used as a comparison population. When smoking rates are taken into account, the strength of the association between silica exposure and lung cancer is reduced—suggesting that smoking is a confounder that needs to be considered in the association.[19]

How can bias due to confounding be controlled? One should attempt to make certain that the effects of potential confounders are controlled by using study groups that are comparable with respect to such confounders. Possible approaches would be to match study groups on age and sex (a procedure called matching) or to use statistical procedures such as multivariate analyses (not discussed in this text).

CONCLUSION

Epidemiologic study designs encompass descriptive and analytic approaches. One of the most common epidemiologic approaches, whether descriptive or analytic, is an observational study design. Examples of observational analytic study designs covered in this chapter were ecologic studies, case-control studies, and cohort studies. Ecologic studies are distinguished by the use of the group as the unit of analysis; the other study designs use individual subjects as the unit of analysis.

Differing from the observational approach are experimental designs (intervention studies). By definition, the investigator controls who is and who is not exposed to the study factor in an intervention study. Experimental designs include randomized controlled trials (RCTs) and quasi-experimental designs. RCTs are used to test new medications, vaccines, and medical procedures. Among the applications of quasi-experimental designs is the assessment of the effects of public health interventions. One must be aware of the strengths, weaknesses, and appropriate uses of each type of study design. Also, one must examine carefully possible biases such as confounding that can affect the validity of epidemiologic research. Increasingly, the Internet is being used as a platform for conducting RCTs. This innovation may help to speed results and lower costs.[20]

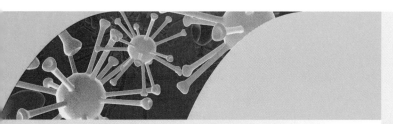

Study Questions and Exercises

1. Describe the two major approaches (observational and experimental) used in analytic studies. What circumstances would merit use of either of these approaches?

2. List the seven factors that characterize study designs and explain each one.

3. Define each of the following terms used by the U.S. Census Bureau:
   a. Census tract
   b. Census block
   c. Metropolitan area

4. State one of the most important ways in which ecologic studies differ from other observational study designs used in epidemiology. What is meant by the ecologic fallacy? Using your own ideas, suggest a possible design for an ecologic study; how might the study design be affected by the ecologic fallacy?

5. Define the term case-control study. Describe how to calculate an odds ratio.

6. Define the term cohort study. What measure of association is used in a cohort study?

7. Interpret the following values for an odds ratio (OR) and a relative risk (RR):
   a. OR = 1.0; OR = 0.5; OR = 2.0
   b. RR = 1.0; RR = 0.5; RR = 2.0

8. Compare and contrast randomized controlled clinical trials and quasi-experimental designs.

9. Identify the type of study design that is described by each of the following statements:
   a. The association between average unemployment levels and mortality from coronary heart disease was studied in counties in California.
   b. A group of women who had been diagnosed with breast cancer were compared with a group of cancer-free women; participants were asked whether they used oral contraceptives in the past.
   c. A group of recent college graduates (exercisers and nonexercisers) were followed over a period of 20 years in order to track the incidence of coronary heart disease.
   d. A pharmaceutical company wanted to test a new medicine for control of blood sugar. Study participants were assigned randomly to either a new medication group or a group that used an older medication. The investigator and the participants were blinded as to enrollment in the study conditions.

10. Define the terms attributable risk and population risk difference. What types of information do these measures provide?

11. Construct a grid that compares the advantages and disadvantages of the following study designs: ecologic, case-control, and cohort.

12. Define what is meant by bias in epidemiologic studies. Give examples of four types of bias.

Young Epidemiology Scholars (YES) Exercises

The Young Epidemiology Scholars Web site provides links to teaching units and exercises that support instruction in epidemiology. The YES program is administered by the College Board and supported by the Robert Wood Johnson Foundation. The Web address of YES is www.collegeboard.com/yes. The following exercises relate to topics discussed in this chapter and can be found on the YES Web site.

1. Kaelin MA, Bayona M. Case-control study.

2. Kaelin MA, Bayona M. Attributable risk applications in epidemiology.

3. Bayona M, Olsen C. Observational studies and bias in epidemiology.

4. Bayona M, Olsen C. Measures in epidemiology.

5. Huang FI, Stolley P. Testing ephedra: Using epidemiologic studies to teach the scientific method.

REFERENCES

1. Porta M. *A Dictionary of Epidemiology*. 5th ed. New York: Oxford University Press; 2008.

2. Pollán M, Ramis R, Aragonés N, et al. Municipal distribution of breast cancer mortality among women in Spain. *BMC Cancer*. 2007;7(78): no page numbers. Available at: http://www.biomedcentral.com/1471-2407/7/78. Accessed August 1, 2008.

3. Shi L, Macinko J, Starfield B, et al. Primary care, social inequalities, and all-cause, heart disease, and cancer mortality in US counties, 1990. *Am J Public Health*. 2005;95:674–680.

4. Breslin FC, Smith P, Dunn JR. An ecological study of regional variation in work injuries among young workers. *BMC Public Health*. 2007;7(91):no page numbers. Available at: http://www.biomedcentral.com/1471-2458/7/91. Accessed August 1, 2008.

5. U.S. Census Bureau. *Census 2000 Basics*. Washington, DC: U.S. Government Printing Office; 2002.

6. Blair A, Hayes RB, Stewart PA, Zahm SH. Occupational epidemiologic study design and application. *Occup Med*. 1996;11:403–419.

7. Miyake Y, Iki M. Ecologic study of water hardness and cerebrovascular mortality in Japan. *Arch Environ Health*. 2003;58:163–166.

8. Reynolds P, Von Behren J, Gunier RB, et al. Childhood cancer and agricultural pesticide use: An ecologic study in California. *Environ Health Perspect*. 2002;110:319–324.

9. Bhopal R. *Concepts of Epidemiology: An integrated introduction to the ideas, theories, principles and methods of epidemiology*. New York: Oxford University Press; 2002.

10. Schoenfeld ER, O'Leary ES, Henderson K, et al. Electromagnetic fields and breast cancer on Long Island: A case-control study. *Am J Epidemiol*. 2003;158:47–58.

11. Taskinen HK. Epidemiological studies in monitoring reproductive effects. *Environ Health Perspect*. 1993;101(Suppl 3):279–283.

12. Beard J, Sladden T, Morgan G, et al. Health impacts of pesticide exposure in a cohort of outdoor workers. *Environ Health Perspect*. 2003;111: 724–730.

13. Rothman KJ. Methodologic frontiers in environmental epidemiology. *Environ Health Perspect*. 1993;101(Suppl 4):19–21.

14. Prentice RL, Thomas D. Methodologic research needs in environmental epidemiology: Data analysis. *Environ Health Perspect*. 1993;101(Suppl 4): 39–48.

15. Morgenstern H, Thomas D. Principles of study design in environmental epidemiology. *Environ Health Perspect*. 1993;101(Suppl 4):23–38.

16. Fortmann SP, Flora JA, Winkleby MA, et al. Community intervention trials: reflections on the Stanford Five-City Project experience. *Am J Epidemiol*. 142;579–580.

17. COMMIT Research Group. Community Intervention Trial for Smoking Cessation (COMMIT): summary of design and intervention. *J Natl Cancer Inst*. 1991;83:1620–1628.

18. Monson RR. *Occupational Epidemiology*. 2nd ed. Boca Raton, FL: CRC Press; 1990.

19. Steenland K, Greenland S. Monte Carlo sensitivity analysis and Bayesian analysis of smoking as an unmeasured confounder in a study of silica and lung cancer. *Am J Epidemiol*. 2004;160:384–392.

20. Paul J, Seib R, Prescott T. The Internet and clinical trials: Background, online resources, examples and issues. *J Med Internet Res*. 2005;7(1):e5.

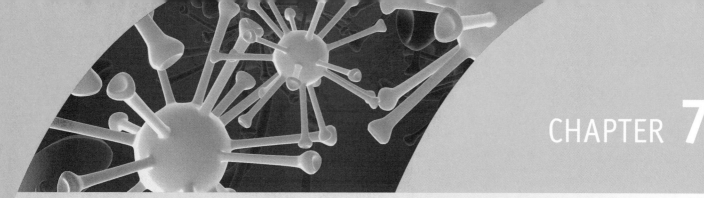

Epidemiology and the Policy Arena

TABLE 7-1 List of Important Terms Used in This Chapter

Cost-effectiveness analysis	Health policy
Decision analysis	Policy cycle
Dose-response assessment	Reliability (precision)
Evidence-based public health	Risk assessment
Exposure assessment	Screening for disease
Hazard identification	Validity (accuracy)

INTRODUCTION

"Researchers are from Mars; policymakers are from Venus"[1(p344)]

Chapter 7 relates epidemiologic methods to the broader issue of policy formulation. Policy issues illustrate a situation in which "the rubber hits the road" for applied epidemiology. Implementation and enforcement of public health policies can require the expenditure of substantial monetary, personnel, and other resources. "Health policies, in the form of laws, regulations, organizational practices, and funding priorities, have a substantial impact on the health and well-being of the population. Policies influence nearly every aspect of daily life, ranging from seat belt use in cars, to where smoking is allowed, to access to health care."[2(p260)]

One of the most noteworthy and perhaps less recognized uses of epidemiology is the application of epidemiologic methods to the policy arena, which is increasingly a concern of epidemiologists, who usually focus their activities on the design of studies and collection and analysis of data. Perhaps the involvement of epidemiologists in policy development arises from the recognition that many significant public health policies are established or abandoned in the absence of specific empirical evidence. Epidemiologists have the expertise to acquire the data needed for policy development.

As noted in the quotation from James Tallon, the worlds of the policy maker and researcher are quite different, "similar to oil and water." Tallon writes that ". . . [at the state level] legislators work within a broader context of state government, which includes governors, executive agencies, executive staffs, budget divisions, and the like. They also work within a context of interest groups, of media attention, and of course of a broader public who are, in a final analysis for legislators, their constituents. . . . But researchers can make their work relevant to state health policy if they are willing to focus on how to operate in that world. Most of us think of our research as our findings, our observations, our analysis. Let me take a step back and remind researchers that they also do two other things —they frame the question and they create the context in which the question is analyzed."[1(p344)]

What is the role of epidemiologists vis-à-vis policy development? They can provide the quantitative evidence for justifying needed policies. In addition, the input of epidemiologists can be helpful in demonstrating the effectiveness of policies once they have been adopted. All too often, health policies are implemented (or fail to be implemented) as a result of political pressures. In some cases, valuable and needed health policies may be abandoned later in response to political backlash or the demands of a self-interested, vociferous minority. Policy making is inherently a political process; the governmental political domain is *terra incognita* for most epidemiologists.

Epidemiologists are able to take an objective stance with respect to data collection. Empirical data gathered in epidemiologic studies may either support or fail to support the need for and efficacy of health policies. For example, policies that prohibit smoking in eating and alcohol-serving establishments initially met resistance because of their possible impact on the economy. Subsequent empirical evidence suggested that the economic impact of smokefree laws was minimal and that the positive health effects of such laws were likely to be substantial. In this case, the data supported the policy.

Chapter 7 provides information regarding the terminology of policy development and examples of major public health policies that have been informed through the application of epidemiologic methods. In summary, the following are ways in which epidemiologists can contribute to health policy:

- "Conducting and disseminating his or her own research
- Serving on expert groups that make policy recommendations
- Serving as an expert witness in litigation
- Testifying before a policy-making body (e.g., city council or state legislature)
- Working as an advocate (e.g., within a health-related coalition) to achieve a specific policy objective"[2(p270)]

WHAT IS A HEALTH POLICY?

Before discussing the epidemiologic aspects of policy development, the author will define the terms *policy* and *health policy*. A **policy** is "a plan or course of action, as of a government, political party, or business, intended to influence and determine decisions, actions, and other matters."[3]

A **health policy** is one that pertains to the health arena, for example, in provision of healthcare services, dentistry, medicine, or public health. Public health policies apply to such aspects of health as water quality, food safety, health promotion, and environmental protection. Policies are not equivalent to laws, which either require or prohibit certain behaviors. Nevertheless, health policies are linked with the development of laws such as those involved in licensing (e.g., licensing medical practitioners and medications), setting standards (e.g., specifying the allowable levels of contaminants in food), controlling risk (e.g., requiring the use of child safety seats), and monitoring (e.g., surveillance of infectious diseases).

How are health policies implemented? Consider a hypothetical example. The policy of many government health agencies is to protect the public from morbidity and mortality caused by infectious diseases. The implementation of this policy would be accomplished via laws and regulations that require the immunization of children against communicable diseases, maintenance of hygienic sanitary conditions in restaurants, and protection of the public water supply from contamination.

News Flash: The state of California introduces a ban on the use of trans fats by restaurants

Beginning on January 1, 2010, all restaurants in the state of California are prohibited from using trans fats. Epidemiologic evidence has suggested that the use of trans fats (hydrogenated fats) is associated with coronary heart disease as well as stroke and diabetes. Consumption of trans fats leads to increases in "bad cholesterol" and the build-up of arterial plaques. With the adoption of this new law (AB 97), California became the first state in the United States to ban the use of trans fats in restaurants. Although the California Restaurant Association strongly opposed the law, members are expected to comply, and some restaurants already follow the policy of not using trans fats.[4]

Some other examples of public health–related laws are the following:

- prohibition of smoking in automobiles when children are present
- requiring the use of hands-free cellular telephones while driving
- regulating the amount of particulate matter that can be emitted from motor vehicles
- regulating the nutritional content of food sold in restaurants (see news flash)
- removing high fat and high sugar content foods from vending machines in schools
- requiring the use of motorcycle helmets

The Policy Cycle

The **policy cycle** refers to the distinct phases involved in the policy-making process[5] (refer to Figure 7-1). The policy cycle comprises several stages: (1) problem definition, formulation, and reformulation; (2) agenda setting; (3) policy establishment (i.e., adoption and legislation); (4) policy implementation; and (5) policy assessment.

The terms subsumed under the policy cycle are explained more fully in Table 7-2. Some definitions of terms used in the table are as follows:

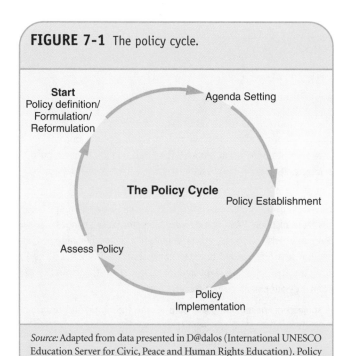

FIGURE 7-1 The policy cycle.

Source: Adapted from data presented in D@dalos (International UNESCO Education Server for Civic, Peace and Human Rights Education). Policy Cycle: Teaching Politics. Available at: http://www.dadalos.org/politik_int/politik/policy-zyklus.htm. Accessed August 22, 2008.

- **Policy actors:** individuals who are involved in policy formulation; these include members of the legislature, citizens, lobbyists, and representatives of advocacy groups.
- **Stakeholders:** individuals, organizations, and members of government who are affected by policy decisions.
- **Legitimization:** the process of making policies legitimate, meaning to be acceptable to the norms of society.
- **Interest group:** "A group of persons working on behalf of or strongly supporting a particular cause, such as an item of legislation, an industry, or a special segment of society."[6]

Problem definition, formulation, and reformulation denote the processes of defining the problem for which the policy actors believe that policies are necessary. This early stage—problem definition and development of alternative solutions—often is regarded as the most crucial phase of the policy development process. The problems chosen should be significant for public health and have realistic and practical solutions. Poorly defined problems are unlikely to lead to successful policy implementation. Note that Figure 7-1 (The policy cycle) shows that following a process of review, problem definitions may need to be reformulated and the steps in the policy cycle repeated.

Agenda setting refers to setting priorities, deciding at what time to deal with a public health problem or issue, and determining who will deal with the problem. Policy makers need to establish priorities in order to reconcile budgetary constraints, resource restrictions, and the complexity of public health problems against the need to develop those policies that are most feasible, realistic, and workable. A successful approach in developing priorities for public health policies is to involve the community and stakeholders.

One of the difficulties in establishing priorities stems from the lack of information on risks.[7] Consider the development of policies related to control of environmental health hazards. (The author will use the example of environmental health throughout the remainder of this discussion because of the extensive track record of policy development in the environmental health field.) For example, there may be concern about the presence of suspected carcinogenic chemicals used in plastic containers for storing food. Suppose that the carcinogenic properties of plastic containers (or whether, in fact, they are indeed carcinogenic) have not been established definitively. Nor is it known how much exposure to the chemical is needed in order to produce an adverse health effect. Given the dearth of information about the level of risk, it would be difficult to establish an appropriate policy for use of the plastic containers. When the nature of the risks associated with an

TABLE 7-2 Components of the Policy Cycle

	Problem definition, formulation, and reformulation	Agenda setting	Policy establishment	Policy implementation	Assessment/ evaluation
What happens?	Define problems and alternatives	Set priorities; involve stakeholders	Formally adopt public policy; legitimization	Put the policy into practice	Assess or evaluate effectiveness
Who performs the function?	Formal and informal policy actors	Formal and informal policy actors	Formal decision makers	Government agencies	Arm of government responsible for assessment
What factors influence policy?	Research and science; interest groups; public opinion; social and economic factors	Research and science; interest groups; public opinion; social and economic factors	Research and science; interest groups; public opinion; social and economic factors	Research and science; interest groups; public opinion; social and economic factors	Research and science; interest groups; public opinion; social and economic factors
What problems are encountered?	Poorly defined problems	Lack of information on risk; lack of coordination	Inability to coordinate and assess research information	Lack of government support	Lack of sound scientific data

Source: Reprinted from Friis RH. *Essentials of Environmental Health.* Sudbury, MA: Jones and Bartlett Publishers; 2007:67.

environmental hazard or toxin is uncertain, planners are left in a quandary about what aspects of the exposure require policy interventions. This scenario occurred in the BPA example cited in the text box.

Another barrier to agenda setting is lack of coordination among government agencies.[10] A criticism levied against the U.S. Congress, which is a crucial policy-formulating body for the government of the United States, is its inability to set pri-

News headline:
California legislature rejects ban on bisphenol A (BPA)

Bisphenol A (BPA) is a chemical ingredient in the manufacture of plastics and resins. This chemical is used extensively in food containers, baby bottles, and many other applications. Human beings are exposed to BPA mainly through food. National biomonitoring studies have suggested that more than 90% of the U.S. population have detectable levels of BPA in their urine. According to the National Toxicology Program,

The scientific evidence that supports a conclusion of *some concern* for exposures in fetuses, infants, and children comes from a number of laboratory animal studies reporting that 'low' level exposure to bisphenol A during development can cause changes in behavior and the brain, prostate gland, mammary gland, and the age at which females attain puberty. These studies only provide limited evidence for adverse effects on development and more research is needed to better understand their implications for human health. However, because these effects in animals occur at bisphenol A exposure levels similar to those experienced by humans, the possibility that bisphenol A may alter human development cannot be dismissed.[8]

Although the National Toxicology Program declared that there was some concern regarding use of BPA, the U.S. Food and Drug Administration stated that studies of BPA "did not indicate a safety concern for BPA at current exposure levels."[9]

California State Senate bill 1713 proposed a ban on BPA in bottles and caps for foods that are consumed by children who are three years old and younger. In 2012, cans and jars that are destined for food consumed by babies and toddlers would have been outlawed. The chemical industry lobbied vigorously against the measure. It was defeated on August 19, 2008, in the California Assembly.

orities because of fragmentation of authority among numerous committees and subcommittees that are involved with environmental policy.

Policy establishment involves the formal adoption of policies, programs, and procedures that are designed to protect society from public health hazards. Once again, in the environmental health arena, a factor that impedes policy establishment is the unavailability of empirical information on the scope of risks associated with environmental hazards. According to Walker, "Limitations on our ability to coordinate, assess, and disseminate research information hampers efforts to translate policy into programs and services designed to reduce environmental risk."[7(p190)]

Policy implementation is the phase of the policy cycle that ". . . focuses on achieving the objectives set forth in the policy decision."[7(p186)] Often this phase of the policy cycle is neglected in favor of the earlier phases of policy development. Barriers to policy implementation can arise from the government administration in power. In the case of the United States, whatever administration is in power may choose to weaken policy prescriptions as a result of political considerations.[11] In order for a policy to be implemented successfully, policy developers may include economic incentives. For example, in order to increase energy efficiency, some states and the federal government have offered rebates for the purchase of energy-saving devices: solar electric panels, solar hot water heating systems, energy-efficient appliances, and fuel-efficient automobiles.

The political and social contexts may stimulate or impede the creation and implementation of public health policies. As Tallon noted, government officials work within the political context and must be able to negotiate this domain if they are to be successful. The impetus for policy development often arises from advocacy groups and lobbyists. Also, special interest groups can mount effective campaigns to block policy initiatives.

Policy assessment/evaluation, the final stage in the policy cycle, refers to the determination of whether the policy has met defined objectives and related goals. This process may be accomplished by applying the methods of epidemiology as well as other tools such as those from economics. The result is a body of quantitative information that can reveal the degree to which the policy has met stated objectives.

Once again, let us turn to environmental policies for an illustration of objectives. In order to facilitate assessment, environmental policies may incorporate **environmental objectives**, which "are statements of policy . . . intended to be assessed using information from a monitoring program. An environmental monitoring program has to be adequate in its quality and quantity of data so that the environmental objectives can be assessed."[12(p144)] An example of an environmental objective is the statement that the amount of particulate matter in an urban area (e.g., Mexico City) will be reduced by 10% during the next five years.

Another example of a statement of objectives can be found in the *Healthy People* Web site (http://www.healthypeople.gov). "Healthy People 2010 is a set of health objectives for the Nation to achieve over the first decade of the new century. It can be used by many different people, States, communities, professional organizations, and others to help them develop programs to improve health."[13] *Healthy People 2010* will make use of ten leading health indicators, which include physical activity, overweight and obesity, and tobacco use.[14]

Policy assessment and evaluation are a function of the quality of evidence that is available to policy makers. **Evidence-based public health** refers to the adoption of policies, laws, and programs that are supported by empirical data. "Evidence reduces uncertainty in decision-making. Evidence is about reality, about what is true and not true."[15(p357)]

Pertinent to the discussion of evidence is the evidence-based medicine movement, which has been attributed to Archie Cochrane who argued that medical care often used procedures that were lacking empirical data with respect to their safety and efficacy.[16] Empirical data varies in quality; one of the most reliable forms of evidence comes from randomized controlled trials. Epidemiologic studies can be arranged according to a hierarchy with respect to their validity for etiologic inference. Less valid are those studies that fall lower on the hierarchy, e.g., case studies, ecologic studies, and cross-sectional studies. However, it is not always feasible to attain the high standard of randomized controlled trials in providing justification for public health interventions that are reflections of policy implementation. Evaluation of most public health policies takes place in the form of quasi-experimental designs, discussed previously. As noted, these designs are inherently methodologically weaker than randomized controlled trials.

As part of policy assessment and evaluation, a cost-effectiveness (cost-benefit) analysis may be conducted. A **cost-effectiveness analysis** is a procedure that contrasts the costs and health effects of an intervention to determine whether it is economically worthwhile. The CDC has made the following statement with respect to HIV cost effectiveness: "The CDC Division of HIV/AIDS Prevention is pleased to make available several tools to help HIV prevention Programs consider cost effectiveness in their planning activities. Cost effectiveness has long been a criterion in setting HIV program priorities. In February 2001, the Institute of Medicine report 'No Time to Lose' recommended that prevention efforts be 'guided by the principles of cost effectiveness.' The basic principle is straightforward: choose those options that pro-vide the greatest outcome for the least cost."[17]

DECISION ANALYSIS BASED ON PERCEPTIONS OF RISKS AND BENEFITS

Decision analysis involves developing a set of possible choices and stating the likely outcomes linked with those choices, each of which may have associated risks and benefits. Ideally, pol-icy makers will select alternatives that minimize health risks and at the same time maximize desirable health outcomes and other benefits. Let us examine the concept of risk briefly. Be aware of the fact that life is not free from risks that have the po-tential to harm our health and well-being. Even the most be-nign activities carry risk: while riding on a busy street, a bicyclist may be struck by a car. Once the author heard about a retired professor who had struggled during most of his pro-fessional life, eagerly anticipating retirement; eventually the awaited moment arrived. A short time after his retirement, the campus received the sad news that the professor had choked to death on his meal while viewing an intense sports event on television. In summary, many aspects of life involve weighing risks—e.g., buying versus renting a house, investing in stocks versus purchasing a certificate of deposit, or choosing a po-tential life partner—and then making a decision about what action to take.

In simple terms, a **risk** involves the likelihood of experi-encing an adverse effect. The term **risk assessment** refers to ". . . a process for identifying adverse consequences and their as-sociated probability."[18(p611)] Risk assessment provides "the qualitative or quantitative estimation of the likelihood of ad-verse effects that may result from exposure to specified health hazards or from the absence of beneficial influences. Risk as-sessment uses clinical, epidemiologic, toxicologic, environ-mental, and any other pertinent data. [It is t]he process of determining risks to health attributable to environmental or other hazards."[19] In environmental health, "risk research ad-dresses the identification and management of situations that might result in losses or harm, immediate or delayed, to indi-viduals, groups, or even to whole communities or ecosystems, often as a result of the interaction of human activities with natural processes."[20(px)]

The meaning of the term risk varies greatly not only from one person to another but also between laypersons and profes-sionals; the latter characterize risk mainly in terms of mortal-ity.[21] In a psychometric study, Slovic reported that laypersons classified risk according to two major factors. His methods en-abled risks to be portrayed in a two-dimensional space so that their relative positions could be compared. The two factors that Slovic identified were the following:

Factor 1, labeled "dread risk," is defined at its high (right-hand) end by perceived lack of control, dread, catastrophic po-tential, fatal consequences, and the inequitable distribution of risks and benefits. . . .

Factor 2, labeled "unknown risk," is defined at its high end by hazards judged to be unobservable, unknown, new, and de-layed in their manifestation of harm.[21(p283)]

Refer to Figure 7-2, which maps the spatial relationships among a large number of risks. For example, nuclear reactor accidents fall in the space that defines uncontrollable dread factors that are of unknown risk. In other words, nuclear reac-tor accidents fall in the quadrant defined by both high levels of unknown risk and high levels of dread risk. Another example is home swimming pools, which pose risks that are not dreaded but are known to those exposed.

Risk assessment generally takes place in four steps: (1) haz-ard identification, (2) dose-response assessment, (3) exposure assessment, and (4) risk characterization.[22,23] Refer to Figure 7-3 for an illustration.

Let us examine each one of the foregoing terms in more detail.

Hazard Identification

Hazard identification applies generally to public health, but is particularly well developed in environmental health research with toxic substances. **Hazard identification** (hazard assess-ment) ". . . examines the evidence that associates exposure to an agent with its toxicity and produces a qualitative judgment about the strength of that evidence, whether it is derived from human epidemiology or extrapolated from laboratory animal data."[23(p286)] Evidence regarding hazards linked to toxic sub-stances may be derived from the study of health effects among exposed humans and animals. These health effects may range from dramatic outcomes such as mortality or cancer to lower-level conditions such as developmental delays in children and reductions in immune status.[22]

A **hazard** is defined as the "inherent capability of an agent or a situation to have an adverse effect. A factor or exposure that may adversely affect health."[19] Hazards may originate from chemicals, biological agents, physical and mechanical energy and force, and psychosocial influences. Toxic agents such as organic toxins and chemicals are examples of potential sources of hazards. Physical hazards arise from ionizing radiation emit-ted by medical x-ray devices or from naturally occurring back-ground radiation. Other hazards originate from non-ionizing radiation—sunlight, infrared and ultraviolet light, and elec-tromagnetic radiation from power lines and radio transmis-sions. In urban and work environments, mechanical energy is associated with high noise levels that can be hazardous for

FIGURE 7-2 Location of 81 hazards on factors 1 and 2 derived from the relationships among 15 risk characteristics.

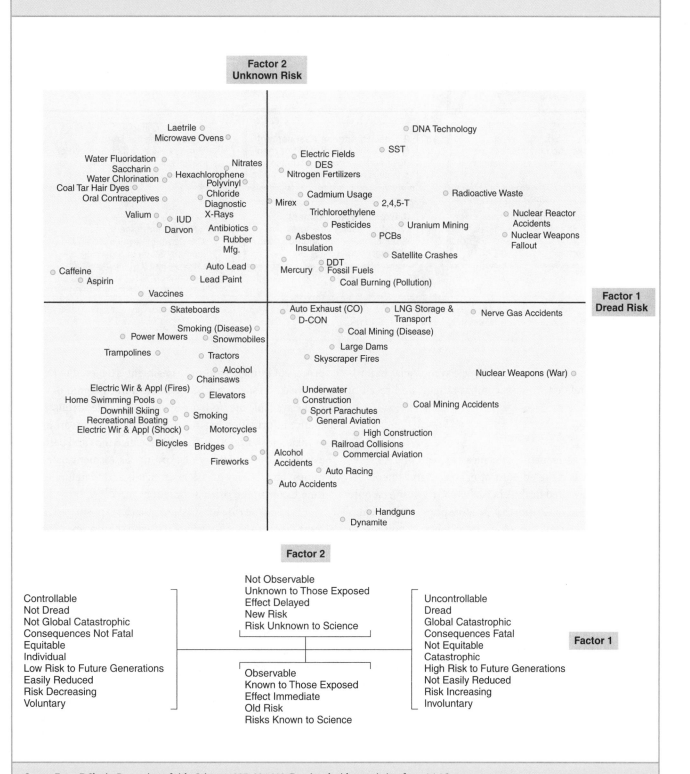

Source: From P Slovic, Perception of risk. *Science.* 1987; 236:282. Reprinted with permission from AAAS.

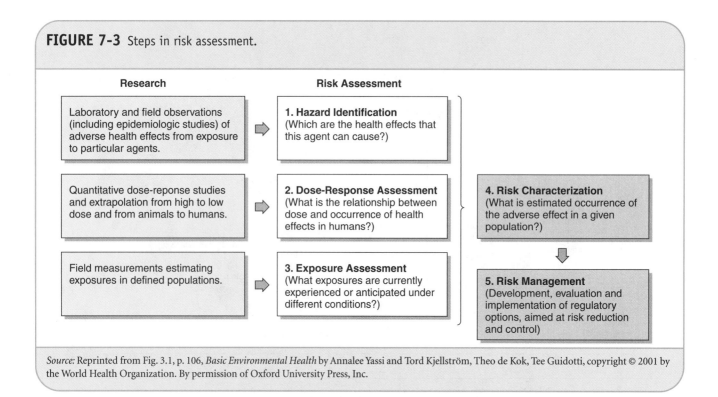

FIGURE 7-3 Steps in risk assessment.

Source: Reprinted from Fig. 3.1, p. 106, *Basic Environmental Health* by Annalee Yassi and Tord Kjellström, Theo de Kok, Tee Guidotti, copyright © 2001 by the World Health Organization. By permission of Oxford University Press, Inc.

hearing and psychological well-being. Psychosocial hazards include work-related stresses, combat fatigue, and recall of posttraumatic events.

Dose-Response Assessment

Dose-response assessment is the measurement of "... the relationship between the amount of exposure and the occurrence of the unwanted health effects."[22(p38)] (A dose-response curve was defined in Chapter 5.) Dose-response assessment is one of the activities of toxicology, the science of poisons. In their research, some toxicologists examine biologic responses to exposure to toxicants, which are toxic substances created by human activity or natural processes. According to Russell and Gruber, "Dose-response assessment examines the quantitative relation between the experimentally administered dose level of a toxicant and the incidence or severity or both of a response in test animals, and draws inferences for humans. The presumed human dosages and incidences in human populations may also be used in cases where epidemiological studies are available."[23(p286)]

Exposure Assessment

Exposure assessment is defined as the procedure that "... identifies populations exposed to the toxicant, describes their composition and size, and examines the roots, magnitudes, frequencies, and durations of such exposures."[23(p286)] The

process of human exposure assessment is believed to be one of the weakest aspects of risk assessment in epidemiology. Many of the available methods are unable to provide adequate quantitative information regarding how much humans are exposed to toxic substances as well as the specific kinds and patterns of exposure.[24] The quality of exposure assessment data determines the accuracy of risk assessments and therefore is a limiting factor in the risk assessment process.[25]

When referring to a toxic substance, exposure assessment must take into account where the exposure occurs, how much exposure occurs, and how the substance is absorbed by the body. The process of human exposure assessment examines "... the manner in which pollutants come into actual contact with the human body—the concentration levels at the points of contact and the sources of these pollutants making contact. The key word here is 'contact'—the occurrence of two events at the same location and same time."[26(p449)] The methods by which human beings are exposed to toxic substances include encountering them in water, air, food, soil, and various consumer products and medications. High-quality data on exposure are necessary for making valid interpretations of a study's findings.[27] This criterion is often difficult to satisfy in epidemiologic research. Several methods of exposure assessment, e.g., personal exposure monitoring and use of biological markers, are used in toxicology, environmental epidemiology, and other environmental health disciplines. (See text box.)

What is an exposure assessment?

An exposure assessment attempts to answer the following questions for a particular substance or chemical:

• Who or what is exposed (e.g., people, aquatic ecosystems)?
• Does the exposure occur through breathing air, drinking water, skin contact or any other routes?
• How much exposure occurs?
• How often and for how long does exposure occur, that is, what is its frequency and duration?

Exposure occurs through contact with a chemical. Such contact can occur by inhaling air, drinking water, eating food, or touching a variety of products that contain the chemical. The concentration of the chemical and the extent of the contact are important components of exposure assessment. The results of an exposure assessment are often considered with a hazard assessment of the chemical. A hazard assessment provides an understanding of the potential for the chemical to cause adverse effects to humans and plant and animal life. Together, the exposure assessment and the hazard assessment can be combined into a risk assessment, which reaches conclusions about the likelihood of adverse effects in the exposed population. . . .

Estimating Concentrations in the Environment Using Models: Before environmental concentrations can be predicted, releases to the environment need to be estimated. Chemicals can be released to air, water, or landfill. Release estimates are generated using industrial data, engineering expertise, and information on the production process. Manufacturing and processing operations are reviewed to determine potential releases in the work place (e.g., vapors from processing equipment, etc.) that could result in worker exposure and releases to the environment. Releases from consumer products should also be considered.

A number of databases and tools allow the user to gather information about the environment into which the chemical is discharged, and to estimate chemical concentrations in air and water. These tools range from mathematical equations to predict simple dilution in a room to complex computer models which estimate the path of the chemical through the environment over time. Some of these computer models can account for chemical decay in the environment and estimate overlapping concentrations from multiple chemical releases.

Assessing Exposures: The last step in an exposure assessment involves estimating the level of contact of the exposed population with the chemical. For people who live near a discharge location, the level of contact involves two factors: the location of nearby populations and the daily human activities that influence how often people come in contact with the chemical. For consumer product exposures and worker exposures, the frequency of use, duration of exposure, and use conditions are important factors.

Assessing Exposures Using Monitoring Data: The most accurate way to obtain environmental concentrations and human exposures is usually to conduct a well-designed exposure monitoring study. Elements of a well-designed exposure monitoring study include: establishing quality assurance objectives that will allow exposure assessors to make estimates of average and high end exposures with a known level of reliability; where possible, using sampling and analytical chemistry methods that have been found acceptable by an independent authoritative body . . .; and ensuring that quality control procedures have been employed and documented. [Also, monitors should be placed so that they obtain representative samples that relate to the actual exposure of the population under study.]

Assessing Exposures Using Models: The screening level tools often make simplifying assumptions which are protective by design (for example, assuming that people live near chemical discharge locations). Higher tier tools are more complex and allow for more realistic exposure assessments, such as using census data and a measure of the distance between the location of the chemical release and the populations living nearby. Daily activities include the amount of time people spend at home as well as the amount of air they breathe and the amount of water they drink. For workers, daily activities include the amount of time they spend handling the chemical during the day. The amount of chemical that an individual breathes, comes into contact via the skin, or drinks via water is the final product of an exposure assessment.

Source: Adapted and reprinted from U.S. Environmental Protection Agency. Exposure assessment tools and models: What is an exposure assessment? Available at: http://www.epa.gov/oppt/exposure/pubs/exposurep.htm. Accessed August 22, 2008.

During a review of records to assess exposure, the investigator may select a study population from personnel records maintained by a company. If the records of former and retired workers are retained by the company, a complete data set spanning long time periods may be available. Ideally, every previous and current worker exposed to the factor should be included. Selection bias may occur if some workers are excluded because their records have been purged from the company's database.[28] Data collected from employment records may include:

- personal identifiers to permit record linkage to Social Security Administration files and retrieval of death certificates
- demographic characteristics, length of employment, and work history with the company
- information about potential confounding variables, such as the employee's medical history, smoking habits, lifestyle, and family history of disease

Some environmental studies use biomarkers (discussed in Chapter 10) that may be correlated with exposures to potential carcinogens and other chemicals. These biomarkers involve changes in genetic structure that are thought to be the consequence of an exposure.

Risk Characterization

Risk characterization develops ". . . estimates of the number of excess unwarranted health events expected at different time intervals at each level of exposure."[22(p38)] Risk characterization follows the three foregoing steps by integrating the information from hazard identification, dose-response assessment, and exposure assessment.[29] The process of risk characterization yields "a synthesis and summary of information about a hazard that addresses the needs and interests of decision makers and of interested and affected parties. Risk characterization is a prelude to decision making and depends on an iterative, analytic-deliberative process."[30(p216)] "Risk characterization presents the policy maker with a synopsis of all the information that contributes to a conclusion about the nature of the risk and evaluates the magnitudes of the uncertainties involved and the major assumptions that were used."[23(p286)]

Risk Management

Oriented toward specific actions, **risk management** ". . . consists of actions taken to control exposures to toxic chemicals in the environment. Exposure standards, requirements for premarket testing, recalls of toxic products, and outright banning of very hazardous materials are among the actions that are used by governmental agencies to manage risk."[22(p37)]

POLICY IMPLEMENTATION: THE EXAMPLE OF WORLDWIDE SMOKEFREE BARS LAWS

A significant public policy development concerns smokefree bars laws that were first adopted in California and then spread across the United States and eventually to Europe and many countries across the world. The impetus for the implementation of these laws was the growing body of information about the health hazards that secondhand cigarette exposure presented in the work setting. These hazards endangered the employees of alcohol-serving establishments, as well as customers. Epidemiologic studies were one of the sources of data that demonstrated the adverse health effects of smoking and exposure to secondhand cigarette smoke. Exhibit 7-1 presents a case study that reviews the status of smokefree bars laws.

HEALTH POLICY AND SCREENING FOR DISEASE

A topic that is closely related to health policy is screening for disease. The process of **screening for disease** is defined as the presumptive identification of recognized disease or defects by the application of tasks, examinations, or other procedures that can be applied rapidly. Screening provides only preliminary information; a diagnostic confirmation of any positive results of a screening test is required. Usually this confirmation involves additional procedures, including clinical examinations and additional testing.

There are a number of policy and related issues that pertain to the use of screening tests. Simple policy questions (without simple answers!) are: who should be screened; what conditions should be screened; under which circumstances should screening tests be used; and at what age should screening begin? For example, consider who should be screened and the age groups for which screening programs should be applied. **Mass screening** refers to application of screening tests to total population groups, regardless of their risk status. **Selective screening** is the type of screening applied to high risk groups such as those at risk for sexually transmitted diseases. Selective screening is likely to result in the greatest yield of true cases and to be the most economically efficient. Controversy surrounds the age at which routine screening for breast cancer should begin. Similarly, opinion is divided on the timing and application of screening tests for prostate cancer. Considerations regarding the appropriate use of screening tests include whether the condition being screened is sufficiently important for the individual and the community. Also, the screening test should have a high cost-benefit ratio; this means that the condition needs to be sufficiently prevalent in the population to justify the cost of screening. In addition, the screening test should be applied mainly to conditions for which an effective treatment is available.

Exhibit 7-1

CASE STUDY
Status of Smokefree Bars Laws, United States and Europe

- Background: In 1998, the California state legislature passed a law (AB 3037) that prohibited smoking in all workplaces including alcohol-serving establishments. The purpose of AB 3037 was to protect workers from the health effects associated with secondhand smoke. Initially, it was feared that the law would be opposed or ignored by the public and the business community and thus be doomed to failure. A survey of the residents of a large city (Long Beach) in California found strong approval of the prohibition of smoking in all indoor public places. Two-thirds and three-fourths of the respondents approved of the law in 1998 and 2000, respectively.[31] It is noteworthy that tobacco control policies such as the smokefree bars law in California have been correlated with a decline in the percentage of adult smokers in that state; as of late 2008, the prevalence of smoking had fallen to about 15%.
- The strong endorsement of the smokefree bars law in California has major public health and policy implications. For example:
  - Should there be restriction of smoking in other venues such as public beaches?
  - Should tobacco taxes be increased further to fund smoking cessation programs and research?
  - What are the economic effects of the law, e.g., how have businesses been impacted?
  - Are smokefree policies being enforced?
  - Are businesses complying?
  - Does banning of cigarette smoking result in increases in the use of other forms of tobacco?
  - Should films be prevented from showing smoking by glamorous movie stars?

Since the adoption of California's smokefree bars law, other states and government agencies have adopted similar laws:
- Eighteen U.S. states ban smoking in bars and restaurants (as of early 2008).
- Eleven states ban smoking in worksites.
- The U.S. government prohibits smoking on commercial aircraft; smoking is prohibited in airports and many other confined public areas.

Smokefree bars laws have also been implemented in Europe. Some countries that have such laws are the United Kingdom, Denmark, Czech Republic, Ireland, Norway, and Italy. The Netherlands, Spain, and Sweden have areas set aside for smokers in bars so that nonsmokers will be protected.
- France: On January 1, 2008, bars and cafés joined nightclubs, restaurants, and casinos in becoming 100% smoke free.
- Turkey: A new smokefree law (implemented on January 3, 2008) restricts tobacco use in restaurants, bars, and teahouses.
- Germany: As of January 2008, 11 out of 16 German states had introduced smokefree bars laws. However, during July 2008, the Federal Constitutional Court ruled against smoking bans in small bars and restaurants.

In addition, many other countries across the globe have adopted smokefree laws or are considering such legislation.

Source: Data from American Nonsmokers' Rights Foundation. Smokefree status of hospitality venues around the world. Available at: www.no-smoke.org. Accessed August 23, 2008; Campaign for Tobacco-Free Kids, International Resource Center. New laws in Turkey, France and Germany show smokefree movement is spreading globally. Available at: http://www.tobaccofreecenter.org/en/print/133. Accessed August 23, 2008; BBC News. German court rejects smoking bans. Available at: http://newsvote.bbc.co.uk/mpapps/pagetools/print/news.bbc.co.uk/2/hi/europe/7533132.stm. Accessed August 23, 2008.

Screening tests need to demonstrate reliability and validity. The term **reliability** (synonym: **precision**) refers to the ability of a measuring instrument to give consistent results on repeated trials. In comparison with reliability is **validity** (synonym: **accuracy**), which is the ability of the measuring instrument to give a true measure of the entity being measured. The "true measure" sometimes is called the gold standard.

Reliability and validity are interrelated terms; it is possible for a measure to be invalid and reliable, but not the converse. An example would be a bathroom weight scale that has been tampered with so that it does not give a correct weight measurement but consistently gives the same incorrect measurement that is invalid.

However, it is never possible for a measure that is unreliable to be valid. A valid measure must give a true measure of an attribute on repeated occasions; an unreliable measure would give different results each time a measurement is taken. Consider the analogy of a bullet hitting a target. For several

TABLE 7-3 Fourfold Table for Classification of Screening Test Results

Definitions: True positives are individuals who have been both screened positive and truly have the condition; false positives are individuals who have been screened positive but do not have the condition; false negatives are individuals screened negative who truly have the condition; and true negatives are individuals who have been both screened negative and do not have the condition.

Condition According to Gold Standard

		Present	Absent	Total	
Test Result	**Positive**	a = True positives	b = False positives	a + b	Predictive Value (+) $\dfrac{a}{a+b}$
	Negative	c = False negatives	d = True negatives	c + d	Predictive Value (−) $\dfrac{d}{c+d}$
	Total	a + c	b + d	**Grand Total** a + b + c + d	
		Sensitivity $\dfrac{a}{a+c}$	Specificity $\dfrac{d}{b+d}$		

rifle shots at a target, when the bullet hits the bull's-eye consistently, this outcome is analogous to validity (and also to a reliable, valid measure). A situation that would be analogous to an unreliable, invalid measure would be when the bullet hits several different places on the target (not the bull's-eye every time). Ideally, a screening test should be both reliable and valid.

In the context of screening, there are four measures of validity that must be considered: sensitivity, specificity, predictive value (+), and predictive value (−). A good screening test needs to be high in sensitivity, high in specificity, high in predictive value (+) and high in predictive value (−). Table 7-3 represents a sample of individuals who have been examined with both a screening test for disease (rows) and a definitive diagnostic test or gold standard (columns). Thus, we are able to determine how well the screening test performed in identifying individuals with disease.

- **Sensitivity:** the ability of the test to identify correctly all screened individuals who actually have the disease. In Table 7-3, a total of a + c individuals were determined to have the disease, according to some established **gold standard**, a definitive diagnosis that has been determined by biopsy, surgery, autopsy, or other method[32] and has been accepted as the standard. Sensitivity is de-

fined as the number of true positives divided by the sum of true positives and false negatives. Suppose that in a sample of 1,000 individuals there were 120 who actually had the disease. If the screening test correctly identified all 120 cases, the sensitivity would be 100%. If the screening test was unable to identify all these individuals, then the sensitivity would be less than 100%.

- **Specificity:** the ability of the test to identify only nondiseased individuals who actually do not have the disease. It is defined as the number of true negatives divided by the sum of false positives and true negatives. If a test is not specific, then individuals who do not actually have the disease will be referred for additional diagnostic testing.

- **Predictive value (+):** the proportion of individuals screened positive by the test who actually have the disease. In Table 7-3, a total of a + b individuals were screened positive by the test. Predictive value (+) is the proportion a/(a + b) who actually have the condition, according to the gold standard; this is the probability that an individual who is screened positive actually has the disease.

- **Predictive value (−):** an analogous measure for those screened negative by the test; it is designated by the formula d/(c + d); this is the probability that an individual who is screened negative does not have the disease. Note that the only time these measures can be estimated is when the same group of individuals has been examined using both the screening test and the gold standard.

Additional interpretations of Table 7-3 are the following: a false positive result could unnecessarily raise the anxiety levels of persons who are screened positive and subjected to invasive medical tests. On the other hand, a false negative test result would not detect disease in persons who actually have the disease and require treatment. For example, if a screening test missed a case of breast cancer (false negative result), the disease could progress to a more severe form.

Calculation example: Suppose that a pharmaceutical company wishes to evaluate the validity of a new measure for screening persons who are suspected of having diabetes. (Refer to Table 7-4.) A total of 1,473 persons are screened for diabetes; 244 of them have been confirmed as diabetics according to the gold standard. Here are the results of the screening test: true positives (a = 177); false positives (b = 268); false negatives (c = 67); true negatives (d = 961).

CONCLUSION

The worlds and realities of the epidemiologist and policy maker are often quite different. Epidemiologists are able to maintain objectivity, and their focus is on designing studies and collecting data. Policy makers must function in the world of politics and are subject to the influences of elected officials, constituents, and special interest groups. This chapter has stressed the importance of increasing the input of epidemiologists into the policy-making process because of their expertise in study design. Another important role for epidemiologists is in policy assessment and evaluation, which require the establishment of clearly articulated objectives, the use of evidence-based approaches, and cost-effectiveness analysis. Policies often are developed as a consequence of risk assessment, which culminates in risk management. The method of risk assessment has been used extensively in the study and control of environmental health problems, for example, hazards associated with smoking and exposure to secondhand cigarette smoke. In response to the perceived hazards associated with these exposures, governments in the United States and abroad have developed smokefree bars laws. This chapter concluded with the policy-related issue of screening for disease; policy determinations affect the application of screening tests. Finally, the chapter discussed reliability and validity of screening tests and presented calculation examples for measures such as sensitivity and specificity.

TABLE 7-4 Calculation Example

	Gold standard (present)	Gold standard (absent)	Total
Positive test result	a = 177	b = 268	445
Negative test result	c = 67	d = 961	1,028
Total	244	1,229	1,473

Sensitivity = 177/244 = 72.5%
Specificity = 961/1,229 = 78.2%
Predictive value (+) = 177/445 = 39.8%
Predictive value (−) = 961/1,028 = 93.5%
[This test has moderate sensitivity and specificity, low predictive value (+), and fairly high predictive value (−).]

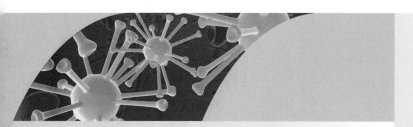

Study Questions and Exercises

1. Define the following terms:
   a. cost-effectiveness analysis
   b. evidence-based public health
   c. environmental objectives

2. Discuss the role of epidemiologists in policy making. How do the roles of epidemiologists differ from those of policy makers?

3. Discuss the differences between health policies and health laws.

4. Describe the stages of the policy cycle. Which of these stages is the most important for epidemiology? Or, would you assign them equal importance?

5. What is meant by risk assessment? Describe the process of risk assessment for a potentially toxic chemical used in containers for food storage.

6. Name five public health laws that have been implemented within the past few years. Invite a public health official to your classroom and ask the individual to discuss policy issues that currently confront his or her organization.

7. How does screening for disease relate to health policy considerations?

8. Define the following terms that are related to screening tests:
   a. reliability and validity
   b. sensitivity and specificity
   c. predictive value positive and negative

9. The following table presents the results of a screening test. Calculate sensitivity, specificity, predictive value (+), and predictive value (−).

TABLE 7-5 Data for Question 9

	Gold standard: disease present	Gold standard: disease absent
Screening test positive	55	5
Screening test negative	11	145

Answers:

Sensitivity = 55/66 × 100 = 83.3%

Specificity = 145/150 × 100 = 96.7%

Predictive Value (+) = 55/60 × 100 = 91.7%

Predictive Value (−) = 145/156 × 100 = 92.9%

Young Epidemiology Scholars (YES) Exercises

The Young Epidemiology Scholars Web site provides links to teaching units and exercises that support instruction in epidemiology. The YES program is administered by the College Board and supported by the Robert Wood Johnson Foundation. The Web address of YES is www.collegeboard.com/yes. The following exercises relate to topics discussed in this chapter and can be found on the YES Web site.

1. Novick LF, Wojtowycz M, Morrow CB, Sutphen SM. Bicycle helmet effectiveness in preventing injury and death.

2. Huang FI, Stolley P. Epidemiology and public health policy: Using the smoking ban in New York City bars as a case study.

REFERENCES

1. Tallon J. Health policy roundtable—View from the state legislature: Translating research into policy. *HSR: Health Services Research.* 2005;40(2):337–346.

2. Brownson RC. Epidemiology and health policy. In: Brownson RC, Petitti DB. *Applied Epidemiology: Theory to Practice.* 2nd ed. New York: Oxford University Press; 2006.

3. The American Heritage® Dictionary of the English Language: Fourth Edition. 2000.

4. *Los Angeles Times.* Schwarzenegger signs law banning trans fats in restaurants. July 26, 2008.

5. D@dalos (International UNESCO Education Server for Civic, Peace and Human Rights Education). Policy Cycle: Teaching Politics. Available at: http://www.dadalos.org/politik_int/politik/policy-zyklus.htm. Accessed August 22, 2008.

6. Answers.com. Interest group. Available at: http://www.answers.com/topic/interest-group. Accessed July 26, 2008.

7. Walker B Jr. Impediments to the implementation of environmental policy. *J Public Health Policy.* 1994;15:186–202.

8. National Institute of Environmental Health Sciences-National Institutes of Health. The National Toxicology Program (NTP) Draft Brief On Bisphenol A (BPA). Available at: http://www.niehs.nih.gov/news/media/questions/sya-bpa.cfm#6. Accessed August 22, 2008.

9. U.S. Food and Drug Administration. Bisphenol A (BPA). Available at: http://www.fda.gov/oc/opacom/hottopics/bpa.html. Accessed August 22, 2008.

10. Rabe BG. Legislative incapacity: The congressional role in environmental policy-making and the case of Superfund. *J Health Polit Policy Law.* 1990;15:571–589.

11. Natural Resources Defense Council. The EPA's Changes to New Source Review. Available at: http://www.nrdc.org/air/pollution/pnsr.asp. Accessed May 23, 2008.

12. Goudey R, Laslett G. Statistics and environmental policy: Case studies from long-term environmental monitoring data. *Novartis Found Symp.* 1999;220:144–157.

13. U.S. Department of Health and Human Services, Office of Disease Prevention and Health Promotion. What is Healthy People? Available at: http://www.healthypeople.gov/About/whatis.htm. Accessed August 22, 2008.

14. U.S. Department of Health and Human Services, Office of Disease Prevention and Health Promotion. What are the leading health indicators? Available at: http://www.healthypeople.gov/LHI/lhiwhat.htm. Accessed August 22, 2008.

15. Raphael D. The question of evidence in health promotion. *Health Promotion International.* 2000;15:355–367.

16. Ashcroft RE. Current epistemological problems in evidence based medicine. *J Med Ethics.* 2004;30:131–135.

17. Centers for Disease Control and Prevention. HIV cost effectiveness. Available at: http://www.cdc.gov/hiv/topics/prev_prog/ce/index.htm. Accessed July 24, 2008.

18. McKone TE. The rise of exposure assessment among the risk sciences: An evaluation through case studies. *Inhal Toxicol.* 1999;11:611–622.

19. Porta M, ed. *A Dictionary of Epidemiology.* 5th ed. New York: Oxford University Press; 2008.

20. Amendola A, Wilkinson DR. Risk assessment and environmental policy making. *J Hazard Mater.* 2000;78:ix–xiv.

21. Slovic P. Perception of risk. *Science.* 1987;236:280–285.

22. Landrigan PJ, Carlson JE. Environmental policy and children's health. *The Future of Children.* 1995;5(2):34–52.

23. Russell M, Gruber M. Risk assessment in environmental policy-making. *Science.* 1987;236:286–290.

24. Department of Health and Human Services, National Toxicology Program. Human Exposure Assessment. Available at: http://webharvest.gov/peth04/20041020135705/ntp.niehs.nih.gov/index.cfm?objectid=06F6F41D-9B12-8FD0-63E4048B173CC36A. Accessed August 22, 2008.

25. Lippmann M, Thurston GD. Exposure assessment: Input into risk assessment. *Arch Environ Health.* 1988;43:113–123.

26. Ott WR. Human exposure assessment: The birth of a new science. *J Expos Anal Environ Epidem.* 1995;5:449–472.

27. Gardner MJ. Epidemiological studies of environmental exposure and specific diseases. *Arch Environ Health.* 1988;43:102–108.

28. Monson RR. *Occupational Epidemiology.* Boca Raton, FL: CRC Press; 1990.

29. Duffus JH. Risk assessment terminology. *Chemistry International.* 2001;23(2):34–39.

30. Stern PC, Fineberg HV, eds. National Academy of Sciences' National Research Council, Committee on Risk Characterization. *Understanding Risk: Informing Decisions in a Democratic Society.* Washington, D.C.: National Academy Press; 1996.

31. Friis RH, Safer AM. Analysis of responses of Long Beach, California residents to the smoke-free bars law. *Public Health.* 2005;119:1116–1121.

32. Haynes RB. How to read clinical journals, II: to learn about a diagnostic test. *Can Med Assoc J.* 1981;124:703–710.

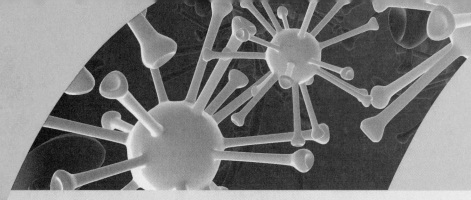

CHAPTER **8**

Infectious Diseases and Outbreak Investigation

INTRODUCTION

Infectious diseases (synonym: communicable diseases) are important causes of morbidity and mortality in the United States

TABLE 8-1 List of Important Terms Used in This Chapter

Agent	Fomite	Point source epidemic
Antigen	Generation time	Portal of entry/portal of exit
Attack rate	Herd immunity	Reservoir
Carrier	Host	Resistance
Determinant (environmental)	Immunity (passive vs. active)	Subclinical (inapparent) infection
Direct vs. indirect transmission	Incubation period	Toxin
Emerging infection	Index case	Vector
Endemic	Infectious disease (infection)	Vehicle
Environment	Infectivity	Virulence
Epidemiologic triangle	Parasitic disease	Zoonosis

and worldwide. During the past century, chronic health problems such as heart disease have replaced infectious diseases as the leading killers in developed countries and to a lesser extent in developing nations. Nevertheless, infectious diseases remain significant worldwide. For example, in the United States the category of influenza and pneumonia was the eighth leading cause of death in 2005 (63,001 deaths); infectious disease agents contributed to several of the other fourteen leading causes of death. Additional examples of major infectious diseases are the sexually transmitted diseases, such as HIV/AIDS, emerging infections, such as avian influenza and West Nile virus, and illnesses transmitted by foods, including *E. coli* infections. Table 8-1 provides a summary of major terms that will be defined in this chapter.

Infectious/parasitic diseases and respiratory infections account for almost 20% and 7%, respectively, of mortality worldwide. Table 8-2 presents data on the worldwide frequency of mortality from selected communicable diseases. (The most recently available data are from 2002.)

THE EPIDEMIOLOGIC TRIANGLE: AGENT, HOST, AND ENVIRONMENT

An **infectious disease** (or **communicable disease**) is "an illness due to a specific infectious agent or its toxic products that arises through transmission of that agent or its products from an infected person, animal, or reservoir to a susceptible host, either directly or indirectly through an intermediate

plant or animal host, vector, or the inanimate environment."[1] A **parasitic disease** (for example, amebiasis) is an infection caused by a parasite, which ". . . is an organism that lives on or in a host organism and gets its food from or at the expense of its host."[2] An infection is defined as "the entry and development or multiplication of an infectious agent in the body of persons or animals."[3(p708)]

One of the long-standing models used to describe the etiology of infectious diseases is the **epidemiologic triangle**, which includes three major factors: agent, host, and environment. Although this model has been applied to the field of infectious disease epidemiology, it also provides a framework for organizing the causality of some other types of health outcomes such as those associated with the environment. Refer to Figure 8-1 for an illustration of the epidemiologic triangle.

- The term **environment** is defined as the domain in which disease-causing agents may exist, survive, or originate; it consists of "all that which is external to the individual human host."[1]
- The **host** is "a person or other living animal, including birds and arthropods, that affords subsistence or lodgment to an infectious agent under natural conditions."[1] A human host is a person who is afflicted with a disease; or, from the epidemiologic perspective, the term host denotes an affected group or population.
- An **agent** refers to "a factor—such as a microorganism, chemical substance, or form of radiation—whose presence, excessive presence, or (in deficiency diseases) rel-

TABLE 8-2 Number of Deaths from Communicable Diseases, Worldwide, 2002 Estimates

World population = 6,224,985,000	Data are for both sexes combined	
Cause	Number × 1,000	% of Total
Total deaths	57,027	100
Infectious and parasitic diseases	11,122	19.5
HIV/AIDS	2,821	4.9
Diarrheal diseases	1,767	3.1
Childhood diseases	1,360	2.4
Malaria	1,222	2.1
Tropical diseases	130	0.2
Respiratory infections	3,845	6.7

Source: Data from World Health Organization. *The World Health Report: 2003: shaping the future.* Geneva, Switzerland: World Health Organization; 2003:154.

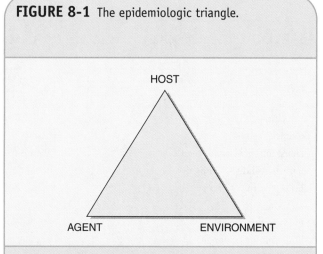

FIGURE 8-1 The epidemiologic triangle.

Source: Reprinted from Friis RH, Sellers TA. *Epidemiology for Public Health Practice.* 4th ed. Sudbury, Massachusetts: Jones and Bartlett Publishers; 2009:439.

ative absence is essential for the occurrence of a disease. A disease may have a single agent, a number of independent alternative agents (at least one of which must be present), or a complex of two or more factors whose combined presence is essential for the development of the disease."[1]

Disease transmission involves the interaction of the three major components, as you will learn subsequently. Although the model provides a simplified account of the causality of infectious diseases, in reality the etiology of infectious diseases is often complex.

INFECTIOUS DISEASE AGENTS

With respect to infectious and communicable diseases, agents include specific microbes and vectors involved in the cycle of disease transmission. Examples of infectious agents are microbial agents such as bacteria, rickettsia, viruses, fungi, parasites, and prions. Infectious disease agents vary in their **infectivity**, which refers to the capacity of an agent to enter and multiply in a susceptible host and thus produce infection or disease. The term **virulence** refers to the severity of the disease produced, i.e., whether the disease has severe clinical manifestations or is fatal in a large number of cases.

Some infectious disease agents enter the body and cause illness when they multiply; they act directly. Other disease agents produce a toxin; it is the action of this toxin that causes illness. A **toxin** usually refers to a toxic substance (a material that is harmful to biologic systems) made by living organisms. Foodborne intoxications are examples of illness caused by the actions of microbial toxins. Refer to the example of botulism discussed later in this text.

The consequences of infectious diseases are manifested in diverse ways—to name a few examples, subclinical and clinically apparent infections, zoonotic illnesses, foodborne illnesses, infectious disease outbreaks that are associated with specific occupations, and infectious disease occurrences linked with water pollution. Figure 8-2 illustrates four infectious disease agents: bacteria, viruses, fungi, and parasites (protozoa).

HOST CHARACTERISTICS

A second component identified in the epidemiologic triangle is the host. Whether human or animal, hosts vary in their responses to disease agents. A host characteristic that can limit the ability of an infectious disease agent to produce infection is known as **immunity**, which refers to the host's ability to resist infection by the agent. Immunity is defined as "a status usually associated with the presence of antibodies or cells having a specific action on the microorganism concerned with a particular infectious disease, or on its toxin."[3(p707)] Susceptible hosts are those at risk (capable) of acquiring an infection. Generally speaking, immune hosts are at lowered risk of developing the infection, although they may be susceptible in some situations, for example, if they receive large doses of an infectious agent or they are under treatment with immunosuppressive drugs.

Immunity may be either **active** or **passive**, the former referring to immunity that the host has developed as a result of a natural infection with a microbial agent; active immunity also can be acquired from an injection of a vaccine (immunization) that contains an **antigen** (a substance that stimulates antibody formation). Examples of antigens are live or attenuated microbial agents. (Chapter 1 illustrated the development of an immunization against smallpox.) Active immunity is usually of long duration and is measured in years. **Passive immunity** refers to immunity that is acquired from antibodies produced by another person or animal. For instance, one type is the newborn infant's natural immunity conferred transplacentally from its mother. Another example is artificial immunity that is conferred by injections of antibodies contained in immune serums from animals or humans. Passive immunity is of short duration, lasting from a few days to several months.

From the epidemiologic perspective, the immune statuses of both individual hosts and the entire population are noteworthy. The term **herd immunity** denotes the resistance (opposite of susceptibility) of an entire community to an infectious agent as a result of the immunity of a large proportion of individuals in that community to the agent. Herd immunity can limit epidemics in the population even when not every member of the population has been vaccinated.

A clinically apparent disease is one that produces observable clinical signs and symptoms. The term **incubation period** denotes the time interval between invasion by an infectious agent and the appearance of the first sign or symptom of the disease.

In some hosts, an infection may be **subclinical** (also called **inapparent**), meaning that the infection does not show obvious clinical signs or symptoms. For example, hepatitis A infections among children and the early phases of infection with HIV are largely asymptomatic. Nevertheless, individuals who have inapparent infections can transmit them to others; thus inapparent infections are epidemiologically significant and part of the spectrum of infection.

After an infectious organism has lodged and reproduced in the host, the agent can be transmitted to other hosts. The term **generation time** is defined as the time interval between lodgment of an infectious agent in a host and the maximal communicability of the host. The generation time for an infectious disease and the incubation time may or may not be equivalent.

FIGURE 8-2 Four infectious disease agents. Upper left, *Bacillus anthracis* bacteria; Lower left, herpes simplex virions; Upper right, dermatophytic fungus (causes ringworm infections of the skin and fungal infections of the nail bed); Lower right, *Cryptosporidium parvum* oocysts.

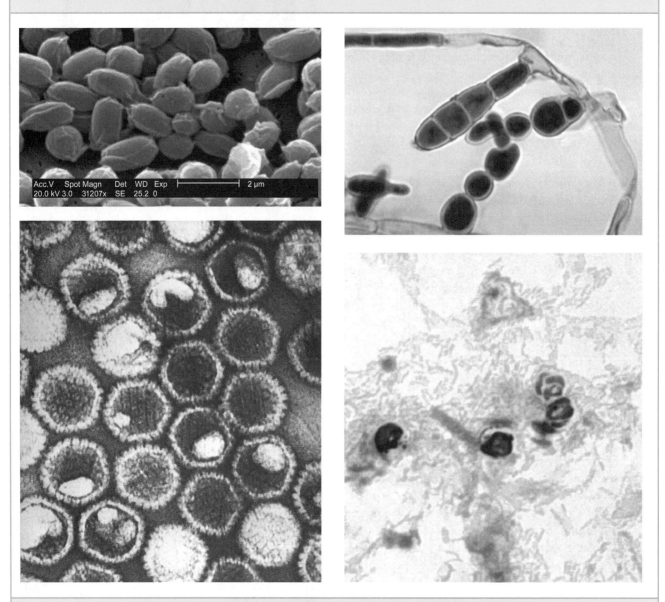

Source: Reprinted from Centers for Disease Control and Prevention. Public Health Image Library, ID# 10123 (upper left); ID# 10230 (lower left); ID# 4207 (upper right); ID# 7829 (lower right). Available at: http://phil.cdc.gov/phil/details.asp. Accessed July 3, 2008.

For some diseases, the period of maximal communicability precedes the development of active symptoms. The term incubation period applies only to clinically apparent cases of disease, whereas the term generation time applies to both inapparent and apparent cases of disease.

Related to inapparent infections is carrier status; a **carrier** is "a person or animal that harbors a specific infectious agent without discernible clinical disease, and which serves as a potential source of infection."[3(p703)] When carrier status is longstanding, the host is called a chronic carrier.

A famous example of an infectious disease carrier was "Typhoid Mary" Mallon, who worked as a cook in New York City during the early 1900s and was alleged to be a typhoid carrier. Several cases of typhoid fever were traced to households where she was employed. Typhoid fever, caused by *Salmonella* bacteria (*S. typhi*), is a systemic infection associated with a 10% to 20% case fatality rate when untreated. After the first cases of typhoid were associated with her, Mallon was quarantined for three years on Brother Island in New York City and then released with the proviso that she no longer work as a cook. However, after she continued working as a cook and was linked to additional typhoid outbreaks, she again was confined to Brother Island until she died in 1938. Refer to Figure 8-3 for an image of "Typhoid Mary."

FIGURE 8-3 Typhoid Mary as a cook.

Source: © Mary Evans Picture Library/Alamy Images.

The foregoing example illustrated an outbreak of typhoid fever. An outbreak of infectious disease may trigger an epidemiologic investigation. The term **index case** is used in an epidemiologic investigation of a disease outbreak to denote the first case of a disease to come to the attention of authorities.

ENVIRONMENT AND INFECTIOUS DISEASES

The third component of the epidemiologic triangle is the **environment**. The external environment is the sum of total influences that are not part of the host; it comprises physical, climatologic, biologic, social, and economic components. Here are some examples of how environmental factors may act as determinants of diseases and other health outcomes.

- Physical environment. The availability of clean and abundant water supplies is instrumental in maintaining optimal sanitary conditions; waterborne diseases such as cholera are associated with pathogens that can contaminate water. Other pathogens such as fungi may be present naturally in the soil in some geographic areas. An example is the fungus *Coccidioides immitis*, found in California's San Joaquin Valley. This fungus is the agent for San Joaquin Valley fever.
- Climatologic environment. In warm, moist, tropical climates, disease agents and arthropod vectors such as the *Anopheles* mosquito, the vector for malaria, are able to survive and cause human and animal diseases. These same vectors and the diseases associated with them are not as common in drier, colder, temperate climates. However, with global warming observed in recent years, it may be possible for disease vectors to migrate to regions that formerly were much colder.
- Biologic environment. The biologic environment includes the presence of available plant and animal species that can act as reservoirs for disease agents. These species may be part of the cycle of reproduction of the disease agent. An example is the disease schistosomiasis, which depends on the presence of intermediate hosts (certain species of snails) in order to reproduce. Schistosomiasis, a major cause of illnesses including liver cirrhosis, is found in Africa, the Middle East, parts of South America and Asia, as well as some other geographic areas.
- Social and economic environments. While the world becomes increasingly urbanized as inhabitants search for improved opportunities, cities will become ever more crowded. The overcrowded urban environment can contribute to the spread of infections through person-to-person contact and creation of unsanitary conditions such as improper disposal of human wastes.

When an infectious disease agent is habitually present in an environment (either a geographic or population group), it is said to be **endemic**. In illustration, plague is endemic among certain species of rodents in the western United States. Another term to describe the presence of an infectious agent in the environment is a **reservoir**, which is a place where infectious agents normally live and multiply; the reservoir can be human beings, animals, insects, soils, or plants. The term **zoonosis** refers to "an infection or infectious agent transmissible under natural conditions from vertebrate animals to humans."[3(p716)] An example of a zoonotic disease is rabies, a highly fatal viral disease that affects the brain (causing acute viral encephalomyelitis) and that can be transmitted by the bite of an infected dog or other rabid animal.

MEANS OF TRANSMISSION OF INFECTIOUS DISEASE AGENTS

Now that the three elements of the epidemiologic triangle have been defined, the author will explain two methods for the spread of disease agents: directly from person to person and indirectly. Some modes of indirect transmission are by means of vehicles (defined later) and vectors. In order for infection to occur, the agent needs to move from the environment (an infected person or a reservoir) to a potential host. For an infected person, a **portal of exit** is the site from which the agent leaves that person's body; portals of exit include respiratory passages, the alimentary canal, the genitourinary system, and skin lesions.

Person to Person (Direct Transmission)

The term **direct transmission** refers to "direct and essentially immediate transfer of infectious agents to a receptive portal of entry through which human or animal infection may take place. This may be by direct contact such as touching, kissing, biting, or sexual intercourse or by the direct projection (droplet spread) of droplet spray . . ."[1] See Figure 8-4, which illustrates that when one sneezes, potentially infectious droplets are dispersed over a wide area. When a person is infected with a microbial agent such as a cold virus and sneezes, other individuals in the vicinity can inhale the virus-containing droplets. Then, what happens next?

In order for an infectious agent to lodge in a host, it must gain access to a **portal of entry**, or site where the agent enters the body. Examples of portals of entry are the respiratory system (through inhalation), a skin wound (such as a break in skin), and the mucus membranes, which line some of the body's organs and cavities—e.g., nose, mouth, and lungs.

Depending upon several factors, including the type of microbial agent, access to a portal of entry, the amount of the agent to which the potential host is exposed, and the immune status of the host, an active infection may result.

FIGURE 8-4 The model demonstrates that a sneeze releases a cloud of droplets into the nearby environment.

Source: Photo courtesy of Andrew Davidhazy, RIT.

Indirect Transmission

Indirect transmission of infectious disease agents involves intermediary sources of infection such as vehicles, droplet nuclei (particles), and vectors. The terms used to describe indirect transmission of disease agents by these sources are as follows:

- Vehicle-borne infections
- Airborne infections
- Vector-borne infections

Vehicle-Borne Infections.

These infections result from contact with **vehicles**, which are contaminated, nonmoving objects. Vehicles can include fomites (defined later), unsanitary food, impure water, or infectious bodily fluids. For example, used injection needles may contain bloodborne pathogens; such was the case during a 2008 suspected hepatitis C virus (HCV) transmission by unsafe injection practices. In January 2008, the Nevada State Health Department reported three cases of acute hepatitis C to the Centers for Disease Control and Prevention (CDC). Investigations by state and local health departments in collaboration with the CDC discovered that all three individuals had procedures performed at the same endoscopy clinic.

Endoscopy is a procedure for viewing the inside of a body cavity or organ (for example, the esophagus) by using an instrument such as a flexible tube. Laboratory and epidemiologic research findings suggested that syringes from single-use medication vials had been reused and that this unsafe practice could have been the cause of the outbreak. Health authorities notified approximately 40,000 patients who had been treated in the clinic of their possible exposure to HCV and other pathogens carried in blood. Figure 8-5 portrays the unsafe injection practices that might have led to the outbreak.

A **fomite** is an inanimate object that carries infectious disease agents; fomites include the classroom doorknob, used towels found in a locker room, or carelessly discarded tissues. Medical wastes and unsanitary linen in hospitals can cause outbreaks of hospital-acquired (nosocomial) infections. For this reason, hospital epidemiologists seek to minimize exposure of patients and staff to these types of fomites by requiring hand-washing procedures, disposal of medical wastes in sealed bags (often red and marked "biohazard"), and frequent disinfection of floors and surfaces.

Foodborne diseases are those caused by ingestion of contaminated food. Such contamination can be from arsenic, heavy metals, toxins naturally present in foods, and toxic chemicals including pesticides. Other sources of contamination are microbial agents that have entered the food supply during growth and harvesting of crops, storage of ingredients, and preparation and storage of foods that are consumed. One of the most important causes of foodborne infections in the United States is *Salmonella*, which was identified as the cause of a foodborne disease outbreak during mid-2008. Initially, the source of the outbreak was thought to be contaminated tomatoes; later, however, authorities stated that the cause was jalapeño and Serrano peppers imported from Mexico.

Waterborne infections are those caused by the presence of infectious disease agents that contaminate the water supply and in which water is the vehicle of infection. Examples of waterborne infections are bacterial infections (e.g., cholera, typhoid fever), parasitic infections (e.g., giardiasis, cryptosporidiosis) caused by enteric protozoal parasites, and viral infections (e.g., Norwalk agent disease, winter vomiting disease) caused by noroviruses. Waterborne infections take a great toll in morbidity and mortality in developing nations and present a hazard to tourists visiting these areas. In the United States, outbreaks of waterborne diseases occur sporadically, a case being the 1993 infamous cryptosporidiosis outbreak in Milwaukee, Wisconsin. The incident, which affected more than 400,000 people, was attributed to inadequate treatment of the water supply during heavy precipitation.

Airborne infections.

Another type of indirect transmission involves the spread of droplet nuclei (particles) that are present in the air, for example, by stirring up dust that carries fungi or microbes. Some venues for the airborne transmission of disease agents are closed, poorly ventilated environments: movie theaters, doctors' examination rooms, classrooms, and motor vehicles. Passengers who are confined in closed environments, such as compartments of airplanes, are at risk of exposure to airborne infectious agents emitted by infected passengers.

On March 15, 2003, a 72-year-old man in Hong Kong, China, boarded a Boeing 737-300 aircraft for a three-hour

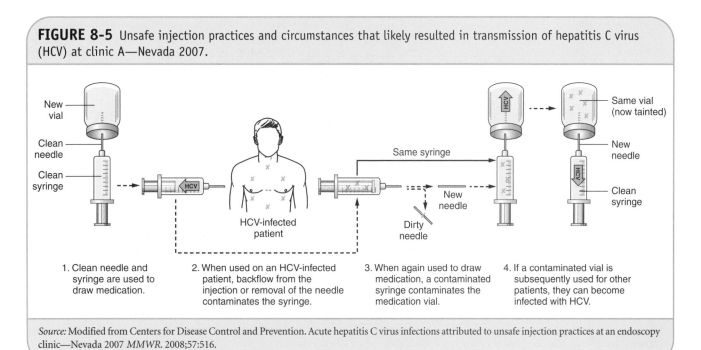

FIGURE 8-5 Unsafe injection practices and circumstances that likely resulted in transmission of hepatitis C virus (HCV) at clinic A—Nevada 2007.

1. Clean needle and syringe are used to draw medication.
2. When used on an HCV-infected patient, backflow from the injection or removal of the needle contaminates the syringe.
3. When again used to draw medication, a contaminated syringe contaminates the medication vial.
4. If a contaminated vial is subsequently used for other patients, they can become infected with HCV.

Source: Modified from Centers for Disease Control and Prevention. Acute hepatitis C virus infections attributed to unsafe injection practices at an endoscopy clinic—Nevada 2007 *MMWR.* 2008;57:516.

flight that was bound for Beijing. The man (called the index case) had developed a fever on March 11; he was hospitalized when he arrived at his destination, was diagnosed with atypical pneumonia, and died on March 20. Between March 4 and March 9, the index case had visited his brother in a Hong Kong hospital. The brother, who died on March 9, was diagnosed with severe acute respiratory syndrome (SARS); several other patients on the same ward also were reported to have SARS. During the flight to Beijing, the index case shared the aircraft with 111 other passengers and eight crew members. Investigations later revealed that twenty-two persons (18% of the individuals on board the aircraft) were believed to have become infected with SARS and five subsequently died. A total of 65 of the 112 passengers were interviewed, and eighteen of these (28%) met the World Health Organization (WHO) definition of a probable case of SARS.

The seat locations of the cases were mapped in relation to the index case. Passengers who sat closest to the index case had the highest risk of contracting SARS in comparison with passengers who sat farther away.[4] Figure 8-6 shows the seating arrangement of the aircraft, the location of the index case, and the location of the probable cases of SARS.

Vector-Borne Infections.

A **vector** is an animate, living insect or animal that is involved with the transmission of disease agents. Transmission of an infectious disease agent may happen when the vector feeds on a susceptible host. Examples of vectors are arthropods (insects such as lice, flies, mosquitoes, and ticks) that bite their victims and feed on the latter's blood. Vectors also include some species of rodents (rats and mice that harbor fleas). Figure 8-7 illustrates common vectors.

EXAMPLES OF SIGNIFICANT INFECTIOUS DISEASES

Infectious diseases are often grouped in categories that are defined according to the method by which they are spread (e.g., foodborne) or by using other criteria such as being vaccine preventable or newly discovered. The categories are not mutually exclusive; several of the diseases could be included in more than one category. The following list presents categories of significant infectious diseases, some of which are discussed in the next section.

- Sexually transmitted diseases
- Foodborne diseases
- Waterborne diseases (discussed earlier in the chapter)
  - Bacterial conditions—e.g., cholera and typhoid fever (see Chapter 1). Note that cholera and typhoid fever also can be transmitted in food.
  - Parasitic diseases—e.g., giardiasis and cryptosporidiosis (see previous example)

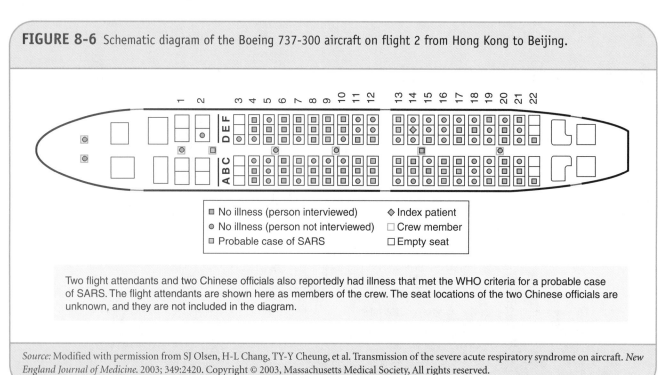

FIGURE 8-6 Schematic diagram of the Boeing 737-300 aircraft on flight 2 from Hong Kong to Beijing.

■ No illness (person interviewed)   ◆ Index patient
● No illness (person not interviewed)   □ Crew member
■ Probable case of SARS   □ Empty seat

Two flight attendants and two Chinese officials also reportedly had illness that met the WHO criteria for a probable case of SARS. The flight attendants are shown here as members of the crew. The seat locations of the two Chinese officials are unknown, and they are not included in the diagram.

Source: Modified with permission from SJ Olsen, H-L Chang, TY-Y Cheung, et al. Transmission of the severe acute respiratory syndrome on aircraft. *New England Journal of Medicine.* 2003; 349:2420. Copyright © 2003, Massachusetts Medical Society, All rights reserved.

FIGURE 8-7 Four vectors of infectious diseases. Upper left, a female louse; Upper right, a female *Aedes aegypti* mosquito acquiring a blood meal; Lower left, a tick; Lower right, a Norway rat.

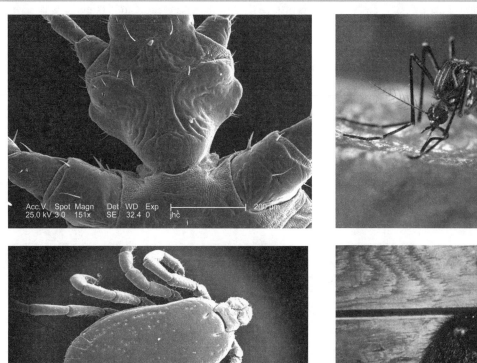

Source: Reprinted from Centers for Disease Control and Prevention. Public Health Image Library, ID# 9250 (upper left); ID# 9255 (upper right); ID# 9959 (lower left); ID# 5445 (lower right). Available at: http://phil.cdc.gov/phil/details.asp. Accessed July 3, 2008.

- Vector-borne (e.g., arthropod-borne) diseases
- Vaccine-preventable diseases
- Zoonotic diseases
- Emerging infections
- Bioterrorism-related diseases

Sexually Transmitted Diseases

Table 8-3 lists eight examples of infectious diseases and related conditions (such as crab lice) that can be spread by sexual contact. In addition to those shown, many other infections may be transmitted through sexual contact; these diseases include salmonellosis, viral hepatitis B, and viral hepatitis C.

TABLE 8-3 Examples of Sexually Transmitted Diseases

Acquired immunodeficiency syndrome (AIDS)*	Gonococcal infections (gonorrhea)*
Anogenital herpes infections (caused by herpes simplex virus type 2)	Lymphogranuloma venereum
Chlamydial genital infections*	Syphilis (discussed in Chapter 1)
Crab lice	Venereal warts

*Discussed in text.

HIV/AIDS.

The first example of a sexually transmitted disease cited in this section is acquired immunodeficiency syndrome (AIDS), which is a late clinical stage of infection with the human immunodeficiency virus (HIV). The term HIV/AIDS covers persons who are infected with HIV but who may not have been diagnosed with AIDS, as well as persons infected with HIV who have developed AIDS.

The infectious agent of HIV is a type of virus called a retrovirus. Among the possible modes for transmission of the agent are unprotected sexual intercourse and contact with infected blood (e.g., through transfusions and accidental needle sticks). Transmission from infected mother to child (known as vertical transmission) is also possible. As noted, HIV can progress to acquired immunodeficiency syndrome (AIDS), the term used to describe cases of a disease that began to emerge in 1981. Successful treatment programs have helped to limit the progression of HIV to AIDS. Because early infection with HIV is often asymptomatic, screening at-risk persons is essential for limiting the spread of this condition.

The CDC maintains confidential, name-based public health disease surveillance systems for collecting reports of HIV infection. As of 2006, thirty-three states and five dependent areas of the United States participated in this surveillance system. As shown in Table 8-4, in 2006 the estimated numbers of cases among male adults or adolescents exceeded the number of female cases in the corresponding age group by a factor of three to one. Among males the highest transmission category was male-to-male sexual contact; among females transmission occurred most frequently among those who had high-risk sexual contact.

TABLE 8-4 Estimated Numbers of Cases of HIV/AIDS, by Year of Diagnosis and Selected Characteristics, 2003–2006—33 States and 5 U.S. Dependent Areas with Confidential Name-Based HIV Infection Reporting

	Year of diagnosis			
	2003	2004	2005	2006
Transmission category				
Male adult or adolescent				
Male-to-male sexual contact	15,409	15,880	16,833	17,465
Injection drug use	3,514	3,083	2,978	3,016
Male-to-male sexual contact and injection drug use	1,349	1,299	1,247	1,180
High-risk heterosexual contact[a]	4,269	3,959	3,871	4,152
Other[b]	125	110	107	114
Subtotal	24,666	24,331	25,036	25,928
Female adult or adolescent				
Injection drug use	2,027	1,856	1,720	1,712
High-risk heterosexual contact[a]	7,731	7,182	7,216	7,432
Other[b]	134	107	97	109
Subtotal	9,892	9,145	9,033	9,252
Child (<13 yrs at diagnosis)				
Perinatal	190	157	147	115
Other[c]	23	27	23	20
Subtotal	213	184	170	135
Subtotal for 33 states	34,770	33,659	34,239	35,314

Note: These numbers do not represent reported case counts. Rather, these numbers are point estimates, which result from adjustments of reported case counts. The reported case counts have been adjusted for reporting delays and for redistribution of cases in persons initially reported without an identified risk factor, but not for incomplete reporting.

Data include persons with a diagnosis of HIV infection (not AIDS), a diagnosis of HIV infection and a later diagnosis of AIDS, or concurrent diagnoses of HIV infection and AIDS.

[a]Heterosexual contact with a person known to have, or to be at high risk for, HIV infection.
[b]Includes hemophilia, blood transfusion, perinatal exposure, and risk factor not reported or not identified.
[c]Includes hemophilia, blood transfusion, and risk factor not reported or not identified.

Source: Adapted and reprinted from Centers for Disease Control and Prevention. *HIV/AIDS Surveillance Report, 2006.* Vol. 18. Atlanta: U.S. Department of Health and Human Services, Centers for Disease Control and Prevention; 2008:11.

Gonococcal infections.

A second example of a sexually transmitted disease is the category of gonococcal infections. These infections result from sexual activity that can spread the bacteria *Neisseria gonorrhoeae*. Possible outcomes include several forms of morbidity—urethritis, pelvic inflammatory disease, pharyngitis, and gonococcal conjunctivitis of the newborn, which can result in blindness if not treated promptly. Among adults, more severe and less frequent consequences of gonococccal infections are septicemia, arthritis, and endocarditis. Reported cases of gonorrhea in the United States showed a decline of 74% between 1975 and 1997. Figure 8-8 demonstrates that after about 1997, the incidence rate leveled off until 2004, when it began to increase slightly. For the past few years, the incidence of gonorrhea has been slightly higher among women than among men.

Chlamydial genital infections.

These infections, which stem from the sexual transmission of the bacterial agent *Chlamydia trachomatis*, are the third exam-ple of an STD discussed in this chapter. A large proportion of infections with *C. trachomatis* are asymptomatic (up to 70% in women and 25% in men). Among the sequelae of infections are male and female infertility. Among women, chlamydial infections are associated with chronic pelvic pain and preterm delivery; these infections can be transmitted to the fetus during pregnancy, possibly resulting in conjunctivitis and pneumonia among newborn infants. Figure 8-9 portrays the geographic incidence of *Chlamydia* among women in the United States. The incidence rate was 511.7 cases per 100,000 population in 2006.

Foodborne Illness

Biologic agents of foodborne illness include bacteria, parasites, viruses, and prions (linked to mad cow disease). Some names of bacterial agents of foodborne illnesses can be found in Table 8-5.

From the worldwide perspective, foodborne illness is a major cause of morbidity. In the United States, the Foodborne Diseases Active Surveillance Network (FoodNet)—part of the CDC's Emerging Infections Program—monitors foodborne

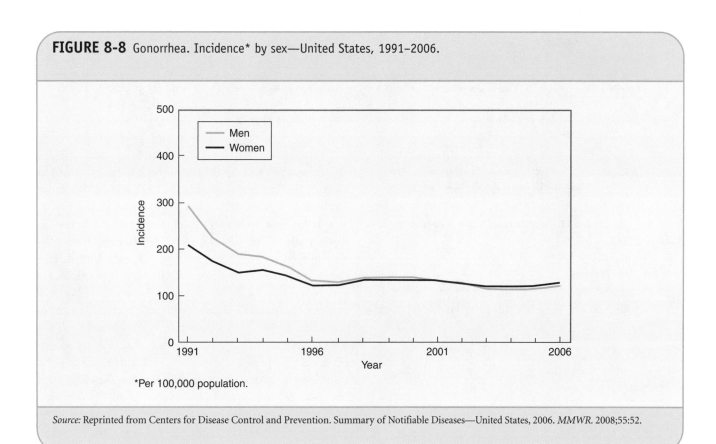

FIGURE 8-8 Gonorrhea. Incidence* by sex—United States, 1991–2006.

*Per 100,000 population.

Source: Reprinted from Centers for Disease Control and Prevention. Summary of Notifiable Diseases—United States, 2006. *MMWR.* 2008;55:52.

FIGURE 8-9 Chlamydia. Incidence* among women—United States and U.S. territories, 2006.

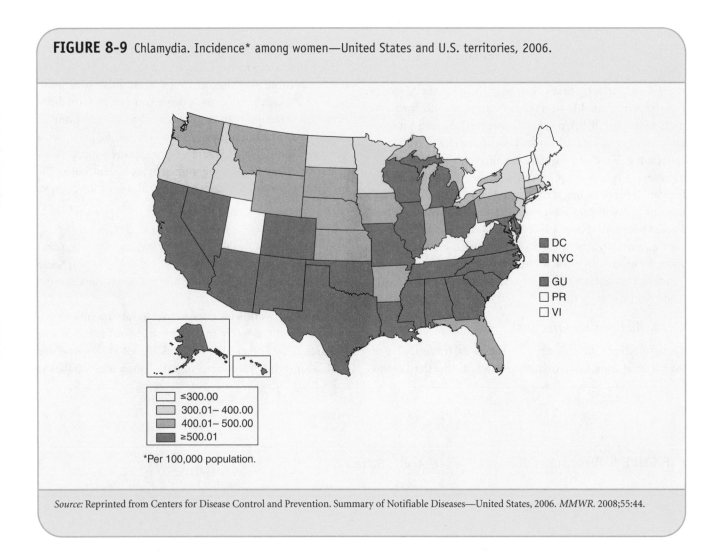

DC
NYC
GU
PR
VI

☐ ≤300.00
▨ 300.01– 400.00
▨ 400.01– 500.00
▨ ≥500.01

*Per 100,000 population.

Source: Reprinted from Centers for Disease Control and Prevention. Summary of Notifiable Diseases—United States, 2006. *MMWR.* 2008;55:44.

diseases in ten states: Connecticut, Georgia, Maryland, Minnesota, New Mexico, Oregon, Tennessee, and parts of California, Colorado, and New York. The FoodNet surveillance program identified 17,883 laboratory-confirmed cases of foodborne infection in 2007.

TABLE 8-5 Examples of Bacterial Agents of Foodborne Illness

Campylobacter	*Listeria monocytogenes*
Clostridium botulinum	*Salmonella*
Clostridium perfringens	*Shigella*
Escherichia coli O157:H7	*Staphylococcus aureus*

An example of a foodborne illness is botulism caused by *Clostridium botulinum*, reported in Figure 8-10. *C. botulinum* produces a potent toxin when it multiplies in food. When ingested, this toxin causes serious illnesses; fortunately, cases of foodborne botulism are uncommon. Approximately twenty-five cases of foodborne botulism are reported in the United States each year, although there are periodic increases in the number of cases as a result of outbreaks. (Refer to Figure 8-10.) Botulism outbreaks have been associated with improperly processed or canned foods. The CDC reports that "home-canned foods and Alaska Native foods consisting of fermented foods of aquatic origin remain the principal sources of foodborne botulism in the United States. During 2006, a multistate outbreak of foodborne botulism was linked to commercial carrot juice."[5(p42)] The most common form of botulism is infant botulism (97 cases in 2006), which has been correlated with ingestion of raw honey.

Refer to the text box for tips about how to prevent foodborne illness.

FIGURE 8-10 Botulism, foodborne. Number of reported cases, by year—United States, 1986–2006.

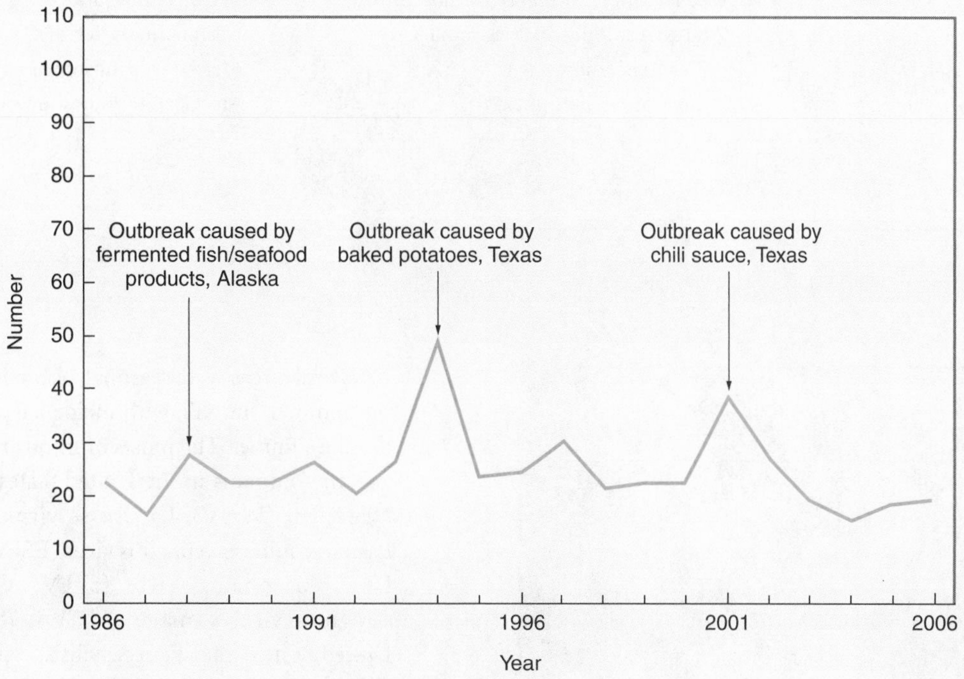

Source: Reprinted from Centers for Disease Control and Prevention. Summary of Notifiable Diseases—United States, 2006. *MMWR.* 2008;55:42.

Preventing foodborne illness

Foodborne illness can be prevented through the following procedures:

- Thoroughly wash hands and surfaces where food is being prepared.
- Avoid cross-contamination—e.g., keep juices from raw chicken and meats away from other foods.
- Cook foods at correct temperatures that are sufficient to kill microorganisms, e.g., 180°F for poultry.
- Use proper storage methods—i.e., in a refrigerator below 40°F. (Don't let your lunch stay in a hot car without refrigeration.)

Vector-Borne Diseases

Table 8-6 presents examples of vector-borne diseases, which include those caused by bacteria, viruses, and parasites. Four bacterially associated vector-borne conditions are Lyme disease, plague, tick-borne relapsing fever, and tularemia. The agent for Lyme disease is *Borrelia burgdorferi*, transmitted by a species of ticks. Lyme disease cases occur in most of the continental United States but have endemic foci on the Atlantic coast, Wisconsin, Minnesota, and sections of California and Oregon. Figure 8-11 shows the distinctive "bull's-eye" skin lesions found in Lyme disease, which can cause arthritis and other serious conditions.

Arthropod-borne viral (arboviral) diseases are responsible for many forms of morbidity including encephalitis and severe neurologic complications. See Figure 8-12 for information on the number of reported cases of arboviral diseases in the United States. According to the CDC,

TABLE 8-6 Examples of Vector-Borne Diseases (Name of vector in parentheses)

Bacterial diseases	Arthropod-borne viral (arboviral) diseases*	Parasitic diseases
Lyme disease (tick)*	Eastern equine encephalitis (mosquito)	Malaria (mosquito)
Plague (flea)	West Nile encephalitis (mosquito)	Leishmaniasis (sandfly)
Tick-borne relapsing fever	Yellow fever (mosquito)	African trypanosomiasis (tsetse fly)
Tularemia (tick—in the United States	Dengue fever (mosquito)*	American trypanosomiasis (kissing bug)

*Discussed in text.

FIGURE 8-11 Lesions of Lyme disease.

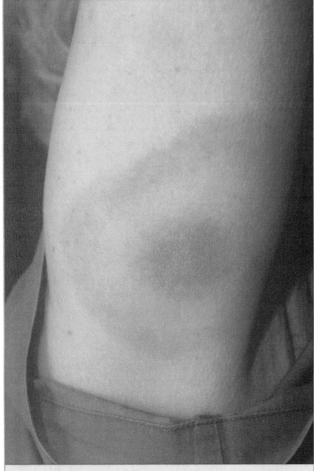

Source: Reprinted from Centers for Disease Control and Prevention. Public Health Image Library ID# 9874. Available at: http://phil.cdc.gov/phil/details.asp. Accessed July 8, 2008.

Arboviral diseases are seasonal, occurring during the summer and fall, with incidence peaking in the late summer. The most common arboviruses affecting humans in the United States are West Nile virus (WNV), La Crosse virus (LACV), Eastern equine encephalitis virus (EEEV), and St. Louis encephalitis virus (SLEV). California serogroup viruses (mainly LACV in the eastern United States) cause encephalitis, especially in children. In 2006, California serogroup virus were [sic] reported from 12 states (Florida, Indiana, Iowa, Louisiana, Michigan, Minnesota, North Carolina, Ohio, South Carolina, Tennessee, West Virginia, and Wisconsin). During 1964–2006, a median of 68 (range: 29–167) cases per year were reported in the United States. EEEV disease in humans is associated with high mortality rates (>20%) and severe neurologic sequelae. In 2006, EEEV cases were reported from four states (Georgia, Louisiana, Massachusetts, and North Carolina). During 1964–2006, a median of five (range: 0–21) cases per year were reported in the United States. Before the introduction of West Nile virus to the United States, SLEV was the nation's leading cause of epidemic viral encephalitis. In 2006, SLEV cases were reported from six states (Arizona, Kentucky, Louisiana, Missouri, New Hampshire, and Ohio). During 1964–2006, a median of 26 (range: 2–1,967) cases per year were reported in the United States.[6(p48)]

Referring back to Table 8-6, you will note that dengue fever is one of the types of arboviral diseases. Transmitted mainly by the *Aedes aegypti* mosquito, the dengue virus has caused epi-

FIGURE 8-12 Domestic arboviral diseases. Number* of reported cases, by year—United States, 1997–2006.

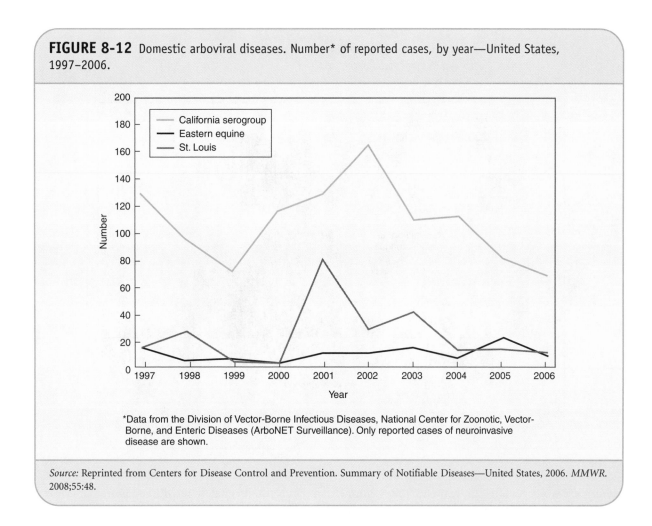

*Data from the Division of Vector-Borne Infectious Diseases, National Center for Zoonotic, Vector-Borne, and Enteric Diseases (ArboNET Surveillance). Only reported cases of neuroinvasive disease are shown.

Source: Reprinted from Centers for Disease Control and Prevention. Summary of Notifiable Diseases—United States, 2006. *MMWR.* 2008;55:48.

demics in Asia and South and Central America. A large proportion of dengue fever infections are asymptomatic. However, dengue fever is a potentially serious infection; the severe form, dengue hemorrhagic fever, causes bleeding at various sites of the body and can progress to life-threatening shock. Figure 8-13 shows the epidemic curve for an outbreak of more than 1,600 cases of dengue fever that occurred along the U.S.-Mexico border in Matamoros, Mexico, and Cameron County in south Texas. Almost all the cases took place in Matamoros, mainly between the months of July and November 2005; the greatest number happened from August through October. The presence of the *Aedes aegypti* mosquito as well as other favorable environmental conditions suggest that the spread of dengue fever is at least a theoretical possibility in south Texas.

Vaccine-Preventable Diseases

Vaccine-preventable diseases (VPDs) are conditions that can be prevented by vaccination (immunization), a procedure in which a vaccine is injected into the body. Some vaccinations are given routinely to children aged 0 to 6 years. Examples of diseases that can be prevented by vaccines include diphtheria, tetanus, whooping cough (pertussis), hepatitis A and hepatitis B, poliomyelitis, pneumococcal diseases, *Haemophilus influenzae* type B, rotavirus gastroenteritis, and measles. With advances in medical science, the list of diseases that can be prevented through vaccination continues to grow. As a result of successful vaccination programs, some diseases, in illustration, poliomyelitis and measles, have shown marked drops in incidence over the span of recent years. Nevertheless, despite these advances, from the global perspective approximately 2.5 million children younger than five years of age died by vaccine-preventable diseases (see Figure 8-14).

Measles is a noteworthy example of a VPD. Caused by the measles virus, the disease can produce a number of significant complications: middle ear infections, pneumonia, and encephalitis. Often a fatal disease in developing countries, the case fatality rate for measles infections can be as high as 30%.[3(p348)] In developed countries, measles occurs mainly

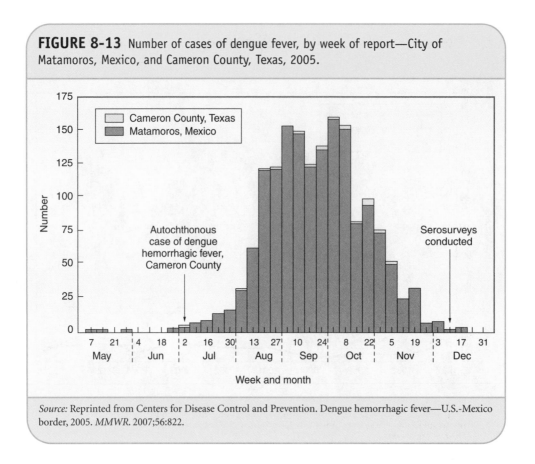

FIGURE 8-13 Number of cases of dengue fever, by week of report—City of Matamoros, Mexico, and Cameron County, Texas, 2005.

Source: Reprinted from Centers for Disease Control and Prevention. Dengue hemorrhagic fever—U.S.-Mexico border, 2005. *MMWR.* 2007;56:822.

among unimmunized persons. With the introduction of measles immunizations, the number of deaths worldwide from measles has dropped dramatically, as shown in Figure 8-15. In 2006, slightly more the 200,000 deaths were estimated to have occurred globally.

Zoonotic Diseases

Zoonotic diseases were defined previously as diseases that can be transmitted from vertebrate animals to human beings. Examples of such diseases are the following:

- Rabies (discussed previously)
- Anthrax (discussed in the section on bioterrorism)
- Avian influenza (bird flu): a form of influenza caused by the H5N1 virus that began to appear in the late 1990s. It is a highly fatal condition that has been linked to transmission between poultry and human beings.
- Hantavirus pulmonary syndrome: an acute viral disease that produces a range of symptoms including fever, muscle pain, stomach ache, respiratory diseases, and low blood pressure. The case fatality rate is about 50%. Certain species of rodents (for example, deer mice) can serve as reservoirs for hantaviruses in the United States. The disease may be transmitted when aerosolized urine and droppings from infected rodents are inhaled.

- Toxoplasmosis: a protozoal infection transmitted from cats. Infection may occur when children ingest dirt that contains the protozoal oocysts from cat feces. Infection during pregnancy can cause death of the fetus.
- Tularemia (rabbit fever): the reservoir of tularemia is wild animals, particularly rabbits. This condition, which is caused by the bacterium *Francisella tularensis*, can in some cases cause fatalities when untreated. The disease can be transmitted by several methods including tick bites, ingestion of inadequately cooked, contaminated food, and inhalation of microbe-laden dust.

As noted for tularemia, some zoonotic diseases are also foodborne illnesses; a second example is trichinosis (trichinellosis), which is associated with the agent *Trichinella spiralis*, the larva of a species of worm. Trichinosis can be acquired by eating raw or undercooked pork and pork products. A third example is variant Creutzfeldt-Jakob disease (vCJD), which has been linked to mad cow disease (bovine spongiform encephalopathy—BSE). Consumption of meat from cattle that have developed BSE (caused by an agent known as a prion) is suspected of causing Creutzfeldt-Jakob disease in humans.

FIGURE 8-14 Percentage of deaths from vaccine-preventable diseases (VPDs) among children aged <5 years, by disease—worldwide, 2002.

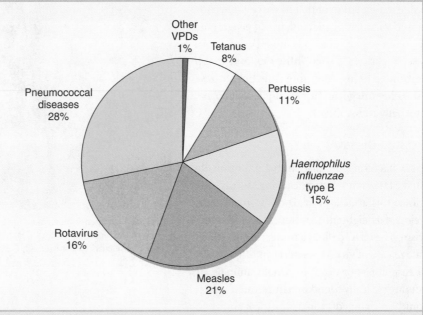

Source: Reprinted from Centers for Disease Control and Prevention. Vaccine preventable deaths and the global immunization vision and strategy, 2006–2015. *MMWR.* 2006;55:512.

FIGURE 8-15 Estimated number of measles deaths, by year—worldwide, 2000–2006.

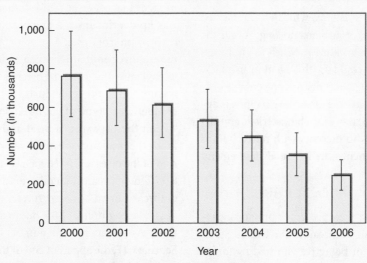

*Uncertainty bounds. Based on Monte Carlo simulations that account for uncertainty in key input variables (e.g., vaccination coverage and case-fatality ratios).

Source: Reprinted from Centers for Disease Control and Prevention. Progress in global measles control and mortality reduction, 2000–2006. MMWR. 2007;56:1240.

Emerging Infectious Diseases (Emerging Infections)

An **emerging infectious disease** is "an infectious disease that has newly appeared in a population or that has been known for some time but is rapidly increasing in incidence or geographic range."[7] Examples of emerging infections are HIV infection, Ebola virus disease, hepatitis C, avian influenza, and *E. coli* O157:H7. In addition to being emerging infections, these diseases also fit into other categories (for example, foodborne, vector-borne, or sexually transmitted).

Bioterrorism-Related Diseases

In fall 2001, anthrax bacteria were distributed intentionally through the United States mail system causing twenty-one cases of illness. Since this attack, officials domestically and globally have developed a heightened awareness of and readiness for bioterrorism. The CDC defines a **bioterrorism attack** as "... the deliberate release of viruses, bacteria, or other germs (agents) used to cause illness or death in people, animals, or plants. These agents are typically found in nature, but it is possible that they could be changed to increase their ability to cause disease, make them resistant to current medicines, or ... increase their ability to be spread into the environment."[8]

The CDC groups agents for bioterrorism according to how easily they may be disseminated and the degree of morbidity and mortality that they produce. The highest priority agents, called category A agents, cause the following diseases: anthrax, botulism, plague, smallpox, tularemia, and viral hemorrhagic fevers such as Ebola.

Consider the example of smallpox, which was eradicated in 1977. Although natural cases of smallpox no longer occur, the virus has been stockpiled in laboratories, which might be accessed by terrorists, who then could use this agent in an attack. Smallpox is a contagious, untreatable disease preventable only by vaccination. The case fatality rate of severe smallpox is approximately 30%. Figure 8-16 shows the characteristic appearance of a smallpox patient, who presents with raised bumps that later can produce permanent scarring and disfigurement.

METHODS OF OUTBREAK INVESTIGATION

Several examples of outbreaks were presented previously: typhoid fever, the salmonellosis outbreak in the United States that initially was suspected of being transmitted by tomatoes, and cryptosporidiosis from inadequately treated water in Wisconsin. In the United States, local health departments (often at the county level and sometimes at the city level), state health departments, and federal agencies (for example, CDC) are charged with the responsibility for tracking the

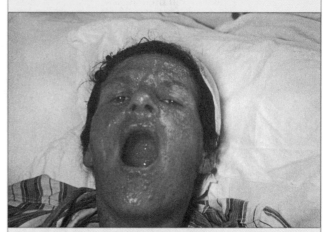

FIGURE 8-16 Smallpox victim.

Source: Reprinted from Centers for Disease Control and Prevention. Public Health Image Library ID# 3333. Available at: http://phil.cdc.gov/phil/details.asp. Accessed July 7, 2008.

cause of infectious disease outbreaks. Several procedures are common to the investigation of such outbreaks. Table 8-7 lists the steps involved in the investigation of an infectious disease outbreak.

Explanations of terms used in Table 8-7:

Clinical observations: The pattern of symptoms suggests possible infectious agents. Disease detectives are interested in a wide range of symptoms such as fever, nausea, diarrhea, vomiting, headache, rashes, and stomach pain.

Epidemic curve: "A graphic plotting of the distribution of cases by time of onset."[1] An epidemic curve may reflect a **common-source epidemic**, which is defined as an "outbreak due to exposure of a group of persons to a noxious influence that is common to the individuals in the group."[1] A **point-source epidemic** is a type of common-source epidemic that occurs "when the exposure is brief and essentially simultaneous, [and] the resultant cases all develop within one incubation period of the disease ..."[1] (Refer also to Chapters 4 and 5.) Figure 8-17 illustrates an epidemic curve for a school gastroenteritis outbreak caused by norovirus, an agent for gastrointestinal illness. The beginning of the outbreak was on February 4, when three cases occurred; the number of cases declined to one on February 17, the apparent end of the outbreak. The number of cases peaked on February 7.

Incubation period: As noted previously, the incubation period is the time interval between invasion of an infectious agent and the appearance of the first signs or symptoms of disease. As part of the investigation of a disease outbreak, the

TABLE 8-7 Steps in the Investigation of an Infectious Disease Outbreak

Procedure	Relevant questions and activities
Define the problem	Verify that an outbreak has occurred; is this a group of related cases that are part of an outbreak or a single sporadic case?
Appraise existing data	Case identification: Track down all cases implicated in the outbreak.
	Clinical observations: Record the pattern of symptoms and collect specimens.
	Tabulations and spot maps: • Plot the epidemic curve • Calculate the incubation period • Calculate attack rates • Map the cases (helpful for environmental studies)
Formulate a hypothesis	Based on a data review, what caused the outbreak?
Confirm the hypothesis	Identify additional cases; conduct laboratory assays to verify causal agent.
Draw conclusions and formulate practical applications	What can be done to prevent similar outbreaks in the future?

Source: Adapted from Friis RH, Sellers TA. *Epidemiology for Public Health Practice,* 4th ed. Sudbury, MA: Jones and Bartlett Publishers; 2009:456–457.

FIGURE 8-17 Number of identified cases (N = 103) in a school gastroenteritis outbreak, by date of symptom onset—District of Columbia, February 2–18, 2007.

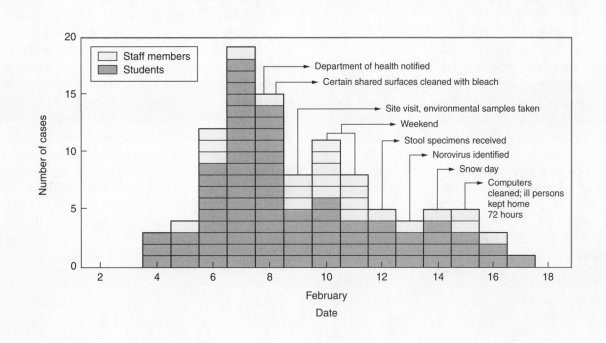

Source: Reprinted from Centers for Disease Control and Prevention. Norovirus outbreak in an elementary school—District of Columbia, February 2007. *MMWR.* 2008;56:1341.

incubation period for each affected person is estimated. From this information, the average and range of incubation periods for the affected group can be computed. In conjunction with information about symptoms, the incubation period provides clues regarding possible infectious disease agents that caused the outbreak. For example, in a foodborne illness outbreak caused by *Salmonella* bacteria, the incubation period would range from 6 to 72 hours, with most cases having an incubation period of 12 to 36 hours.

Attack rate: a type of incidence rate used when the occurrence of disease among a population at risk increases greatly over a short period of time, often related to a specific exposure. The attack rate is frequently used to describe the occurrence of foodborne illness, infectious diseases, and other acute epidemics. The formula for an attack rate is:

$$\text{Attack rate} = \frac{Ill}{Ill + Well} \times 100 \text{ during a time period}$$

Calculation example: Fifty-nine persons ate roast beef suspected of causing a *Salmonella* outbreak. Thirty-four persons fell ill; 25 remained well.
Number ill = 34
Number well = 25
Attack rate = 34/(34 + 25) = 100 = 57.6%

Case mapping: Early in the history of epidemiology (mid-1800s), John Snow used this method to show the location of cholera cases. Mapping procedures can be used to locate cases in relation to environmental exposures to pollution, identify contacts of cases of infectious diseases, and conduct many other innovative health research investigations. The process of case mapping is facilitated by computer hardware and software known as Geographic Information Systems (GIS).

Hypothesis formulation and confirmation: With the foregoing types of information at hand, the epidemiologist is now in a position to suggest (hypothesize) the causative agent for the outbreak and attempt to confirm the hypothesis by trying to locate additional cases and conducting additional laboratory analyses.

Draw conclusions: Once the cause of an outbreak has been determined, the final stage in the investigation is to develop plans for the prevention of future outbreaks. For example, if the outbreak was a foodborne illness that occurred in a restaurant, the epidemiologist could recommend procedures to the management for improved methods of storing and preparing foods. Public health authorities in many localities are required to shut down restaurants that maintain unsanitary conditions until the deficiencies have been corrected.

CONCLUSION

At the beginning of the 1900s, infectious diseases were the leading causes of mortality in the United States. During the twentieth century, improvements in social conditions and advances in medical care led to a reduction in mortality caused by infectious diseases. At present (the beginning of the second decade of the twenty-first century), chronic diseases—heart disease, cancer, and stroke—are the leading causes of death in developed countries. Nevertheless, infectious diseases remain as significant causes of morbidity and mortality in both developed and developing countries. Infectious diseases take a particularly high toll in developing countries. Additionally, they remain a threat to all societies for several reasons. First, new types of diseases, known as emerging infections, are constantly evolving and imperiling public health; second, infectious disease outbreaks caused by acts of bioterrorism are a potential threat; and finally, some of the infectious disease agents, for example, bacteria, have mutated into forms that resist conventional antibiotic treatment, meaning that they could cause increased levels of morbidity and mortality. Outbreaks caused by drug-resistant organisms (e.g., methicillin-resistant *Staphylococcus aureus*—MRSA) in hospitals are potential threats to patients and staff. Foodborne illnesses transmitted by contaminated foods are another infectious disease hazard; foodborne illnesses are capable of creating havoc until their sources have been identified and controlled. With the growing internationalization of the food supply, public health officials are experiencing formidable challenges in tracing the causes of foodborne disease outbreaks. Consequently, given these challenges, infectious disease epidemiology will continue to remain an important application of epidemiology.

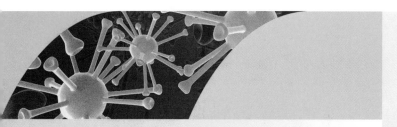

Study Questions and Exercises

1. Define the following terms:
   a. infectious (communicable) disease
   b. parasitic disease
   c. zoonotic disease

2. Explain what is meant by the epidemiologic triangle. Define the three elements of the triangle.

3. Describe the defense mechanisms that can protect a host from infection. Be sure to include the terms immunity (active or passive) and herd immunity.

4. Why are subclinical (also called inapparent) diseases significant for epidemiology and public health?

5. Describe the main differences between direct and indirect transmission of disease agents. Be sure to give examples.

6. What are vectors and how are they involved with the transmission of disease agents? Name three diseases transmitted by vectors.

7. Do the risk patterns for transmission of the HIV virus differ between men and women? Describe gender differences in transmission of the virus.

8. What is the mode of action of the foodborne illness botulism, that is, how does botulism cause its victims to become ill?

9. Describe the steps in investigating an infectious disease outbreak. Why do investigators collect information about clinical symptoms, attack rates, and the incubation period?

10. In your opinion, why are there so many worldwide deaths caused by vaccine-preventable diseases? What would you do in order to reduce this death toll?

Young Epidemiology Scholars (YES) Exercises

The Young Epidemiology Scholars Web site provides links to teaching units and exercises that support instruction in epidemiology. The YES program is administered by the College Board and supported by the Robert Wood Johnson Foundation. The Web address of YES is www.collegeboard.com/yes. The following exercises relate to topics discussed in this chapter and can be found on the YES Web site.

1. Fraser DW. An outbreak of Legionnaires' disease.

2. Huang FI, Bayona M. Disease outbreak investigation.

3. Klaucke D, Vogt R. Outbreak investigation at a Vermont community hospital.

REFERENCES

1. Porta M, ed. *A Dictionary of Epidemiology.* 5th ed. New York: Oxford University Press; 2008.

2. Centers for Disease Control and Prevention. About parasites. Available at: http://www.cdc.gov/ncidod/dpd/aboutparasites.htm. Accessed June 30, 2008.

3. Heymann DL, ed. *Control of Communicable Diseases Manual.* 19th ed. Washington, DC: American Public Health Association; 2008.

4. Olsen SJ, Chang H-L, Cheung TY-Y, et al. Transmission of the severe acute respiratory syndrome on aircraft. *N Engl J Med.* 2003; 349:2416–2422.

5. Centers for Disease Control and Prevention. Summary of Notifiable Diseases—United States, 2006. *MMWR.* 2008;55:42.

6. Centers for Disease Control and Prevention. Summary of Notifiable Diseases—United States, 2006. *MMWR.* 2008;55:48.

7. MedicineNet.com. Definition of emerging infectious disease. Available at: http://www.medterms.com/script/main/art.asp?articlekey=22801. Accessed July 23, 2008.

8. Centers for Disease Control and Prevention. Bioterrorism Overview: What is bioterrorism? Available at: http://www.bt.cdc.gov/bioterrorism/overview.asp. Accessed August 25, 2008.

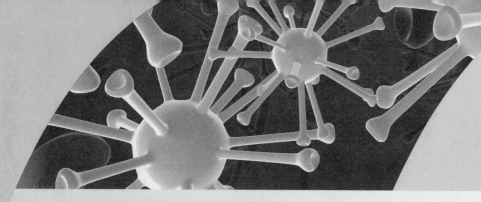

CHAPTER 9

Social and Behavioral Epidemiology

LEARNING OBJECTIVES

By the end of this chapter you will be able to:

- Give two examples of how lifestyle is associated with negative health outcomes
- State the linkage between tobacco use and adverse health outcomes
- Describe the epidemiology of one form of substance abuse
- Describe the epidemiology of two important mental disorders

CHAPTER OUTLINE

INTRODUCTION

Social and behavioral dimensions that impact human health include social adversities (for example, poverty and discrimination), stress, and lifestyle practices. **Lifestyle** is defined as the choice of behavioral factors that affect how we live; these choices often are a function of social influences. Epidemiologists have developed an increasing awareness of the associ-

TABLE 9-1 List of Important Terms Used in This Chapter

Autism	Passive smoking
Behavioral epidemiology	Posttraumatic stress disorder
Binge drinking	Psychiatric comorbidity
Body mass index (BMI)	Psychiatric epidemiology
Chronic strains	Social epidemiology
Coping skills	Social support
Lifestyle	Stress
Meth mouth	Stressful life events

Source: Author.

ation of social and behavioral factors with human illnesses. There is a strong relationship between personal behavior and many chronic diseases, including heart disease, cancer, and stroke. Consequently, by encouraging people to adopt healthful lifestyles, the public health community might be able to prevent or limit the effects of chronic diseases and other conditions related to behavioral practices. Nevertheless, the impact of these factors on human health tends to be unrecognized and needs to be given more attention.

Tied in with the broad topic of social and behavioral factors related to health are mental disorders. Such disorders can be the consequence of social factors, including stress and social adversities. Mental disorders are also associated with choice of lifestyle, as in the case of depressive symptomatology that leads to inactivity and substance use disorders that are associated with abuse of legal and illegal drugs. Later in the chapter, the applications of epidemiology to the study of mental disorders will be covered in more detail. Refer to Table 9-1 for a list of important terms used in this chapter.

Social epidemiology is the discipline that examines ". . . the social distribution and social determinants of states of health."[1(p6)] Some of the topics that the discipline covers are the relationship between socioeconomic status and health, the effect of social relationships (social support) upon health outcomes, the epidemiology of mental disorders (e.g., the association of stress with mental disorders), and how social factors affect the choice of health-related behaviors. Many social determinants are a function of how society is structured and are beyond the control of the individual; others are related to modifiable personal behavioral choices and lifestyle characteristics.

The term **behavioral epidemiology** is defined as the study of the role of behavioral factors in health. The contributions of unhealthful behaviors (e.g., consumption of high-fat foods, sedentary lifestyle, and cigarette smoking) to adverse health outcomes (e.g., obesity, diabetes, and asthma) have been documented.[2] These behavioral choices often begin during childhood and adolescence and carry over into the adult years. For example, teenage smoking and binge drinking represent personal choices, although peer pressure and advertising influence their uptake. Other lifestyle dimensions relate to improper dietary choices, substance abuse (e.g., methamphetamine and cocaine use), and avoiding exercise.

STRESS AND HEALTH

The term **stress** has been defined in a number of ways, one being ". . . a physical, chemical, or emotional factor that causes bodily or mental tension and may be a factor in disease causation."[3] Figure 9-1 symbolizes the effect of stress upon the human brain. Stress has been studied in relation to a range of adverse health effects:

- cardiovascular disease
- substance abuse
- mental disorders including posttraumatic stress disorder
- work-related anxiety and neurotic disorders
- chronic diseases such as cancer and asthma
- impaired immune function

Stressful life events are stressors (sources of stress) that arise from happenings such as job loss, financial problems, and death of a close family member. Events fall into domains

such as health related, monetary, employment associated, and interpersonal. Stressful life events may be classified as either positive or negative. Those events that are associated with adverse life circumstances are called **negative life events**; examples of negative life events are being fired at work or being arrested and incarcerated. Examples of **positive life events** are graduation from school, marriage, and the birth of a new child. According to the theory of stressful life events, the more salient the life event and the higher the frequency of events, the greater is the chance that an adverse health outcome will occur. Life events that are sustained over a long period of time are known as **chronic strains**.

Although there are several measures of stress, one common approach for its measurement is to tally the number of stressful life events that an individual has experienced during a defined time period. Some life events measures use a weighting scheme that assigns more importance to some events than others; other measures give equal weight to each item. Researchers Holmes and Rahe are credited with the development during the late 1960s of the life events approach to measurement of stress; their measure was a weighted checklist (the Schedule of Recent Experiences) that comprised forty-three items.[4] Subsequently, longer checklists and other modifications have been developed. However, it has been noted that ". . . researchers still lack a coherent definition of stress or a

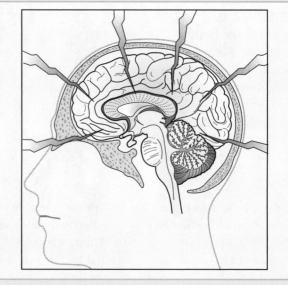

FIGURE 9-1 Illustration of brain under stress. Stress is hypothesized to impact the brain, causing physical and mental health effects.

Source: Reprinted from National Institutes of Health, National Institute on Drug Abuse (NIDA). Available at: http://www.drugabuse.gov/DrugPages/PSAartcards/stress.pdf. Accessed July 23, 2008.

classification of stressors, stress responses, and long-term effects of stress that can be applied across species and environments."[5]

Several investigations have explored the association between experience of stressful life events and physical and mental health outcomes.[6] A prospective study followed children with asthma, measuring the association between strongly negative life events and risk of a new asthma attack. Stressful life events were followed with new attacks immediately after the event; a delayed response after about 5–7 weeks also followed severe events.[7] In a Finnish cohort study, stressful life events were examined in relationship to breast cancer. The data came from 10,808 women from the Finnish Twin Cohort. Three negative life events (divorce or separation, death of a husband, and death of a close relative or friend) each predicted increased breast cancer risk.[8]

Posttraumatic Stress Disorder

The term **posttraumatic stress disorder (PTSD)** refers to ". . . an anxiety disorder that some people develop after seeing or living through an event that caused or threatened serious harm or death. Symptoms include flashbacks or bad dreams, emotional numbness, intense guilt or worry, angry outbursts, feeling 'on edge', or avoiding thoughts and situations that remind them of the trauma. In PTSD, these symptoms last at least one month."[9] PTSD may affect people who have undergone traumatic events in the community. Also vulnerable are soldiers (Figure 9-2) and civilians during wartime. PTSD was found to affect mothers responsible for child rearing who were exposed to traumatic events during armed conflict in Kabul Province, Afghanistan[10]; such events included shelling or rocket attacks, bomb explosions, and the murder of family members or relatives. As a result of armed conflict, these women experienced hardships in meeting their basic needs for food, water, and shelter. Their ability to take care of their children also was impaired.

The Veterans Health Study is a longitudinal investigation of the health of a repre-sentative sample of male veterans who are outpatients at Department of Veterans Affairs hospitals.[11] Data from this study indicated that 20% of the sample met the screening criteria of PTSD. In comparison with veterans who had not been so diagnosed, those who had PTSD reported higher levels of both health problems and healthcare utilization. This generalization applies to male veterans who had higher rates of health services use[12] as well as female veterans.[13]

Not all people who are under stress develop illnesses; in fact, for some people stress may be a positive experience that challenges one toward greater accomplishment. One of the factors associated with ability to deal with stress is **social support**, which refers to help that we receive from other people when we are under stress. Friends, relatives, and significant others often are able to provide material and emotional support during times of stress.

Coping skills are techniques for managing or removing sources of stress. Effective coping skills help to mitigate the effects of stress. Here is an example: Suppose that a person does not have enough money to pay for routine living expenses. An effective coping skill would be to either lower one's expenses or find employment that pays a higher income. That individual might also request a loan from friends or family members.

FIGURE 9-2 Military conflict: a setting for posttraumatic stress disorder.

Work-Related Stress

Stress, a common feature of most occupations, includes work overload, time pressures, threat of job layoff and unemployment, interpersonal conflicts, and inadequate compensation. The National Institute for Occupational Safety and Health states that "The nature of work is changing at whirlwind speed. Perhaps now more than ever before, job stress poses a threat to the health of workers and, in turn, to the health [of] organizations."[14]

The United States Bureau of Labor Statistics (BLS) collects information on fatal and nonfatal work-related injuries as well as anxiety, stress, and neurotic disorders. The "BLS reported 5,659 anxiety, stress, and neurotic disorder cases involving days away from work in 2001.... Rates declined 25% between 1992 and 2001, from 0.8 per 10,000 full-time workers in 1992 to 0.6 in 2001 ... [refer to Figure 9-3]. In 2001, most cases involved workers who were aged 25–54 (78.3%) ..., female ..., and white, non-Hispanic (64.8%).... Two occupational groups accounted for more than 63% of all anxiety, stress, and neurotic disorder cases in 2001: technical, sales, and administrative support (39.9% or 2,250 cases) and managerial and professional specialty occupations (23.6% or 1,331 cases)...."[15 (p34)] High rates of anxiety, stress, and neurotic disorders were reported for the finance, insurance, and real estate fields.

TOBACCO USE

Cigarette smoking and other forms of tobacco use (e.g., inhalation of tobacco smoke from water pipes and chew tobacco) increase the risk of many forms of adverse health outcomes. These conditions include lung diseases, coronary heart disease, stroke, and cancer. The second leading cause of death in the United States is cancer (malignant neoplasms); lung cancer is the leading cause of cancer death among both men and women. Lung cancer is causally associated with smoking, as are cancer of the cervix, kidney, oral cavity, pancreas, and stomach. Pregnant women who smoke risk damage (e.g., stillbirth, low birth weight, and sudden infant death syndrome) to their developing fetuses.

Between 1965 and 2005, the prevalence of adult current smokers in the United States declined sharply among men, from more than 50% to about 23%, and less steeply from about 30% to about 19% among women.[16] (In 2007, 22.7% of men and 17.4% of women were current smokers.[17]) There also was a declining trend in the percentage of women who smoked during pregnancy—from about 20% in the late 1980s to about 10% in 2002 (refer to Figure 9-4). The figure also shows the percentage of high school students who smoked. The line for high school students begins in 1990. Until the mid-1990s, smoking among high

FIGURE 9-3 Annual rates of anxiety, stress, and neurotic disorder cases involving days away from work in private industry, 1992–2001.

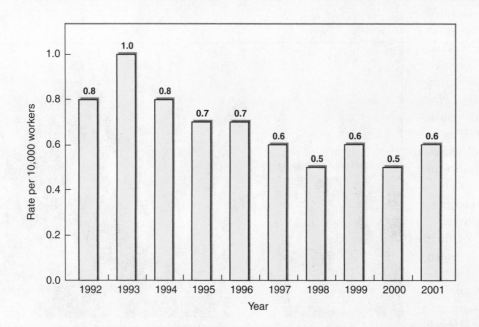

Source: Reprinted from Centers for Disease Control and Prevention, National Institute for Occupational Safety and Health. *Worker Health Chartbook, 2004.* Cincinnati, OH: DHHS (NIOSH) Publication No. 2004-146. September 2004:35.

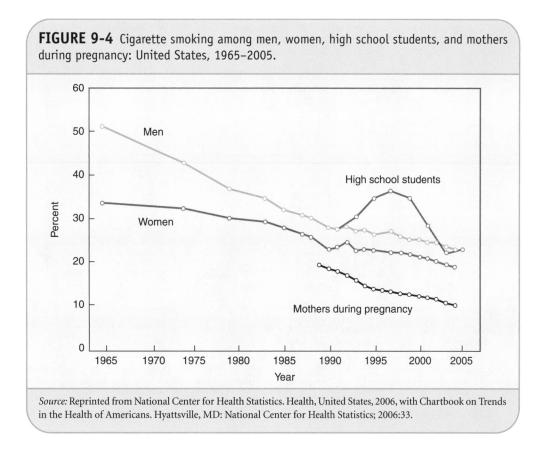

FIGURE 9-4 Cigarette smoking among men, women, high school students, and mothers during pregnancy: United States, 1965–2005.

Source: Reprinted from National Center for Health Statistics. Health, United States, 2006, with Chartbook on Trends in the Health of Americans. Hyattsville, MD: National Center for Health Statistics; 2006:33.

school students showed an increasing trend to a prevalence of almost 40%. Following this increase, the prevalence decreased.

In 2002, the overall percentage of high school students (both genders) who were current cigarette smokers was similar to the level among adult men in the United States. According to the National Youth Tobacco Survey (NYTS) conducted in 2002, the prevalence of current cigarette smokers was 22.5% (Figure 9-5), with 23.9% among male students and 21.0% among female students.[18] At the middle school level, the prevalence of current cigarette smoking was 9.8% and was not significantly different between male and female students.

Regarding use of any tobacco product by high school students, 28.2% were current users (32.6% for male students versus 23.7% for female students). The percentage of middle school students who were current users of any tobacco product was 13.3% (14.7% and 11.7% among males and females, respectively). Among both middle school and high school students, current use of tobacco was most common for the following three products: cigarettes followed by cigars and smokeless tobacco.

The NYTS also queried respondents about "ever use" of tobacco. Cigarettes were the most common form of tobacco that was ever used; a total of 57.4% of high school students

reported ever use of cigarettes. (See Figure 9-6.) "Ever use of tobacco products was determined by asking students if they had ever tried cigarettes, even one or two puffs; tried smoking cigars, cigarillos, or little cigars, even one or two puffs; used chewing tobacco, snuff, or dip, such as Redman®, Levi Garrett®, Beechnut®, Skoal®, Skoal Bandits®, or Copenhagen®; tried smoking bidis, even one or two puffs; or tried smoking kreteks, even one or two puffs."[18(p4)]

The NYTS questioned middle school and high school students who currently smoke cigarettes regarding how they obtain cigarettes, e.g., purchase them in a store or from a vending machine, ask other people to purchase the cigarettes, borrow them, or even steal them. Middle school students acquired their cigarettes most typically by borrowing them from someone, having someone else buy them, or stealing them. High school students obtained their cigarettes by asking someone else to buy them, buying them in a store, or borrowing them from someone else. (Refer to Figure 9-7.)

Exposure to Secondhand Smoke

The term **passive smoking**, also known as secondhand or side-stream exposure to cigarette smoke, refers to the involuntary breathing of cigarette smoke by nonsmokers in an environ-

FIGURE 9-5 Percentage of all middle school and high school students who were current users of any tobacco product,* by type of tobacco product—National Youth Tobacco Survey, United States, 2002.

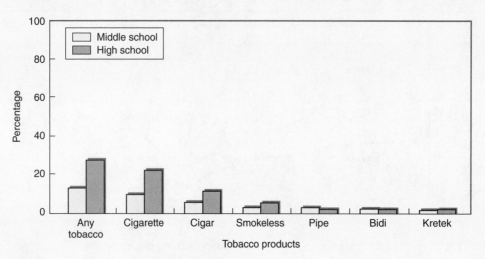

* Use of cigarettes, cigars, smokeless tobacco, pipe tobacco, bidis, or kreteks on ≥1 of the 30 days preceding the survey.

Source: Reprinted from Marshall L, Schooley M, Ryan H, et al. Youth tobacco surveillance—United States, 2001–2002. In: Surveillance Summaries, May 19, 2006. *MMWR.* 2006;55(No. SS-3):5.

FIGURE 9-6 Percentage of all middle school and high school students who ever used tobacco, by type of tobacco product—National Youth Tobacco Survey, United States, 2002.

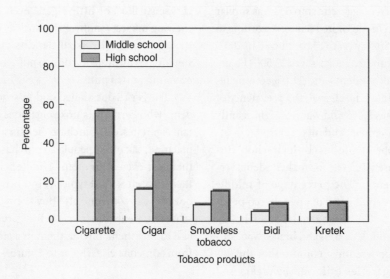

Source: Reprinted from Marshall L, Schooley M, Ryan H, et al. Youth tobacco surveillance—United States, 2001–2002. In: Surveillance Summaries, May 19, 2006. *MMWR.* 2006;55(No. SS-3):4.

FIGURE 9-7 Percentage of current cigarette smokers* aged <18 years in middle school and high school who obtained cigarettes, by usual methods of obtainment—National Youth Tobacco Survey, United States, 2002.

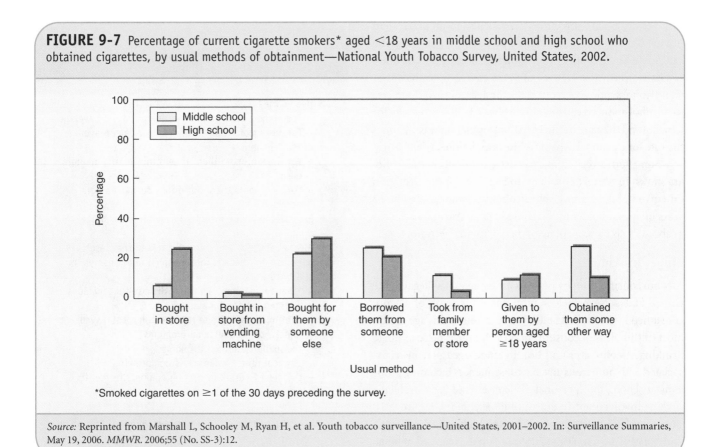

*Smoked cigarettes on ≥1 of the 30 days preceding the survey.

Source: Reprinted from Marshall L, Schooley M, Ryan H, et al. Youth tobacco surveillance—United States, 2001–2002. In: Surveillance Summaries, May 19, 2006. *MMWR.* 2006;55 (No. SS-3):12.

ment where there are cigarette smokers present. Exposure to secondhand smoke may occur in work settings, airports, restaurants, bars, and any other area where smokers gather. In June 2006, the U.S. Surgeon General published a report titled *The Health Consequences of Involuntary Exposure to Tobacco Smoke*, which concluded that "Secondhand smoke exposure causes disease and premature death in children and in adults who do not smoke."[19(p9)] The adverse health effects of such exposure among adults include heart disease and lung cancer. Among children, secondhand smoke increases the "risk for sudden infant death syndrome (SIDS), acute respiratory infections, ear problems, and more severe asthma. (Refer to Figure 9-8.) Smoking by parents causes respiratory symptoms and slows lung growth in their children."[19 (p9)]

ALCOHOL CONSUMPTION

Data from the CDC's National Center for Health Statistics indicate that alcohol consumption is a significant cause of mortality in the United States. In 2005, the age-adjusted death rate for alcohol-induced causes was 7.3 per 100,000 population. "In 2005, a total of 21,634 persons died of alcohol-induced causes in the United States. . . .The category 'alcohol-induced causes'

FIGURE 9-8 Secondhand smoke is dangerous to children. Smoking around children can cause sudden infant death.

Source: © Adam Borkowski/ShutterStock, Inc.

includes not only deaths from dependent and nondependent use of alcohol but also accidental poisoning by alcohol. The category excludes unintentional injuries, homicides, and other causes indirectly related to alcohol use as well as deaths due to fetal alcohol syndrome.... In 2005, the age-adjusted death rate for alcohol-induced causes for males was 3.2 times the rate for females, and the rate for the Hispanic population was 1.3 times the rate for the non-Hispanic white population...."[20(p10)]

Some terms related to excessive consumption of alcohol are shown in the text box. Refer to Figure 9-9 for information on current, binge, and heavy alcohol use among persons 12 years of age and older in the United States. Alcohol use peaks at about 21 to 25 years of age, when drinking becomes legal.

Binge Drinking

Alcohol consumption by persons under age 21 is illegal in the United States. Nevertheless, more than one-tenth of alcohol consumed in the United States is by persons in this age group; most of this alcohol consumption (90%) takes place as binge drinking. Alcohol consumption by underaged persons is associated with numerous adverse consequences including problems at school, interpersonal difficulties, and legal problems such as involvement in automobile accidents. Figure 9-10 shows levels of binge drinking among high school students; more than 30% of males and 25% of females engaged in binge drinking during 2005.

Alcohol terms

- Heavy drinking
  - For women, more than one drink per day on average
  - For men, more than two drinks per day on average
- Binge drinking
  - For women, more than three drinks during a single occasion
  - For men, more than four drinks during a single occasion
- Excessive drinking includes heavy drinking, binge drinking, or both
- Alcohol abuse is a pattern of drinking that results in harm to one's health, interpersonal relationships, or ability to work
- Alcohol dependence, a chronic disease that includes
  - a strong craving for alcohol
  - continued use despite repeated physical, psychological, or interpersonal problems
  - the inability to limit drinking
  - physical illness when one stops drinking
  - the need to drink increasing amounts to feel its effects

Source: Adapted from Centers for Disease Control and Prevention. Alcohol Terms. Available at: http://www.cdc.gov/alcohol/terms.htm. Accessed July 24, 2008.

FIGURE 9-9 Current, binge, and heavy alcohol use among persons aged 12 or older, by age: 2006.

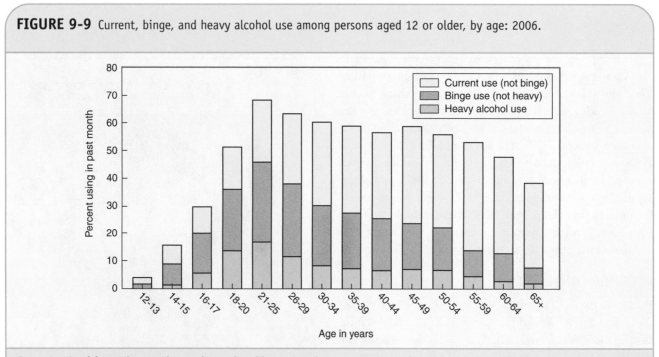

Source: Reprinted from Substance Abuse and Mental Health Services Administration. *Results from the 2006 National Survey on Drug Use and Health: National Findings* (Office of Applied Studies, NSDUH Series H-32, DHHS Publication No. SMA 07-4293). Rockville, MD; 2007:32.

FIGURE 9-10 Binge drinking among high school students, by sex, grade level, and year: United States, 1991, 1993, 2003, and 2005.

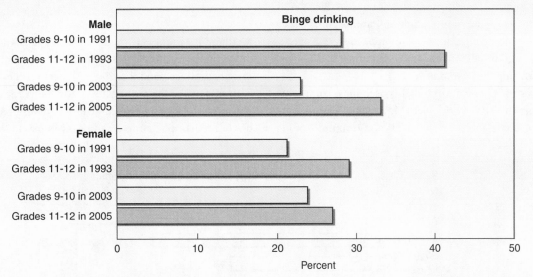

NOTE: In this study, binge drinking is drinking five or more drinks of alcohol in a row on one or more of the 30 days preceding the Youth Risk Behavior Survey.

Source: Adapted and reprinted from National Center for Health Statistics. *Health, United States, 2006, with Chartbook on Trends in the Health of Americans.* Hyattsville, MD: National Center for Health Statistics; 2006:35.

Binge drinking among college students is also a matter of concern because of its association with health problems such as increased rates of sexually transmitted diseases, unintended pregnancies, violence, unintentional injuries, and possible alcohol poisoning. In 2005, 19.5% of full-time college students and 13.0% of part-time college students reported heavy alcohol use. Thus, persons aged 18 to 22 who were enrolled in college full-time were more likely to be heavy users of alcohol than those who were enrolled part-time or were not currently enrolled in college.[21] (Refer to Figure 9-11.)

FIGURE 9-11 Heavy alcohol use among adults aged 18 to 22, by college enrollment: 2002–2006.

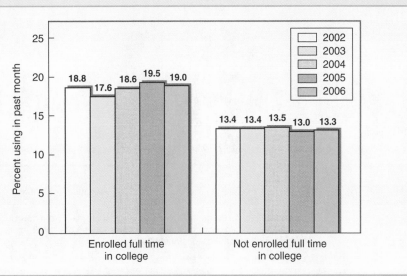

Source: Reprinted from Substance Abuse and Mental Health Services Administration. *Results from the 2006 National Survey on Drug Use and Health: National Findings* (Office of Applied Studies, NSDUH Series H-32, DHHS Publication No. SMA 07-4293). Rockville, MD; 2007:36.

SUBSTANCE ABUSE

Figure 9-12 shows estimates of the numbers of illicit drug users during 2006. The figure presents the distribution of use during the past month according to different types of illicit drugs such as marijuana, methamphetamines, and heroin. Other drugs that are abused include prescription painkillers. Approximately 5.2 million persons indicated that they had abused painkillers during the past month.

Marijuana is the illicit drug that is used most commonly among all persons aged 12 or older (14.8 million "past month" users during 2006). Use of marijuana is also common among high school students; approximately 25% of male high school students reported using marijuana in 2005; the percentage for female students was slightly less than 20%. (Refer to Figure 9-13.)

Methamphetamines

Methamphetamines are highly addictive substances that have powerful, stimulating effects upon the body. In most cases the drug is produced and distributed illegally. Ingestion of large amounts of the drug can cause body temperature to rise to dangerous levels and also can cause convulsions. Long-term use of methamphetamines can result in psychotic symptoms

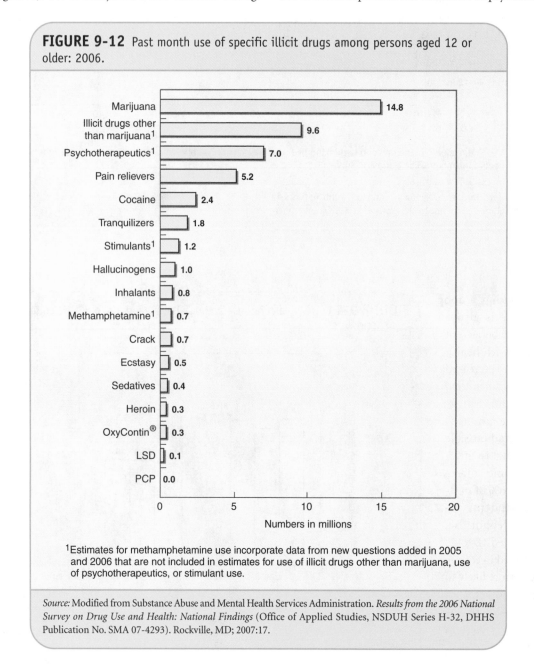

FIGURE 9-12 Past month use of specific illicit drugs among persons aged 12 or older: 2006.

[1]Estimates for methamphetamine use incorporate data from new questions added in 2005 and 2006 that are not included in estimates for use of illicit drugs other than marijuana, use of psychotherapeutics, or stimulant use.

Source: Modified from Substance Abuse and Mental Health Services Administration. *Results from the 2006 National Survey on Drug Use and Health: National Findings* (Office of Applied Studies, NSDUH Series H-32, DHHS Publication No. SMA 07-4293). Rockville, MD; 2007:17.

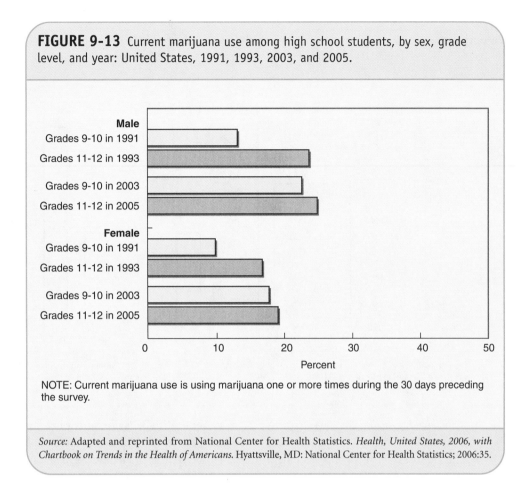

FIGURE 9-13 Current marijuana use among high school students, by sex, grade level, and year: United States, 1991, 1993, 2003, and 2005.

NOTE: Current marijuana use is using marijuana one or more times during the 30 days preceding the survey.

Source: Adapted and reprinted from National Center for Health Statistics. *Health, United States, 2006, with Chartbook on Trends in the Health of Americans.* Hyattsville, MD: National Center for Health Statistics; 2006:35.

such as paranoia. Some users are affected with the crank bug, a sensation of bugs crawling underneath or on top of the skin, causing victims to abrade their skin until it is raw and bleeding. Another consequence of methamphetamine use is known as **meth mouth**, a condition that contributes to decay and loss of teeth. The cause is reduced output of saliva, increased consumption of sugary carbonated beverages, and neglect of personal hygiene (e.g., tooth brushing). Refer to Figure 9-14 for a picture of meth mouth.

Use of methamphetamines is fairly common in the United States. The Substance Abuse and Mental Health Services Administration reported that "in 2004, 1.4 million persons aged 12 or older (0.6 percent of the population) had used methamphetamine in the past year, and 600,000 (0.2 percent) had used it in the past month."[22] Figure 9-15 (left side) shows the number of methamphetamine users who used methamphetamine in the past month classified according to whether they met the criteria for abuse of or dependence on one or more illicit drugs in the past 12 months. The number of people who were either dependent on or an abuser of a stimulant drug or had a history of other illicit

FIGURE 9-14 Meth mouth.

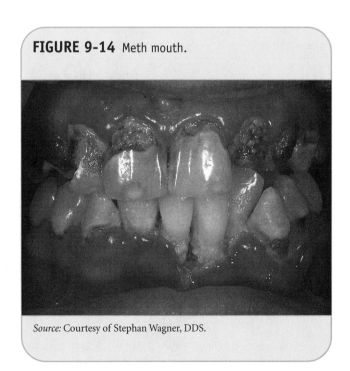

Source: Courtesy of Stephan Wagner, DDS.

FIGURE 9-15 Methamphetamine use in past month among persons aged 12 or older, by dependence and abuse: 2002, 2003, and 2004 (left); and methamphetamine use in past year among persons aged 12 or older, by gender and age: 2002, 2003, and 2004 (right).

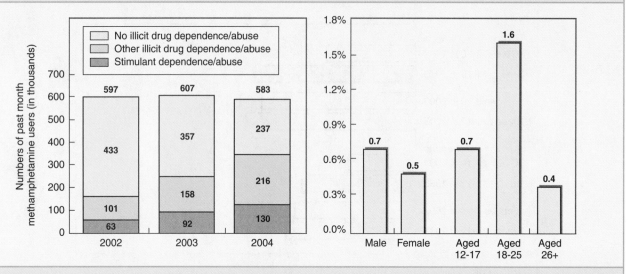

Source: Reprinted from U.S. Department of Health and Human Services, Substance Abuse & Mental Health Services Administration, Office of Applied Studies. *The NSDUH Report: Methamphetamine Use, Abuse, and Dependence: 2002, 2003, and 2004.* September 16, 2005. Available at: http://oas.samhsa.gov/2k5/meth/meth.pdf. Accessed August 31, 2008.

drug dependence or abuse increased from 2002 to 2004. Figure 9-15 (right side) shows the prevalence of methamphetamine use by demographic group. The prevalence of methamphetamine use was higher among males than among females and highest among young adults aged 18 to 25 years (1.6%).

The Youth Risk Behavior Survey investigated high school students' lifetime use of heroin or methamphetamines during 2007. The percentage of lifetime use of heroin among U.S. high school students was 2.3%; for methamphetamines it was 4.4%. (Refer to Table 9-2.)

TABLE 9-2 Percentage of High School Students Who Used Heroin* and Who Used Methamphetamines,† by Sex, Race/Ethnicity, and Grade—United States, Youth Risk Behavior Survey, 2007

	Lifetime heroin use						Lifetime methamphetamine use					
	Female		Male		Total		Female		Male		Total	
Category	%	CI§	%	CI	%	CI	%	CI	%	CI	%	CI
Race/ Ethnicity												
White¶	1.3	0.9–2.0	2.1	1.4–3.2	1.7	1.2–2.4	4.5	3.3–6.0	4.4	3.4–5.6	4.5	3.5–5.6
Black¶	0.7	0.3–1.5	2.9	1.8–4.7	1.8	1.2–2.7	0.8	0.4–1.5	3.0	1.9–4.8	1.9	1.3–2.9
Hispanic	3.3	1.8–6.0	4.0	2.8–5.7	3.7	2.5–5.2	5.3	3.6–7.8	6.1	4.2–8.7	5.7	4.1–7.9
Grade												
9	2.1	1.2–3.7	3.0	2.2–4.2	2.6	1.9–3.5	3.4	2.3–4.9	3.7	2.5–5.3	3.6	2.7–4.7
10	1.6	1.0–2.6	1.9	1.3–2.8	1.8	1.3–2.4	4.2	3.0–5.9	4.0	2.9–5.5	4.1	3.2–5.3
11	1.2	0.7–2.0	2.4	1.6–3.6	1.8	1.2–2.6	5.3	3.7–7.7	5.4	4.1–7.1	5.4	4.1–7.1
12	1.3	0.7–2.4	4.0	2.7–5.8	2.6	1.9–3.6	3.5	2.5–4.8	5.6	4.1–7.6	4.5	3.4–6.0
Total	**1.6**	**1.1–2.3**	**2.9**	**2.3–3.6**	**2.3**	**1.8–2.8**	**4.1**	**3.2–5.3**	**4.6**	**3.8–5.5**	**4.4**	**3.7–5.3**

*Used heroin (also called "smack," "junk," or "China White") one or more times during their life.
†Used methamphetamines (also called "speed," "crystal," "crank," or "ice") one or more times during their life.
§95% confidence interval.
¶Non-Hispanic.
Source: Reprinted from Eaton DK, Kann L, Kinchen S, et al. Youth risk behavior surveillance—United States, 2007. In: Surveillance Summaries, June 6, 2008. *MMWR.* 2008;57(No. SS-4):83.

OVERWEIGHT AND OBESITY

Media reports inform us that both overweight and obesity are increasing in prevalence in the United States. Being overweight or obese impacts the quality of one's life and increases the risk of chronic diseases such as coronary heart disease and diabetes. Obesity is related to higher healthcare costs and premature death.[23] Among the factors associated with overweight and obesity are inactivity (sedentary lifestyle) and consumption of high-calorie foods.

A measure of overweight and obesity, body mass index (BMI) takes into account both a person's weight and height. **BMI** is defined as body weight in kilograms divided by height in meters squared. A BMI of 25.0 to 29.9 classifies a person as being overweight; a BMI of 30 or higher classifies a person as being obese. (Refer to Table 9-3, which shows BMI levels for a person who is 5'9" tall.)

Figure 9-16 shows trends in child and adolescent overweight. From the mid-1960s until 2003–2004, the percentages of children and adolescents who were overweight rose steadily. Almost 15% of children aged 2 to 5 years were overweight in 2003; nearly 20% of preadolescents and adolescents were overweight. This phenomenon has ominous implications for the future incidence of chronic diseases and reduced life expectancy in the United States.

TABLE 9-3 Determining Overweight and Obesity

Height	Weight Range	BMI	Considered
	124 lbs or less	Below 18.5	Underweight
	125 lbs to 168 lbs	18.5 to 24.9	Healthy weight
5'9"	169 lbs to 202 lbs	25.0 to 29.9	Overweight
	203 lbs or more	30 or higher	Obese

Source: Reprinted from Centers for Disease Control and Prevention. Defining Overweight and Obesity. Available at: http://www.cdc.gov/nccdphp/dnpa/obesity/defining.htm. Accessed July 24, 2008.

FIGURE 9-16 Trends in child and adolescent overweight.

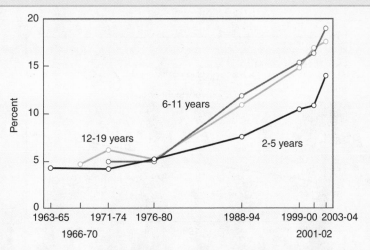

NOTE: Overweight is defined as BMI ≥ gender- and weight-specific 95th percentile from the 2000 CDC Growth Charts. Source: National Health Examination Surveys II (ages 6-11) and III (ages 12-17), National Health and Nutrition Examination Surveys I, II, III and 1999-2004, NCHS, CDC.

Source: Reprinted from Centers for Disease Control and Prevention, National Center for Health Statistics. Prevalence of Overweight Among Children and Adolescents: United States, 2003-2004. Available at: http://www.cdc.gov/nchs/products/pubs/pubd/hestats/overweight/overwght_child_03.htm. Accessed July 27, 2008.

Similar to the trends for children and teenagers, the levels of obesity among adults aged 20 years and older have increased. The National Health and Nutrition Examination Survey III (NHANES III) in 1988 through 1994 found that 56% of U.S. adults were either overweight or obese and 22.9% were obese; in 2003 through 2004, the NHANES survey indicated that 66.3% of adults were either overweight or obese and 32.2% were obese. These data are reported in Table 9-4 and Figure 9-17.

In 2007, the overall prevalence of obesity among adults in the United States was 25.6%. However, the prevalence of obesity showed substantial regional variations, being higher in the South (27.3%) and Midwest (26.5%) and lower in the Northeast (24.4%) and West (23.1%). Among states, the prevalence of obesity ranged from 18.7% in Colorado to 32.0% in Mississippi. In addition to Mississippi, the two other states that had a prevalence of obesity greater than 30% were Alabama (30.3%) and Tennessee (31.1%). (Refer to Figure 9-18.)

TABLE 9-4 Age-Adjusted* Prevalence of Overweight and Obesity among U.S. Adults, Age 20 Years and Over

	NHANES III (1988–94) (n = 16,679)	NHANES (1999–2000) (n = 4,117)	NHANES (2001–02) (n = 4,413)	NHANES† (2003–04) (n = 4,431)
Overweight or obese (BMI greater than or equal to 25.0)	56.0	64.5	65.7	66.3
Obese (BMI greater than or equal to 30.0)	22.9	30.5	30.6	32.2

*Age-adjusted by the direct method to the year 2000 U.S. Bureau of the Census estimates using the age groups 20–39, 40–59, and 60 years and over.
†Crude estimates (not age-adjusted) for 2003–4 are 66.5% with a BMI ≥ 25 and 32.3% with a BMI ≥ 30.
Source: Reprinted from Centers for Disease Control and Prevention, National Center for Health Statistics. Prevalence of Overweight and Obesity among Adults: United States, 2003-2004. Available at: http://www.cdc.gov/nchs/products/pubs/pubd/hestats/overweight/overwght_adult_03.htm. Accessed July 24, 2008.

FIGURE 9-17 Trends in adult overweight and obesity, ages 20–74 years.

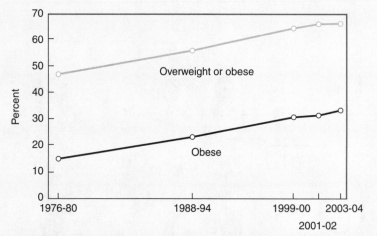

NOTE: Age-adjusted by the direct method to the year 2000 U.S. Bureau of the Census estimates using the age groups 20-39, 40-59 and 60-74 years. Overweight defined as BMI ≥ 25; Obesity defined as BMI ≥ 30.

Source: Reprinted from National Center for Health Statistics. Prevalence of overweight and obesity among adults: United States, 2003–2004. Available at: http://www.cdc.gov/nchs/products/pubs/pubd/hestats/obese03_04/obese_fig2.gif. Accessed July27, 2008.

FIGURE 9-18 Prevalence of obesity* among adults aged ≥18 years—Behavioral Risk Factor Surveillance System, United States, 2007.

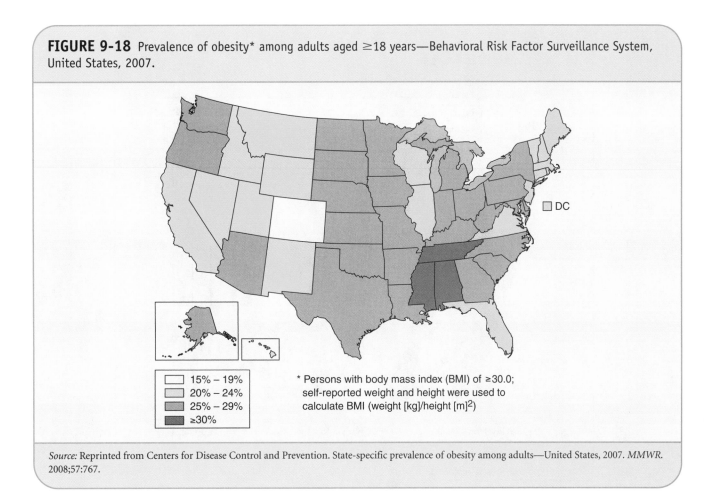

DC

15% – 19%
20% – 24%
25% – 29%
≥30%

* Persons with body mass index (BMI) of ≥30.0; self-reported weight and height were used to calculate BMI (weight [kg]/height [m]^2)

Source: Reprinted from Centers for Disease Control and Prevention. State-specific prevalence of obesity among adults—United States, 2007. *MMWR.* 2008;57:767.

EPIDEMIOLOGY AND MENTAL HEALTH

Epidemiologic methods have been applied for many years to the study of mental health phenomena in order to unravel the mysteries of mental disorders. The field of **psychiatric epidemiology** studies the occurrence of mental disorders in the population. As with other health conditions, mental disorders have characteristic distributions according to the categories of person, place, and time. Psychiatric epidemiology studies the incidence of mental disorders according to variables such as age, sex, and social class; the discipline measures the frequency of occurrence of mental disorders and factors related to their etiology. The DSM-IV-TR, which refers to the *Diagnostic and Statistical Manual of Mental Disorders*, Fourth Edition, Text Revision (2000), is used to classify psychiatric disorders. Examples of groups of mental disorders defined by the DSM-IV-TR are anxiety disorders, mood disorders, impulse-control disorders, and substance use disorders. Epidemiologic research findings suggest that more than one-quarter of the U.S. population is afflicted with a mental disorder during a given year.

As part of the NHANES III (conducted between 1988 and 1994), the Diagnostic Interview Schedule (DIS) was administered to almost 8,000 participants in order to obtain information on the lifetime prevalence of mood disorders. The DIS assesses the occurrence of major psychiatric disorders as defined in the DSM-IV. One of the categories of disorders for which information was collected was mood disorders; these include the following:

1. Major depressive episode (MDE)
2. Major depressive episode with severity (MDE-s)
3. Dysthymia (a less severe form of depression)
4. Dysthymia with MDE-s
5. Any bipolar disorder
6. Any mood disorder

In the overall sample, men and women combined, the most common diagnoses were MDE (8.6%), MDE-s (7.7%), and dysthymia (6.2%). The results for men and women separately are shown in Figure 9-19. The lifetime prevalence of MDE

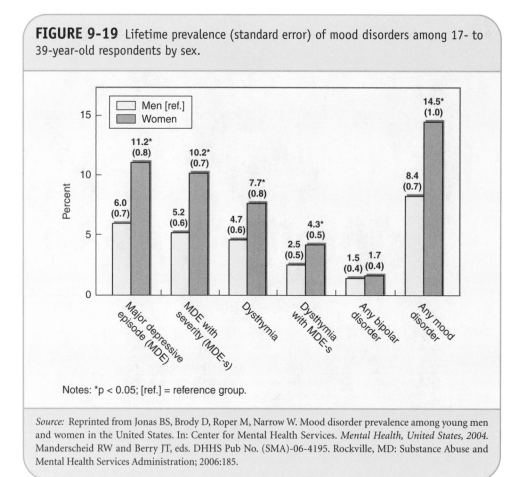

FIGURE 9-19 Lifetime prevalence (standard error) of mood disorders among 17- to 39-year-old respondents by sex.

Notes: *p < 0.05; [ref.] = reference group.

Source: Reprinted from Jonas BS, Brody D, Roper M, Narrow W. Mood disorder prevalence among young men and women in the United States. In: Center for Mental Health Services. *Mental Health, United States, 2004.* Manderscheid RW and Berry JT, eds. DHHS Pub No. (SMA)-06-4195. Rockville, MD: Substance Abuse and Mental Health Services Administration; 2006:185.

among women was higher than that among men (11.2% versus 6.0%).

The lifetime prevalence of mood disorders varied according to education level (see Figure 9-20). Lower levels of education were associated with higher levels of mood disorders; the lifetime prevalence of mood disorders was higher among women than men.

One of the topics of interest to psychiatric epidemiologists is **psychiatric comorbidity**, defined as the co-occurrence of two or more mental disorders, for example, major depression and substance use disorder. The 2006 National Survey on Drug Use and Health found that adults who had experienced a major depressive disorder episode within the past year were more likely to engage in illicit drug use, smoke cigarettes daily, and use alcohol heavily in comparison with those who did not experience a major depressive episode. (See Figure 9-21.)

Mental health issues are significant for children because such disorders are associated with impaired emotional, social, and behavioral development. During 2001 through 2003, approximately 12% (6.8 million) of children aged 4–17 years were diagnosed with a disorder that affected behavior or learning. Frequently reported severe emotional or behavioral difficulties included a triad of disorders: attention deficit hyperactivity disorder (ADHD), learning disability, and developmental delay (found commonly among both boys and girls). "Among boys with severe/definite difficulties, 59 percent had ever been diagnosed with ADHD, 48 percent with learning disability, and 21 percent with developmental delay."[24(p193)] With the exception of ADHD (higher among boys), the corresponding percentages for girls were similar to those of boys. (Refer to Figure 9-22.)

Autism (autism spectrum disorder-ASD) is a condition that impairs functioning in the social, communication, and be-

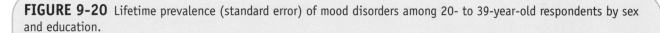

FIGURE 9-20 Lifetime prevalence (standard error) of mood disorders among 20- to 39-year-old respondents by sex and education.

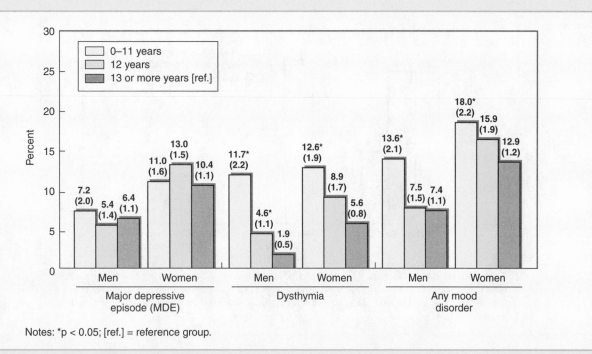

Notes: *p < 0.05; [ref.] = reference group.

Source: Reprinted from Jonas BS, Brody D, Roper M, Narrow W. Mood disorder prevalence among young men and women in the United States. In: Center for Mental Health Services. *Mental Health, United States, 2004.* Manderscheid RW and Berry JT, eds. DHHS Pub No. (SMA)-06-4195. Rockville, MD: Substance Abuse and Mental Health Services Administration; 2006:185.

havioral domains. Generally the condition appears by 3 years of age and is manifested by difficulties in cognitive functioning, learning, and processing sensory information. During 2002, the CDC collected information on the occurrence of autism among 8-year-old children in six states, as shown in Figure 9-23. Cases of autism were identified from multiple sources ". . . including education sources (i.e., public schools) and health sources (e.g., state health facilities, hospitals, clinics, diagnostic centers, and other clinical providers for children with developmental disabilities . . . ."[25 (pp3–4)] The prevalence of autism ranged from 4.5 per 1,000 children in West Virginia to 9.9 per 1,000 children in New Jersey; boys were more likely to be affected than girls.

CONCLUSION

One theme of this chapter was the association among social factors, lifestyle (how we live), and health outcomes; a second theme was the epidemiology of mental disorders. With re-

spect to the first topic, tobacco use, excessive alcohol consumption, substance abuse, and being under stress play a significant role in health. Sedentary habits and poor nutritional choices are associated with increasing levels of overweight and obesity in the United States. Lifestyle (directly or indirectly) is implicated in many of the leading causes of death such as heart disease and cancer.

Another topic covered in this chapter was the epidemiology of mental disorders. Psychiatric epidemiology studies the occurrence of mental disorders in the population. The prevalence of mental disorders among adults in the U.S. population is more than 25%. Some disorders, such as major depression, are associated with cigarette smoking, alcohol consumption, and illicit drug use. Mental health issues are common and significant for children in the United States. Autism, which appears early in life, is a serious disorder that affects many realms of functioning.

FIGURE 9-21 Substance use among adults aged 18 or older, by major depressive episode in the past year: 2006.

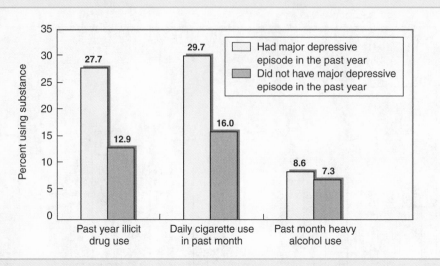

Source: Reprinted from Substance Abuse and Mental Health Services Administration. *Results from the 2006 National Survey on Drug Use and Health: National Findings.* (Office of Applied Studies, NSDUH Series H-32, DHHS Publication No. SMA 07-4293). Rockville, MD: Substance Abuse and Mental Health Services Administration; 2007:88.

FIGURE 9-22 Selected diagnosed disorders among children 4–17 years of age by level of emotional or behavioral difficulties and sex: United States, 2001–2003.

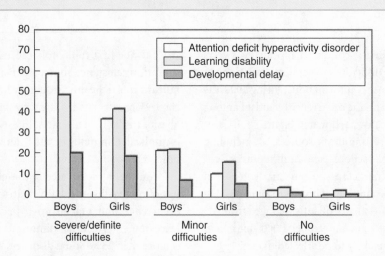

Note: A child may have more than one diagnosis.

Source: Reprinted from Pastor PN, Reuben CA, Falkenstern A. Parental reports of emotional or behavioral difficulties and mental health service use among U.S. school-age children. In: Center for Mental Health Services. *Mental Health, United States, 2004.* Manderscheid RW and Berry JT, eds. DHHS Pub No. (SMA)-06-4195. Rockville, MD: Substance Abuse and Mental Health Services Administration; 2006:193.

FIGURE 9-23 Percentage of children aged 8 years identified as having an autism spectrum disorder, by data source—Autism and Developmental Disabilities Monitoring Network, six sites, United States, 2000.

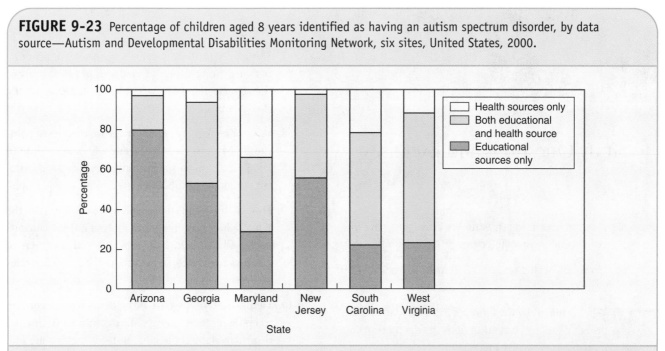

Source: Reprinted from Centers for Disease Control and Prevention. Prevalence of autism spectrum disorders—Autism and Developmental Disabilities Monitoring Network, six sites, United States, 2000. In: Surveillance Summaries, 2007. *MMWR* 2007;56(No. SS-1):5.

Our behavioral choices are modifiable factors that contribute to positive and negative health status. Although it is often difficult to change one's lifestyle, adoption of a desirable lifestyle would go a long way toward improving the health of both the individual and the population. Many successful interventions have been developed to encourage the adoption of healthful habits; examples are smoking cessation protocols and alcohol recovery programs, such as those operated by Alcoholics Anonymous. One of the greatest challenges for applied epidemiologists is to design programs that are successful for positive lifestyle modification.

Study Questions and Exercises

1. Distinguish among stressful life events, negative life events, and positive life events.

2. How are chronic strains different from stressful life events?

3. What is meant by the term posttraumatic stress disorder? What are some situations in which posttraumatic stress disorder might occur?

4. How common are anxiety, stress, and neurotic disorders in the work setting? What has been the trend in the rates of these disorders during the past 10 years?

5. Describe three major health effects associated with tobacco use. In your opinion, why has the prevalence of current smokers declined sharply since 1965?

6. The following questions relate to cigarette smoking among middle school and high school students:
   a. How frequent is cigarette smoking among this group?
   b. What kinds of epidemiologic research studies would you conduct to further explore the issue of cigarette smoking?
   c. What types of data would you collect?
   d. How would you apply the results of your research?

7. Aside from the fact that alcohol consumption among persons younger than 21 is illegal, what are some of the adverse consequences of binge drinking among this group?

8. What three kinds of illicit drugs are used most commonly by persons aged 12 and older, according to 2006 data? Can you suggest any methods for the prevention of illegal substance use among young people?

9. How do the trends for overweight and obesity in the United States compare for children and adolescents versus adults? Why is it important for members of our society to be concerned about the increasing rates of overweight and obesity?

10. Define the term psychiatric epidemiology. According to epidemiologic surveys, how common are mental disorders in the United States? Does this finding surprise you? How are gender and education related to the lifetime prevalence of mental disorders? Give an explanation for the associations you have stated.

REFERENCES

1. Berkman LF, Kawachi I. A historical framework for social epidemiology. In: Berkman LF, Kawachi I, eds. *Social Epidemiology*. New York, NY: Oxford University Press; 2000.

2. Centers for Disease Control and Prevention. Youth risk behavior surveillance—selected Steps communities, 2005. In: Surveillance Summaries, February 23, 2007. *MMWR*. 2007;56(SS-2):1–18.

3. Merriam-Webster Online Dictionary. Stress. Available at: http://www.merriam-webster.com/dictionary/stress. Accessed July 4, 2008.

4. Holmes T, Rahe R. The social readjustment rating scale. *J Psychosom Res*. 1967;11:213–218.

5. National Institutes of Health, National Institute of Mental Health. Meeting Summary: Cognition and stress: Advances in basic and translational research. Available at: http://www.nimh.nih.gov/research-funding/scientific-meetings/2007/cognition-and-stress-advances-in-basic-and-translational-research/summary.shtml. Accessed August 27, 2008.

6. Scheller-Gilkey G, Thomas SM, Woolwine BJ, Miller AH. Increased early life stress and depressive symptoms in patients with comorbid substance abuse and schizophrenia. *Schizophrenia Bulletin*. 2002;28(2): 223–231.

7. Sandberg S, Järvenpää S, Penttinen A, et al. Asthma exacerbations in children immediately following stressful life events: a Cox's hierarchical regression. *Thorax*. 2004;59:1046–1051.

8. Lillberg K, Verkasalo PK, Kaprio J, et al. Stressful life events and risk of breast cancer in 10,808 women: A cohort study. *Am J Epidemiol*. 2003; 157:415–423.

9. National Institutes of Health, National Institute of Mental Health. Post traumatic stress disorder research fact sheet. Available at: http://www.nimh.nih.gov/health/publications/post-traumatic-stress-disorder-research-fact-sheet.shtml. Accessed August 27, 2008.

10. Seino K, Takano T, Mashal T, et al. Prevalence of and factors influencing posttraumatic stress disorder among mothers of children under five in Kabul, Afghanistan, after decades of armed conflicts. *Health Qual Life Outcomes*. 2008 Apr 23;6:29.

11. Hankin CS, Spiro A 3rd, Miller DR, Kazis L. Mental disorders and mental health treatment among U.S. Department of Veterans Affairs outpatients: the Veterans Health Study. *Am J Psychiatry*. 1999;156:1924–1930.

12. Calhoun PS, Bosworth HB, Grambow SC, et al. Medical service utilization by veterans seeking help for posttraumatic stress disorder. *Am J Psychiatry*. 2002;159:2081–2086.

13. Dobie DJ, Maynard C, Kivlahan DR, et al. Posttraumatic stress disorder screening status is associated with increased VA medical and surgical utilization in women. *J Gen Intern Med*. 2006;21(Suppl 3):S58–S64.

14. Centers for Disease Control and Prevention. National Institute for Occupational Safety and Health (NIOSH). Stress . . . at work. NIOSH publication number 99-101. Available at: http://www.cdc.gov/Niosh/stresswk.html. Accessed July 4, 2008.

15. National Institute for Occupational Safety and Health (NIOSH). *Worker Health Chartbook, 2004*. Cincinnati, OH: DHHS (NIOSH) Publication No. 2004-146; 2004.

16. National Center for Health Statistics. *Health, United States, 2006, with Chartbook on Trends in the Health of Americans*. Hyattsville, MD: National Center for Health Statistics; 2006.

17. Centers for Disease Control and Prevention. Early release of selected estimates based on data from the January-September 2007 National Health Interview Survey. Available at: http://www.cdc.gov/nchs/data/nhis/earlyrelease/200803_08.pdf. Accessed August 28, 2008.

18. Marshall L, Schooley M, Ryan H, et al. Youth tobacco surveillance—United States, 2001-2002. In: Surveillance Summaries, May 19, 2006. *MMWR*. 2006;55(SS-3):1–56.

19. U.S. Department of Health and Human Services. *The Health Consequences of Involuntary Exposure to Tobacco Smoke: A Report of the Surgeon General—Executive Summary*. U.S. Department of Health and Human Services, Centers for Disease Control and Prevention, Coordinating Center for Health Promotion, National Center for Chronic Disease Prevention and Health Promotion, Office on Smoking and Health, 2006.

20. Kung HC, Hoyert DL, Xu JQ, Murphy SL. Deaths: Final data for 2005. *National vital statistics reports*, vol 56 no 10. Hyattsville, MD: National Center for Health Statistics; 2008.

21. Substance Abuse and Mental Health Services Administration. *Results from the 2006 National Survey on Drug Use and Health: National Findings* (Office of Applied Studies, NSDUH Series H-32, DHHS Publication No. SMA 07-4293). Rockville, MD: Department of Health and Human Services; 2007.

22. U.S. Department of Health and Human Services, Substance Abuse & Mental Health Services Administration, Office of Applied Studies. *The NSDUH Report: Methamphetamine Use, Abuse, and Dependence: 2002, 2003, and 2004*. September 16, 2005. Available at: http://oas.samhsa.gov/2k5/meth/meth.pdf. Accessed August 31, 2008.

23. Centers for Disease Control and Prevention. State-specific prevalence of obesity among adults—United States, 2007. *MMWR*. 2008;57:766–768.

24. Pastor PN, Reuben CA, Falkenstern A. Parental reports of emotional or behavioral difficulties and mental health service use among U.S. school-age children. In: Center for Mental Health Services. *Mental Health, United States, 2004*. Manderscheid RW and Berry JT, eds. DHHS Pub No. (SMA)-06-4195. Rockville, MD: Substance Abuse and Mental Health Services Administration; 2006.

25. Centers for Disease Control and Prevention. Prevalence of autism spectrum disorders—Autism and Developmental Disabilities Monitoring Network, six sites, United States, 2000. In: Surveillance Summaries, 2007. *MMWR*. 2007;56(No. SS-1):1–11.

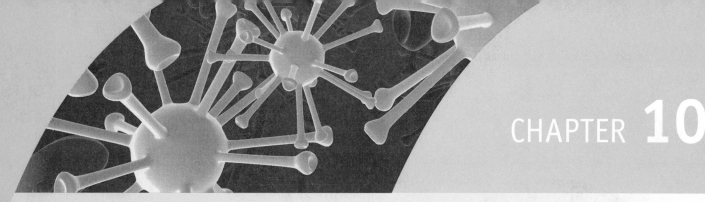

Special Epidemiologic Applications

TABLE 10-1 List of Important Terms Used in This Chapter

Autosomal dominant	Global warming
Autosomal recessive	Human Genome Project
Congenital malformation	Injury epidemiology
Environmental epidemiology	Molecular epidemiology
Genetic epidemiology	Occupational epidemiology
Genetic marker	Sewage epidemiology

INTRODUCTION

Scientists utilize epidemiologic methods and concepts with respect to a wide range of health-related phenomena. Several of the earlier chapters of this book covered the most familiar applications of epidemiology, for example, descriptive epidemiologic investigations of infectious disease outbreaks and studies of the role of social and behavioral factors in health. Chapter 10 covers health-related applications not discussed previously, including cutting-edge molecular and genetic techniques. Other uses are in the fields of environmental epidemiology and injury epidemiology, which fits epidemiologic methods to the study of various types of injuries such as intentional and unintentional injuries; the latter was the fifth leading cause of death in the United States in 2005. In addition, several uses are indirectly related to health; examples cited in this chapter include screen-based media use (e.g., television and computer games) and "sewage epidemiology." See Table 10-1 for a list of important terms used in this chapter.

MOLECULAR AND GENETIC EPIDEMIOLOGY

The application of molecular and genetic methods to the study of diseases in the population is an exciting development that has expanded in recent years. Traditionally, epidemiologic research uncovers associations between exposures and health outcomes, often without fully developing an explanation for the observed associations. This type of epidemiologic research is called "black box" epidemiology: the associations are "black boxes" in which the mechanisms for the associations are hidden and unknown. Molecular and genetic methods have increased the ability of scientists to peer inside these black boxes in order to expand the knowledge base of disease causality.

FIGURE 10-1 Human Genome Project logo.

Source: Reprinted from U.S. Department of Energy Human Genome Project Program. Available at: http://genomics.energy.gov/gallery/logos/detail.np/detail-10.html. Accessed July 22, 2008.

Jointly coordinated by the U.S. Department of Energy and the National Institutes of Health, the **Human Genome Project (HGP)** was completed in 2003. One of the goals of the HGP was to identify all of the genes (20,000 to 25,000) in human DNA. This project will continue to provide valuable information for epidemiologic research for many years. As an example, the HGP will aid in studying genetic and environmental interactions. The fields of both molecular and genetic epidemiology make use of genetic methods.

Molecular epidemiology is a subfield of epidemiology that uses molecular markers in addition to genes to establish exposure-disease relationships. "A genetic marker of susceptibility is a host factor that enhances some step in the progression between exposure and disease such that the downstream step is more likely to occur. The term *genetic marker* is used here in reference to susceptibility genes."[1] Certain genes are markers for exposure and do not confer risk on their own; health effects occur in conjunction with specific exposures. When these genes are present, the person may have increased susceptibility to specific exposures. While more detailed information is beyond the scope of this text, an example is the linkage between the gene CYP2D6 and susceptibility to the effects of exposure to benzo-a-pyrene, a hazardous chemical released by incomplete combustion of petroleum-based chemicals.

The field of **genetic epidemiology**, which has a narrower focus than molecular epidemiology, is concerned with ". . . the identification of inherited factors that influence disease, and how variation in the genetic material interacts with environmental factors to increase (or decrease) risk of disease."[2(p536)] Examples of research questions addressed by genetic epidemiology are whether diseases cluster in families and whether the patterns of diseases within families are consistent with the laws of inheritance.

Genetic factors have been implicated in a wide range of conditions. According to the World Health Organization, insufficient data are available regarding epidemiology of genetic diseases, despite growing knowledge about their importance in chronic and infectious diseases.[3] Examples of conditions that are known or believed to have a genetic basis are:

- Hemophilia: The inherited form of hemophilia is a sex-linked disorder, which is caused by an abnormal gene carried on an X chromosome. Hemophilia is a bleeding disorder in which the blood does not clot normally. The condition is rare; approximately 18,000 persons (almost always males) are affected in the United States. How is the condition inherited? Females have two X chromosomes. In most cases, females who are carriers of the abnormal gene for hemophilia are not themselves affected. Males have an X and a Y chromosome. The affected male inherits the abnormal gene on the X chromosome from his mother, should she have the carrier trait. A father who has hemophilia can transmit the affected gene on his X chromosome to his daughter, who usually will not be affected but will be a carrier. The father's son also will not be affected; he cannot inherit the trait from his father because he receives only a Y chromosome from his father.

- Tay-Sachs disease: This condition is an uncommon inherited disease. Infants born with Tay-Sachs disease develop severe neurologic symptoms such as blindness, deafness, and inability to swallow. A highly fatal condition, Tay-Sachs disease causes the death of most patients by age four. Persons of Eastern European and Ashkenazi Jewish descent have a higher incidence of Tay-Sachs disease than other groups. Tay-Sachs disease is caused by a genetic mutation that is inherited in an autosomal recessive pattern. (**Autosomal recessive** denotes those diseases for which two copies of an altered gene are required to increase risk of the disease; **autosomal dominant** refers to a situation in which only a single copy of an altered gene located on a nonsex chromosome is sufficient to cause an increased risk of disease.) In order for a child to be affected, he or she must receive the gene from both parents.

- Sickle cell disease: This condition is a genetic disease that is characterized by red blood cells that have an abnormal form of hemoglobin, called hemoglobin S; the disease is caused by a genetic mutation. The hemoglobin-containing red blood cells appear to be sickle shaped, hence the name sickle cell anemia. The mutation is thought to have evolved as a protection against malaria. The trait is found among people whose ancestors came from sub-Saharan Africa, Saudi Arabia, India, and some Mediterranean countries. The condition is caused by an autosomal recessive gene; in order to develop sickle cell anemia, a child must inherit the trait from both parents.

- BRCA1 and BRCA2 genes: BRCA1 and BRCA2 stand for breast cancer gene one and breast cancer gene two. Mutations in these two types of genes have been linked to hereditary breast and ovarian cancer; it has been estimated that about 5% to 10% of women who have breast cancer have the hereditary form of the disease. The National Cancer Institute indicates that "the likelihood that breast and/or ovarian cancer is associated with BRCA1 or BRCA2 is highest in families with a history of multiple cases of breast cancer, cases of both breast and ovarian cancer, one or more family members with two primary cancers (original tumors at different sites), or an Ashkenazi (Eastern European) Jewish background. However, not every woman in such families carries an alteration in BRCA1 or BRCA2, and not every cancer in such families is linked to alterations in these genes."[4]

- Down syndrome: This disorder is caused by a chromosomal abnormality associated with the presence of an extra twenty-first chromosome (either all or part). Persons who are afflicted with Down syndrome tend to have reduced cognitive ability and also may have distinctive facial and bodily characteristics. One of the epidemiologic characteristics of Down syndrome is that its frequency among newborns increases with increasing age of mothers (refer to Figure 10-2). The rate of Down syndrome births begins to increase among mothers who are in their twenties; the rate approaches eighty cases per 10,000 live births among mothers who are older than 39 years of age. Persons of Hispanic origin have a higher rate than whites or blacks: about 120 cases per 10,000 live births.

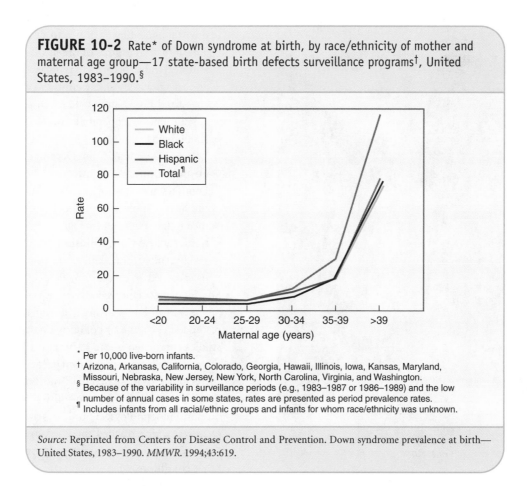

FIGURE 10-2 Rate* of Down syndrome at birth, by race/ethnicity of mother and maternal age group—17 state-based birth defects surveillance programs†, United States, 1983–1990.§

* Per 10,000 live-born infants.
† Arizona, Arkansas, California, Colorado, Georgia, Hawaii, Illinois, Iowa, Kansas, Maryland, Missouri, Nebraska, New Jersey, New York, North Carolina, Virginia, and Washington.
§ Because of the variability in surveillance periods (e.g., 1983–1987 or 1986–1989) and the low number of annual cases in some states, rates are presented as period prevalence rates.
¶ Includes infants from all racial/ethnic groups and infants for whom race/ethnicity was unknown.

Source: Reprinted from Centers for Disease Control and Prevention. Down syndrome prevalence at birth—United States, 1983–1990. *MMWR.* 1994;43:619.

- Congenital malformations (birth defects): **Congenital malformations** are defects present at birth. Birth defects include structural birth defects and those that are produced by chromosomal abnormalities (e.g., Down syndrome). "Major structural birth defects are defined as conditions that 1) result from a malformation, deformation, or disruption in one or more parts of the body; 2) are present at birth; and 3) have a serious, adverse effect on health, development, or functional ability."[5(p1302)] An example of a congenital malformation is a cleft foot (see Figure 10-3).

ENVIRONMENTAL EPIDEMIOLOGY

The term **environmental epidemiology** refers to the study of diseases and conditions (occurring in the population) that are linked to environmental factors. Examples of topics included under the purview of this field are health effects of exposure to air pollution, pesticides and toxic chemicals, heavy metals (e.g., lead, mercury, and arsenic—technically a crystalline metalloid), contaminated drinking water, and radiation.

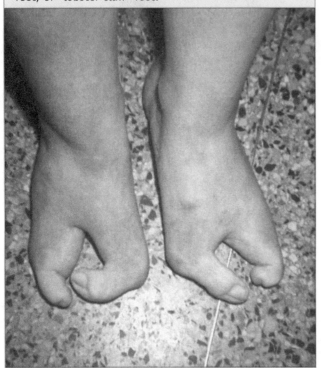

FIGURE 10-3 A photograph of a child with cleft feet, or "lobster claw" feet.

Source: Reprinted from Centers for Disease Control and Prevention. Public Health Image Library, ID# 2631. Available at: http://phil.cdc.gov/phil/details.asp. Accessed July 21, 2008.

Air Pollution

Epidemiologic research has examined a number of adverse health outcomes as possible consequences of exposure to air pollution—mortality, coronary heart disease, chronic obstructive pulmonary disease, asthma, and lung cancer. Air pollution represents potential health risks to the residents of cities (e.g., Beijing and Mexico City) in developing countries of the world as well as in the United States (e.g., the Los Angeles Basin and Houston). With the growing use of fossil fuels such as coal and oil to power increasing numbers of industries and automobiles, the threat of air pollution will escalate as an environmental health issue. Epidemiologic approaches to the study of air pollution include the following:

- Observations of the health effects of extreme air pollution episodes: several noteworthy severe air pollution episodes are historically important; two of these were the event in Donora, Pennsylvania, in 1948 and the incident in London, England, during 1952; both were linked to increases in morbidity and mortality.
  - Donora is a small town located on the Monongahela River about 30 miles south of Pittsburgh. An atmospheric condition known as an inversion layer caused a thick layer of fog combined with particles from industrial and other facilities to descend on Donora. The industrial sources of the contaminants were iron and steel mills, factories that burned coal, coke ovens, and metal works. Other emitters of smoke included coal-fired home stoves. This episode caused widespread illnesses, hospitalizations, and deaths in the small town.
  - Between December 5 and December 9, 1952, a severe air pollution event confronted London, England. London's normally foggy climate in combination with the heavy combustion of coal and other fossil fuels meant that "pea-souper" fogs were common. The particularly heavy air pollution episode in December 1952 resulted in a "killer fog" that was reported to have caused an excess of 3,000 deaths.
- Studies of associations between mortality and increased air pollution levels at much lower levels than those recorded in extreme air pollution events: several research studies conducted in the 1970s and 1980s showed that increased pollution levels (from particles in the air) were correlated with increased daily mortality.
- Examinations of total communities: noteworthy is the Tucson Epidemiological Study of Airways Obstructive Diseases, which tracked the etiology and natural history of chronic obstructive pulmonary disease and other conditions.

- Studies of the possible associations between air pollution and specific diseases and adverse health outcomes.
  - Coronary heart disease exacerbates the risk of adverse health effects of air pollution.
  - Asthma, one of the most common chronic diseases in the United States, has increased in prevalence, despite improving air quality.
- Examinations of traffic patterns and air pollution health effects: residents who live near heavily traveled motorways, highways, and city streets may have increased risk of mortality and other adverse health effects.

Global Warming

The term **global warming** refers to the gradual increase in the earth's temperature over time. Global warming is a controversial topic because some have argued that it is merely a transitory phenomenon and is not supported by scientific evidence. Nevertheless, historical data indicate that the earth's temperature has warmed approximately 0.6°C since the end of the nineteenth century and about 0.4°C within the past 25 years. Some estimates suggest that the earth's temperature may increase by about 1 1/2° to 4°C by the mid-twenty-first century. Factors that contribute to global warming include the use of fossil fuels such as coal and petroleum-based fuels that release greenhouse gases—carbon dioxide, methane, chlorofluorocarbons, and nitrous oxide. Widespread deforestation in many parts of the world, particularly the Brazilian Amazon jungle, has reduced the capacity of trees in the forest ecosystem to absorb carbon dioxide in the atmosphere. The potential impacts of global warming include northward movement of disease-carrying arthropods such as the *Aedes aegypti* mosquito. Over the past half century, glaciers in many parts of the world have receded. Evidence also suggests that global warming is associated with extreme climatic conditions including heat waves and severe rainstorms. During mid-1995, Chicago, Illinois, experienced episodes of heat-related mortality caused by abnormal heat waves. In August 2003 a blistering heat wave descended on France, incurring a death toll of almost 15,000 persons.

Toxic Chemicals

Chemicals and pesticides are used extensively in industry, at home, and in agriculture; two examples are DDT and dioxins. Concerns about the safety of DDT (a pesticide from the organochlorine family) led to its prohibition in 1972. DDT, a highly effective agent for the control of malaria-bearing mosquitoes, became a focus of awareness because of its possible adverse animal and human health effects. For example, in North America DDT endangered bird species such as the brown pelican. With the discontinuance of DDT spraying, the *Anopheles* mosquito has re-established itself, with corresponding increases in malaria cases.

Dioxins, highly toxic chemicals that persist in the environment, have been associated with disruption of the immune, endocrine, reproductive, and nervous systems. They have been reported to cause cancer in laboratory animals. Polychlorinated biphenyls (PCBs) are classified as dioxin-like chemicals; shown to cause cancer in laboratory animals, they have been designated as probable human carcinogens. Agent Orange, the defoliant used in the Vietnam War, was found to contain minute levels of dioxins. Returning veterans from the battle theater reported unusual adverse health outcomes including cancer and skin rashes among themselves and birth defects among their children.

Heavy Metals

Industrial sites, metal smelters, some mining operations, and coal-fired power plants can release heavy metals into the environment, endangering the health of persons who live near such facilities. Also at risk are employees who come into contact with heavy metals in their work environment. Heavy metals from these sources also can permanently contaminate the soil. Other sources for release of heavy metals into the environment are waste disposal sites. Used electronic equipment and old automobile tires that have been deposited in these sites contain toxic heavy metals, for example, lead, mercury, cadmium, and arsenic. Improperly designed disposal sites can allow toxic metals to leach into the groundwater, which often is used for human consumption.

Lead.

Formerly lead was an additive in paints and motor vehicle fuels, before its use was prohibited for these purposes. Lead is also a component of automobile batteries and solder used in electronics. Lead exposure is associated with serious central nervous system effects and other adverse health consequences, even when ingested at low levels. Among children, lead exposure is associated with intellectual impairment and behavioral deficits. Children may come into contact with lead from playground equipment or paint chips that are peeling off the surfaces in older buildings.

Mercury.

A highly toxic metal that is a particular hazard to the unborn children of pregnant women, mercury is released into the environment as a by-product of industrial processes. Certain types of fish (e.g., shark, swordfish, tilefish, king mackerel, and canned albacore) are believed to contain unhealthful mercury levels; frequent consumption of such fish may expose one to unacceptably high levels of mercury.

Nuclear Facilities

Potential sources for exposure of the population to ionizing radiation, nuclear facilities include weapons production plants, test sites, and nuclear power plants. A well-publicized incident was the unintentional release of radiation into the community from the Three-Mile Island nuclear power plant in Pennsylvania on March 28, 1979. This release occurred as a result of a partial meltdown of the reactor core. Apparently, ionizing radiation exposure levels from this accident were very low.

A much more serious accident (involving explosions and fires) occurred at the nuclear power plant in Chernobyl, Ukraine, on April 26, 1986. This accident caused substantial radiation exposure of the population nearby as well as in many neighboring European countries. In fact, the Chernobyl accident resulted in the second largest major exposure of a large population to radiation. (The largest exposure occurred in 1945 among the Japanese population during the detonation of atomic bombs over Hiroshima and Nagasaki.) The most common health effect associated with Chernobyl was an increase in thyroid cancer among persons who were exposed as children.[6]

EPIDEMIOLOGY AND OCCUPATIONAL HEALTH

Occupational epidemiology focuses on adverse health outcomes associated with the work environment. In many instances, the work environment can present health hazards to workers employed in a variety of positions. Sometimes these hazards are similar to those that affect the general environment. However, in the work environment, the levels of exposures that occur among employees are often much higher than exposure levels that the general population encounters in the ambient environment. Potential hazards that are encountered at work are high noise levels, fumes and dusts, toxic chemicals, biohazards, and stress (discussed in Chapter 9).

Applications of epidemiology to environmental health include the study of health effects related to environmental exposures that occur at work as well as occupational injuries. The field of occupational health and safety is closely related to environmental epidemiology and focuses on identifying, preventing, and remediating adverse health effects related to the occupational environment. Occupational injuries and illness are major causes of morbidity and mortality and have significant economic impacts on society because of lost work time and the cost of treating occupational illnesses, some of which may last a lifetime.

The U.S. Department of Labor, Bureau of Labor Statistics, collects information on occupational injuries and illnesses in private industry; more than 4 million cases were reported during 2006. Injuries accounted for more than 94% of this total. The leading causes of illnesses were skin diseases, hearing loss, and respiratory conditions (refer to Figure 10-4). The skin, au-

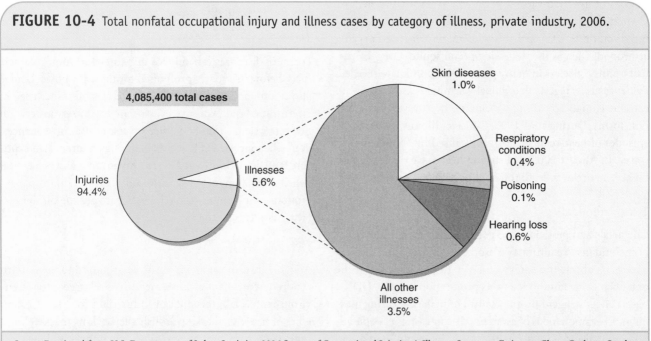

FIGURE 10-4 Total nonfatal occupational injury and illness cases by category of illness, private industry, 2006.

Source: Reprinted from U.S. Department of Labor Statistics. *2006 Survey of Occupational Injuries & Illnesses Summary Estimates Charts Package, October 16, 2007*:15. Available at: http://www.bis.gov/iif/oshwc/osh/os/osch0035.pdf. Accessed July 28, 2008.

ditory system, and respiratory system are the sites that come into most direct contact with disease-causing agents.

Workers in many industries are exposed to hazardous agents. An example is the high-tech industry that manufactures semiconductors and electronic equipment. Chip manufacturing requires the use of dangerous solvents, acids, and gases. Many of these agents are potentially carcinogenic; some of the solvents used in high-tech processes may contaminate nearby groundwater, posing a hazard to residents of the area. Fortunately, it is possible to prevent exposures of employees and the community to hazardous agents. Methods for limiting exposures include requiring workers to use personal protective devices, designing safer manufacturing processes, and controlling emissions from factories.

Figure 10-5 shows geographic variation in occupational injuries and illness by state in the United States. The national average for injuries and illness was 4.4 per 100 workers. A total of twenty-three states exceeded this average.

UNINTENTIONAL INJURIES

Injury epidemiology studies the distribution and determinants of injuries (such as intentional and unintentional) in the population. The use of the term unintentional injury is preferred to accident; the term accident implies a random event that cannot be prevented. An **accident** is defined as "an unanticipated event—commonly leading to INJURY or other harm—in traffic, the workplace, or a domestic or recreational setting. . . . Epidemiological studies have demonstrated that the risk of accidents is often predictable and that accidents are preventable. This word is preferably avoided in many types of scientific works."[7]

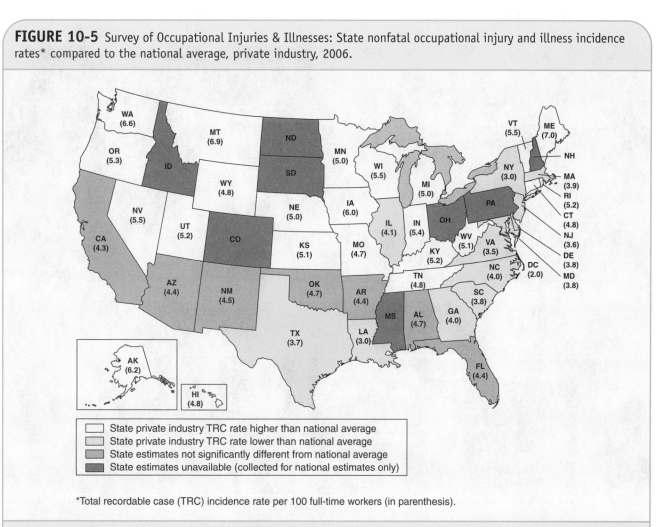

FIGURE 10-5 Survey of Occupational Injuries & Illnesses: State nonfatal occupational injury and illness incidence rates* compared to the national average, private industry, 2006.

State private industry TRC rate higher than national average
State private industry TRC rate lower than national average
State estimates not significantly different from national average
State estimates unavailable (collected for national estimates only)

*Total recordable case (TRC) incidence rate per 100 full-time workers (in parenthesis).

Source: Reprinted from U.S. Department of Labor, Bureau of Labor Statistics. *2006 Survey of Occupational Injuries & Illnesses Summary Estimates Charts Package, October 16, 2007:*24. Available at: http://www.bis.gov/iif/oshwc/osh/os/osch0035.pdf. Accessed July 28, 2008.

As noted previously, unintentional injuries are the fifth most frequent cause of mortality in the United States. During 2005, almost 118,000 deaths from unintentional injuries (4% of the total deaths) were recorded.[8] The crude death rate for this cause was 39.1 per 100,000 population. The category of unintentional injuries includes transport injuries (motor vehicle injuries, other land transport injuries, and injuries that occur on water and in the air and space) and nontransport injuries (falls, accidental discharges of firearms, and accidental poisonings). Unintentional injuries are highly preventable; for example, laws that require lap belts and air bags in cars have contributed to a decline in motor vehicle driver and passenger deaths. Descriptive epidemiologic studies aid in the development of policies and procedures to prevent unintentional injuries.

In the United States, the three leading causes of unintentional injury deaths are motor vehicle traffic deaths, firearm deaths, and poisonings. Motor vehicle accidents were the leading cause of unintentional deaths in 2005 and accounted for 45,343 fatalities. The largest number (10,908) occurred among persons aged 15 to 24 years. Figure 10-6 illustrates the destruction that can be caused by a severe automobile crash.

Age adjusted death rates for the leading causes of injury death are presented in Figure 10-7. According to the CDC, "During 1979–2004, the three leading causes of injury death in the United States were motor-vehicle traffic, firearm, and poisoning (including drug overdose). In 2004, for the first time since 1968, when such data first became available, the number of reported poisoning deaths (30,308) and the age-adjusted poisoning death rate (10.3 per 100,000 population) exceeded

FIGURE 10-6 An overturned car with first responders.

Source: © Jack Dagley/ShutterStock, Inc.

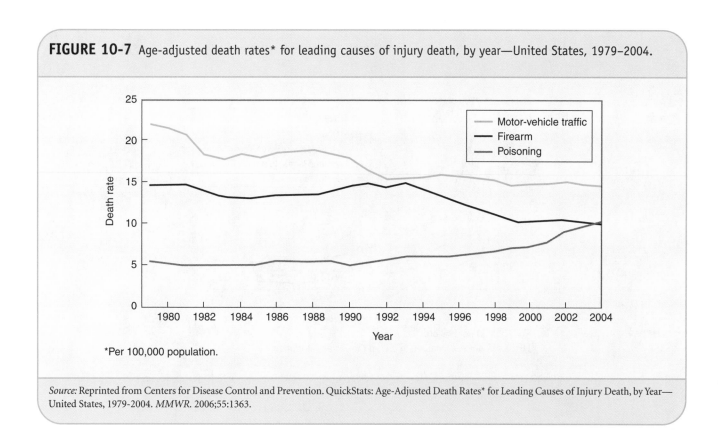

FIGURE 10-7 Age-adjusted death rates* for leading causes of injury death, by year—United States, 1979–2004.

*Per 100,000 population.

Source: Reprinted from Centers for Disease Control and Prevention. QuickStats: Age-Adjusted Death Rates* for Leading Causes of Injury Death, by Year—United States, 1979-2004. *MMWR.* 2006;55:1363.

the number of firearm deaths (29,569) and the firearm death rate (10.0), respectively. During 1999–2004, the poisoning death rate increased 45%, whereas the firearm death rate declined 3%; during the same period, no change occurred in the rate (14.7%) for motor-vehicle traffic deaths."[9(p1363)]

Several other categories of unintentional injuries are significant causes of mortality; these include all types of injuries among children and young adults, sports-related injuries among children, and falls among the elderly.

The rate of injury death for all types of injuries among children aged 0 to 9 years by race/ethnicity in the United States (1999–2002) is shown in Figure 10-8. The highest death rates from injuries among children and young adults occur during the first five years of life and then stabilize at age 9. These data suggest the need for improved interventions for reducing the toll of unintentional injuries among children and young adults.

Sports-related children's injuries include traumatic brain injuries. Almost 40 million children and adolescents take part in organized sports; about 170 million adults engage in physical activity not connected with work. Participation in these activities incurs the risk of traumatic brain injury (TBIs), which can cause long-lasting adverse health effects such as behavioral changes and memory loss.

The CDC reported that, "During 2001–2005, an estimated 207,830 patients with [sports and recreation] SR-related TBIs were treated in U.S. hospital [emergency departments] EDs each year, accounting for 5.1% of all SR-related ED visits. . . . Overall, males accounted for approximately 70.5% of SR-related TBI ED visits. The highest rates of SR-related TBI ED visits for both males and females occurred among those aged 10–14 years, followed by those aged 15–19 years (Figure 10-9). Activities associated with the greatest number of TBI-related ED visits included bicycling, football, playground activities, basketball, and riding all-terrain vehicles. Activities for which TBI accounted for greater than 7.5% of ED visits for that activity included horseback riding (11.7%), ice skating (10.4%), riding ATVs (8.4%), tobogganing/sledding (8.3%), and bicycling (7.7%)."[10(p733)] Table 10-2 gives a detailed listing of hospitalizations for all nonfatal and nontraumatic brain injuries related to sports and recreation activities. The data are provided for all ages and ages 5 through 18 years for the United States during 2001 through 2005.

Participation in collegiate sports, e.g., volleyball, is sometimes a cause of traumatic injuries. The National Collegiate Athletic Association collected injury surveillance data for participation in women's volleyball from 1988–1989 through 2003–2004. Results indicated 2,216 injuries reported from

FIGURE 10-8 Rate* of injury death among children aged 0–9 years, by race/ethnicity†—United States, 1999–2002.

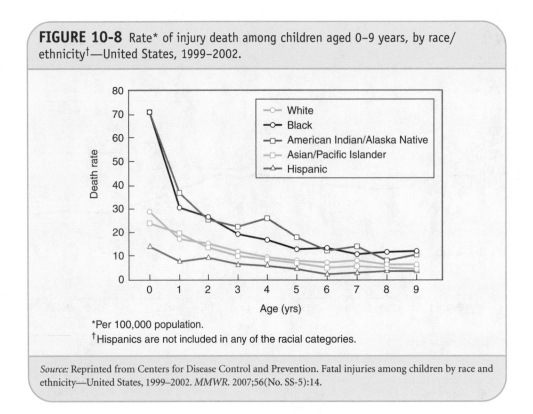

*Per 100,000 population.
†Hispanics are not included in any of the racial categories.

Source: Reprinted from Centers for Disease Control and Prevention. Fatal injuries among children by race and ethnicity—United States, 1999–2002. *MMWR.* 2007;56(No. SS-5):14.

FIGURE 10-9 Estimated annual rate* of nonfatal, sports- and recreation-related traumatic brain injuries treated in emergency departments, by age group and sex—National Electronic Injury Surveillance System—All Injury Program, United States, 2001–2005.

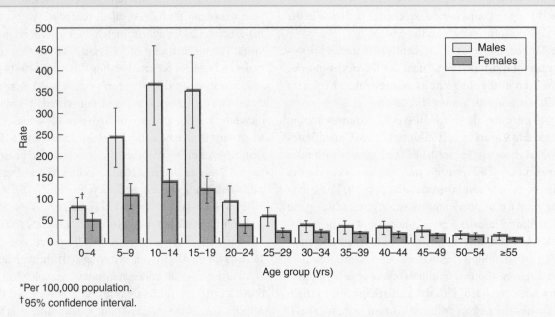

*Per 100,000 population.
†95% confidence interval.

Source: Reprinted from Centers for Disease Control and Prevention. Nonfatal traumatic brain injuries from sports and recreation activities—United States, 2001–2005. *MMWR.* 2007;56:735.

TABLE 10-2 Estimated Annual Number of Hospitalizations* for All Nonfatal Injuries and Nonfatal Traumatic Brain Injuries (TBIs) Related to Sports and Recreation Activities, for All Ages and for Ages 5–18 Years, by Selected Activity—National Electronic Injury Surveillance System—All Injury Program, United States, 2001–2005

Activity	All ages						Ages 5-18 yrs					
	All injuries		TBIs				All injuries		TBIs			
	No.†	(95% CI§)	No.	(95% CI)	% of all injury hospitalizations¶	% resulting in hospitalization**	No.	(95% CI)	No.	(95% CI)	% of all injury hospitalizations	% resulting in hospitalization
Bicycle	25,062	(17,858–32,267)	6,296	(3,636–8,957)	25.1	15.6	11,396	(8,958–13,835)	3,026	(1,993–4,059)	26.6	12.9
All-terrain vehicle	16,503	(10,195–22,810)	3,383	(1,649–5,117)	20.5	30.2	6,413	(3,897–8,929)	1,622	(698–2,545)	25.3	31.1
Moped/minibike/ dirt bike††	6,095	(3,848–8,341)	1,039	(442–1,636)	17.0	21.9	2,653	(1,683–3,623)	517	(233–801)	19.5	20.5
Football	6,809	(5,588–8,030)	891	(633–1,148)	13.1	3.9	5,639	(4,590–6,688)	775	(521–1,029)	13.7	3.8
Baseball/softball	3,759	(2,895–4,623)	811	(491–1,130)	21.6	5.6	1,926	(1,481–2,371)	419	(198–640)	21.8	4.5
Playground	9,669	(7,714–11,624)	529	(332–727)	5.5	3.3	7,398	(5,727–9,069)	349	(200–497)	4.7	3.3
Basketball	4,816	(4,057–5,575)	465	(274–656)	9.7	3.2	2,674	(2,110–3,238)	365	(218–513)	13.6	3.2
Skateboard	3,068	(1,700–4,437)	432	(216–647)	14.1	8.2	2,304	(1,389–3,219)	350	(170–529)	15.2	7.9
Scooter	2,011	(1,586–2,437)	372	(191–552)	18.5	10.5	1,429	(1,090–1,769)	329	(154–504)	23.0	11.8
Golf§§	1,586	(1,016–2,156)	366	(159–573)	23.1	13.6	504	(299–708)	178	(87–269)	35.3	15.8
Swimming/diving	3,915	(2,380–5,449)	352	(155–549)	9.0	6.0	1,304	(820–1,789)	198	(81–315)	15.2	5.1
Skating¶¶	2,946	(2,148–3,745)	263	(126–399)	8.9	4.8	1,571	(1,114–2,029)	153	(63–243)	9.7	4.0
Soccer	2,653	(1,625–3,681)	198	(84–312)	7.5	2.1	1,602	(999–2,206)	161	(66–256)	10.0	2.1
Other specified***	37,790	(27,470–48,110)	5,916	(3,264–8,567)	15.7	11.5	13,557	(10,359–16,755)	2,351	(1,340–3,361)	17.3	8.2
Total	126,683	(97,146–156,220)	21,311	(13,258–29,364)	16.8	10.3	60,372	(49,416–71,329)	10,790	(7,461–14,120)	17.9	8.0

*Includes those for patients hospitalized and those for patients transferred to another facility for additional care.

†Estimates might not sum to totals because of rounding.

§Confidence interval.

¶Percentage of all hospitalizations attributed to TBI = (number of TBI hospitalizations for activity/number of all hospitalizations for activity) × 100.

**Percentage of TBIs resulting in hospitalization = (number of TBI hospitalizations for activity/number of TBI-related emergency department visits for activity) × 100.

††Includes other two-wheeled, powered off-road vehicles and dune buggies.

§§Includes injuries related to golf carts.

¶¶Includes ice, in-line, and roller skating.

***Includes trampoline, toboggan/sled, go-cart, gymnastics, bowling, hockey, racquet sports, volleyball, miscellaneous ball games, track/field, combative exercise, amusement attractions, water skiing, surfing, personal watercraft, snow skiing, snowmobile, snowboarding, camping, fishing, archery, darts, table tennis, nonpowder/BB guns, and billiards. Nonfatal traumatic brain injuries from sports and recreation activities—United States, 2001–2005.

Source: Reprinted from Centers for Disease Control and Prevention. Nonfatal traumatic brain injuries from sports and recreation activities—United States, 2001–2005. *MMWR.* 2007;56:735.

50,000 games and 4,725 injuries from 90,000 practices. The majority of reported injuries affected the lower extremities; ankle injuries were the most frequently reported type of injury.[11]

Still another type of sports-related injury is associated with the use of all-terrain vehicles (ATVs). An ATV has a motor and low-pressure tires to enable it to travel off road. According to data for the 1990s, West Virginia had death rates from ATV crashes that were about eight times higher than the national average.[12] The state enacted several laws to reduce ATV fatalities; these laws reduced the distance that is permitted to travel on paved roads, reduced the speed of the vehicle, and required helmet use. Nevertheless, between 1999 and 2006, fatal ATV crashes increased by about 14% per year (refer to Figure 10-10). During this period, 250 people died from ATV crashes in West Virginia. Factors related to ATV fatalities were lower socioeconomic status, being single or divorced, and having lower levels of education.

Falls among the elderly represent a final category of unintentional injuries discussed in this chapter. According to the CDC, falls are the leading cause of fatal and nonfatal injuries for persons aged 65 years and older.[13] The prevalence of falls among persons in this age group was estimated by using data from the 2006 behavioral risk factor surveillance system. Overall, 15.9% of the sample reported falling during the pre-

ceding three months; among those who fell, 31.3% were injured at least one time. Among persons aged 80 years and older, the prevalence of falls increased to 20.8%. Race and ethnicity were related to falling, with the greatest prevalence occurring among American Indian/Alaska natives; the highest prevalence of injuries among those who fell occurred among Hispanic persons. The prevalence of falling was similar for men and women, although women had a greater percentage of fall-related injuries than men.

OTHER APPLICATIONS OF EPIDEMIOLOGY

Sewage Epidemiology

Sewage epidemiology refers to monitoring levels of excreted drugs in the sewer system in order to assess the level of illicit drug use in the community. Sewage wastewater systems contain measurable levels of human metabolic end-products of drugs that are consumed. These end-products include those from both prescription medications and illicit drugs. The drugs that are measured in wastewater are called drug target residues (DTRs). Zuccato et al.[14] measured the DTRs for cocaine, opiates, cannabis, and amphetamines in wastewater from sewage treatment plants in Milan, Italy; Lugano, Switzerland; and London, England. The investigators found that cocaine consumption rose on the weekends in Milan. Heroin consumption (measured in milligrams per day per 1,000 people) varied among the three cities. The highest consumption was 210 mg in London, followed by 100 mg in Lugano and 70 mg in Milan. This methodology could be used to test for levels of drug use in specific communities and even at the household level, raising the specter of privacy issues.

Descriptive Epidemiology of Screen-Based Media Use

Chapter 9 demonstrated that levels of obesity in the population are increasing in many developed areas of the world; obesity is also a health issue in the developing world. Of par-

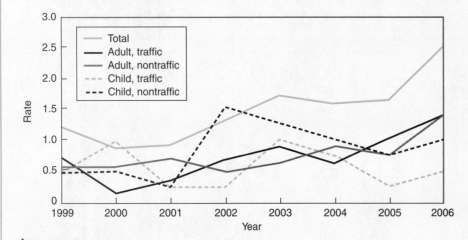

FIGURE 10-10 Death rate* attributed to fatal all-terrain vehicle crashes, by age group[†] and crash classification[§]—West Virginia,[¶] 1999–2006.

* Per 100,000 population.
[†] Adult is defined as a person aged ≥18 years; child is defined as a person aged <18 years.
[§] Based on *International Classification of Deaths,* 10th Revision. Traffic crash defined as occurring on a public highway; nontraffic crash occurs entirely in any place other than a public highway.
[¶] Includes only decedents who were West Virginia residents involved in crashes that occurred in West Virginia (N = 215).

Source: Reprinted from Centers for Disease Control and Prevention. All-terrain vehicle fatalities—West Virginia, 1999–2006. *MMWR.* 2008;57:314.

ticular concern are rising levels of obesity among young people. This phenomenon may be attributed in part to contemporary sedentary lifestyles. Instead of engaging in active free-time activities, more and more youths spend their free hours watching television or playing computer games. Marshall et al. conducted a systematic review in order to ". . . (i) estimate the prevalence and dose of television (TV) viewing, video game playing and computer use, and (ii) assess age-related and (iii) secular trends in TV viewing among youth (≤18 yr)."[15(p333)] Researchers found that young people watched TV for an average of 1.8 to 2.8 hours per day. Boys and girls used video games for about one hour and half an hour, respectively. Those who had computers used them for about half an hour per day. The authors concluded that ". . . it is likely that media-based inac-

tivity, and TV viewing in particular, is being unfairly implicated in the 'epidemic' of youth sedentariness."[15(p345)]

Physical Dating Violence

"Dating violence is defined as physical, sexual, or psychological violence within a dating relationship."[16(p532)] The CDC examined the occurrence of physical dating violence by using information from the Youth Risk Behavior Surveillance System (see Table 10-3). This program ". . . measures the prevalence of health risk behaviors among high school students through biennial national, state, and local surveys." One item on the questionnaire used in the 2003 survey queried ". . . During the past 12 months, did your boyfriend or girlfriend ever hit, slap, or physically hurt you on purpose?" The overall prevalence of

TABLE 10-3 Prevalence of Physical Dating Violence Victimization* among High School Students, by Sex and Selected Characteristics—United States, 2003

Characteristic	Total		Male		Female	
	%	(95% CI†)	%	(95% CI)	%	(95% CI)
Overall	8.9	(7.9–9.9)	8.9	(7.7–10.2)	8.8	(7.9–9.8)
Grade level						
9	8.1	(7.0–9.5)	7.8	(6.3–9.5)	8.6	(6.7–10.8)
10	8.8	(7.0–10.9)	9.3	(7.3–11.8)	8.2	(6.4–10.3)
11	8.1	(6.9–9.6)	7.9	(6.5–9.6)	8.2	(6.7–10.1)
12	10.1	(8.5–12.0)	10.1	(7.8–13.0)	10.2	(8.4–12.4)
Race/Ethnicity						
White, non-Hispanic	7.0	(6.2–7.9)	6.6	(5.8–7.5)	7.5	(6.2–9.0)
Black, non-Hispanic	13.9	(12.3–15.5)	13.7	(11.8–16.0)	14.0	(11.8–16.5)
Hispanic	9.3	(7.6–11.3)	9.2	(6.7–12.6)	9.2	(7.7–11.1)
Geographic region§						
Northeast	10.6	(8.4–13.2)	10.8	(8.7–13.3)	10.4	(7.8–13.7)
Midwest	7.5	(5.8–9.7)	8.3	(6.2–10.9)	6.5	(4.9–8.5)
South	9.6	(8.3–11.1)	9.3	(7.6–11.4)	9.9	(8.6–11.5)
West	6.9	(5.2–9.1)	6.1	(3.7–10.0)	7.8	(6.3–9.5)
Self-reported grades						
Mostly A's	6.1	(5.0–7.4)	6.6	(4.9–8.9)	5.7	(4.6–7.1)
Mostly B's	7.7	(6.8–8.7)	7.4	(6.3–8.7)	8.0	(6.7–9.6)
Mostly C's	11.2	(9.8–12.8)	10.4	(8.8–12.3)	12.3	(10.3–14.8)
Mostly D's or F's	13.7	(11.1–16.7)	13.0	(10.1–16.7)	14.9	(10.7–20.4)

*Defined as a response of "yes" to a single question: "During the past 12 months, did your boyfriend or girlfriend ever hit, slap, or physically hurt you on purpose?"

†Confidence interval.

§*Northeast:* Connecticut, Maine, Massachusetts, New Hampshire, New Jersey, New York, Pennsylvania, Rhode Island, and Vermont. *Midwest:* Illinois, Indiana, Iowa, Kansas, Michigan, Minnesota, Missouri, Nebraska, North Dakota, Ohio, South Dakota, and Wisconsin. *South:* Alabama, Arkansas, Delaware, District of Columbia, Florida, Georgia, Kentucky, Louisiana, Maryland, Mississippi, North Carolina, Oklahoma, South Carolina, Tennessee, Texas, Virginia, and West Virginia. *West:* Alaska, Arizona, California, Colorado, Hawaii, Idaho, Montana, Nevada, New Mexico, Oregon, Utah, Washington, and Wyoming.

Source: Reprinted from Centers for Disease Control and Prevention. Physical dating violence among high school students—United States, 2003. *MMWR.* 2006;55:533.

physical dating violence was 8.9% and was similar for both males and females. Factors related to physical dating violence victimization were being currently sexually active, having attempted suicide, episodic heavy drinking, and physical fighting. Survey results suggested that the prevalence of physical dating violence is quite high and affects approximately one in eleven students.

Forensic Epidemiology

Forensic epidemiology pertains to "the use of epidemiological reasoning, knowledge, and methods in the investigation of public health problems that may have been caused by or associated with intentional and/or criminal acts."[7] One of the stimuli for the development of this specialization was the 2001 bioterrorism attack (distribution of anthrax bacteria through the postal system) in the United States. Since this event, public health and law enforcement officials worldwide have become increasingly alert for additional bioterrorism attacks; advance preparedness would enable responsible jurisdictions to respond to future attacks in a coordinated fashion and thus limit the impact of intentional dissemination of harmful biologic and other agents upon society. Forensic epidemiology applies standard epidemiologic methods to detect and respond to bioterrorism and other criminal acts that can affect the population. These methods include detection of unusual occurrence of disease (e.g., smallpox), use of ongoing surveillance systems, case identification and confirmation, and development of a descriptive epidemiologic profile of a group of cases. During a bioterrorism attack, surveillance systems might detect an increase in the number of patients who present with infectious diseases in hospital emergency rooms, increases in ambulance services, and increases in the sales of antibiotics. A specific type of surveillance, known as a syndromic surveillance system, records information on syndromes of diseases (e.g., influenza-like conditions) reported in ambulatory care settings; information from syndromic surveillance systems can aid in the detection of disease clusters—from natural disease outbreaks and bioterrorism attacks. By applying the information gathered during a forensic epidemiologic investigation, officials can formulate and implement plans for response to bioterrorism-associated events.

CONCLUSION

This chapter presented information on additional uses of epidemiology not covered previously in the textbook. Examples of these uses were taken from the fields of molecular and genetic epidemiology, environmental health, and injury epidemiology. Miscellaneous uses—some of which were not specifically health related—also were described. The examples presented in Chapter 10 demonstrated that epidemiology is a growing field with many applications, even outside the worlds of medicine and public health. And, with society's increasing awareness of epidemiology, the number of applications of this discipline is likely to increase in the future. Many opportunities exist for additional study as well as for employment in positions that use epidemiologic skills. The author hopes that this textbook will motivate you to consider the many research and employment possibilities that exist in this field; these opportunities can be found in both the public sector and private industry.

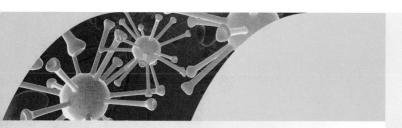

Study Questions and Exercises

1. Define the following terms:
   a. genetic epidemiology
   b. genetic marker
   c. environmental epidemiology
   d. occupational epidemiology
   e. injury epidemiology

2. Give an example of a disease that has the following genetic characteristic:
   a. autosomal recessive
   b. sex linked
   c. mutation in one of the BRCA1 or BRCA2 genes

3. Why should you be concerned about the health effects of air pollution? What types of adverse health outcomes and conditions have been associated with air pollution?

4. Why are dioxins regarded as potentially dangerous chemicals? What hazards do they present for the environment?

5. Name three types of occupational injuries and illnesses that occur in the work environment. In your opinion, what could be done to prevent them?

6. What unusual applications of epidemiology (especially non-health related) have you heard about that were not mentioned in Chapter 10?

Exercises

1. Invite a trauma specialist to your classroom and ask him or her to discuss the types of injuries treated in the hospital trauma center.

2. Arrange a debate in your classroom to discuss the causes and consequences of unintentional injuries. Assume that little can be done to prevent such events because they are random occurrences. Ask one group of students to present the pro side of this assumption and another group to present the con side of the assumption.

REFERENCES

1. Schulte PA, Lomax GP, Ward EM, Colligan ML. Ethical Issues in the Use of Genetic Markers in Occupational Epidemiologic Research. Available at: http://www.cdc.gov/genomics/population/file/print/ethical.pdf. Accessed August 7, 2008.

2. Friis RH, Sellers TA. *Epidemiology for Public Health Practice.* 4th ed. Sudbury, MA: Jones and Bartlett Publishers; 2009.

3. World Health Organization. Control of genetic diseases: Report by the Secretariat. Available at: http://www.who.int/gb/ebwha/pdf_files/EB116/B116_3-en.pdf. Accessed August 7, 2008.

4. U.S. National Institutes of Health, National Cancer Institute. Genetic testing for BRCA1 and BRCA2: It's your choice. Available at: http://www.cancer.gov/cancertopics/factsheet/risk/brca. Accessed July 6, 2008.

5. Centers for Disease Control and Prevention. Improved national prevalence estimates for 18 selected major birth defects—United States, 1999-2001. *MMWR.* 2006;54:1301–1305.

6. Baverstock K, Williams D. The Chernobyl accident 20 years on: An assessment of the health consequences and the international response. *Environ Health Perspect.* 2006;114:1312–1317.

7. Porta M, ed. *A Dictionary of Epidemiology.* 5th ed. New York: Oxford University Press; 2008.

8. Kung HC, Hoyert DL, Xu JQ, Murphy SL. Deaths: Final data for 2005. National vital statistics reports; vol 56 no 10. Hyattsville, MD: National Center for Health Statistics. 2008.

9. Centers for Disease Control and Prevention. QuickStats: Age-Adjusted Death Rates for Leading Causes of Injury Death, by Year—United States, 1979–2004. *MMWR.* 2006;55:1363.

10. Centers for Disease Control and Prevention. Nonfatal traumatic brain injuries from sports and recreation activities—United States, 2001–2005. *MMWR.* 2007;56:733–737.

11. Agel J, Palmieri-Smith RM, Dick R, et al. Descriptive epidemiology of collegiate women's volleyball injuries: National Collegiate Athletic Association Injury Surveillance System, 1988–1989 through 2003–2004. *Journal of Athletic Training.* 2007;42:295–302.

12. Centers for Disease Control and Prevention. All-terrain vehicle fatalities—West Virginia, 1999–2006. *MMWR.* 2008;57:312–315.

13. Centers for Disease Control and Prevention. Self-reported falls and fall-related injuries among persons aged ≥65 years—United States, 2006. *MMWR.* 2008;57:225–229.

14. Zuccato E, Chiabrando C, Castiglioni S, et al. Estimating community drug abuse by wastewater analysis. National Institutes of Health, National Institute of Environmental Health Sciences. *Environ Health Perspect.* 2008; 116:1027–1032.

15. Marshall SJ, Gorely T, Biddle SJH. A descriptive epidemiology of screen-based media use in youth: A review and critique. *J Adolesc.* 2006;29: 333–349.

16. Centers for Disease Control and Prevention. Physical dating violence among high school students—United States, 2003. *MMWR.* 2006;55:532–535.

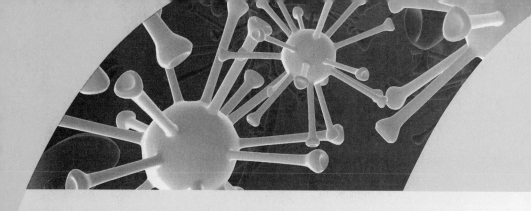

Glossary

NOTE: Some definitions are quoted from other sources; refer to text for citations.

A

Adjusted rate

Rate of morbidity or mortality in a population in which statistical procedures have been applied to permit fair comparisons across populations by removing the effect of differences in the composition of various populations; an example is age adjustment.

Agent

In the epidemiologic triangle, the cause of a disease; in infectious diseases, often the agent is a microbe such as a virus or bacterium.

Age-specific rate

Frequency of a disease in a particular age stratum divided by the total number of persons within that age stratum during a time period.

Analytic epidemiology

A type of epidemiology that examines causal (etiologic) hypotheses regarding the association between exposures and health conditions. The field of analytic epidemiology proposes and evaluates causal models for etiologic associations and studies them empirically.

Analytic study

A type of research design concerned with the determinants of disease and the reasons for relatively high or low frequency of disease in specific population subgroups. Analytic studies iden-

tify causes of the problem, test specific etiologic hypotheses, generate new etiologic hypotheses, and suggest mechanisms of causation; they also may include some types of ecologic studies, case-control studies, and cohort studies.

Antigen

A substance that stimulates antibody formation.

Attack rate

An alternative form of the incidence rate that is used when the nature of a disease or condition is such that a population is observed for a short time period. The attack rate is calculated by the formula ill/(ill + well) $\times$ 100 (during a time period). The attack rate is not a true rate because the time dimension is often uncertain.

Attributable risk

A measure of risk difference. In a cohort study, refers to the difference between the incidence rate of a disease in the exposed group and the incidence rate in the nonexposed group.

Autosomal dominant

A situation in which only a single copy of an altered gene located on a nonsex chromosome is sufficient to cause an increased risk of disease.

Autosomal recessive

Denotes those diseases for which two copies of an altered gene are required to increase risk of disease.

Availability of the data

Refers to the investigator's access to data (e.g., patient records and databases in which personally identifying information has been removed).

B

Behavioral epidemiology

The study of the role of behavioral factors in health at the population level.

Bias (also, systematic errors)

Refers to deviations of results, or inferences, from the truth.

Blinding (also, masking)

An aspect of study design wherein the subject is not aware of his/her group assignment of placebo or treatment; seeks to alleviate bias in study results.

C

Carrier

A person or animal that harbors a specific infectious agent without discernible clinical disease and serves as a potential source of infection.

Case clustering

An unusual aggregation of health events grouped together in space or time.

Case-control study

A study that compares individuals who have a disease with individuals who do not have the disease in order to examine differences in exposures or risk factors for the disease.

Case fatality rate

Number of deaths caused by a disease among those who have the disease during a time period.

Cause

Act, event, or state of nature that initiates/permits, alone or in conjunction with other causes, a sequence of events resulting in an effect.

Cause-specific rate

Measure that refers to mortality (or frequency of a given disease) divided by the population size at the midpoint of a time period times a multiplier.

Clinical trial

A carefully designed and executed investigation of the effects of a treatment or technology that uses randomization, blinding of subjects to study conditions, and manipulation of the study factor.

Cohort

A group of individuals who share an exposure in common and who are followed over time; an example is an age cohort.

Cohort study (also, prospective or longitudinal study)

A type of study that collects data and follows a group of subjects who have received a specific exposure. The incidence of a specific disease or other outcome of interest is tracked over time. The incidence in the exposed group is compared with the incidence in groups that are not exposed, that have different levels of exposure, or that have different types of exposures.

Confidence interval

A computed interval of values that, with a given probability, is said to contain the true value of the population parameter; a measure of uncertainty about a parameter estimate. An example is the confidence interval about a relative risk measure.

Confounding

Distortion of an association between an exposure and an outcome because of the influence of a third variable that was not considered in the study design or analysis.

Congenital malformation

A type of defect present at birth; for example, cleft foot.

Continuous variable

A type of variable that can have an infinite number of values within a specified range (e.g., blood pressure measurements, height, and weight).

Cost-effectiveness analysis

A procedure that contrasts the costs and health effects of an intervention to determine whether it is economically worthwhile.

Count

Total number of cases of a disease or other health phenomenon being studied.

Crossover design

Any change of treatment for a patient in a clinical trial that involves a switch of study treatments.

Cross-sectional study (also, prevalence study)

A type of descriptive study (e.g., a population survey) designed to estimate the prevalence of a disease or exposure.

Crude birth rate

Number of live births during a specified period of time per the resident population during the midpoint of the time period (expressed as rate per 1,000).

Crude death rate

Number of deaths in a given year divided by the reference population (during midpoint of the year) times 100,000.

Crude rate

A summary rate based on the actual number of events in a population over a given time period. An example is the crude death rate, which approximates the proportion of the population that dies during a time period of interest.

Cyclic fluctuation

An increase or decrease in the frequency of a disease or health condition in a population over a period of years or within each year.

D

Demographic transition

Historical shift from high birth and death rates found in agrarian societies to much lower birth and death rates found in developed countries.

Descriptive epidemiology

Epidemiologic studies that are concerned with characterizing the amount and distribution of health and disease within a population.

Descriptive epidemiologic study

A type of study designed to portray the health characteristics of a population with respect to person, place, and time. Such studies are utilized to estimate disease frequency and time trends, and include case reports, case series, and cross-sectional surveys.

Determinant

A factor or event that is capable of bringing about a change in the health status of a population.

Direct transmission

Spread of infection through person-to-person contact.

Dose-response curve

Graphical representation of the relationship between changes in the size of a dose or exposure and changes in response. This curve generally has an "S" shape.

Double-blind design

Feature of a clinical trial in which neither the subject nor the experimenter is aware of the subject's group assignment in relation to control or treatment status.

E

Ecologic comparison study

Type of research design that assesses the correlation (association) between exposure rates and disease rates among different groups or populations over the same time period. The unit of analysis is the group.

Ecologic fallacy

A misleading conclusion about the relationship between a factor and an outcome that occurs when the observed association obtained between study variables at the group level does not necessarily hold true at the individual level.

Ecologic trend study

Type of study that examines the correlation of changes in exposure and changes in disease over time within the same community, country, or other aggregate unit.

Emerging infection

An abrupt increase in the incidence or geographic scope of a seemingly new infectious disease (e.g., hantaviral pulmonary syndrome found in the southwestern United States).

Endemic

Donates a disease or infectious agent habitually present in a community, geographic area, or population group. Often an endemic disease maintains a low but continuous incidence.

Environment

Domain in which a disease-causing agent may exist, survive, or originate.

Environmental epidemiology

The study of diseases and conditions (occurring in the population) that are linked to environmental factors.

Epidemic

Occurrence of a disease clearly in excess of normal expectancy.

Epidemiologic transition

A shift in the pattern of morbidity and mortality from causes related primarily to infectious and communicable diseases to causes associated with chronic, degenerative diseases; is accompanied by demographic transition.

Epidemiologic triangle

A model that includes three major factors: agent, host, and environment; used to describe the etiology of infectious diseases.

Epidemiology

Concerned with the distribution and determinants of health and disease, morbidity, injuries, disability, and mortality in populations. Epidemiologic studies are applied to the control of health problems in populations.

Evidence-based public health

The adoption of policies, laws, and programs that are supported by empirical data.

Experimental study

Research design in which the investigator manipulates the study factor and randomly assigns subjects to exposed and nonexposed conditions.

Exposure

Contact with a disease-causing factor; the amount of the factor that impinges upon a group or individuals.

External validity

Measure of the generalizability of the findings from the study population to the target population.

F

Family recall bias

A type of bias that occurs when cases are more likely to remember the details of their family history than are controls (see Bias).

Fertility rate (see General fertility rate)

Fetal death rate

Number of fetal deaths after 20 weeks or more gestation divided by the number of live births plus fetal deaths after 20 weeks or more gestation during a year (expressed as rate per 1,000 live births plus fetal deaths).

Fomite

An inanimate object that carries infectious disease agents.

G

Gene

A particular segment of a DNA molecule on a chromosome that determines the nature of an inherited trait in an individual.

General fertility rate

Number of live births reported in an area during a given time interval divided by the number of women aged 15 to 44 years in that area (expressed as rate per 1,000 women aged 15–44).

Generation time

An interval of time between lodgment of an infectious agent in a host and the maximal communicability of the host.

Genetic epidemiology

Field of epidemiology concerned with inherited factors that influence risk of disease.

Global warming

The gradual increase in the earth's temperature over time.

H

Hawthorne effect

Participants' behavioral changes as a result of their knowledge of being in a research study.

Healthy migrant effect

In studies of migration and health, a bias that results from the migration of younger, healthier persons in comparison with those who remain at home (see Bias).

Healthy worker effect

Error linked to the observation that employed persons tend to have lower mortality rates than the general population; stems from the fact that good health is necessary for obtaining and maintaining employment (see Bias).

Herd immunity

Resistance of an entire community to an infectious disease due to the immunity of a large proportion of individuals in that community to the disease.

Host

Person (or animal) who (that) has a lodgment of an infectious disease agent under natural conditions.

Hypothesis

Supposition tested by collecting facts that lead to its acceptance or rejection.

I

Immunity

The host's ability to resist infection by a disease agent.

Inapparent infection

A type of infection that shows no clinical or obvious symptoms.

Incidence rate

(Number of new cases of a disease—or other condition—in a population divided by the total population at risk over a time period) times a multiplier (e.g., 100,000).

Incubation period

Time interval between invasion by an infectious agent and the appearance of the first signs or symptoms of disease.

Index case

In an epidemiologic investigation of a disease outbreak, the first case of disease to come to the attention of authorities (e.g., the initial case of Ebola virus).

Infant mortality rate

Number of infant deaths among infants aged 0 to 365 days during a year divided by the number of live births during the same year (expressed as the rate per 1,000 live births).

Infectious disease (communicable disease)

An illness due to a specific infectious agent or its toxic products that arises through transmission of that agent or its products from an infected person, animal, or reservoir to a susceptible host, either directly or indirectly through an intermediate plant or animal host, vector, or the inanimate environment.

Infectivity

Capacity of an agent to enter and multiply in a susceptible host and thus produce infection or disease.

Injury epidemiology

The study of the distribution and determinants of various types of injuries in the population.

Internal validity

Measurement of the extent to which differences in an outcome between or among groups in a study can be attributed to the hypothesized effects of an exposure, an intervention, or other causal factor being investigated. A study is said to have internal validity when there have been proper selection of study groups and a lack of error in measurement (see Validity).

Intervention study

A type of research design that tests the efficacy of a preventive or therapeutic measure. Intervention studies include controlled clinical trials and community interventions.

L

Late fetal death rate

Number of fetal deaths after 28 weeks or more gestation divided by the number of live births plus fetal deaths after 28 weeks or more gestation during a year (expressed as rate per 1,000 live births plus late fetal deaths).

Latency

Time period between initial exposure to an agent and development of a measurable response. The latency period can range from a few seconds (in the case of acutely toxic agents) to several decades (in the case of some forms of cancer).

Life expectancy

Number of years that a person is expected to live, at any particular year.

Lifestyle

The choice of behavioral factors that affect how we live; these choices often are a function of social influences.

M

Matched case-control study

A type of study in which the cases and controls have been matched according to one or more criteria such as sex, age, race, or other variables.

Maternal mortality rate

(Number of maternal deaths ascribed to childbirth divided by the number of live births) times 100,000 live births during a year.

Molecular epidemiology

Field of epidemiology that uses biomarkers to establish exposure–disease associations. Examples of biomarkers are serum levels of micronutrients and DNA fingerprints.

Morbidity

Occurrence of an illness or illnesses in a population.

Mortality

Occurrence of death in a population.

Multiple causality (multicausality)

A portrayal of causality wherein several individual, community, and environmental factors may interact to cause a particular disease or condition.

Mutation

A change in DNA that may adversely affect the organism.

N

Nativity

Place of origin (e.g., native-born or foreign-born) of an individual or his or her relatives.

Natural experiment

A type of research design in which the experimenter does not control the manipulation of a study factor(s). The manipulation of the study factor occurs as a result of natural phenomena or policies that impact health, an example being laws that control smoking in public places.

Nature of the data

Source of the data (e.g., vital statistics, physician's records, case registries, etc.).

Neonatal mortality rate

Number of infant deaths under 28 days of age divided by the number of live births during a year.

Null hypothesis

A hypothesis of no difference in a population parameter among the groups being compared.

O

Observational study

A type of research design in which the investigator does not manipulate the study factor or use random assignment of subjects. There is careful measurement of the patterns of exposure and disease in a population in order to draw inferences about the distribution and etiology of diseases. Observational studies include cross-sectional, case-control, and cohort studies.

Odds ratio

Measure of association between frequency of exposure and frequency of outcome used in case-control studies. The formula is (AD)/(BC), where A is the number of subjects who have the disease and have been exposed, B is the number who do not have the disease and have been exposed, C is the number who have the disease and have not been exposed, and D is the number who do not have the disease and have not been exposed.

Operationalization

Methods used to translate concepts used in research into actual measurements.

Operations research

A type of study of the placement of health services in a community and the optimum utilization of such services.

Outcome

A result that may arise from an exposure. Examples of outcomes in epidemiologic research are specific infectious diseases, disabling conditions, unintentional injuries, chronic diseases, and conditions associated with personal behavior and lifestyle.

P

Pandemic

An epidemic that spans a wide geographic area. A worldwide influenza outbreak is an example of a pandemic.

Passive smoking (also, sidestream exposure to cigarette smoke)

Involuntary breathing of cigarette smoke by nonsmokers in an environment where cigarette smokers are present.

Pathogenesis

Process and mechanism of interaction of disease agent(s) with a host in causing disease.

Perinatal mortality rate

Number of late fetal deaths after 28 weeks or more gestation plus infant deaths within 7 days of birth divided by the number of live births plus the number of late fetal deaths during a year (expressed as rate per 1,000 live births and fetal deaths).

Period prevalence

All cases of a disease within a period of time. When expressed as a proportion, refers to the number of cases of illness during a time period divided by the average size of the population.

Point epidemic

Response of a group of people circumscribed in place to a common source of infection, contamination, or other etiologic factor to which they were exposed almost simultaneously.

Point prevalence

Number of cases of illness in a group or population at a point in time divided by the total number of persons in that group or population.

Population

All the inhabitants of a given country or area considered together.

Population at risk

Those members of the population who are capable of developing a disease or condition.

Population-based cohort study

A type of cohort study that includes either an entire population or a representative sample of the population (see Cohort study).

Population risk difference

Difference between the incidence rate of disease in the nonexposed segment of the population and the overall incidence rate. It measures the benefit to the population derived by modifying a risk factor.

Postneonatal mortality rate

Number of infant deaths from 28 days to 365 days after birth divided by the number of live births minus neonatal deaths during a year (expressed as rate per 1,000 live births).

Posttraumatic stress disorder (PTSD)

An anxiety disorder that some people develop after seeing or living through an event that caused or threatened serious harm or death.

Predictive value (positive and negative)

(+) Proportion of individuals who are screened positive by a test and actually have the disease. (−) Proportion of individuals who are screened negative by a test and actually do not have the disease.

Prepathogenesis

Period of time that precedes the interaction between an agent of disease and a host.

Prevalence

Number of existing cases of a disease or health condition in a population at some designated time.

Primary prevention

Activities designed to reduce the occurrence of disease that occur during the period of prepathogenesis (i.e., before an agent interacts with a host).

Probability sample

Type of sample in which every element in the population has a nonzero probability of being included in the sample.

Program evaluation

The determination of whether a community intervention program meets stated goals and is justified economically.

Prophylactic trial

A type of clinical trial designed to evaluate the effectiveness of a treatment or substance used to prevent disease. Examples are clinical trials to test vaccines and vitamin supplements.

Proportion

Fraction in which the numerator is a part of the denominator.

Proportional mortality ratio (PMR)

Number of deaths within a population due to a specific disease or cause divided by the total number of deaths in the population during a time period such as a year.

Prospective cohort study

A type of cohort study design that collects data on exposure at the initiation (baseline) of a study and follows the population in order to observe the occurrence of health outcomes at some time in the future.

Protective factor

A circumstance or substance that provides a beneficial environment and makes a positive contribution to health.

Psychosocial epidemiology

Field of epidemiology that examines the role of psychological, behavioral, and social factors in health.

P value

An assessment that indicates the probability that the observed findings of a study could have occurred by chance alone.

Q

Quasi-experimental study

Type of research design in which the investigator manipulates the study factor but does not assign subjects randomly to the exposed and nonexposed groups.

R

Randomization

A process whereby chance determines the subjects' likelihood of assignment to either an intervention group or a control group. Each subject has an equal probability of being assigned to either group.

Rate

A ratio that consists of a numerator and denominator in which time forms part of the denominator. Example: The crude death rate refers to the number of deaths in a given year divided by the size of the reference population (during the midpoint of the year) (expressed as rate per 100,000).

Rate difference

Measure of the difference between two rates (for example, incidence rates) between exposed and nonexposed populations (see Risk difference).

Ratio

A fraction in which there is not necessarily any specified relationship between the numerator and denominator.

Recall bias

A type of bias associated with the ability of the cases to remember an exposure more clearly than the controls.

Reference population

Group from which cases of a disease (or health-related phenomenon under study) have been taken; also refers to the group to which the results of a study may be generalized.

Registry

Centralized database for collection of information about a disease.

Relative risk

Ratio of the risk of disease or death among the exposed to the risk among the unexposed. The formula used is relative risk = Incidence rate in the exposed/Incidence rate in the nonexposed.

Reliability (also, precision)

Ability of a measuring instrument to give consistent results on repeated trials.

Reportable disease statistics

Statistics derived from diseases that physicians and other health-care providers must report to government agencies according to legal statute. Such diseases are called reportable diseases.

Representativeness (also, external validity)

Refers to the generalizability of the findings of an epidemiologic study to the population.

Resistance (host)

Immunity of the host to an infectious disease agent.

Retrospective cohort study

Type of cohort study that uses historical data to determine exposure level at some time in the past; subsequently, follow-up measurements of occurrence(s) of disease between baseline and the present are taken.

Risk

The probability that an event will occur, e.g., that an individual will become ill or die within a stated period of time or by a certain age.

Risk difference (also, attributable risk)

Difference between the incidence rate of disease in the exposed group and the incidence rate of disease in the nonexposed group.

Risk factor

An exposure that is associated with a disease, morbidity, mortality, or adverse health outcome.

S

Sampling error

As a result of sampling methods, the misrepresentation of the sample selected for a study in relation to the target population.

Screening

Presumptive identification of unrecognized disease or defects by the application of tests, examinations, or other procedures that can be applied rapidly.

Secondary prevention

Intervention designed to reduce the progress of a disease after the agent interacts with the host; occurs during the period of pathogenesis.

Secular trends

Gradual changes in disease frequency over long time periods.

Selection bias

Error that occurs when the relationship between exposure and disease is different for those who participate in a study versus those who would be theoretically eligible for the study but do not participate (see Bias).

Selective screening (also, targeted screening)

A type of presumptive identification of unrecognized disease or defects applied to subsets of the population at high risk for disease or certain conditions as the result of family history, age, or environmental exposures (see Screening).

Sensitivity

Ability of a test to identify correctly all screened individuals who actually have the disease being screened for.

Social epidemiology

The discipline that examines the social distribution and social determinants of states of health.

Social support

Perceived emotional support that one receives from family members, friends, and others; may mediate against stress.

Socioeconomic status (SES)

A measure that takes into account three interrelated dimensions: a person's income level, education level, and type of occupation. Some measures of SES use only one dimension such as income.

Spatial clustering

Concentration of cases of a disease in a particular geographic area.

Specific rate

Statistic referring to a particular subgroup of the population defined in terms of race, age, or sex; also may refer to the entire population but is specific for some single cause of death or illness.

Specificity

Ability of a test to identify nondiseased individuals who actually do not have a disease.

Statistical significance

The assertion that the observed association is not likely to have occurred as a result of chance.

Stress

A physical, chemical, or emotional factor that causes bodily or mental tension and may be a factor in disease causation.

Surveillance

Systematic collection, analysis, interpretation, dissemination, and consolidation of data pertaining to the occurrence of a specific disease.

T

Temporal clustering

Association between common exposure to an etiologic agent at the same time and the development of morbidity or mortality in a group or population.

Temporality

Timing of information about cause and effect; whether the information about cause and effect was assembled at the same time point or whether information about the cause was garnered before or after the information about the effect.

Tertiary prevention

Intervention that takes place during late pathogenesis and is designed to reduce the limitations of disability from disease.

Therapeutic trial

A type of study designed to evaluate the effectiveness of a treatment in bringing about an improvement in a patient's health. An example is a trial that evaluates a new curative drug or a new surgical procedure.

Threshold

Lowest dose (often of a toxic substance) at which a particular response may occur.

Toxin

A material that is harmful to biologic systems and that is made by living organisms.

V

Vaccination

Procedure in which a vaccine (a preparation that contains a killed or weakened pathogen) is introduced into the body to invoke an immune response against a disease-causing microbe such as a virus or bacterium. Also called inoculation, immunization.

Validity (also, accuracy)

Ability of a measuring instrument to give a true measure (how well the instrument measures what it purports to measure).

Vector

An animate, living insect or animal that is involved with the transmission of disease agents.

Vehicle

A contaminated, nonmoving object involved with indirect transmission of disease; examples are fomites, unsanitary food, impure water, and infectious bodily fluids.

Virulence

Severity of the clinical manifestations of a disease.

Vital events

Deaths, births, marriages, divorces, and fetal deaths.

Vital statistics

Mortality and birth statistics maintained by government agencies.

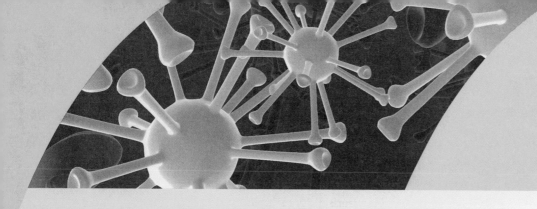

Index

Page numbers with *ex, f,* or *t* indicate exhibits, figures, or tables respectively.